A MARKET TO EXPLORE

THIS PUBLICATION
HAS BEEN MADE POSSIBLE
BY A GENEROUS GRANT FROM

A MARKET TO EXPLORE

*A history of public-private partnership
in the promotion of trade and investment
between the Netherlands and the United States*

Dr. Walter H. Salzmann

Published by:

The Netherlands Chamber of Commerce in the United States, Inc.

This book is dedicated to the members of the board of the Netherlands Chamber of Commerce in the United States:

Mr. Peter E.J. Boost	Philips Electronics North America Corporation
Mr. Ton J. de Boer	ABN Amro North America, Inc.
Mr. Jan Dix	Océ-USA, Inc.
Mr. W.F. Dutilh	Krediet & Effectenbank N.V.
Mr. Maurits E. Edersheim	Smith Barney International
Mr. Allen R. Freedman	Fortis, Inc.
Mr. C.J. Freriks	Bond van Bloembollenhandelaren
Mr. Lane C. Grijns	ING Capital Holdings, Inc.
Mr. Guy F. Jonckheer	Nationale Nederlanden NV
Mr. Jilles J. Hoek	Mees Pierson Holdings, Inc.
Mr. Martin J. Hoek	CGR Advisors
Mr. W.H. Peter Keesom	Boyden/Zay & Co
Mr. Mario J.P.M. Mol	Mees and Zoonen
Mr. Lloyd B. Morgan	Arthur Andersen & Company
Mr. Alex J. Postma	Moret Ernst & Young
Mr. Peter Roorda	Stibbe Simont Monahan Duhot
Dr. H. Onno Ruding	Citicorp/Citibank N.A.
Mr. Karl W. Schroff, Sr.	Karl Schroff & Associates, Inc.
Mr. Steven R. Schuit	Loeff Claeys Verbeke
Mr. Richard C. Spikerman	Republic National Bank
Mr. W.F.C. Stevens	Caron & Stevens
Mr. Frederick E. Tetzeli	J.P. Morgan & Company
Mr. Maarten van Hengel	Brown Brothers Harriman & Co.
Mr. Jacob van Namen	Vans Incorporated
Mr. J.J. van Steenbergen	
Mr. Philip W. van Verschuer	Loeff Claeys Verbeke
Mr. Peter van Vliet	KLM Nederland
Prof. Willem F. van Vliet	Coleman, Hull & van Vliet
Mr. Cor H. Verhagen	Aegon Insurance Group
Mr. Herman A. Vonhof	Grand Cypress Development Corp.
Mr. Toon H. Woltman	KLM Royal Dutch Airlines
Mr. Dennis J. Ziengs	RABOBank Nederland

CIP information
ISBN: 90-71056-09-0
© 1994, The Netherlands Chamber of Commerce in the United States, Inc.
    Six Art Promotion bv, Amsterdam.

Illustration cover:
Dutch ships on the coast of Texel, Holland; in the middle the "Gouden Leeuw",
the flagship of Admiral Cornelis Tromp, 1671
Painting by Ludolf Bakhuizen (1631-1708)
Rijksmuseum, Amsterdam

CONTENTS

*Three figures,
with New Amsterdam in
the background, c. 1700
The New-York Historical
Society*

*Queen Beatrix of the
Netherlands, 1985
Portrait by
Andy Warhol,
(1930-1987)
Private collection,
Chicago*

FOREWORD

This interesting and highly informative book which you have before you shows that the Netherlands Chamber of Commerce in the United States, Inc. has had a close working relationship with the Netherlands Government since its inception at the start of the century. I am happy to continue this tradition of cooperation in my function of Honorary Member. The enthusiasm and dedication on the part of the Chamber's representatives with whom I have had an opportunity to work for the promotion of the Netherlands' commercial interests has been most impressive.

One of the reasons why I hold the Chamber and our relationship in such high esteem is that good cooperation between Government and the private sector does not always develop naturally. So when we have such cooperation, we should value it highly, safeguard it and create the conditions for its healthy continuation.

Government and the private sector each have their own particular strengths and weaknesses. Only by pooling our talents and resources will our efforts become most effective. Without the cooperation of the Chamber and the Government, the promotion of the Netherlands in the United States, including the country's economic interests, would have been a different proposition indeed. Great things would have remained undone.

While the Chamber's main task is export promotion, I should like to recall that the activities of the Chamber reach much further than that. The Chamber also performs a vital role in improving the awareness and promoting the image of the Netherlands in the United States; its share in the overall promotion of the Netherlands in the United States is very major indeed. The Chamber is equally active in the Netherlands Community in the United States. Its unstinting generosity in the material and moral support of that Community in times of difficulty will not be forgotten.

In conclusion, I extend my compliments to Walter H. Salzmann on this insightful study. It gives the reader the opportunity to get acquainted with a "public-private partnership" that came into being well before the phrase was coined. I hope that, by showing how effective this partnership has been and remains, the book will contribute to the awareness that the twain can, and do, meet.

Adriaan Jacobovits de Szeged
Netherlands Ambassador to the United States

Chart of the world, 1626
"Nova Totius Terrarum
Orbis Geographica ac
Hydrographica Tabula"
Engraving by
Johannes Janssonius,
1626
Six Archives

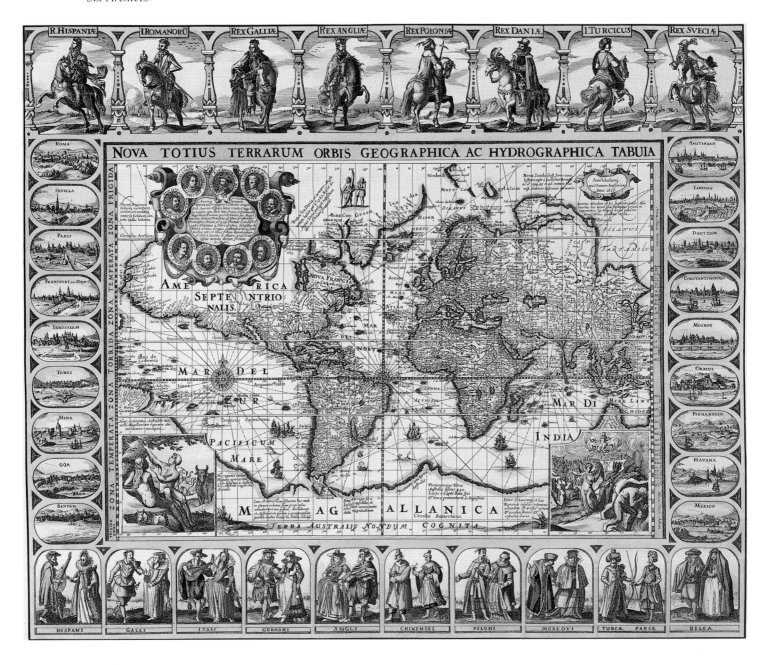

PREFACE

Contrasting images are an effective medium for conveying the essence of complicated situations. Using this approach in typifying relations between the Dutch authorities and private enterprise in the field of trade promotion, such terms as 'a love-hate relationship' or 'a comedy of errors' would seem to be a fair approximation of reality. But inherent in the apparent honed simplicity of attributions of this kind is the danger of over-emphasizing the moments of discord between the two parties.

Reflected in the 90-year history of the promotion of Dutch trade with the United States is the more elaborate picture of long channels of development and permanent undercurrents side by side with short-term initiatives and the need to act promptly at moments of crisis. On closer examination, it is in any event evident that the trade promotion activities of government and of industry and commerce were not mutually opposed. Through their fundamentally different naturethey were of course each inclined to present the other's initiatives in that light. In making up the balance of those 90 years, however, an inevitably evolving element of cooperation is discernible in constantly changing forms and with varying measures of success.

Trade promotion on a collective basis made its appearance towards the end of the nineteenth century. In the two or more preceding centuries it was the usual practice for individual merchants, bankers and investors themselves to find their clients, to investigate their creditworthiness and, in general, to follow trends on the American market. With the advent of industrialisation in the late nineteenth century, many of the newcomers to the American market lacked the knowledge and experience of the established merchant houses and exporters. Efforts to solve the problem followed two different approaches: the business community set about organising commercial information by founding the Netherlands Chamber of Commerce in the United States; and the government was asked to do something about the poor quality of the commercial information supplied by the consular officers abroad. The appeal to the government was a logical step, for since the mid-nineteenth century it had come to play an ever larger part in the social and economic life of the Netherlands.

So the elements comprising the main theme of this study are these: first, the efforts of newly emergent Dutch exporters and branches of industry to gain entry to the American market; second, the success they achieved; and third, the government as the representative of the nation as a whole, for whom exports meant greater prosperity. The role of the government as a financial and organisational partner in the provision of commercial information and the promotion of trade is portrayed against this background.
No one concerned had any doubt of the significance of the American market for the Dutch economy, but they were not invariably in agreement about the most effective way of stimulating trade with the United States. In this context individuals were of cardinal importance: an active chairman and an alert executive secretary of a chamber of commerce could accomplish much more than any campaign strategy. A rational division of tasks between those working in the United States, government representatives and the central organisations of industry and commerce was equally essential for exports. And finally, the approach to trade promotion changed under the impact of technological advances and new marketing methods. Yet no matter how these and other developments are described, no words can provide an adequate picture of the ever-changing pattern of Netherlands-American trade relations in those 90 years. The situation was in a constant state of flux: the philosopher's stone could never be found.

Creativity, rivalry, collaboration, consultation, adapting to new circumstances and clinging doggedly to past gains were all part of the overall picture. It reveals that there are limits to what government and pri-

9

vate enterprise can do to further the interests of trade: the market remains beyond their control. It also accentuates the fact that they each have their own distinct part to play in the promotion of trade. So what progress was made in those 90 years of trade relations? Did the results show an upward curve, an ever better input-output ratio? Though intrinsic to economic activity, trade promotion defies quantification. There are no statistics registering its effects in hard currency or export percentages. Nevertheless, it is not unreasonable to assert that the endeavours described in this study were not without their reward. Why else would so many outstanding individuals have found the effort worthwhile? They are a collective part of the economic history of the twentieth century that to date has received too little notice. It is a remarkable omission at the end of a century in many ways characterised by the growth of international trade.

Albert E. Kersten
Professor of Diplomatic History
Leiden University

Brandywine bowl Made in New York, silver, ca. 1710 by Gerrit Onckelbag (1691-1732). Engraved "MB" on the base for Maria Brockholst (1682-1766), and on the inside with arms. Museum of the City of New York Bequest of Miss Charlotte A. Van Cortlandt

CHAIRMANS MESSAGE

Looking back at the history of trade and investment between the Netherlands and the United States, certain threads that bind the centuries stand out.

First, from the modest start made by the Dutch East India Company in 1609, when it sent Henry Hudson on the first Dutch mission to the New World, to its present position as the third largest foreign investor in the United States, the Netherlands has continually expanded on its goodwill and business relationship with the United States.

Secondly, sound infrastructure and geographical locations enhanced opportunities for both countries to flourish economically - the Netherlands during its 17th century "Golden Age" when it was recognized as a powerful force in shipping and international trade, and the United States during the late 19th century when its rise to an economic superpower was stimulated by westward migration tapping the continent's vast resources. Indeed, it seems natural that an American of Dutch descent, Commodore Vanderbilt, became one of the important architects of the modern American economy by leading the expansion of American rail and shipping lines.

Finally, a spirit of friendship and a long and mutual commitment among both countries for upholding every right to liberty, tolerance and democracy, has further strengthened mutual bonds, making the Netherlands Europe's most American-minded country where the United States has invested more per capita than in any other country in the world.

So like the Dutch East and West India Companies before, the Netherlands Chamber of Commerce in the United States is an indispensable link between the two countries, working tirelessly to advance mutual business opportunities. A shining example of public-private partnership, the Chamber is an essential aspect of the commercial infrastructure upon which both countries depend.

As a bridge between Dutch and American companies, the Chamber enhances and promotes open communication for mutual benefit. And like the countless Dutch who have settled in the United States and the many Americans working in the Netherlands, the Chamber contributes daily to the strengthening of ties between Dutch and American people.

The Chamber is proud to be the vehicle through which Dutch and American companies and citizens can uphold and extend the centuries of fraternal relations. This book is a testament to that shared pride and lasting commitment!

Peter E.J. Boost
Chairman
The Netherlands Chamber of Commerce in the United States, Inc

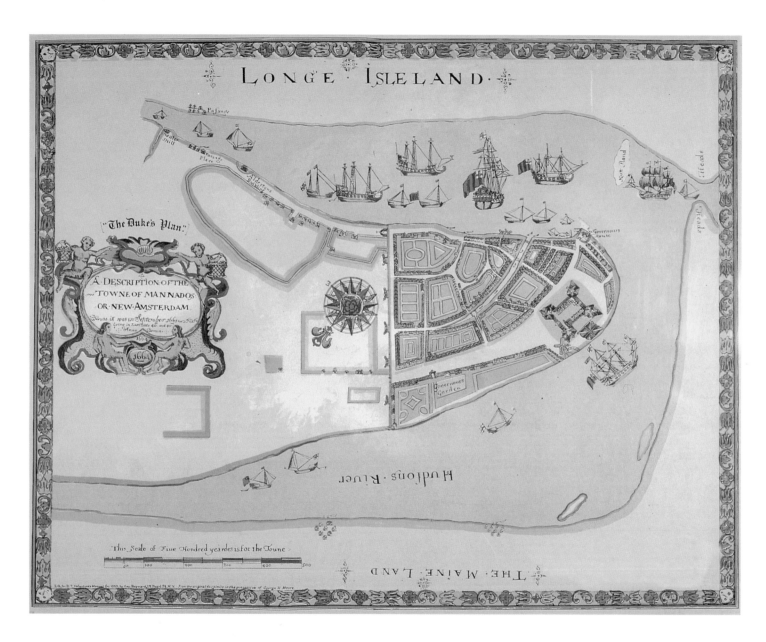

Chart of Long Island,
1664
Drawing by
unknown artist
The Kings Library,
British Museum

INTRODUCTION

The colony of New Netherland was founded in 1626, when Peter Minuit acquired Mannahattanik, or Manhattan, for the Dutch West India Company in exchange for ten shirts, eighty pairs of stockings, ten muskets, thirty rounds of shot, thirty pounds of gunpowder, thirty axes, thirty cooking pots, and a copper roasting pan. Relations between the Netherlands and America had begun a few years earlier when Henry Hudson, in search of an ice-free northwest passage to the Orient, reached the North American coast in the summer of 1609. Sighting a broad river on September 12, 1609, he sailed ninety miles upstream, hoping that he had found an entrance to the long sought passage to the East. After his return to Europe, wildly exaggerated reports about the Hudson River and its abundant flora and fauna circulated in the Republic, and notwithstanding its long icy winters, New Netherland was soon reputed to be a land of milk and honey. Although Hudson had consulted a wealth of geographical material before setting out on his voyage, the reports themselves subsequently proved to be based on nothing more than conjecture and supposition, and his great discovery was made purely by chance. However, it marked the beginning of Dutch expansion in the Americas.

This shows that no matter how scant or unreliable, information lies at the heart of all commercial transactions. The Netherlands developed into the staple market of Europe thanks to the fact that Dutch traders had more and better information on international trade than their foreign competition. Despite the fact that the Netherlands had lost its economic primacy in Europe by the second half of the eighteenth century, information on foreign markets allowed the Netherlands to remain Europe's financial center. After the defeat of Napoleon and the end of French rule in the Netherlands by 1814, it was evident that the Dutch commercial classes had lost touch with developments abroad. Therefore, in 1824 King Willem I established the Netherlands Trading Society, which together with the consular service of the Ministry of Foreign Affairs, were to keep Dutch companies informed of commercial developments at home and abroad. Dutch businessmen who were in search of new export markets but who lacked sources of information abroad, were dependent throughout the nineteenth century on the Dutch consular service which largely consisted of honorary officials. Criticism and complaints were voiced ever more frequently as the century drew to a close. Career consuls were both too few in number and too uninformed about commercial matters, while the honorary consuls rarely troubled to answer enquiries from the Netherlands. In 1891 the Dutch business community in London took matters into their own hands and set up a Chamber of Commerce. Their example was followed twelve years later in New York. With the aid of the Netherlands Ministry of Foreign Affairs, and in close collaboration with leading American businessmen of Dutch descent, representatives of Dutch private enterprise founded the Netherland Chamber of Commerce in America on May 28, 1903. Also in 1903, the first information center in the Netherlands, the Trade Information Center, was opened in Amsterdam to improve the situation on the home front, and in 1906 a trade division was set up at the Netherlands Ministry of Agriculture, Trade and Industry to collect and disseminate foreign commercial information received from consuls and diplomats.

The basic structure for providing commercial information on foreign markets was now established: it was to be provided by and for private enterprise, while the Netherlands government would play a supportive role in the background. Foreign and national political and economic factors determined its further development. The activities of the Chamber were suspended during the first world war, but shortly after the armistice the Netherlands government and business community organized a restructured Chamber in 1920. In that same year a counterpart office was established in Amsterdam to maintain and strengthen contact with government and business circles in the Netherlands. It gave the Chamber a solid base in the Netherlands. But the principal change was the growing role of the Netherlands government, which aban-

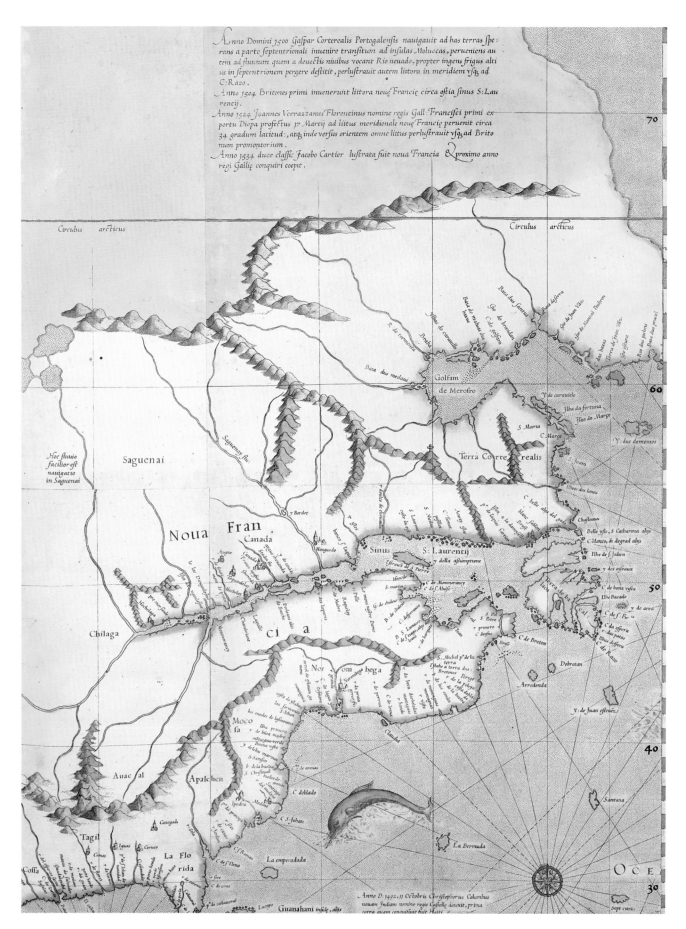

Anno Domini 1500 Gaspar Corterealis Portogalensis nauigauit ad has terras spe-
rans a parte septentrionali inuenire transitum ad insulas Moluccas, perueniens autem ad fluuium quem a deuectis niuibus vocant Rio neuado, propter ingens frigus alti-
us in septentrionem pergere destitit, perlustrauit autem littora in meridiem ysq; ad
C: Razo.
Anno 1504. Britones primi inuenerunt littora nouę Francię circa ostia sinus S: Laurentij.
Anno 1524. Joannes Verrazzanus Florentinus nomine regis Gall: Francisci primi ex-
portu Diepa profectus 17 Martij ad littus meridionale nouę Francię peruenit circa
34 graduum latitud:, atq; inde versus orientem omne littus perlustrauit ysq; ad Brito-
num promontorium.
Anno 1534. duce classis Jacobo Cartier lustrata fuit noua Francia Qproximo anno
regi Gallię conquiri coepit.

70

Circulus arcticus   Circulus arcticus

Baia dus sartis
Baia de michaoi haia   Gio de brendan   Baia dasserra
Illha de carauella   C: do Beffun   Gio de Juan Vaz
R: de tormentas   Brasil   Gio de Manuel Padrouss
Baia dus medaus   C: das bauas   Gio: gisares
Golfam   terra do frio   Baia das preces
de Merofro

Hoc fluuio   Y: de carauelo
facilior est   Jlha da fortuna
nauigatio   Jlha do Março
in Saguenai   Saguenai   S. Maria   C. Março   Y: dus demones
Saguenay flu.   S: Joam
Terra Corte realis
Ulhos das lanes
Y bordet   C: belle   alta del gado
dance S Jaque   p. de cristmal   Jlha   a la damoisl   Chasteaus
Noua Fran   Canada   Hanguedo   S: Nicolas   Jlha, alta del gado   Belle ysle, S Catharina alijs
Aruge   C:Sasoes   C:lanco, di degrad alijs
Canada   Sinus   S: Laurentij   Ilhe de S:Julien
cia   y della assumptione   Y des oyseaux
Chilaga   C: de bona vista
Ilhe Bacalao   C de Breton   Ilhe Bacalao
Nor   om   bega   Terra de baccal
C de S: Fr:
C da espera
Dobretan   dau patas
Moco   Ilha dasserra
sa   C de Razo
Arredonda
Ilha primera   Y: de Juan esteues
Auacal   Apalchen   de boca madre
Buena vista   40
Claudia
Tagil   Santana
La Flo   La Bermuda
Coffa   rida   La emperadada   O C E
30
Guanahani insule, alijs   Anno D: 1492. 11 Octobris Christophorus Columbus
nouan Indiam nomine regis Castelle detexit, prima
terra quam conspisiit fuit Haiti
Sept citra:

14

doned its passive attitude and expanded the official information services in the 1930s and started to lend increasing support to private organizations.

In the first two decades after the second world war the Chamber functioned as a semi-public institution, dependent on subsidies and acting on the instructions of the Netherlands Ministry of Economic Affairs, which had taken over the task of export promotion. Fairly detailed information on foreign markets was made available to companies in search of new outlets. In the early 1960s, after stimulating the process of industrialization which necessarily included export promotion, the Netherlands government gradually withdrew its support and the task of introducing Dutch exporters to foreign markets was again left largely to private organizations. Since 1972 official export promotion budgets were reduced and government policy was geared increasingly to privatization.

The kind of information needed by a Dutch exporter before entering a foreign market has barely changed since the Chamber was founded in 1903. Besides specific aspects like customs duties and regulations, the political and economic climate of the particular country needs to be assessed as well in order to determine

⇐
Map of the coast of North America,
Engraving by
Gerard Mercator
Maritime Museum
Prince Hendrik,
Rotterdam

Hollandia Leonis, 1648
Engraving by
Nicolas Johannis Visscher
(1649-1702)
Six Archives

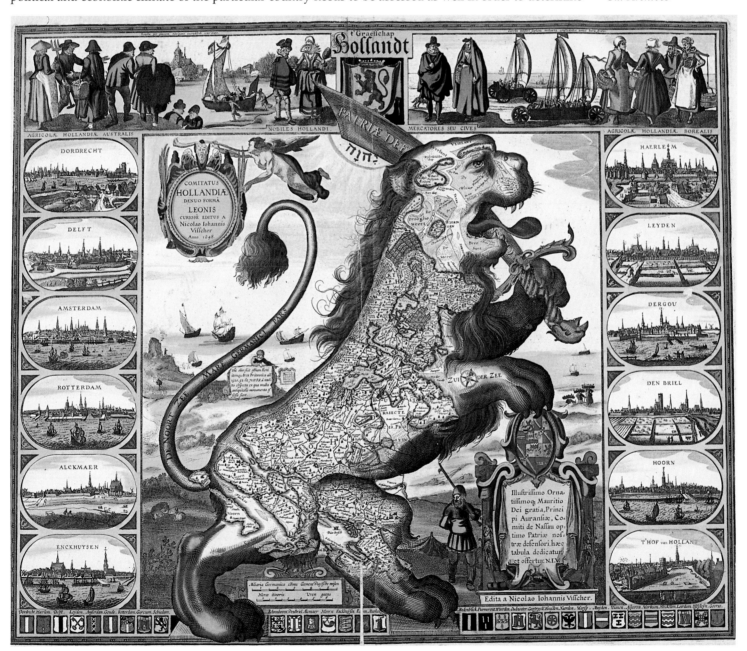

the chances of success. Hygiene regulations, for instance, may have a prohibitive effect on imports even if customs duties are low or non-existent, and restrictions may be imposed by statutory measures like quota systems or specifications for production methods. Furthermore, each market has its own conventions regarding business methods and terms of payment, and its own standards governing quality, quantities, and packaging. A point of crucial importance for early twentieth-century Dutch exporters was the financial standing of potential buyers. In seeking buyers on whom they could rely, Dutch exporters also had to be keenly aware of the differences between European and American business practices.

Although the aims of the private and government agencies were basically the same, a division of tasks gradually evolved. Wherever possible, the Netherlands' government delegated specific tasks to private organizations and focused on collecting general commercial information on foreign markets, on enhancing the image of the Netherlands abroad, and on encouraging Dutch firms to look further afield.

Only three earlier studies of the development of non-public organizations that provided commercial information on foreign markets have appeared in the Netherlands, all dating from before the second world war. Since 1945 only oblique references have been made to the subject. This is especially the case with the development of economic relations with the United States. Although it is widely known that the Dutch are among the foremost foreign investors in the United States, research in this area has been sadly lacking to date. The two most recent monographs on Dutch trade with and investments in the United States date from 1923 and 1948.

This book traces the history of business relations between the Netherlands and America and the history of the Chamber in the twentieth century. The Chamber occupies a prominent position among private trade promotion organizations. As the largest such organization outside Europe, the Chamber has been operating in a market that made exceptionally heavy demands on the competitiveness of the individual Dutch exporter. Not only the distance separating the United States from Europe, but also the wide disparities in business practice in the two countries was an additional obstacle to overcome. Notwithstanding these barriers, the American market has consistently accounted for 3 to 5 percent of annual Dutch exports.

The export promotion policy of the Netherlands government is a recurrent theme in the study. Large corporations and small and medium-sized businesses have different demands for commercial information on foreign markets. The former had sufficient resources to gather all information needed to facilitate exports, but smaller companies were dependent on commercial information agencies, official institutions like embassies and consulates, and special services such as the rudimentary information service operated by the Trade Division of the Netherlands Ministry of Agriculture, Trade and Industry. Not until the reorganization of the Economic Information Division in 1936 did the Ministry of Economic Affairs finally have the benefit of a fully professional unit, which thereafter played a pivotal role in the organization of private and official commercial information and export promotion. Two central factors are the Ministry's export promotion policy, especially as it related to the United States, and the extent to which that policy was influenced by the business community and the organizations concerned with commercial information about the United States. Given the growing influence of the Netherlands government on the Dutch economy, it is likely that working closely together with private enterprise in providing commercial information on foreign markets, its influence in this area must have increased as well. Another major element is the development of the private promotion of trade with the United States.

The Vechte Cortelyou House is a Dutch mansion built by Nicholas Vechte in 1699. Vechte was appointed Governor at that time. During the blood and cruel battle of Long Island, August 27th, 1776, General Stirling with a few soldiers fortified this house and kept the British at bay for a long time.

The Vechte Cortelyou House
Watercolor-drawing by James Ryder Van Brunt (1820-1916), who was a descendant of Rutger Joosten Van Brunt, who settled in New Utrecht in 1657.
The Brooklyn Historical Society

*Chart of coast of North
America near
New York, 1614
Drawing by
Cornelis Doetsz
General State Archives,
The Hague*

CHAPTER I

1609 - 1903: NEW NETHERLAND, ST. EUSTATIUS, AND THE INDUSTRIAL REVOLUTION

The Golden Age and New Netherland: 1609 - 1674

For the young Dutch Republic of the United Provinces the seventeenth century was a period of spectacular economic, political, and cultural growth. The northern Netherlands, which had risen in revolt against Spain, rapidly developed into a world power. Amsterdam became the financial and economic center of Europe, a vast colonial empire was established in Asia, and in 1667, during the Second Anglo-Dutch War, Dutch admiral Michiel Adriaanszoon de Ruyter sailed his ships up the Medway and destroyed much of the English fleet at Chatham. The Dutch achievements in North America lacked the drama of these successes. Colonial expansion in the Indonesian archipelago continued up to the early years of the twentieth century, but in the Western hemisphere, after New Netherland was taken over by the English in 1664, Dutch territory dwindled to a number of Caribbean islands and a small colony on the South American mainland. Yet the efforts made in the Western Hemisphere were in no way less impressive than those in Asia.

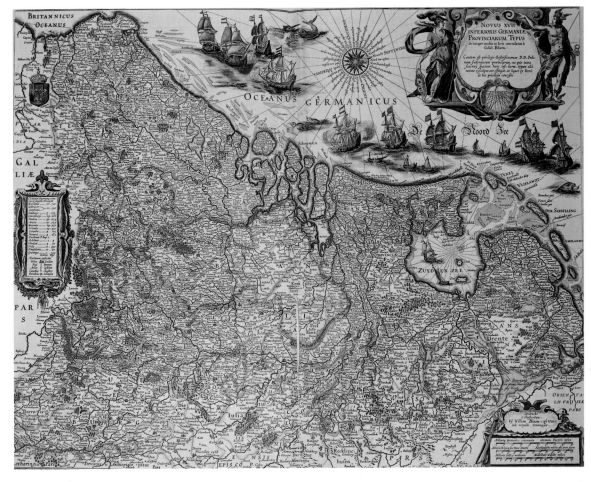

Chart of the 17 provinces
Engraving by
Willem Jansz Blaeu
(1571-1638)
Six Archives

Henry Hudson's expedition in 1609 marks the beginning of European colonization in the area watered by the river which was later to bear his name. But he was not the first European to explore the region; Spaniards and French had preceded him by several decades, and the Italian Giovanni da Verrazano had sailed into the mouth of the Hudson in 1518. It is even said that the French built a small blockhouse on Castle Island near today's Albany in about 1540.

The history of commercial relations between Holland and North America actually begins with the rediscovery - quite accidentally - of the Manhattan peninsula in September, 1609. Hudson had set out in that year to find a northwest passage to the Orient for the Dutch East India Company, not, like his colleague Willem Barentszoon, via the north coast of Russia, but by sailing westward. It was the English navigator's third attempt. In 1607 he had reached Spitsbergen, but icebergs and heavy storms forced him to return to England. His reports of huge whale populations in the waters around the island inspired English whalers to set sail for Spitsbergen in 1610, followed two years later by Dutch ships.

The search for a new passage to the East became an obsession for Hudson. In 1608 he persuaded the English Muscovy Company to finance a second expedition which got as far as Novaya Zemlya in the Arctic Ocean before the early onset of winter forced him to turn back. The patience of his English backers was now exhausted, so in 1609 Hudson approached the Dutch East India Company. Though the Company had doubts about the feasibility of his plan, it agreed to finance the expedition which was to make Hudson famous. The discovery of a northwest passage would, after all, vastly improve the Company's competitive position. The known routes to the East via the Strait of Magellan and the Cape of Good Hope were not only long and costly, but they also led past the Portuguese possessions in southern

DUTCH COTTAGE IN BEAVER ST IN 1679.

Africa. Ever since the beginning of the sixteenth century Portugal had held the extremely lucrative monopoly of the spice trade, which the Dutch Republic was determined to gain for itself. A northwest passage would not only considerably reduce the length of the passage to East Asia, but would have the additional merit of bypassing the Portuguese settlements.

On April 6, 1609 Hudson set sail in the small seventy-ton *Halve Maen* (Half Moon) in a final effort to find the elusive northwest passage. He first headed for the Barents Sea north of Russia, but menaced by storms and icebergs, the crew forced him to change course before the ship had reached Novaya Zemlya. The crew then coursed south-east in the direction of North America. In July landfall was made at Newfoundland, and after repairing the storm-battered *Halve Maen*, Hudson charted the American coast. South of Cape Cod a broad, navigable river was sighted on September 12, 1609. Hudson followed the river upstream in the hope that here at last was the entrance to the northwest passage, but after ninety miles shallow waters forced him to acknowledge that he had failed again. The winter storms were approaching, and he had no choice but to return to Europe.

Hudson's discovery became a point of contention between England and the Dutch Republic. When Hudson docked at Dartmouth, England on the homeward voyage, the English authorities seized his log book, notes, and maps, and he was detained for some time before they allowed him to proceed to Holland to report to his principals in Amsterdam. As he had brought no news of a northwest passage, the Dutch East India Company evinced little interest in the Hudson's exploits. The costs of Hudson's voyage were written off and the Company refocused its attention on finding other passages to Asia.

It was because of a few Dutch fur traders that Hudson's account of "a Great River" with thickly wooded banks and abundant wildlife was not forgotten in the Republic. Because the French had assigned the

"Nieuw Amsterdam ofte Nue Nieuw Iork op 'T EYLANT MAN"
Engraving by Johannes Vingboons (c. 1650-1670)
General State Archives, The Hague

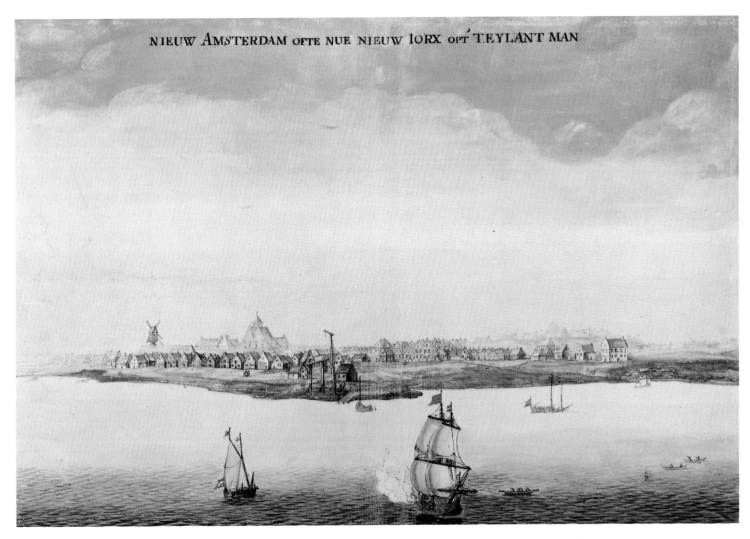

NIEUW AMSTERDAM OFTE NUE NIEUW IORX OPT T.EYLANT MAN

View on the River Y at Amsterdam, 1605 Painting by Hendrick Vroom (1566-1640) Amsterdams Historisch Museum

Canadian fur trade as a monopoly of French merchants, Dutch traders were compelled to buy their beaver and otter skins in Rouen, France, and now it seemed that Hudson's discovery might enable them to break the French monopoly. After a failed first attempt in 1610, the Dutch tried again with five ships in 1613. Later a more southerly route past the Canary Islands and the West Indies was followed to take advantage of the currents and trade winds, but the 1613 expedition followed in Hudson's wake via Newfoundland, reaching "Prince Maurice's River" as Hudson's Great River was now called. The Connecticut River was explored and along the "Great River" the Dutch built Fort Nassau, the first Dutch trading post in North America, on top of the ruins of the French blockhouse dating from 1540. The small fleet returned to Holland laden with furs.

The geographical data collected on this voyage were even more significant than its commercial success. On the basis of the famous "Figurative Map on Vellum" showing the Hudson, Manhattan, and Long Island, the Dutch merchants were granted a three-year trade monopoly for New Netherland, the new name of the area extending from New France and New England in the north to Virginia in the south. The United New Netherlands Company, which ran the new colony, did so well that the Dutch States General did not renew its charter in 1618. Instead, discussions began on the foundation of a company which, like the Dutch East India Company in Asia, would conduct all commercial activities in the Atlantic regions and carry on economic warfare against Spain and Portugal. In 1621 the States General granted the Chartered West India Company a monopoly of the trade with the Americas and Africa and the Atlantic regions in between.

At first the West India Company concentrated on privateering against Spain and Portugal, which were united under one Crown since 1580. Although not unsuccessful - in 1628 Dutch admiral Piet Heyn captured the Spanish treasure fleet in the Cuban Bay of Matanzas, Spain's only such loss in 300 years - privateering proved to be less profitable than expected. In 1630 the West India Company changed tactics and focused its attention on trade. In a trade network between Europe, Africa, and the Americas, the West India Company concentrated on a three-part plan: on transporting a workforce from Africa to the American

colonies; on shipping sugar, tobacco, and dye-woods from the plantations in Portuguese Brazil to the staple markets of the Dutch Republic; and on settling colonists in New Netherland to enhance the agrarian nature of the Dutch colony and to grow food. For this plan to work, the success of the Dutch West India Company was dependent on conquering parts of Portuguese Brazil. The attack on Pernambuco by a fleet of 76 ships on February 15, 1630 started a war that was to drag on until 1654 and which would bring about the financial ruin of the Company. Waging war proved less rewarding than hoped, for the first victories were followed by mounting losses. Virtually bankrupt by the end of the following decade, the West India Company was dependent on loans to finance all further large-scale activities. In 1648, for instance, the city of Amsterdam assumed the costs of fitting out a new fleet.

Since the original purpose of the Dutch West India Company was to wage economic warfare against Spain and Portugal, its directors, the *Heeren XIX* (the Nineteen Gentlemen), took little interest in the colonization of New Netherland. It was not until 1624, three years after the Company's foundation, that the first group of settlers crossed the Atlantic, and then only because France and England were laying claim to the area. As a relative newcomer to the colonial scene, the Dutch West India Company could not base its territorial claims on the grounds advanced by other countries, namely the "right of discovery" or allocation by the Pope. It therefore argued that territorial rights could proceed only from permanent settlement. When the Dutch West India Company learned in 1624 that a ship financed by French entrepreneurs was about to leave the Dutch port of Hoorn for North America, it decided to act. The Company seized the ship and gave the first group of colonists permission to settle in New Netherland. Thirty Walloon families set out for America on board the *Nieu Nederlandt* in May, 1624.

High Island on what is today Delaware, near present-day Gloucester, was the site chosen for the Company's first settlement. The *Nieu Nederlandt* sailed from High Island to the mouth of the Connecticut River, Governor's Island, and Fort Nassau, which was rebuilt on a larger scale and renamed Fort Orange.

The Mariner,
late 17th century
Sepia drawing by
Jan Luyken (1649-1712)
Amsterdams Historisch
Museum

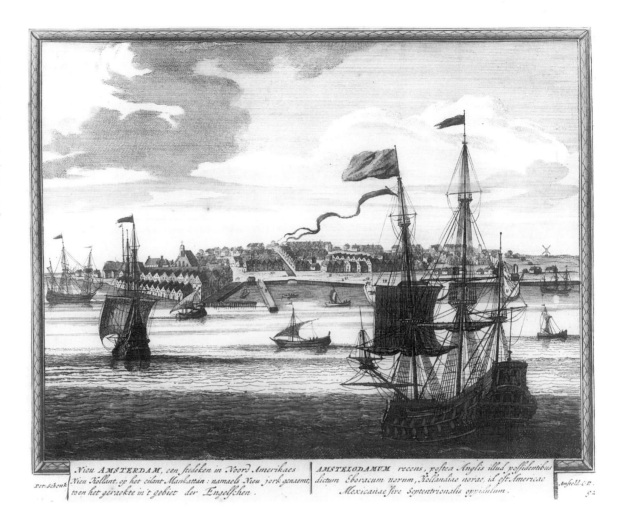

Nieu AMSTERDAM, een ſtedeken in Noord Amerikaes Nieu Hollant, op het cilant Mankattan: namaels Nieu Jork genaemt, toen het geraekte in 't gebiet der Engelſchen.

AMSTELODAMUM recens, poſtea Anglis illud poſsidentibus dictum Eboracum novum, Hollandis novae, id eſt Americae Mexicanae ſive Septentrionalis oppidulum.

The colony's frontiers were thus demarcated, enabling the Company to dispute any claims made by the surrounding English colonies. New Netherland comprised a large part of what later became Connecticut, New York, New Jersey, and almost the whole of Delaware. The colonists were settled at the mouth of large rivers to guard against attack from the sea. Moreover, as furs were mainly transported from the interior by boat, the Company intended that the settlements would serve a dual purpose.

In 1625 the tiny group of Walloons was reinforced by several hundreds of new arrivals. Despite this increase in numbers, the director general New Netherland, Peter Minuit, decided in the following year to concentrate his sparse resources on the southern tip of the island Manhattan around the planned Fort New Amsterdam. Not only were Fort Orange and the other settlements on the Delaware and the Connecticut in constant danger of attack by American Indians, but supplying them by sea was often fraught with difficulty. In May, 1626 Minuit purchased the entire island of Manhattan from the American Indians for 60 guilders worth of gewgaws. In order to strengthen New Amsterdam's defenses Minuit later added Staten Island to the colony. By the end of 1626 New Amsterdam comprised thirty loghouses, a stone counting-house, a mill and a provisional fort consisting of a fortified blockhouse enclosed by a wooden stockade.

Although New Amsterdam expanded considerably in the years that followed, the population remained relatively small, especially in comparison with the surrounding English colonies. In 1633 it still had only 300 inhabitants, and ten years later the entire population of New Netherland was estimated at 2,000. It was only during the last ten years of the Company's administration that immigration dramatically increased. With the loss of Brazil in 1654, the Dutch West India Company's territorial possessions in the New World were reduced to a few Caribbean islands and New Netherland. Determined to retain the colony at all costs, the Company actively encouraged immigration. Adventurers and single men had constituted the majority of the first colonists, but most of the newcomers after 1657 were young families. In 1664

24

the population of New Netherland was an estimated 9,000. England's North American colonies, by contrast, had 25,000 inhabitants by the mid-1640s, ranging from New Haven with 2,500 to Bay Colony with 15,000. Boston was already a thriving port with a population of 5,000 to 6,000. Even by 1660 New Amsterdam still had no more than 243 houses and approximately 1,500 inhabitants. By that time the Walloon families who had founded the colony forty years before were already in the minority. Dutch company officials, clerks, sailors, and fur traders made up the greater part of the population, together with the colonists brought to New Netherland by 'proprietors' since the beginning of the 1630s.

When the ship *Nieu Nederlandt* returned to Amsterdam at the end of 1624, it was carrying the Company's first shipment of beaver and otter pelts bought from the American Indian tribes living along the banks of the Hudson. The fur trade expanded rapidly in the following years. The 63,000 pelts shipped from the colony between 1624 and 1632 fetched 454,000 guilders at auction in Holland. Despite heavy competition from the English colonies, the fur trade reached its peak in the 1650s, when Fort Orange alone was despatching 46,000 pelts each year.

Furs and timber remained New Netherland's chief exports, but they did not yield enough to prevent the colony from being a financial drain on the Dutch West India Company after the first few years. No precious metals were found, and the fur trade turned out to be considerably less profitable than expected, partly because the Company's monopoly rights were widely infringed by traders and Company officials. Various attempts to transform the colony into a major producer of tobacco, wheat, and silk in the course of the years met with little success; furs and timber remained its principal exports. At the end of the 1620s the Company was obliged to develop a different form of administration so that New Netherland would at last become a profitable colony. The war in Brazil ruled out the possibility of additional investment in New Netherland. The Company had a choice between strengthening its hold on the colony to enforce its monopoly of the fur trade - which implied controlling immigration and concentrating the population

Unloading merchandise from the West Indies on the Amsterdam harbour quai, 1660
Painting attributed to Abraham Storck
(c. 1635-c. 1710)
Private collection

around New Amsterdam - or attracting private capital. The *Heeren XIX* opted for the latter. They decided to transform New Netherland into a farming colony divided into large holdings known as "proprietorships". In return for financing the passage and settlement of thirty to sixty colonists over a period of three years, the proprietor was allocated a large tract of land with ownership rights. The Company thus in effect transferred to private individuals the administrative rights and obligations vested in it by the Dutch States General. The proprietor was entitled to 10 percent of the revenues from agriculture, trapping, hunting, fishing, and mining. With the exception of the fur trade, the proprietor was also granted free trading and shipping rights along the entire Atlantic seaboard. In order to impose some restraint on the powers of the proprietors and because there was such a dearth of colonists, the Company also promised land to all wishing to settle in New Netherlands at their own expense. Among those applying in 1629 was Kiliaen van Rensselaer, one of the plan's most active promoters and the future owner of Rensselaerwyck near Fort Orange.

Despite the initial enthusiasm of Dutch entrepreneurs, the proprietorships did not provide a permanent solution. The Company steadily whittled down the proprietors' rights, whose returns were lower than anticipated. The number of colonists remained disappointingly small. The Republic had reached a high level of prosperity, and trade, shipping, and industry provided the country with virtually full employment. Why abandon hearth and home for an uncertain future? Van Rensselaer was forced to offer wages 25 percent higher than those paid in the Republic. Smuggling colonists and fraudulent officials added the finishing touches to the failure of the project. The Company therefore decided in 1639 to open New Netherland to unrestricted immigration.

Unlike the surrounding English colonies, New Netherland was a commercial rather than an agricultural settlement, which benefited from its fine natural harbor, its location as a crossroads for shipping along the Atlantic seaboard, and the Company's free trade policy. But it was not until 1639, when the last vestiges of the Company monopoly disappeared and private trade was allowed to develop freely. From then on the Company confined itself to governing the colony and levying taxes. Even by the standards of the time, the number of ships plying between the Dutch Republic and North America was small. Compared to the annual volume of Asia-bound shipping, North Atlantic traffic was negligible. Four large companies dominated trade during the last twenty years of the Company's administration, and they often fitted out ships jointly in order to minimize the risks. The interest paid by merchants on so-called bottomry bonds, which were loans secured by the 'bottom' or keel of the ship, give some indication of the risks involved. In peacetime 20 percent, it rose to much higher levels in times of war. During the First Anglo-Dutch War, when Dutch shipping suffered heavy losses at the hands of the English navy, it soared to 39 percent. Compared to the Republic's other shipping routes, including 'the mother trade' to the Baltic, trade with New Netherland was a high-cost and high-risk affair. In view of the substantial profits that could be made elsewhere, it is surprising that merchants were still prepared to take such risks. Cargo costs were also high. In the 1630s Van Rensselaer put them at 50 percent of the vendor price of the supplies he shipped to Rensselaerwyck.

Trade between Amsterdam and New Netherland consisted primarily of the bartering of furs and tobacco for the food, livestock, tools, etc. that the colony did not produce itself.

Many of the goods that reached Europe via New Netherland were first imported into the colony. Thanks to its natural harbor, by the beginning of the 1650s New Amsterdam lay at the center of the shipping routes along the eastern seaboard, an advantage the Company sought to maintain. Governor Pieter Stuyvesant carried out the first improvement to the harbor in 1647 by building a small dock in East River. This was followed in 1659 by a further expansion, and the pier had to be lengthened again the following year to accommodate the growing volume of shipping.

The English Navigation Act of 1651 prompted a rapid increase in smuggling trade between the English colonies and New Netherland. Large numbers of Dutch, English, French, and Spanish ships now sailed to New Amsterdam every year. Beef, sheep, wheat, flour, fish, butter, cider apples, iron, tar, and barrel staves were imported from New England and tobacco, ox hides, pork, and fruit from Virginia. Dutch merchants traded linen canvass, tape, thrid, cordage, brasse, Hading cloth, stuffs, stockings, spices, fruit, all sorts of ironwork, wine, brandy, anise, and salt in exchange. The American Indians continued to supply furs.

By the beginning of the 1660s New Amsterdam was a lively, bustling town viewed with covetous eyes by the English. In 1653 Stuyvesant and the Company acknowledged that the enterprising inhabitants of New Amsterdam were the colony's greatest asset. Stuyvesant appointed two burgomasters, five aldermen and a Council secretary on February 2, 1653. The meeting-place of America's first City Council was the City Tavern, where it assembled on February 20, 1653. On December 16, 1654 the Governor presented the Council with a municipal coat of arms.

Governor
Peter Stuyvesant
(1592-1620), c.1620.
[... Peter Stuyvesant was
the last Director-General
of New Netherland. He
was intelligent, efficient,
and always loyal to the
Company, but dictatorial
and fiery-tempered.]
Attributed to
Henri Couturies
The New-York Historical
Society

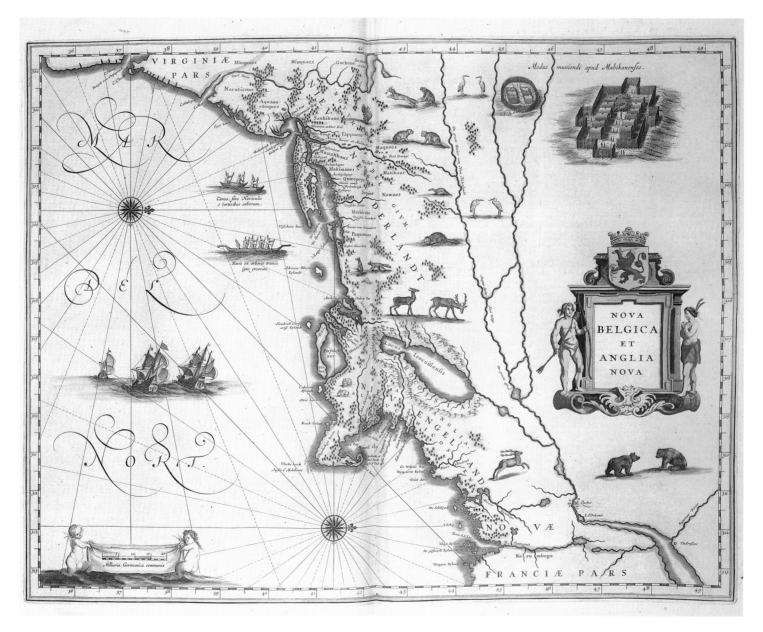

"Nova Belgica et Anglia Nova"
Engraving by
Willem Jansz. Blaeu
(1571-1638)
Six Archives

Economic prosperity changed the appearance of New Amsterdam. A canal, the Herengracht, was dug between 1657 and 1659 on the site of what is now Broad Street, but could only be used for transport at high tide. Stuyvesant was eager to attract as much commerce and shipping as possible. The Company had retained its right to levy a 10 percent duty on all goods imported into New Netherland, but considering an increase in trade to be more beneficial to the colony, Stuyvesant sometimes turned a blind eye to smuggling activities. Like so many Dutch settlements, New Amsterdam was a Dutch town in miniature. "Most of the houses are built in the old way", noted a visitor, "with the gable end toward the street; the gable end of brick and all the other walls of planks ... The street doors are generally in the middle of the houses and", as in every small town and village in the Republic, "on both sides are seats, on which during fair weather, the people spend almost the whole day". A later visitor described some of the houses as "very stately and tall. The bricks are of diverse colours and laid in checkers, being glazed, look very agreable". As many of the houses were built of wood, fire was a constant danger. Not only did New Amsterdam look like a small town in the mother country, it also smelled like one. Shocked by the custom of building privies in the street in front of the houses, Stuyvesant ordered them to be removed in August, 1658. Brouwerstraat (Stone Street) was the first street to be paved at the request of the residents in 1658.

But despite its prosperity, New Amsterdam could not be compared with the commercial center of Boston, whose Puritan merchants traded with the West Indies and Newfoundland, England, France, Holland, Spain, and Portugal. Visiting Boston in 1663, Stuyvesant saw a city that was wealthier and more dynamic than the capital of the Dutch colony. The differences were striking. Most of New Amsterdam's streets were still unpaved, while those in Boston were well laid out and well kept. Its shops were filled with goods, and its houses were built of stone. And Boston boasted three churches, as compared with the Dutch colony's small St. Nicholas Church built in 1642.

The last years of New Netherland were dominated by territorial conflicts with the surrounding American Indian tribes and the neighboring English colonies. From the time of the founding of the colony in 1624, clashes with the Indians alternated with peaceful intervals sometimes lasting several years. Control of the fur trade and the ownership of cultivable land were at the root of the trouble. As the use of firearms spread, otters and beavers became increasingly scarce, and competition between hunters and trappers grew ever fiercer. The two cultures' contrasting attitudes to property rights inevitably gave rise to disputes about who actually owned specific plots of land. The collective ownership of the Indians, in force as long as the land was in use, was at variance with the colonists' European conception of permanent individual ownership. Because the European population of New Netherland was so much smaller than the surrounding American Indian population, Company officials sought to avoid strife, and in 1641 Governor Willem Kieft imposed heavy penalties for the sale of alcohol to Indians.

Yet Governor Kieft was also responsible for the war with the American Indians which erupted in 1643 and almost led to the destruction of New Netherland. Taking advantage of inter-tribal warfare, Kieft tried to evict the Indians from the west bank of the Hudson. In the irregular fighting that followed, settlers took refuge in Fort New Amsterdam, and only their superior weapons saved them from annihilation. By 1645 both sides had had enough, and a truce was declared. Large parts of Long Island and Manhattan had gone up in flames, food was scarce, trade had come to a halt, and Fort New Amsterdam was crowded with refugees.

The *Heeren XIX* recalled Kieft, and in May, 1647 Peter Stuyvesant made his debut in the history of New Netherland when he landed in America as the new director-general of the Dutch colony. Born in the Frisian hamlet of Peperga in 1610 or 1611 to a clergyman and the daughter of a patrician family from Gelderland, Stuyvesant entered the service of the West India Company and made a name for himself in Brazil and Curaçao. In 1644 he led an unsuccessful attack on the Spanish island of St. Maarten, losing a leg in the fray. By the time he arrived in New Netherland it was no longer the American Indians who posed the greatest threat to the Dutch colony, but the English.

When news arrived of the discovery by Hudson in 1609, the English had promptly laid claim to the area. Since the frontiers of New Netherland had not been formally demarcated, the surrounding English colonies constantly encroached on the Company's territory. Knowing that the colony's survival depended on reaching a compromise with the English, Stuyvesant opened negotiations in 1649, claiming the entire region between the Connecticut and the Delaware but at the same time demonstrating his good will by banning further sales to the American Indians of the weapons they used to attack the English colonists in Connecticut Valley. Through divisions in the English community, an agreement was concluded in 1650. Though Stuyvesant thereby relinquished his claim to large parts of New Netherland, the Company remained securely in possession of all the land settled by Dutch colonists. It meant giving up areas that were in effect already held by the English, such as Connecticut Valley and the eastern part of Long Island. The agreement was never formally acknowledged by either the English or Dutch governments, but it was nonetheless honored by local administrators until New Netherland passed into the hands of the English in 1664.

The situation on the banks of the Delaware in the south was if anything even more complicated owing to the presence of a third competitor. In 1637 Peter Minuit, who had commanded the garrison of Fort New Amsterdam a decade earlier and was now in the service of the Swedish West India Company, founded Fort Christina, named in honor of Queen Christina of Sweden, near present-day Wilmington. The Swedish settlement rapidly extended its control over the valley after 1643, and the Dutch Fort Casimir, on

the lower reaches of the river, was captured in 1654. A year later, however, New Sweden was taken by a small Dutch army led by Stuyvesant.

The English threat assumed serious proportions with the outbreak of the First Anglo-Dutch War in 1652. Only the timely arrival of the news of a truce saved New Netherland from attack by four frigates despatched by English dictator Cromwell in February, 1654 to assist the New England militia in a campaign against the Dutch colony. The ships were about to open fire on New Amsterdam when a merchant-man arrived with the news that peace had been concluded. The American Indians, however, continued their sporadic attacks on New Netherland. Although the Second Anglo-Dutch War did not begin until

1665, it was preceded by constant skirmishing. In 1663 the English Royal African Company captured several of the West India Company's forts on the African Gold Coast with the object of gaining control of the trade to America. The news that four ships carrying 300 soldiers had left Portsmouth on May 15, 1664 caused consternation in New Netherland. Though the Company's headquarters in Amsterdam reported that the English fleet was being sent to suppress religious unrest in New England, it was in fact under orders to seize Long Island and, if possible, New Amsterdam. It was sighted off New Amsterdam by August. With a force of only 150 men under his command, the fortifications in disrepair, and a population too fearful to take up arms, Stuyvesant had no option but to surrender on September 8, 1664.

Though the Dutch Republic soon gained the upper hand in the Second Anglo-Dutch War, New York, as New Netherland had been renamed by the English, did not return under Dutch sovereignty. Under the Treaty of Breda of July 11, 1667, each country retained the territory it had conquered. The situation remained unchanged even after New York was retaken in August, 1673 in the Third Anglo-Dutch War by a fleet of eight Dutch warships and a small army of 600 marines under the admirals Cornelius Evertsen the Younger and Jacob Binckes. Although briefly renamed New Orange by the Dutch, the Republic exchang-

The House of the West India Company, 1664
Engraving by
Jacob de Maris
Museum of the City of New York
Gift of G.C.J. Boissevain

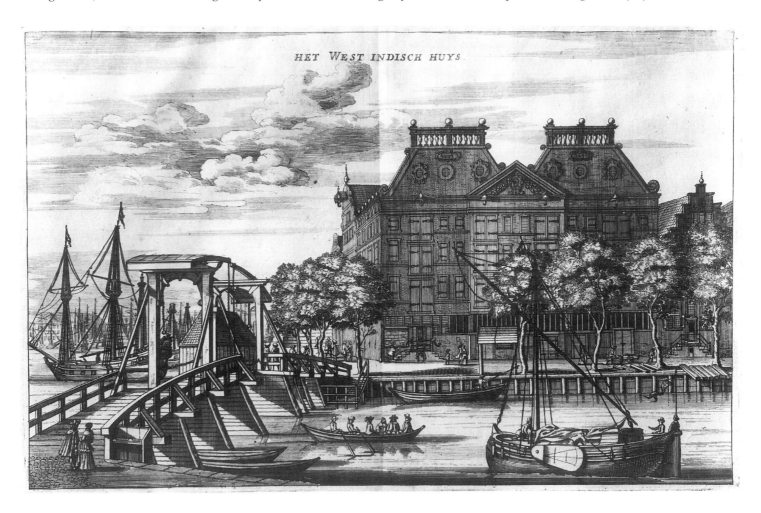

HET WEST INDISCH HUYS.

ed New York for the much more profitable colony of Suriname in South America under the terms of the peace treaty concluded at Westminster on February 19, 1674. On November 10, 1674 the Dutch flag was lowered for the last time in the only Dutch colony ever established on the mainland of North America.

The capture by the Dutch of the English flagship the "Royal Prince" on June 13th, 1666 during the second Anglo Dutch war 1665-1667. Painting by Willem van de Velde (1633-1707) Rijksmuseum, Amsterdam

A Century of Contraband Trade: 1674 - 1783

The transfer of New Netherland to England by no means put an end to commercial relations between the colony and the former mother country. English mercantilism, which prohibited trade between the colonies and other countries, now necessitated a detour via the West Indies. During the eighteenth century Dutch merchants profited handsomely from the growing discontent in the American colonies with England's trade monopoly. But mercantilism also had its advantages. England held a monopoly of North American tobacco, and the cultivation of indigo was subsidized. Hemp, tar, pitch, and other naval stores were reserved for the English merchant fleet and navy, and the English government accordingly helped to finance their production. There was nevertheless a wide range of products that could be traded freely.

The colonists' growing resentment stemmed largely from the fact that the North American colonies and England were producing the same commodities, yet the colonies were forbidden to establish their own industries. The money needed to import English luxury goods and manufactured products had to be earned in other ways. Large quantities of food and timber were exported from the colonies to the sugarcane plantations in the British West Indies, from which American merchantmen returned with cargoes of molasses, the basic ingredient of the cheap rum that was so important to the colonial economy: it paid for the furs bought from the American Indians for export to England and for the forced labor that were put to work at the plantations in the southern colonies. But as the British colonies in the West Indies were too small to absorb the entire North American timber and food output, it was not long before trade relations were established with the French and Dutch settlements in the Caribbean. Though the North American merchants often traded quite openly, the British government never succeeded in halting their illicit activities. The West Indies, with its many small islands, was a smugglers' paradise. When the British navy blockaded French colonies in times of war, trade was switched to one of the neutral colonies. The Dutch colony of St. Eustatius, famous as the *Golden Rock* of the West Indies, served as the principal depot for French and North American merchants during the Seven Years' War (1756-1763) between France and Britain. Salted meat, wheat, butter, lard, potatoes, peas, and brandy from North America were traded for sugar, rum, cotton, indigo, cocoa, and hides from the French and Spanish colonies, and European goods. When the British navy systematically began searching all Dutch ships carrying French colonial goods to St. Eustatius, trade was diverted to Spanish Hispaniola.

The Stadthuys of New York, corner of Pearl St. and Coentijs Slip, 1679 Published by G. Hayward The Brooklyn Historical Society

*Mount Pleasant
(Beekman Mansion),
New York City, 1874
Watercolor by
Abram Hosier
The New-York Historical
Society*

Trade between the Dutch colonies in the West Indies and North America was concentrated on New York, where the majority of the population were still of Dutch origin. In 1790 about half of all 106,000 North Americans of Dutch descent lived there, and many shop signs were still in Dutch. New Year's Day was celebrated in traditional Dutch style, and the feast of St. Nicholas was an annual event in Albany. Dutch remained the language of the Reformed Church up to 1763. In order to strengthen trade relations, merchants from Curaçao and St. Eustatius, the two most important Dutch islands in the Caribbean, settled in New York, where they mixed with members of prominent Amsterdam and Rotterdam mercantile families, and sent their sons to the Republic to complete their commercial training. Though direct trade with the former mother country had been banned after the transfer of New Netherland to England, the prohibition was never effective.

Linen, canvas, rope, tea, and gunpowder were exported to New York, Boston, and Rhode Island. Through its proximity to the English channel ports, Rotterdam evolved into a major import center for North American tobacco and rice which, after clearance through English customs, were destined for other parts of Europe. Seeking cargo for the return voyage, English shipowners channelled the stream of German emigrants bound for Philadelphia through Rotterdam, which soon became one of the main West European ports of embarkation. Of the 319 ships carrying emigrants to Philadelphia between 1727 and 1775, 253 gave Rotterdam as their port of departure.

The economic, political, and military brilliance of the Dutch Republic's *Golden Age* faded in the course of the eighteenth century. In the seventeenth century the Republic had been the foremost European carrier, largely thanks to the Amsterdam staple market; thereafter international trade was gradually lost to other countries. The trade from the Baltic to the Mediterranean, known as 'the mother trade' in the seventeenth century because it constituted the base of the staple market, now bypassed Amsterdam. Industry also rapidly lost ground. The processing of tobacco and the distillation of alcohol from grain were the sole industries for which the Republic was still renowned. In 1791-1792 Amsterdam, Rotterdam, and Schiedam distillers exported over 14.5 million liters of Dutch gin to the United States. Amsterdam however retained its reputation as the financial center of Europe.

*"t' Stadt-Huys op
DelftsHaven"
Engraving, 17th century
Six Archives*

*'t Nieuw Hooft,
Rotterdam Harbor
Engraving by
Johannes de Vou
(1690-1705)
Six Archives*

In 1608 the Pilgrim Fathers fled religious suppression in England and sailed to Holland, "where they heard of freedom of Religion for all men". After a short stay in Amsterdam, the Pilgrim Fathers lived and worked in the Dutch city of Leiden for over ten years. In 1620, the Pilgrims decided to resettle in the New World where they could better retain their English language and avoid the wars of Europe. On July 22, 1620, the entire congregation assembled at what today is known as the Pilgrim Fathers' Church in Delfshaven, now a part of Rotterdam, to pray for a safe voyage across the Atlantic. The Pilgrims then boarded the "Speedwell" for the trip to Portsmouth, England, where they transferred to the "Mayflower" for their historic journey to the New World where they founded the colony of Plymouth, Massachusetts.

Chart of Rotterdam, c. 1640
Engraving by Willem Jansz Blaeu (1571-1638)
Six Archives

St. Eustatius and Foreign Loans

Britain and her North American colonies drifted ever further apart between 1763 and 1775. When the French in Canada no longer represented a threat, the colonists questioned ever more insistently the need for the British presence in North America. The desire for autonomy and the removal of stifling economic restraints became priorities for the colonists. Feelings ran high. The first explosion occurred in Boston in 1770. What went down in history as the Boston Massacre started as a snowball fight between citizens and British soldiers; when the snowballs became stones, the British guards opened fire. The award of the tea monopoly to the English East India Company provoked the Boston Tea Party on December 16, 1773. Disguised as American Indians, Bostonians dumped three shiploads of tea in the harbor. Tension mounted to the point where the colonies banned all imports from Britain as from December 1, 1774, but actual hostilities did not break out for another six months. On April 19, 1775, when British troops tried to seize weapons and munitions from a warehouse in Concord, Massachusetts, the local population fired on them. The American Revolution had begun.

View of Amsterdam from the Y, in the Golden Age Painting by Abraham Storck (c. 1635-c. 1710) Nederlands Historisch Scheepvaart Museum

Policy Description Mees & Zoonen Insurance, 18th century cargo/ship to coast of Africa for trade and from there to America, 1765.

Today Mees & Zoonen provides insurance brokerage services in the United States in partnership with Johnson & Higgins.

Though the Dutch Republic complied with the British government's request, made directly after the start of the American Revolution, to prohibit all trade with North America, many Dutch merchants chose to ignore the ban. The Dutch government, afraid of unrest in its own colonies, might have felt a certain sympathy for the British, but the mercantile class saw the American rebellion as a golden opportunity to make a quick profit. The British envoy at The Hague lodged his first protest against the rapidly increasing Dutch contraband trade with North America in November, 1774. The captains of two British frigates lying in the River Y at Amsterdam noted which ships were being loaded for America and the nature of their cargoes. On March 20, 1775, the Dutch Republic again banned the exports of weapons and munitions to the British colonies in America. It had little effect. Amsterdam merchants used the free port of St. Eustatius as a transit hub for trade with the American rebels. They were soon joined by French, Spanish, and even British traders. Arms, munitions, and ships' stores from Europe, and molasses and sugar from the West Indies were stored on the Dutch island, where they were traded for North American tobacco, indigo, timber, and horses. American ships carried the goods to their port of destination, usually Philadelphia or Charleston.

Opportunities for profit-making were as great as the risks. Profits of 120 percent per voyage had not been unusual in previous years; during the American Revolution some merchants entered a profit of 500 percent in their books. This meant that they could count on a handsome return, even if the British navy intercepted two out of every three ships. An average of 2,500 vessels a year called on St. Eustatius during the 1770s, reaching a peak of 3,500 in 1779. One of them was the *Andrew Doria*, the U.S. brig-of-war which was saluted by the cannons of Fort Orange on St. Eustatius on November 16, 1776, the first foreign recognition of an American ship sailing under the flag of the new nation after the American Declaration of Independence. It did not imply, however, that the Dutch Republic of the United Provinces accorded formal recognition to the United States of America, which did not follow until 1782, when the rebel colonies had achieved de facto independence. It was chiefly as a supplier of war materials that the Dutch Republic made a substantial contribution to the success of the American Revolution.

The American rebels gained a number of victories in quick succession at the beginning of the war. In 1776 the English were forced to withdraw from Boston, the rebel colonies' economic center, and the loyalists were driven out of North Carolina. Then the tide of war suddenly turned. The rebels lost New York, followed by Philadelphia in 1777. Their financial resources were virtually exhausted, and their situation seemed hopeless. Yet before the end of the year the pendulum had swung back: in October a British army surrendered at Saratoga. This was the signal for France, Britain's traditional enemy, to accord formal recognition to the United States and to conclude an official alliance after two years of unofficial support. It was what Benjamin Franklin, heading a diplomatic mission to the Court of Louis XVI, had been trying to achieve since 1776, and at last his efforts were rewarded. Viewing every British loss as a gain for itself,

France had given the rebels free access to its military stores in 1776. Up to 1783 France also made available loans and gifts amounting to millions of livres which were used, inter alia, to purchase arms in the Dutch Republic.

That the Dutch Republic of the United Provinces did not officially recognize the United States of America until 1782 was due primarily to its role as arms supplier and because of its position as Europe's major capital market. It was in the rebels' interest that a neutral power should act as the supplier of the material and capital needed to fight the war. Had the Republic openly declared its support for the rebels, this crucial yet neutral support would not have been possible. The United States nevertheless sent its first unofficial envoy, the Swiss immigrant Charles Guillaume Frédéric Dumas, to the Dutch Republic in 1776. He was succeeded in 1780 by John Adams, who was later to become the second president of the United States. Adams was appointed the first official U.S. envoy to the Republic in 1782.

Stock Exchange,
Amsterdam
Painting by
Gerrit A. Berckheyde
(1638-1698)
Amsterdams Historisch
Museum

The United States made its first appearance on the Amsterdam capital market a good two years before it was formally recognized by the Dutch Republic. The uncertain outcome of the hostilities in North America inhibited Dutch investors from subscribing to American bonds, and a mere Dfl. 51,000 was raised. A number of changes were required before Amsterdam bankers would consider lending money to the United States: appointment of an official American envoy to the Dutch Republic, the prospect of military victory, and political changes in the Republic itself. It was not until 1782 that these conditions were met.

Recognition of the United States of America gradually became a major issue in the internal politics of the Dutch Republic. The self-styled Patriots, who opposed the pro-British, oligarchic policy of the ruling Stadtholder's faction centered by the House of Orange, pointed with growing enthusiasm to the example of the United States. The American people had claimed and were fighting for their freedom and the right to self-determination. But no amount of sympathy for the American Revolution could persuade

Amsterdam bankers to part with their money. And when the Fourth Anglo-Dutch War broke out at the end of 1780, they were even less inclined to do so. After Fort Orange fired its salute to the *Andrew Doria* in November, 1776, tension between Britain and the Dutch Republic on the question of contraband trade steadily mounted. From 1778, the British navy intercepted and seized Dutch merchantmen suspected of trading with the enemy, which led the Dutch States-General to vote for a policy of 'unlimited convoy' in the following year. Dutch warships were to protect the merchant fleets against British attack. On December 30, 1779 a British squadron opened fire on two Dutch warships which were escorting a number of merchantmen near the Isle of Wight. The threat of war mounted, and in September, 1780 Britain found a pretext to declare war on the Dutch Republic. The British frigate *Vestal* intercepted the American merchantman *Mercury*. On board was Henry Laurens, travelling to the Republic as the new U.S. commissioner. His instructions were to discuss the establishment of diplomatic relations, to negotiate a loan on the Amsterdam capital market, and to conclude, if possible, a trade and friendship treaty. More seriously, he had in his possession a secret trade agreement signed by Samuel W. Stockton and Amsterdam regents on September 8, 1778. The outbreak of hostilities was now only a matter of time, and on December 20, 1780 Britain declared war on the Republic.

On January 27, 1781 the British fleet in the West Indies was ordered to occupy St. Eustatius, the contraband center of the West Indies. Barely a week later, on February 3, a squadron of seventeen British warships appeared at the harbor mouth. A force of 3,000 British soldiers and marines took the harbor and the fort without a shot being fired. Of the 150 ships seized, sixty were American, and another forty were captured off the Dutch island of Saba. Much of the booty, worth 3 to 4 million pounds, was the property of English merchants. St. Eustatius was recaptured by the French and restored to the Dutch Republic shortly afterwards. But even though prosperity returned, the island never regained the dominant position in European contraband trade with the United States it enjoyed before the British occupation.

John Adams (1735-1826), "Minister Plenipotentiaris der XIII Vereenigde Staaten van Noord-Amerika, bij de Republijk der VII Vereenigde Nederlanden", 1782 Engraving by Reinier Vinkeles (1741-1816) The New-York Historical Society

He was the first American Ambassador to the Netherlands, and became President of the United States in 1797.

When war broke out between Britain and the Dutch Republic, one of the American rebels' main supply lines was severed. If the American rebels had hoped that the Amsterdam capital market might be more accommodating now that the Dutch Republic had been forced to take sides openly, these hopes were soon dashed. Directly after the declaration of war John Adams asked Amsterdam financiers if they would lend the young country 15 to 20 million guilders. A direct loan was not possible as the Dutch Republic had not yet officially recognized the United States. The loan was therefore formally made to France, which enabled the United States to take up 5 million shortly after the news of the final British surrender at Yorktown had reached the Dutch Republic. Though fighting was to continue for some time to come, the ultimate independence of the United States was no longer in doubt.

Adams redoubled his efforts to persuade the Dutch States-General to recognize his country. With the support of France, and after a pro-peace party had come to power in Britain, he was at last successful. On April 19, 1782, exactly seven years after the British colonies in North America had risen in revolt, the States-General recognized the "United States of North America". Adams presented his letters of credence the next day. On April 22 he was officially informed that the States-General accepted him as Minister Plenipotentiary and he was invited to pay his respects to the Stadtholder, Prince Willem V of Orange. The Dutch Republic was thus the second state after France to recognize the new American nation.

Formal recognition was welcomed not only in the United States, but with equal enthusiasm in the Dutch Republic, though more for pecuniary reasons than out of idealism. As one versifier put it:

> Rejoice merchant, rejoice at the freedom
> Of wide vista'd America
> which has long pleaded for your wares.
> Load up your ships, do not tarry.
>
> Rejoice, rejoice rightly, you pillars
> Of the Republic! Rejoice, Manufacturers!
> America calls for your wares.
> Onward, onward, replenish your purse.

On May 12, 1782, John Adams took up residence in a stately mansion in Fluwelen Burgwal, a street near the Binnenhof, the seat of the States-General at The Hague. This was the first official diplomatic residence owned by the United States. A few months later Adams was able to report another success to President George Washington: a trade and friendship treaty between the Dutch Republic and the United States signed at The Hague on October 8, 1782. On June 23, 1783, Pieter Johan van Berckel, a former burgomaster of Rotterdam, sailed for America as the Republic's first envoy to the United States.

Binnenhof
(House of Parliament),
The Hague,
18th century
Painting by
unknown artist
Private collection

On hearing the news that the Dutch Republic had recognized the United States, the American government instructed Adams to raise a loan of 4 to 5 million guilders. As a number of countries had borrowed on the Amsterdam capital market during the war, it was several months before Adams was able to conclude a contract with three banking houses in July, 1782. The bankers Nicolaas and Jan van Staphorst, Willem and Jan Willink, and De la Lande & Fynje undertook to provide the required 5 million at an interest rate of 5 percent and 5 percent commission. However, this first American public loan did not appeal to Dutch investors, and by the end of the year only 1.8 million had been subscribed, followed by a further 1.4 million in 1783.

Because of the financial problems besetting the United States after independence and its difficulties in reaching agreement on a system of taxation, it was some time before the loan was fully subscribed. In January, 1784 Adams had to admit that "American credit in this Republic is dead, never to rise again, at least until the United States shall all agree upon some plan of revenue, and make it certain that interest and principal will be paid". Nevertheless, an interest rate of 7 percent and a series of bonuses aroused enough interest to finance a new loan, and the required sum of 2 million guilders was fully subscribed within five months. Interest in the first loan, Dfl. 125,000 of which still remained open at the beginning of 1785, also revived. It was partly due to these loans that the United States was able to pay or consolidate its war debts.

Over the next few years American credit on the Amsterdam capital market rose steadily, albeit not without promotional activities on the part of the banking houses concerned. In 1794, when the United States appealed to Dutch capitalists for the last time - the interest was becoming too high - eleven loans to the

TRACTAAT
VAN
VRUNDSCHAP
EN
COMMERCIE
TUSSCHEN
HAAR HOOG MOGENDE
DE
STAATEN GENERAAL
DER VEREENIGDE NEDERLANDEN,
EN DE
VEREENIGDE
STAATEN VAN AMERICA.

DE Staaten Generaal der vereenigde Nederlanden; Allen den geenen, die deezen zullen zien, falut! Gezien en geëxamineert het Tractaat van Vrundfchap en Commercie tuffchen Ons en de vereenigde Staaten van America, den 8 October 1782, alhier in den Hage geflooten, waar van den inhoud hier na volgt:

Tractaat van Vriendfchap en Commercie tuffchen haar Hoog Mog. de Staaten Generaal der vereenigde Nederlanden, en de vereenigde Staaten van America, te weeten, New-Hamphire, Maffachufetts, Rode Island en Providence Plantations, Connecticutt, New-York, New-Jerfey, Penfylvania, Delaware, Maryland, Virginie, Noord-Carolina, Zuid Carolina en Georgia.

A Treaty of Amity and Commerce between their High Mightineffes the States General of the United Netherlands, and the United States of America, to wit, New-Hampshire, Maffachufetts, Rhode Island and Providence Plantations, Connecticutt, New-York, New-Jerfey, Penfylvania, Delaware, Maryland, Virginia, North-Carolina, South-Carolina and Georgia

HAar Hoog Mogende de Staaten Generaal der vereenig-

Their High-Mightineffes The States General of the Uni-

A 2

The reception of the first Dutch envoy by the Congress of the United States at Princeton, M. J.; engraving by Reinier Vinkeles.

Eerfte Gehoorgeeving aan den Afgezant VAN BERCKEL in America.

The reception of the first Dutch envoy by the Congress of the United States at Princeton, New Jersey Engraving by Reinier Vinkeles (1741-1816)

Cover page of the Treaty of Amity and Commerce between the United Netherlands and the United States, 1783. Municipal Archive Amsterdam

value of 29 million guilders were listed on the Amsterdam Bourse, where foreign loans totalling 200 million guilders had been floated since 1781. The growing interest in American loans was largely due to the reorganization of public finances effected by the American Secretary of the Treasury, Alexander Hamilton. Dutch investors, large and small, gradually sold off their British and French holdings to invest in American bonds, issued to fund both the federal debt and the debts of the individual states. The Club of Six, comprising the banking houses P. Stadnitski, N. & J. van Staphorst, W. & J. Willink, Van Eeghen & Co., Ten Cate & Van Vollenhoven, and R.J. Schimmelpenninck, offered incentives to stimulate small investors' interest in the loans. As the title was registered in the United States, and the interest was paid there, the bankers bought the bonds themselves and then issued certificates on the market with the bonds as security. They handled the administrative side, collected the interest, and saw to the redemption payments. Their profits derived from the difference between the American and the Dutch interest rates, the latter usually being considerably lower. These transactions enabled them to reserve a large part of the trade in American bonds for themselves.

The Club of Six had other interests in the United States as well. They invested heavily - but at a loss - in the first American canal construction companies, including those for the Potomac, Santee, Connecticut, and James rivers. They also invested in the Society for Establishing Usefull Manufactures, a finance company set up by Hamilton to promote the growth of American industry, which failed dismally. Several members of the Club were connected with the first American banks. Willink, among others, owned shares in the Bank of North America in Philadelphia, while the number of Dutch shareholders in the central Bank of the United States, founded in 1791, was such that in 1793 the American government made the dividend payable in Amsterdam.

United States Treasury Bonds as traded in Amsterdam, 1796 Archief voor de Effectenhandel

TREASURY of the UNITED STATES,

No. 1434.   REGISTER's-OFFICE, 15th June 1791.

BE IT KNOWN, That there is due from the UNITED STATES of AMERICA, unto *Nicolaas van Staphorst, Pieter Stad, with Christiaan van Eeghen & Hendrick Vollenhove, of Amsterdam merchants*

or their assigns, the Sum of *Fifty three thousand three hundred thirty three dollars and thirty three cents*

bearing interest at six per centum per annum, from the first day of January A. D. one thousand eight hundred and one, inclusively, payable quarter yearly, and subject to redemption, by payments not exceeding in one year, on account both of principal and interest, the proportion of eight dollars upon a hundred of the stock bearing interest at six per cent. created by virtue of "An Act making provision for the debt of the United States," passed on the fourth day of August 1790;—which debt is recorded in this office, and is transferable only by appearance in person, or by attorney, at the proper office, according to the rules and forms instituted for that purpose. *Signed Joseph Nourse Reg.*

~~53,333~~ Dollars ~~33~~ Cents.

I REINIER JOHN VAN DEN BROEK, NOTARY PUBLIC for the State of NEW-YORK, by letters patent under the great seal of said State, duly appointed and commissioned, Do hereby CERTIFY, DECLARE and MAKE KNOWN

to all whom it may concern, That the foregoing is a just and true copy from the original: Also that *Joseph Nourse* whose signature is affixed to the original Certificate, is REGISTER of the TREASURY of the UNITED STATES of AMERICA, duly appointed and commissioned, and that to all Certificates signed by him in his quality aforesaid, due credit is to be given as a just and lawful debt. Further I DO CERTIFY, That I personally repaired at the request of *Messrs. Le Roy & Bayard* to the Register's-Office of the said United States of America, in the city of Philadelphia, and that the said *Joseph Nourse* did acknowledge his hand-writing before me the said Notary; and that I have seen the said original Certificate of *fifty three thousand three hundred thirty three dollars and thirty three cents* duly entered in the books of the Treasury of the said United States of America, in the name of *Nicolaas van Staphorst Pieter Stad with Christiaan van Eeghen & Hendrick Vollenhove of Amsterdam merchants.*

IN WITNESS whereof, I do also set my Hand and affix my Seal of Office, in the city of PHILADELPHIA, this *fifteenth day of June 1791*

R. J. van den Broek
Not. Pub.

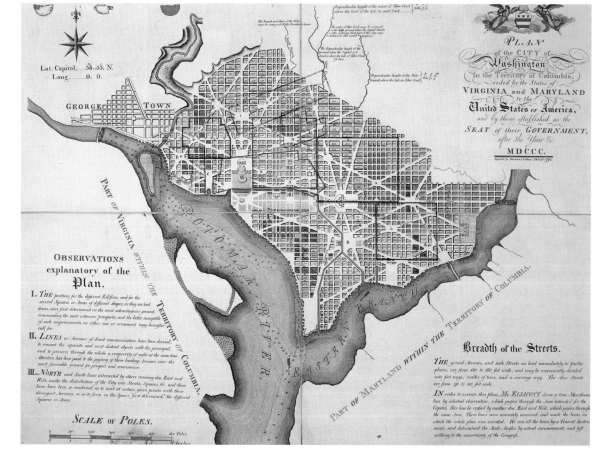

In 1789, four of the six banking houses sent a joint representative, Theophile Cazenove, to the United States with instructions to keep them informed of financial developments and to make investments. One of Cazenove's initiatives was the purchase of large tracts of land which were offered for sale in the Netherlands in the same manner as the state loans. The 3.5 million acres which he bought in New York State alone covered one-seventh of its total area. Another 2 million acres acquired in 1793 were sold to Dutch investors for 6.5 million guilders. It was one of the last major transactions before the French invasion of the Netherlands in 1795 put an abrupt end to the flow of capital to the United States.

The sole exception was the purchase of French Louisiana by the United States in 1803. Almost forty years after the French had left Canada, it looked as if Napoleon was about to realize the long-cherished French dream of a colonial empire in the Western hemisphere. Spain had ceded Louisiana and Florida to France in 1800, rendering British Canada accessible to attack by the French via the Mississippi. Realizing that another colonial war would almost certainly be to the detriment of the United States, President Jefferson sent James Monroe to Paris to negotiate the purchase of Louisiana and Florida. He discovered on arrival that the issue had already been decided. A new war between France and Britain was imminent, funds were in short supply, and Louisiana was indefensible. Moreover, the sale of Louisiana to the United States would keep it safely out of British hands. The bargain was struck in just a few days, and Louisiana and Florida were sold to the United States for 15 million dollars.

To finance the purchase, the United States floated a loan in London and Amsterdam. Francis Baring & Comp. brokered an issue of $ 6.25 million at 6 percent in London, and a consortium headed by Hope & Co., founded in1720 (today called MeesPierson) the remaining $ 5 million at 5.5 percent in Amsterdam. The issue of 12,500 bonds of Dfl. 1000 was a resounding success, and the Dutch consortium was soon able to inform its principal that the loan was fully subscribed. An unknown but undoubtedly large part of the London loan passed into Dutch hands. This success was not surprising. As shipping and industry and commerce had been virtually at a standstill since Britain, Austria, and Russia had resumed the war against France in 1799, there were few opportunities for investment, and the loan for the Louisiana Purchase benefited accordingly.

The end of hostilities between France and Britain in 1802 gave a fresh impulse to Dutch shipping and trade with the United States. But three years later the two countries were again at war. In 1806, in an attempt to bring Britain to its knees, Napoleon proclaimed the so-called Continental System, which prohibited any trade between French-occupied continental Europe and the outside world. Sea traffic between Britain and the United States nevertheless continued virtually unimpeded, and the annual interest was duly paid on time in London. Interest payments in the Netherlands, however, were often subject to considerable delay. The outright annexation of the Netherlands by France in 1809 put an end to seaborne trade with the United States for some years. No American ships sailed into Dutch ports in 1810 or 1811. In order to meet its obligations, the American government sent a consignment of coins aboard the warship *The Constitution* to the Netherlands in 1811. Despite the war with Britain which broke out in 1812, the United States continued to meet all payments until the loan was fully repaid in 1820.

Resumption of Trade: 1783 - 1813

If the Amsterdam bankers' expectations of the trade in U.S. government bonds were fulfilled after the American War of Independence, the situation was different when it came to commerce. When hostilities ended it was soon evident that the contraband trade of Dutch merchants had not created a firm market in the United States. Besides war materials, exports to the rebel colonies had included damask, linen, and cotton fabrics, glass and ceramics, steel products and hardware, tools, household goods, tea, spices, flower and vegetable seeds. But when the war was over, American buyers lost no time in reestablishing contact with suppliers in Britain. The assumption that feelings of hostility towards their erstwhile English oppressors would prevent a resumption of the previous pattern of trade proved to be false. Moreover, there were wide differences between trade practices in the Netherlands and the United States. While Dutch merchants were accustomed to payment in cash, their American counterparts, having no banks of their own, relied on long-term credit, which meant that suppliers sometimes had to wait several years for their accounts to be settled. Not infrequently, the lack of reliable and experienced Dutch agents obliged mer-

Escape of the U.S. Frigate Constitution, 1838
The American government sent a consignment of coins aboard the warship "The Constitution" to the Netherlands in 1811, to pay the interest on their loans to Hope & Co. in Amsterdam.
In 1720, Hope & Co. was one of the founding companies of what today is called MeesPierson.

Painting by Thomas Birch (1779-1851)
The New-York Historical Society

chants to deal with "opportunists of little financial or moral substance who were invariably lacking in money but not in plans". Many of the young Dutchmen who went to America to set up a business indulged in wild, speculative ventures, undeterred by their ignorance of local conditions and possibilities. Only a few had any sort of commercial background. One such young hopeful was J.H.C. Heineken, an Elburg clergyman's son "of pleasing mien", who, having lost everything when the British captured St. Eustatius, decided to try his luck as the representative of a trading company in Philadelphia and was soon faced with mounting losses. Among the firms that were hardest hit was that founded by J. de Neufville, which was declared bankrupt on May 28, 1783. De Neufville had been involved with American attempts to raise loans in the Dutch Republic from the start, and was one of the initiators of the trade agreement concluded between members of the Amsterdam merchant class and the American rebels in 1778.

BROADWAY
New York

The proclamation of the Batavian Republic in 1795 in the Netherlands, making the country a French protectorate and part of the coalition led by France against Britain, dealt a heavy blow to Dutch commerce and shipping. Goods were now carried by neutral American ships bound for Hamburg or Bremen rather than Amsterdam or Rotterdam. Their cargoes were tobacco, train-oil, whalebone, and above all cotton, and American exports soared towards the end of the eighteenth century. Because the war had ended all direct contact between the Netherlands and its West Indian colonies, American ships carried their coffee, sugar, and cocoa to Europe. Dutch exports to the United States were negligible, consisting for the most part of cheese, gin, rope, shoes, soap, madder, goose quills, bulbs, and gunpowder. The bulk of the goods handled in Dutch ports were in transit from the German hinterland, and included crude steel, nails, swords, and firearms, wine, and playing-cards. Various kinds of textiles, paper, and ceramics were sold in the United States as "Haerlem bedticks", "Leyden broadcloth", "Dutch sheetings", "Dutch greatcoats", "Dutch post-paper" and "Delph ware". The renewal of hostilities between France and Britain in 1805 and the introduction of the Continental System, the naval blockade of Britain initiated by Napoleon in 1806, put an end to trade between the Netherlands and the United States over the next few years.

48

Renewed Relations: 1813 - 1850

The decisive battle between Napoleon and Britain, Russia, Austria, and Prussia was fought at Leipzig in October, 1813. The young recruits comprising the core of the French army since the disastrous retreat from Moscow were no match for the coalition forces. A few weeks later Allied troops entered the Netherlands. The country regained its independence, a provisional government was installed, and at the end of November, 1813, the Prince of Orange, son of the last Stadtholder Willem V, returned from exile in England. A constitution was drawn up, and the Prince of Orange ascended the throne of the new Kingdom of the Netherlands as King Willem I.

The end of French rule was greeted with jubilation not only in the Netherlands, but in the United States as well. In Albany and New York the descendants of Dutch colonists celebrated with thanksgiving church services, public parades, and victory banquets. Although at war with Britain since 1812, the United States hoped that commercial relations with the Netherlands could now be reestablished. As *The Boston Sentinel* wrote: "One might daily expect to see the new Dutch Flag floating in the harbors of the United States." Sylvanus Bourne, the American consul in Amsterdam, reported that the Dutch "have still here a considerable share of capital remaining, their talent and genius for trade have only been held dormant by force of events; they will soon rise again into vigor and activity when a peace may be established". He however overestimated the strength and the resources of the new kingdom. The once so powerful Dutch Republic, that had lost its economic and political ascendancy in the eighteenth century, was reduced to the rank of a

Judge Van Aernum in his sleigh, Albany, 1855
Painting by
Thomas K. van Zandt
(1814-1861)
The Albany Institute of History & Art

The old House of
Representatives, 1822
Painting by
Samuel F.B. Morse
(1791-1872)
The Corcoran Gallery of
Art, Washington

[... America was aglow
with nationalistic pride in
the decade following the
constitution of the War of
1812. Samuel Morse's
painting, is the first interior scene of such monu-
mentality that had ever
been painted in America.
His decision to present
the House in night ses-
sion, illuminated by the
Argand Oil lamps of the
great chandelier. The
painting involves both the
Sixteenth and
Seventeenth Congress
(1819-1823).]

Samuel Morse was also
the inventor of the Morse
code, a system of tele-
graphic signals, compri-
sed of dots and dashes or
short and long flashes
representing the letters of
the alphabet and used in
transmitting messages,
contributing greatly to
the acceleration of com-
munication around the
world.

51

second class power. On September 24, 1814, the Dutch envoy, Francois Daniel Changuion, presented his credentials to President James Madison, and on July 20, 1815, the new American envoy to The Hague, former Minister of War William Eustis, was received in audience by King Willem I. The Hague was no longer at the center of European diplomacy. In 1817 Alvert Gallatin, the American envoy to France, described Dutch political and court circles as "absolutely dead", while Alexander Hill Everett (1819-1825) reported, "The unbroken tranquility which prevails here resembles the stillness of an academic retreat more than the ordinary bustle of a court residence". On another occasion he wrote: "Nothing stirs in the Netherlands. The Dutch [...] are dull as their lakes that slumber in the storm, and they displayed little interest in events elsewhere in the world." The time when Dutch newspapers were a valuable source of information on foreign affairs was long past. However, not all early nineteenth-century representatives of the United States were so harsh in their judgments of life in the Netherlands. Christopher Hughes (1826-1830) described The Hague as "a most beautiful country town; it really is the sweetest summer residence possible", and the Netherlands in general as "the most prosperous and happy, because the best governed country in Europe". He was less flattering about the court of King Willem I: "I assure you, Courts are the dullest places, Royal persons are the dullest persons, and presentations are the most insupportable bores imaginable. It is all very fine and dazzling for those at a distance and who read; but for those who are in contact, and behind the curtain, it is all flummery in my eyes!" The fact that as *chargé d'affaires* Hughes was precluded by court etiquette from being invited to dine at the palace may have influenced his opinion. So long as the United States was not represented in The Hague by a minister plenipotentiary, as was the Netherlands in Washington, this situation remained unchanged.

Economic relations with the United States were at first at a low ebb. In 1813 little was left of the thriving trade of the late eighteenth century. Dutch trade, industry, and commerce had suffered heavily from political and economic developments in Europe after 1792. Although Amsterdam merchants had asked the American consul about trade prospects as early as December, 1813, barely a month after the departure of the last French troops from the city, it was another two years before commerce began to revive. The United States was still at war with Britain, and the greatly diminished Dutch merchant fleet was fully employed in European waters and in trade with Asia.

Even after the war ended, trade at first lagged far behind expectations. A large proportion of American exports went to Britain in payment for the manufactured goods not produced in the Netherlands. Only when the demands of the British market had been met, and the Netherlands had lowered customs duties on imports from North America, did American ships and goods again find their way to Dutch ports.

When trade began to pick up it soon became apparent, however, that there was little or no demand in the United States for the products that had formerly constituted the bulk of Dutch exports. Whiskey had replaced brandy and gin in popularity, and American manufacturers had meanwhile mastered the finer points of cheese production. Cotton and woollen fabrics were now produced in such quantities, and linen was imported so inexpensively from Ireland, that there was practically no demand for similar Dutch products. The export potential shrank yet further when an economic crisis in 1819 ushered in protectionist tariff legislation in the United States. Customs duties on such commodities as iron, lead wool, hennep, cotton, woollen goods, and gin were raised sharply in 1824, tipping the balance of trade firmly in favor of the United States. While America's annual export earnings were between 2 and 5 million dollars as from 1820, the Netherlands' exports to the United States did not exceed 1.5 million dollars until 1835.

To give a fresh impetus to trade, the Netherlands and the United States concluded a trade agreement on January 18, 1839. It stipulated that neither country was to discriminate against the other's trade and shipping, though this provision did not apply in respect of the colonies. Dutch trade and shipping reaped few benefits from the agreement, largely because of the economic recession afflicting the United States since 1837. To swell the revenues of the federal government, customs duties were raised in September, 1841, and again in August, 1842. The second round imposed duties of 250 percent on gin, 100 percent on mace, 55 percent on nutmeg, and 40 percent on cloves. But the hardest hit was the coffee trade. Imports from the Dutch East Indies shipped via the Amsterdam staples market had not been liable before to customs duties. Yielding an annual turnover of Dfl. 1 million, coffee comprised approximately 30 percent of total Dutch exports to the United States. In 1842, the U.S. Congress decreed that only coffee imported direct from the

TE KOOP AAN LANDVERHUIZERS.

200,000 Acres Land, gelegen in de Provinciën **Mac Kean** en **Potter** in den Staat van **Pennsylvania**, aan of nabij de grenslijn tusschen de Staten van **New-York** en **Pennsylvania**. — **Smethsport** en **Coudercsport**, Hoofdsteden der Provinciën **Mac-Kean** en **Potter** bevinden zich op dezelven, benevens verscheidene Neêrzettingen, Koorn- en Zaagmolens, Leerlooijerijen, een Smeltoven, enz. en tien Postkantoren.

De Landen worden door drie bevaarbare stroomen doorsneden, als: de rivier **Alleghany** en de beeken **Conowodane** en **Oswage**. Ten zuiden zijn dezelve gelegen aan de wateren van de **Synemahoning**, zich uitgietende in de westelijke tak van de **Susquehanna rivier**, boven **Dunnstown**, alwaar het **Pennsylvania Kanaal** ophoudt.

Een straatweg vereenigt **Jerseyshore**, 17 engelsche mijlen beneden **Dunnstown**, met **Coudercsport**, in de Provincie **Potter**; de afstand bedraagt 70 engelsche mijlen. Een andere straatweg is aangelegen van **Bellefonte**, in de Provincie **Center**, naar de grenslijn van den Staat **New-York**, en leidt door **Smethsport**. — De hoofdstraatweg van het oosten naar het westen van **Pennsylvania** voert 31 engelsche mijlen door de landen.

De Landen zijn heuvelachtig en doorsneden door dalen, ter wijdte van ½ tot 1 engelsche mijl; de heuvels zijn zelden hooger dan 500 voet, en in het algemeen kunnen zij tot aan de toppen bebouwd worden. — De grond is goed en voor alle graansoorten geschikt, in het bijzonder voor weiland; de Landen zijn beplant met mast-, beuken-. eiken-, kersen- en pijnboomen enz. Het pijnhout is geldwaardig en wordt naar **Pittsburg** en **Cincinnati** gezonden. — De Landen zijn goed bevochtigd, van eene gezonde ligging; giftige slangen vindt men er niet. — Men heeft toegang naar dezelven door de reeds vermelde straatwegen en het **Pennsylvania Kanaal**, doch buitendien door eenen meer gemak- gemakkelijken, maar langeren weg van **New-York** langs de **Noord-rivier**, van daar door het **Erie Kanaal** naar **Rochester**, vervolgens door het **Genessee Kanaal** naar **Mount Morris** en eindelijk per postwagen naar **Olean**, gelegen omtrent 11 engelsche mijlen van **Ceres** in de Provincie **Mac-Kean**.

De ontworpen **New-York** en **Erie**-Spoorweg, loopende door de zuidelijke Provinciën van **New-York** en door **Olean**, zal spoedig aangelegd worden; 50 engelsche mijlen van dezelve worden reeds gebezigd en geven eene goede uitdeeling.

Het **Genessee Kanaal** moet tot **Olean** verlengd worden; deszelfs belangrijkheid en de groote, daaraan reeds volbragte werken, geven gegronde uitzigt op de voltooijing.

Men vindt er vele kenteekenen van Steenkool- en Zoutmijnen, doch uit gebrek aan kapitalen, heeft men nadere onderzoeken deswege moeten uitstellen.

In **Smethsport** en **Coudercsport** zijn goede scholen aanwezig.

De tegenwoordige prijzen van het Land zijn van 2 tot 4 Dollars per Acre, naarmate van deszelfs meer of min gunstige ligging bij Wegen of Rivieren.

Ommestaande Kaart toont de ligging van de Landen aan.

Nadere inlichtingen zijn te bekomen bij de Heeren: JOHN KEATING, te *Philadelphia*. — H. W. T. & H. MALI, te *New-York*. — OELRICHS & LURMAN, te *Baltimore*. — JOHN KING, te *Ceres*, Provincie *Mac Kean*. — DE LEPEL & LABOUCHERE, te *Amsterdam*.

Announcement of a land sale to prospective immigrants,
around 1830
Municipal Archive Amsterdam

country of origin and carried on American ships would be exempt from duty; imports from elsewhere, which included the Netherlands, would from now on be subject to a duty of 10 percent. As a result, coffee exports from the Netherlands to the United States fell from 43,090 bags in 1841 to a mere 9,749 bags in 1843. The subsequent increase in direct imports from the East Indies offset only part of the loss. The situation changed when a new administration took office in Washington in 1844. The American economy was no longer in such dire straits, and the free-trade Democrats won both the presidency and a majority in Congress. In 1846, U.S. tariffs were substantially reduced and the duty on coffee was abolished.

The combination of a recession and higher customs duties dealt a heavy blow to Dutch exports to the United States. In 1839 they had amounted for the first time to more than $ 2 million; the figure in 1843 was no higher than $ 557,000. Trade did not begin to revive until U.S. customs duties were lowered in 1846, and it took another five years for the $ 2 million-mark to be passed. Besides coffee, spices, and gin, other important commodities were tobacco, sugar, and tin.

Shipping also suffered. The once-dominant Dutch merchant fleet had to take second place to American ships. Before 1830 Dutch ships carried no more than 10 percent of the trade between the two countries. The share of Dutch shipowners gradually increased after the Dutch government introduced measures to promote shipbuilding. Of the 79 ships leaving American ports for a direct passage to the Netherlands in 1835, 22 were flying the Dutch flag. The tonnage figures are yet more revealing. The cargo volume of American ships leaving American ports for the Netherlands in 1823 was more than 53,000 tons, as compared with the 682 tons of Dutch ships in that year. The ratio gradually changed after 1830, and by 1835 the tonnage of Dutch shipping was equal to that of the United States. The two countries each put 20 to 30 new ships into service each year. The Netherlands' improved position in this respect was attributable less to greater competitiveness than to the fact that American shipowners switched their operations to the more profitable trade with Britain, France, and Germany. Britain in fact functioned as an entrepôt for the Netherlands and Belgium.

If Dutch shipping had been required to bear the full brunt of competition with the American mercantile fleet it would probably have lost. Dutch ships on the whole were too big and cost too much to equip. Moreover, American shipping companies were well ahead in the provision of scheduled services, and played a prominent part in the transport of emigrants to the New World, an area in which the Dutch had long since lost their dominance to ports like Le Havre, Hamburg, and Bremen in particular. Attempts to institute scheduled steamship services to America in 1839 and 1850 had failed before they were properly under way.

The lesser appeal of the United States for Dutch merchants and financiers was also reflected in the Amsterdam capital market. After the 1806 Louisiana issue, trading in American securities was more or less at a standstill for some years. This was partly due to the Dutch government's pressing need for capital, which held interest rates on national loans at a much higher level than in Britain or France. The Dutch had been at war with the princes of Java, the most important island of the Indonesian archipelago, for a number of years. This, together with the secession of Belgium from the union with Holland in 1830 and the lengthy and costly armed peace that followed up to 1839, when King Willem I finally accepted Belgium's independence, was a severe drain on the country's resources.

Nevertheless, it had not been lacking in capital since 1813, as was evident on every occasion when a foreign country or company raised a loan on the Amsterdam capital market. Between 1824 and 1840 Russia borrowed 132 million guilders, while in the same period lack of interest on the part of Dutch capitalists forced the Dutch government to borrow money in London to finance the campaign against the Belgians. The low level of investment in American securities between 1813 and 1850 was attributable to other causes. After the Napoleonic Wars, Europe entered on a period of rapid economic growth which offered numerous opportunities for investment. The financial and economic policies of the United States were directed increasingly towards Britain, whose exports of industrial products to the United States were balanced by its imports of American cotton and grain. The United States, and specifically private persons and business companies, focused to an increasing extent on the capital market in London, the new world financial center. Up to 1835 the American government first paid off its external debts, then turned to repaying the whole of the national debt by means of the sale of public lands, i.e. the lands in federal ownership in territories where American Indian tribes had been displaced by new settlers.

The situation changed however from 1820 onwards. The rapid economic growth of the new American republic placed its inadequate infrastructure under a heavy strain. To remedy this deficiency, the city of New York built the Erie Canal in 1825, giving it direct access to the Great Lakes and converting it into the greatest port in North America, a position it never subsequently lost. This was followed a few years later by the introduction of the railroad, a revolutionary mode of transport which was to have a decisive impact on the development of the American continent. Railroad companies appeared almost overnight, and "railroads from everywhere to everywhere and from nowhere to nowhere were rapidly projected, hastily built and slowly operated". They spread throughout the country "like measles in a boarding school".

But the boom was short-lived. Barely five years after it started in 1835, many banks and railroad companies were in serious financial difficulties. Dutch investors were among those who paid the price.

The Club of Six had been approached in 1817 with a plan for financing the construction of the Erie Canal, but mindful of the disappointing results of earlier canal projects, had turned it down. They realized their mistake later, when the Erie Canal yielded large returns. In 1829 the Amsterdam bankers W. & J. Willink became interested in a similar project, floating a loan of $ 750,000 at 5 percent on behalf of the Morris Canal & Banking Company for the construction of a canal from the Hudson at Jersey City via Newark and Patterson to the Delaware at Easton. Though more than 100 miles had been dug by 1835, it had not reached the Hudson, and the Morris Canal & Banking Company owed the bondholders $ 1.5 million. The interest owing was in fact never paid.

The story was much the same with a second loan raised on the Amsterdam capital market in 1829. Daniël Crommelin & Soonen brokered an issue of 3,750,000 guilders at 5.5 percent for the Chesapeake & Ohio Canal Company, which planned to construct a canal linking Washington D.C. with Lake Erie. The federal government was not inclined to give financial support to the enterprise, and the removal of the first spadeful of earth in 1828 was the beginning of a lengthy drama. By 1834, when the work had progressed

The "Atlantic", 1832
Six Archives

One of the first trains
here pictured between
Baltimore and Ohio.
[... Railroad companies
appeared almost over-
night, and railroads from
everywhere to everywhere
and from nowhere to
nowhere were rapidly
projected, hastily built
and slowly operated.]

160 miles at the cost of 4 million guilders, the company was bankrupt, and despite more millions invested in it by the state of Maryland, the canal never reached Lake Erie. In 1850 it had got as far as Cumberland, the half-way point, where the project was finally abandoned. In that same year of 1828 the first miles of tracks were laid by the Baltimore & Ohio Railroad. This time foreign investors did not lose out. The cities of Georgetown, Alexandria, and Washington guaranteed the loan and the entire enterprise was "under special Guardianship of His Excellency the President of the United States". The company was declared bankrupt in 1834, but Congress, appalled at the prospect of the nation's capital passing into the hands of foreign capitalists other than Dutch investors, and voted in 1836 to assume responsibility for the loan issued in the Netherlands. As a result, the debt was repaid from 1841 onwards in accordance with the prospectus.

As from 1839 Hope & Co. established themselves as the leading brokers of American loans on the Amsterdam capital market. Some of the transactions related to shares in banking institutions like the Bank of the United States in Philadelphia, the Phoenix Bank of New York, and the Farmers Loan and Trust Company of New York, and to bonds issued by states such as Pennsylvania, Ohio, Indiana and Illinois, and the cities of New York and Boston. In 1840 Hope & Co. brokered two loans totalling 10 million guilders at 5 percent on behalf of the Bank of the United States, and also played a prominent part in the issue of securities for the bank by Rothschild in Paris. Up to the period of the Civil War, few new American

Announcement of the sale of U.S. treasury notes for two million guilders at 6% to the public of the Netherlands, 1794 Municipal Archive Amsterdam

BERICHT

Van eene BELEENING, by wyze van *Negotiatie*, groot TWEE MILLIOENEN GULDENS, tegens den Intrest van Zes per Cent in 't Jaar, op authorifatie en voor Reekening van de Wel Edele Heer JAMES GREENLEAF, benoemd Conful; door de VEREENIGDE STAATEN van AMERICA voor deeze Stad, ten Comptoire van de Heeren DANIEL CROMMELIN en SOONEN als Directeuren derzelve.

Deeze Beleening is gevestigd op DRIE DUIZEND ERVEN GRONDS, ofte 1½ Erv Onderpand voor ieder Obligatie van *f* 1000, waar van ieder Erv, door elkander genoomen, ten minften 110 voeten diep en 27 voeten breed; ofte wel 2970 vierkante voeten is houdende, alle gefitueerd tot bouwing van Huizen ofte andere Gestichten; en geleegen binnen den omtrek der nieuwe Stad WASHINGTON, in Noord-America; thans wordende bebouwd, ten einde ook tot de aanftaande en Permanente Zeetel der VEREENIGDE STAATEN te dienen.

Alle deeze Erven Gronds, ofte wel in de bovenftaande Proportie, zullen ten behoeven der Deelneemeren, in deeze Beleening worden gefteld ten Naamen van

de Wel Edele Heeren {PIETER GODEFROY, Mr RUTGER JAN SCHIMMELPENNINCK en ROBERT DANIEL CROMMELIN.

Als bewaarders derzelve.

Tot fecuriteit der Deelneemers zal de Heer *James Greenleaf* ook door *Daniel Crommelin en Zoonen*, doen fourneeren een zodanig Montant van Fondfen, ten laften de VEREENIGDE STAATEN van AMERICA, dewelke, met derzelver Interesfen, zullen goedmaken alle de Renten deezer Beleening, tot den afloop derzelve toe.

Alle deeze Fondfen zullen worden gefteld ten namen van *Daniel Crommelin en Soonen*, en de origineele Certificaten worden gedepofiteerd onder de Notaris *Anthony Mylius*, en waar by teffens door hun zal worden gevoegd eene Acte van afftand, zo voor Capitaal als Intresfen, ten einde ingevalle de gemelde Heer *J. Greenleaf*, niet behoorlyk aan deszelfs Engagement in deeze zoude voldoen, met deeze Fondfen dadelyk ten behoeven der Geinteresfeerdens te kunnen ageeren.

Twaalf

Twaalf Jaaren zal deeze Beleening ftand grypen, aanvang neemende met Primo May 1794. en eindigen met Ultimo April 1806. terwyl by ieder Obligatie zal worden gevoegd 12 Coupons Jaarlyks op Primo May betaalbaar, ten Comptoire van de gemelde Directeuren *Daniel Crommelin en Soonen*, onder deeze referve nogthans dat het de gemelde Heer *Greenleaf* zal vry ftaan omme met de expiratie van het 5de of eenige daar op volgende Jaaren deeze Beleening, 't zy voor het geheel ofte wel in gedeeltens, by Looting te kunnen aflosfen en rembourfeeren, waar van, als dan, door tydige Advertisfementen, in Couranten, de Houders der Aandeelen zullen worden geinformeerd.

Ingevalle van gedeeltelyke aflosfing zal het den gemelden Heer *J. Greenleaf* ook vryftaan een zodanig proportioneel gedeelte der Erven Gronds, als deszelfs Eigendom weder te benaderen, zullende, ten einde deeze benadering op eene billyke wyze gefchiede, ieder Erv Gronds op een hier na te formeere Pordereu worden Genumereerd en by Loting, ten overftaan van Notaris en Getuigen de alzo te rembourfeere Erven worden bepaald, terwyl de gemelde Heer *J. Greenleaf* zig intusfchen ook de vryheid referveerd, ten allen tyde op deeze Erven Gronds na goedvinden te mogen bouwen.

Een Maand, na ieder jaarlykfe verfchyndag en betaaling der Interesfen, zullen de gemelde *Daniel Crommelin en Soonen*, ten behoeven van de gemelde Heer *J. Greenleaf*, als zyn Eigendom uit de gedeponeerde Fondfen intrekken, zo veele Dollars, met de daar op verfcheenen Interesfen, als te famen zullen uitmaken het beloop der alhier betaalde Renten deezer Beleening, zullende egter het in gebreeke blyven der Houders van Aandeelen, omme derzelver Interesfen, binnen de gemelde Maand, te ontfangen, geene præjuditie aan deeze intrekking kunnen te weeg brengen; gelyk ook niet ingevalle van aflosfing, als zullende het Tranfport der Erven, voor zodanig gedeelte, insgelyks een Maand, na de bepaalde tyd, tot rembours der Aandeelen, door voorfz. Heeren Bewaarders gefchieden.

Ieder Dollar 6 pCt. Fonds en 3 pCt in de proportie, zo van Namptisfement als weder intrekking zal tot 50 ft. worden gereekend

Eindelyk zullen alle de Aandeelen in deeze Beleening behoorlyk, door de Notaris voornoemd, worden geprothocolleerd, ten einde het blyke dat geene meerdere Obligatien zyn afgegeeven dan 'er Erven Gronds, in de proportie als voorfz. op naam van Heeren Bewaarders, zyn gefteld geworden.

Ter præftatie en nakoming deezer, verbind de gemelde Heer *James Greenleaf* al verder zyn Perfoon en Goederen, zo roerende als onroerende, en zo alhier als in Noord-America geleegen, afftand doende van alle Wetten en Ufantien, die ten aanzien deszelfs Eigendommen, in Noord-America geleegen, dit zoude kunnen contrarieeren, en verder onder verband alhier als na regten

De intekening gefchied ten Comptoire voormeld, alwaar ook de Fournisfementen, op Recepisfen kunnen gefchieden.

A1

securities were listed on the Amsterdam Bourse. The rapid expansion of American railroads began to attract the interest of Dutch capitalists in 1857, but the extent of Dutch investment in the United States in the preceding decades is difficult to determine. One estimate puts it at 58 million guilders in 1803. The U.S. government's repayment of the public debt must have resulted in a substantial diminution after 1820, so that by 1835 the figure was probably somewhere between 10 and 20 million guilders.

The Netherlands and the Rise of an Economic Superpower: 1850 - 1903

From about 1850 the United States evolved into a major economic power second only to Great Britain in world status. A stream of capital and immigrants flowed into the country, and agricultural and industrial exports showed a rapid increase. Dutch investments in and imports from America grew at a corresponding rate, outstripping the substantial increase in Dutch exports to the United States.

American securities had virtually vanished from the Amsterdam stock exchange, which listed no more than three bond issues, including the ill-fated 1840 loan to the Bank of the United States. This changed a few years later, when American authorities and private enterprises again sought backing on the Dutch capital market. The securities concerned were largely issued by the railroad companies that were rapidly opening up the North American continent, and by the Confederate and Union governments in the years of the Civil War. The Confederate States borrowed mainly in Britain, which was sympathetic to their cause, while the government in Washington concentrated more on the German and French capital markets. There is nothing to indicate that either of the warring parties raised loans on the Dutch market. In 1861, for instance, when the Civil War started, American securities listed on the Amsterdam exchange amounted to no more than 500,000 guilders, as against 77 million guilders in Russian government bonds. The majority of U.S. government bonds traded in Amsterdam during the war were issued in Paris and London, with the sole exception of three new loans in 1863, which were probably conversions of two earlier loans maturing in that year. The development of the market value reflects the lack of interest in Amsterdam for American government bonds. The defeats suffered by the Union armies in 1864 precipitated a sharp fall in value which persisted until after the war. In that year London financiers took advantage of the Confederate successes to unload as many Confederate bonds as possible on to the initially cautious Dutch investor who, with the outcome of the war still uncertain, was willing to speculate. The number of bonds bought at that time, and which subsequently became worthless when General Robert E. Lee surrendered on April 9, 1865, is unknown.

During the rest of the century there was only one more issue of U.S. bonds on the Dutch capital market, namely in 1879 at 4 percent. Their value was consistently well above par, peaking at 128 1/8 in December, 1886. After the last repayment in 1906, it was another twenty years before U.S. government bonds were again listed on the Amsterdam exchange.

Dutch investors were at first equally uninterested in American railroad shares, but this rapidly changed towards the end of the 1850s. Twenty years after the railroad companies had gained a firm foothold in London, the Amsterdam *Beurscourant* reported that Illinois Central was planning to raise $ 3.2 million at 7 percent interest. First floated in London, it was not fully subscribed owing to the Crimean War, whereupon it was transferred to Amsterdam, where it proved to be successful. The debenture stock issued by Illinois Central marked the beginning of Dutch involvement in the financing of American railroads. This new trend was temporarily halted by the outbreak of the Civil War, and it was not until 1868 that an American railroad company again appeared on the Amsterdam exchange, where the lost ground was soon regained. To quote one commentator: "It may be said that the American railroads have conquered our Bourse just as fast as they have opened up the Far West." Around 1875, American securities, of which 90 percent were railroad shares, comprised a third of all foreign securities listed on the Amsterdam exchange. It was not until the twentieth century that Dutch and East Indies securities outnumbered those of foreign origin. In 1900 there were 479 Dutch and 531 foreign securities listed, of which 166 were American. In 1914 there were 956 Dutch and 840 foreign securities. Of the 302 American stocks listed, 194 were issued by railroad companies.

As the railroads arrived fairly late on the scene, the bulk of Dutch capital was invested in the Mississippi Valley and the Far West. Different market quotations often related to the same railroad, which financed specific routes and sections, branch lines, bridges, and terminal stations as separate units. The Union Pacific, for instance, issued special debentures for its "southern branch", while the Atlantic & Pacific had an "Ohio section", the Illinois Central a "Kansas-Mississippi bridge", and the Southern Pacific a "San Francisco Terminal". The number of American securities grew at such a pace that a separate directory, *American Railroads Listed on the Amsterdam Stock Exchange*, was compiled in 1873.

The upsurge of interest in American railroads was attributable to a number of factors. Investors do not appear to have been greatly concerned about the question of solidity. It was often the case that Dutch stockbrokers and banks knew no more about railroad securities than appeared in the financial press, even though all American brokers were prepared to supply full information free of charge by return mail. This made it very easy for malafide American operators to line their own pockets. The advice given by N.J. den Tex, publisher of the American securities directory, was that as a general rule it should be assumed that "the directors of American railroads regard their position first and foremost as an opportunity to enrich themselves". The example of the Union Pacific Railroad is merely one of many. The directors set up a special construction company, Credit Mobilier of America, to build the railroad, and though constantly on the verge of bankruptcy, it paid out annual dividends of up to 300 percent.

Many companies failed to keep their shareholders properly informed, especially in the first years of the boom in American railroad securities. It was often the case that annual reports were not accompanied by any kind of balance sheet. This sometimes resulted in an unpleasant surprise, such as received by the

Train by Niagara waterfalls
Lithograph by unknown artist.
Six Archives

shareholders in the La Crosse & Milwaukee Railroad when they discovered that the debts accumulated over three years had risen by $ 16 million, of which $ 9 million had disappeared into the directors' pockets. This did not enhance the reputation of American railroads. The eminent financial journalist, S.F. van Oss, distinguished between two categories of railroad companies: "those that earned dividends but did not pay them, and those that paid dividends but did not earn them". As another nineteenth-century wit phrased it, "there are cheats, there are liars, and there are railroad presidents".

So if they were not seen as solid investments, what then was the attraction of American railroad securities for Dutch capitalists? Operating in a country with a chronic shortage of capital, American businessmen were accustomed to pay relatively high interest rates. In combination with mortgage securities, an issue price below par and the chance of a rise in prices, the 1 or 2 percent higher interest involved was reason enough for both parties to risk taking the plunge. If it worked, the investor was assured of an annual return of 10 percent or more. Buying American railroad shares was thus primarily a form of speculation for the Dutch investor.

Between 1858 and 1874 sixty new companies were listed on the Amsterdam exchange, all of which, given the issue price, carried an element of risk. Of the thirty-five appearing between 1869 and 1871, only nine were quoted at 80 percent or more. The confidence placed by Dutch investors in American railroads in 1872 was such that the issue price was below that level in only a few instances; indeed the Cleveland & Ohio Railroad was quoted at 90 percent. Then in 1873 Wall Street prices collapsed. The amount of Dutch capital that had meanwhile been invested in the United States is unknown. Proceeding from an estimated $ 72 million before 1871, it may be assumed that it was well above $ 100 million.

The 1873 crash brought the speculators face to face with reality. The many post-Civil War boom was over, railroad companies went bankrupt, banks closed their doors, and panic prevailed on Wall Street. It was six years before the American economy recovered. Dutch dealers and investors incurred heavy losses when many securities were suddenly worthless. More than thirty of the fifty or more listings on the Amsterdam exchange at a nominal value of $ 129 million stopped interest payments in or shortly after 1873, leading almost inevitably some time later to a radical reorganization. No information is available on the losses suffered in the Netherlands. It is known, however, that many of the brokers concerned went out of business. Their place was taken by specialist brokerage firms like Adolphe Boissevain & Co., which together with well-established banking houses like Hope & Co. thereafter assumed responsibility for the issue of American securities in the Netherlands.

But Dutch investments in the United States were not confined to railroads alone. Partly as a consequence of the railroad investments, Dutch capital went into land, mortgage banks, and construction consortiums. The so-called land companies came into being in the wake of the failure of the various railroad companies, which had received large land grants from the federal authorities to finance their construction activities. When interest payments were suspended the bondholders were given the option of accepting payment either in land or in shares in the company proposing to convert the land holdings into cash.

The best-known and indeed most notorious example of such a company was the Maxwell Land Grant & Railway Company, in which the Dutch royal family is said to have owned a substantial interest. Founded in 1867 to construct and operate a railroad through New Mexico and Colorado, it went into liquidation a few years later. An investigation by two representatives of the Dutch shareholders revealed the fact that the books had been kept in pencil. Dutch investors retained a minority interest in the enterprise after its reorganization in 1888 as the Maxwell Land Grant Company. They held approximately 20 percent of the capital of 12 million guilders, and subscribed in large numbers to a $ 3 million loan. The new company focused on the exploitation of the 1.6 million acres it owned in New Mexico and Colorado, operating coal mines and ranches, and selling or leasing as much land as possible. Mining and ranching, however, yielded little in the way of profit, and efforts to attract Dutch settlers were a failure. The inhabitants of Maxwell City, New Mexico, comprised just ten families in 1890, who shortly afterwards were compelled to leave because they were unable to make a living from the unwatered, poor quality soil. A sudden higher yield from one of the gold mines between 1915 and 1917 was not enough to salvage the reputation of the Maxwell Land Grant Company, which had paid no dividends since 1870. The debenture loan was finally redeemed in 1928, but with the reorganization of the company in that year the shareholders lost heavily on the conversion of their shares.

In the 1880s the disparity between interest rates in the United States and the Netherlands gave rise to the establishment of one or two Dutch mortgage banks in America. Shortly after the Civil War two American mortgage banks had made their debut on the Dutch capital market. This example was followed in 1883 by the Netherlands-American Land Company, which covered Minnesota, Iowa, and Indiana from its head office in St. Paul, Minnesota. With a capital of 1.7 million guilders, it issued mortgage bonds to the value of 6.5 million guilders at 4 and 4.5 percent in 1900. A similar institution was the Northwestern & Pacific Mortgage Bank, founded in Amsterdam on July 5, 1889, which operated from Spokane, Washington. Its initial results were promising. The paid-up capital in 1897 was 3.6 million guilders, plus a further 15.9 million in mortgage bonds at 3.5 percent and debentures. In addition, it held mortgages to the value of 4.2 million guilders, and realty worth 9.4 million. Dividends of 44, 36, and 33 percent were paid in 1891, 1892, and 1893, respectively. Three years later, however, the bank announced that it could no longer meet its obligations. The mortgages and other securities had been vastly overvalued in the books, and the director had misappropriated funds. Declared bankrupt in 1898, the Northwestern & Pacific Mortgage Bank was then radically reorganized. Its assets in 1900 were 3.4 million guilders in mortgages and 6.4 million in real estate.

In the early 1890s American mortgage banks again turned their attention to the Dutch capital market. The Northwestern Guaranty Loan Co. issued debenture bonds to the value of 1.5 million guilders at 4.5 percent; the collateral was a 12-floor office building in Minneapolis. Two other mortgage banks were less successful in their bids to attract Dutch capital. The Lombard Investment Co. failed to raise $ 500,000 in mortgage bonds at 5 percent in 1891, and the Equitable Mortgage Bank was equally unsuccessful in raising 700,000 guilders at 5 percent on mortgages in Georgia, Louisiana, and Texas. August Philips, later the Dutch envoy to Washington for a short time in 1917, acted as agent for both institutions. The Equitable Mortgage Bank, hit by the economic crisis of 1893, went bankrupt a year later.

Another notable transaction towards the end of the nineteenth century involved a huge investment in the Kansas City, Pittsburgh & Gulf Railroad (KCPG) by a consortium led by the Amsterdam banking house Tutein Nolthenius & de Haan and Jan de Goeijen Jr., owner of coffee plantations in the Dutch East Indies. The American railroad magnate Arthur E. Stillwell planned to build a railroad linking Kansas City, Missouri, with Port Arthur on the Gulf of Mexico. Prevented by the 1893 crisis from raising capital in the United States for the construction of the section passing through Arkansas and Louisiana, he sought backing in the Netherlands. As collateral for two loans amounting to 13 million guilders, Stillwell deposited the bulk of the shares in the two construction companies concerned with the Amsterdam Trustees Office, a subsidiary of Tutein Nolthenius & de Haan. The Dutch share in Stillwell's enterprise increased over the next few years. To raise more capital, in 1895 De Goeijen and a group of Amsterdam bankers set up an association of KCPG shareholders which floated loans to the value of 5 million guilders. The Amsterdam Trustees Office also traded some 885,000 dollars' worth of KCPG shares, while others sold additional shares amounting to 2 million dollars on the Amsterdam exchange. In the end, Dutch investments in the Stillwell railroad comprised more than 25 million guilders. With sufficient working capital in hand, the project was rapidly completed, and the 750 mile track linking Kansas City with Port Arthur was operational on November 11, 1897. But there were problems from the start. The track was poorly constructed, and trains were regularly derailed. Moreover, there was not enough rolling stock to maintain a regular service. Then a tariff war erupted with the other railroad companies linking the Midwest with the Gulf of Mexico. Unable to weather the storm, the KCPG was declared bankrupt when it failed to meet its financial commitments in April, 1899.

De Goeijen, the railroad tycoon E.H. Harriman and the steel magnate and speculator John W. Gates formed a consortium to buy the KCPG in 1900. The shareholders lost some of their money, but as the new Kansas City Southern Railway Company soon turned out to be a profitable enterprise their losses were not disastrous. After a time the Dutch shareholders bought out first Harriman and then Gates. One of the new directors was Daniël G. Boissevain, the representative of the Amsterdam bankers Adolph Boissevain & Co. who was to be a co-founder of The Netherland Chamber of Commerce in America in 1903.

The success of the Kansas City Southern Railway Company was exceeded by that of the two construction companies that had built the railroad. The shares Stillwell had deposited as collateral passed into Dutch hands when the KCPG was liquidated in 1899. The assets consisted of shares in the railroad company, real estate, and cash. The opening up of the American interior was followed by the exploitation of the forests lining much of the railroad. Then in 1901 oil was discovered at Port Arthur, and the yield from the Spindletop oilfield was reflected in a 1902 dividend of Dfl. 33.60 per nominal share of Dfl. 120.

No more than a rough estimate can be made of Dutch investments in the United States at the end of the nineteenth century. Adolph Boissevain, the founder of the bank of the same name, put their value in 1899 at approximately $ 240 million, but the figure was probably closer to $ 350 million. Total foreign investments in the United States in that year amounted to an estimated $ 3.3 billion.

In the closing decades of the nineteenth century Dutch trade with the United States increased substantially in volume and changed considerably in composition. Up to the early 1880s Dutch exports consisted mainly of spirits, tin, and coffee. Around 1885 the first large shipments of high-quality Sumatra tobacco reached the American market, and about the same time the diamond trade entered a period of rapid expansion. In 1890 exports of these two commodities to the United States amounted to $ 9 million and $ 3.5 million respectively. Coffee, tin, nutmeg, herring, and spirits also sold well on the American market, rising from $ 1.3 million in 1870 to $ 7 million in 1880 and $ 17 million by 1890. Sales in 1901 exceeded $ 20 million.

Visiting card of the Netherlands Fire Insurance Company, established 1845, one of the founding companies that later merged to form Nationale Nederlanden (nowadays ING North America Insurance Corp.). By the year 1900 the company was also represented in San Francisco. Due to bad results in the non-life business in the United States and the danger of large scale fires in cities (Baltimore fire, 1903), the company withdrew from the Pacific Coast, just before San Francisco was hit by the big earthquake in 1906. In 1912 the Netherlands est. 1845 reentered the non-life market in the United States. Today ING Insurance operates 18 life, health, and property and casualty insurance companies over the entire United States. Archief Nationale Nederlanden.

U.S. exports to the Netherlands rose in the same period from $ 6.4 million in 1870 to $ 17 million in 1880 and to $ 22 million in 1890. Impressive though it was, this performance was insignificant compared with the 400 percent growth that followed in the 1890s, with the result that by 1900, American exports to the Netherlands, consisting primarily of raw materials and semi-manufactured products, amounted to almost $ 90 million. They included $ 10 million in animal fats from the Boston and Chicago meatworks imported by the margarine manufacturers Jurgens and Van den Bergh in Rotterdam (part of the Unilever group). Cereals for human and animal consumption accounted for $ 25 million, petroleum $ 8.5 million, cotton-seed oil $ 2.7 million, and tallow $ 4.6 million. There was little demand for American manufactured goods in the Netherlands. American tobacco and cotton, imported in large quantities in 1850, had all but disappeared from the Dutch market by the turn of the century.

By the beginning of the twentieth century the Netherlands had established close economic ties with the United States. As an investor of capital and one of America's five most important trading partners, it occupied a prominent place in the American economy. In addition, more than 200,000 Dutch men and women had settled in the United States between 1820 and 1900 strengthened the bonds between this 75 million-strong superpower and the country that had founded New York in 1626.

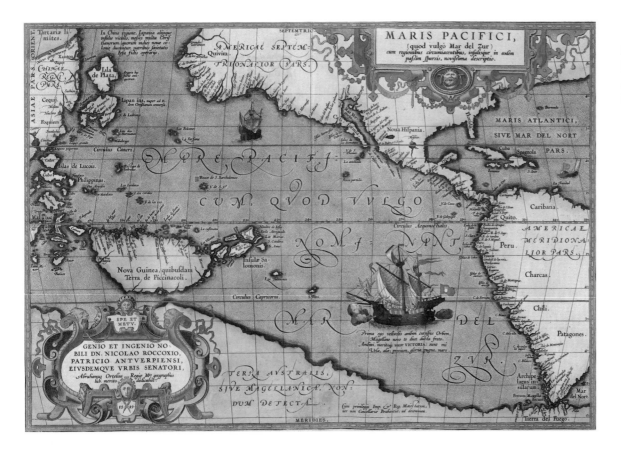

Map of the Pacific, 1589
Engraving by
Abraham Ortelius
(1527-1598)

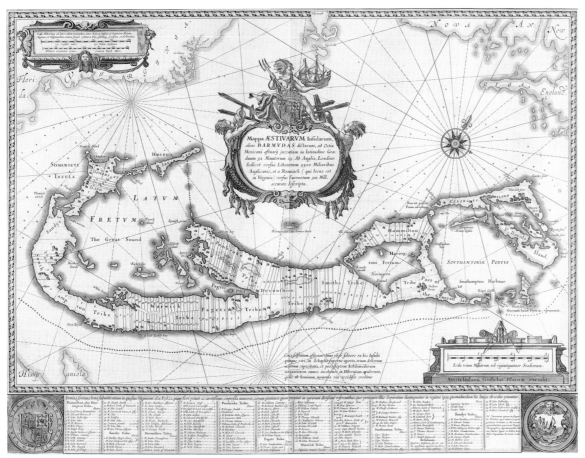

Chart of the island
Bermuda, 1631
Engraving by
Willem Blaeu
(1571-1638)

*George Washington
Vanderbilt
Painting by
John Singer Sargent
(1856-1925)
Biltmore Estate,
Asheville, North Carolina*

*George Washington
Vanderbilt (1862-1914),
one of the founders of the
Netherlands Chamber of
Commerce and grandson
of the "Commodore"
Cornelius Vanderbilt, the
creator of the shipping
and railroad empire. The
Vanderbilts are descen-
dants of Jan Aertsen van
der Bilt, who emigrated
from Holland to New
Amsterdam in 1640.*

CHAPTER II

1903 - 1914: EXPLORATION OF THE MARKET

The Netherland Chamber of Commerce in America: 1903 - 1914

The history of Dutch trade promotion organizations in the United States began in the spring of 1902 when a number of leading representatives of Dutch and American industry and commerce met in New York at the invitation of Baron Gevers, the Dutch envoy to Washington, for the purpose of founding The Netherland Chamber of Commerce in America.

How did this come about? First, the world economy had been booming for some years. The depression prevailing since 1872 had been brought to a halt in the years leading up to 1900 and international trade relations were thriving as never before. Though exact figures are lacking, it is clear that between 1900 and 1913 Dutch exports rose sharply from Dfl. 440 million to Dfl. 650 million. Secondly, through the modernization of agriculture and industry a wide range of new products was shipped abroad and many Dutch entrepreneurs tried their luck on foreign markets. There is little doubt that from the end of the nineteenth century onward, Dutch firms were increasingly active in foreign markets. Thirdly, Dutch exporters encountered numerous problems, especially on a more distant market such as the United States. How would trade be affected by customs and excise duties and import regulations? How could exporters be sure that importers would keep their word and carry out their part of the bargain? Moreover, did both sides speak the same language figuratively as well as literally, or were business practices so different as to doom any form of partnership to failure?

It is easy to forget that at a time when market research was still far in the future, new Dutch exporters often experienced considerable difficulties in ascertaining if there was a demand for their products in foreign markets. It was not that such information was unavailable in the Netherlands, as shown by the volume of foreign trade. But it tended to be concentrated in the traditional commercial networks for which personal contacts were crucial. For exporters in new economic activities like manufacturing, these networks were barely in existence. Whereas trade, shipping, finance and agriculture had accumulated over the years a large pool of knowledge and a dense network of personal relationships, the new entrepreneurs seeking to profit from branching out beyond the confines of the Netherlands had to find their way unaided. Knowledge was now a marketable commodity.

Around the turn of the twentieth century, there were various ways in which a Dutch entrepreneur, who was unable or unwilling to use the services of an established firm, could orient himself in a foreign market. Nevertheless, by gathering information from business firms and contacts, banks, commercial information offices, the Amsterdam and Rotterdam Chambers of Commerce and Industry, the Ministries of Foreign Affairs and of Agriculture, Trade and Industry, and the consular service, he soon discovered that each could provide only a small piece of the puzzle. It is highly unlikely that he was able to form a full and accurate picture of any specific foreign market. This did not deter a Dutch exporter from taking the plunge abroad, but it is impossible to tell to what extent this was a calculated risk.

Dutch industry and commerce found this situation unacceptable. Some Dutch entrepreneurs pressed unsuccessfully for the establishment of a central information office in the Netherlands, while others urged, equally unsuccessfully, for the reorganization of the consular service by the Ministry of Foreign Affairs. On the initiative of the business community, the first Dutch Chamber of Commerce abroad was establish-

Major Van Rensselaer's House near Albany, New York, 1807.
Watercolor by Baroness Hyde de Neuville (1779-1849)
The New-York Historical Society

ed in London in 1891. In 1903, a trade information center was opened in Amsterdam, initiating the systematic collection and processing of economic information on foreign markets to the benefit of Dutch industry and commerce. With the establishment in 1906 of a trade division in the Ministry of Agriculture, Trade and Industry, the Netherlands government took a first cautious step in the direction of the active part it would play many years later in the promotion of Dutch trade. The promotion of exports was one of the first economic policies adopted by the Dutch government, a step prompted by the steadily increasing proportion of foreign trade in total national revenue.

view of major rensselaer's house near albany. 1807.

However, the Netherlands Ministry of Foreign Affairs was not yet ready to promote trade. Its interest was focused on international affairs in general and on preserving Dutch neutrality in particular, since this was regarded fundamental to Dutch independence in Europe and in the Dutch East Indies. In this environment, foreign economic relations were relegated to second place. Discussing trade policy and economic information some forty years later, an unidentified Dutch statesman commented, "A diplomat doesn't discuss cheese". Even though providing economic information was one of the principal tasks of the consular service, the Netherlands Ministry of Foreign Affairs in The Hague left it entirely to the discretion of the individual consulates. Its attitude to commercial information changed gradually, in response to economic developments and political pressure, and it long regarded this as primarily a matter for the business community.

The history of The Netherland Chamber of Commerce in America is to a large extent the history of its members, their commercial sectors, the involvement of its members in exports to the United States, and their measures to promote exports and investment. Of course, trade promotion efforts were affected by the modernization of Dutch exports and of the Dutch economy, the driving force behind many new ventures into international trade, in general. It also relates to furthering the interests of Dutch firms by the business community and government, which encompasses more than trade promotion alone. Dutch diplomatic representatives played an important part in economic relations with the United States, which at that time was pursuing a highly protectionist trade policy. Diplomats were expected to assist Dutch firms wherever possible to gain access to the U.S. market. Besides conducting trade agreement negotiations they also lent support to Dutch commercial interests indirectly when tariff legislation was before Congress. The initiative lay with trade and industry.

The Initial Stages

The group that responded to the invitation of the Dutch envoy and formally established The Netherland Chamber of Commerce in America on June 2, 1903 by signing the constitution and electing a Board of Directors included several well-known names in the American business world. The founding fathers of the Chamber included the two multi-millionaires George Washington Vanderbilt, the grandson of the legendary Commodore Cornelius Vanderbilt, and Colonel John Jacob Astor V, the great-grandson of the founder of the family fortune, Daan G. Boissevain, a member of the New York Stock Exchange and a representative of the Amsterdam bankers Adolphe Boissevain & Co., as well as L. Heyneker and James C. Parrish. Besides Astor and Boissevain, the Board of Directors, which came into being a few days later, also included descendants of seventeenth-century Dutch colonists like Cornelius Vanderbilt II, John van Lansing Pruyn, Stuyvesant Fish, president of the Illinois Central Railroad and the National Park Bank in New York, and the agricultural economist William Bayard van Rensselaer. American importers were represented by John F. Praeger, a textiles importer, and J. Schimmel, director of the Red D Line shipping company. J. Rypperda Wierdsma, the New York general agent for the Holland-America Line, represented Dutch business interests. René J. Jessurun, a lawyer, was the tenth member of the Board of Directors.

The preparations for this charter meeting had been started over a year before in the spring of 1902, when Gevers invited a number of Dutch residents of New York to meet to consider ways of boosting commercial relations between the mother country and the United States. After consultation with Gevers, Boissevain and Rypperda Wierdsma then asked John van Lansing Pruyn to start recruiting a Board of Directors. The result must surely have exceeded their expectations, for Stuyvesant Fish, Cornelius Vanderbilt II, John Jacob Astor and William Bayard van Rensselaer all agreed to take a seat on the Board. Certainly Van Lansing Pruyn was jubilant, writing to Gevers, "... I think that the organization planned by you to strengthen the commercial and traditional ties between the Netherlands and the United States begins its existence under very favorable auspices". Gevers was now assured of what he considered to be the indispensable support of the descendants of Dutch colonists who occupied a prominent position in American business and social life. On May 6, 1902 an organizing committee comprising of Boissevain, Van Lansing Pruyn and the secretary, A. van de Sande Bakhuyzen, the vice-consul designate in New York, drew up a confidential document, "Memorandum Concerning the Founding of a Netherland Chamber of Commerce in America", addressed to the Dutch and American firms trading in the two countries.

Efforts by private enterprise to promote trade were not confined to the United States. In June, 1902, without referring to Boissevain's initiative, the principal Dutch employers' organization, the Netherlands Industrial Association, proposed the idea of establishing an organization in New York similar to the Chambers of Commerce in London, Hamburg and Paris. Reasoning that the Netherlands was the United States' fifth trading partner after Britain, Germany, Canada and France,[1] the Association confidently expected this new initiative to find a ready response in the United States, not only because of the traditional ties of friendship between the two countries, but also because of the prominent position occupied by people of Dutch descent in the American business community.

In November, 1902, the Association and the Boissevain committee launched a joint appeal to the business community to support the establishment of a Dutch Chamber of Commerce in New York. The aims and objectives of the new organization were outlined in the Association's journal. As knowledge about the United States was woefully lacking in all sectors of Dutch society, the committee felt that a Chamber of Commerce, working in close cooperation with the legation in Washington and the consulates throughout the United States, could function as a source of information on the commercial and economic life of the United States for both private enterprise and the government. Ideally, its area of activities would extend further than economic matters alone. The bond between Dutch emigrants and the mother country should not be allowed to weaken, and enterprising young people seeking to gain business experience in the United States or to settle there permanently should be helped to find suitable employment as well.

The idea was welcomed by commercial, industrial, shipping and banking interests in the Netherlands. Within two months of its announcement, the Association had registered one hundred prospective members on behalf of the organizing committee, and by the time of the New York meeting in June, 1903 the number of applications had risen to 144 in total, 96 from the Netherlands and its colonies and 48 from the United States. The Netherland Chamber of Commerce in America was thus the largest of the Dutch Chambers of Commerce which were set up in 1903 in foreign cities with sizeable Dutch business communities. In Paris and Brussels the impetus to establish a Chamber came from businessmen themselves, and in Melbourne the consulate took the initiative; the difference in New York was that businessmen, the Netherlands Industrial Association and representatives of the Netherlands government worked closely together.

Though the preparations were more or less complete by the spring of 1903, the establishment of the new organization was delayed due to the transfer to South Africa of Van de Sande Bakhuyzen, who was to have acted as secretary. When a suitable successor had been found in the person of Jessurun, The Netherland Chamber of Commerce in America was entered in the business register of the state of New York on May 27, 1903. Barely a week later, at a formal inaugural meeting on June 2, the organizing committee became the Board of Directors. An executive committee was appointed at the first meeting of the Board six days later. As the principal initiator, Boissevain was elected president, with Van Lansing Pruyn as vice-president and Jessurun as secretary-treasurer. The Chamber's operations had begun a few days before, on May 28, 1903, at the offices of Jessurun's law practice in the Morris Building, 68 Broad Street in Lower Manhattan. The Chamber's operations were conducted there until T. Greidanus succeeded Jessurun as secretary-treasurer in 1908, when the offices moved to the latter's premises in the Traders Exchange Building on 136 Water Street.

Seal of the Chamber, representing the "Halve Maen", the ship of Henry Hudson

Aims and Objectives

The Memorandum written by the Boissevain committee and the Netherlands Industrial Association to inform the American and Dutch business community of the proposed establishment of The Netherland Chamber of Commerce in America set out the aims of the organization. How the Board of Directors viewed their task, probably unwittingly, is illustrated by their choice of a corporate seal depicting the Dutch flag and the *Halve Maen*, the ship in which Henry Hudson discovered Manhattan in September 1609. In the same way as the *Halve Maen* had served Hudson in opening up the trade route to North America, the Chamber of Commerce was to help industry and commerce gain access to the American market. The ship symbolized the position of Dutch firms in a market that was correctly regarded as one of the biggest and

most formidable in the world. Like the Atlantic winds and storms that had once buffeted the *Halve Maen*, the ups and downs of the American economy and of international economic developments could determine the success or failure of the twentieth-century entrepreneur. Though the Dutch entrepreneur was safe from such perils as shipwreck, scurvy, and hostile American Indians faced by his seventeenth-century ancestor, the commercial dangers were hardly less grave. This was certainly true for the Dutch exporter who ventured into a new, unknown and seemingly boundless market like the United States. The aim of the founders of The Netherland Chamber of Commerce in America was to advise and assist Dutch firms who dared to test the waters on the far side of the Atlantic.

Whitehall Building, Battery Park and entrance to North River, New York, c. 1900

The aims and objectives of the organization, the composition of its Board of Directors and Executive Committee, and the firms and individuals eligible for the various forms of membership were listed in the Bylaws incorporated in all the annual reports from 1903 onward. It was as though the Dutch character of the enterprise had to be emphasized each year anew. Article II stated that the Chamber was:

> "to represent and foster in the United States the interests of the commerce, industry, agriculture, navigation, arts and science of the Netherlands and its Colonies and to increase the commerce of the United States with the Netherlands and its Colonies".

The succeeding articles imposed a number of restrictions on the general nature of the organization. They were first of all geographical. It went without saying that an organization devoted to the promotion of trade would be established in New York, the economic heart of the United States. As the largest seaport in the New World, the foremost consumer market, and the financial and industrial center of the United States, New York was the focal point of foreign trade. Between 1900 and 1914 more than 75 percent of U.S. imports from the Netherlands were unloaded in New York. Though its ascendancy in U.S. exports was less marked, with a share of some 50 percent New York occupied a central position in this respect as well.

The most notable feature of Article III was the stipulation that branch offices could only be opened in the United States, implying that neither then nor in the future the promotion of American exports to the Netherlands was allowed to become one of the Chamber's principal areas of activity. Given the modes of transport and the communications media at that time and the distance between the two countries, the establishment of an office in Amsterdam or Rotterdam was essential for the promotion of American exports to the Netherlands. This was hardly likely to happen in view of the commercial information widely disseminated by the American consular service. The Dutch business community observed this well-equipped and soundly financed organization with something approaching envy, regarding it as the right model to follow.

In the next few articles of its Bylaws, the Chamber's sphere of activity was further restricted to assistance and information for Dutch industry and commerce. Its Dutch character was underscored yet again in Article IV, reserving full membership of the Chamber to Dutch nationals, businesses and institutions, naturalized Americans of Dutch origin, and descendants of Dutch colonists. American citizens and firms were only eligible for associate membership without voting rights. Members of the foreign service comprised a separate category. As was later to become apparent, there were various reasons why The Netherland Chamber of Commerce in America aspired to have a semi-official status. It made it possible for Gevers to be the honorary president, and for J.R. Planten, the honorary consul-general in New York, to be appointed honorary vice-president, while other members of the foreign service could be ordinary members in their official capacity.

The Dutch nature of the Chamber was also reflected in its organizational structure. Article IX specified that five of the ten members of the Board of Directors, including the president and the secretary-treasurer, were to be Dutch nationals or naturalized American citizens of Dutch origin. The remaining five seats were reserved to descendants of Dutch colonists. The president was bestowed with wide powers. He convened the meetings of the Board of Directors, drew up the agenda, and had the casting vote when votes were equally divided. In addition, he supervised the day-to-day activities of the Chamber.

None of these restrictions, however, prevented the working capital from being subscribed by Dutch and American firms and individuals alike. The operational costs of the Chamber were to be met by annual contributions from its members. A reserve fund was formed for one-time donations to the Chamber. The status of Founder was accorded to those who donated $ 200 or Dfl. 200 in the first year of the Chamber's existence, and that of Donor to those contributing $ 100 or Dfl. 100.

The Members

The Dutch character of The Netherland Chamber of Commerce in America is most readily apparent from the composition of its membership, three-quarters of which consisted of firms established in the Netherlands. The approximately 200 members registered at the end of the first two fiscal years dropped to 176 in the two subsequent years. According to the annual report of 1912-1913, the decline in membership did not stem from dissatisfaction with the work of the Chamber, but rather from the fact that the Chamber had become firmly established in the course of its first two years, so that it was no longer perceived to be in need of aid by those individuals and firms that had supported it as a matter of principle. Because of the recession gripping the American economy in 1907, the mark of 200 members was not again reached until 1909, but thanks to favorable economic developments, by 1913 the membership figure had risen to 270.[2]

Even though the Chamber's members were listed in the annual reports, the branches of industry and commerce in which they were engaged are not known in all cases. Those in the Netherlands were largely active in the export and import sector, shipping, banking and the stock market. Members engaged in manufacturing, horticulture, especially bulb-growing and plant breeding, and manufacturing were less common, though the latter increased substantially after 1910.

More than half the members of the new Chamber were based in Amsterdam and Rotterdam, the main centers of economic life in the Netherlands. As the country's financial center and home of the Stock

Exchange, Amsterdam housed the majority of stockbrokers and agencies trading in American securities. Among the Chamber's members were leading merchant banks such as the Netherlands Trading Society, the Amsterdamsche Bank, and the Rotterdamsche Bankvereeniging, as well as smaller banks like the Colonial Bank, H. Oyens & Son, and the Curaçao Bank in Willemstad, Curaçao. Given the extent of portfolio investment in the United States, it is hardly surprising that a considerable number of members were engaged in buying and selling American securities. This explains Daan Boissevain's efforts on behalf of The Netherland Chamber of Commerce in America. In 1870, the Boissevain firm had placed on the Dutch market approximately 30 percent of the shares issued by the Illinois Central Railroad, to whose Board of Directors Stuyvesant Fish was appointed in 1903. In 1872, G.M. Boissevain had listed the first American industrial securities on the Amsterdam Stock Exchange, and thereafter the Boissevain family remained closely associated with the Dutch trade in American securities. At the time of the founding of The Netherland Chamber of Commerce in America, Daan Boissevain was the driving force behind the Boissevain group. As the New York representative of the banking house of Adolphe Boissevain & Co., he was on the Board of Directors of various American concerns as well. Other members of the Boissevain family were involved in The Netherland Chamber of Commerce in America, too. On behalf of Kean van Cortland & Co. of New York, G.L. Boissevain joined as one of the six life members, while in Amsterdam the Boissevain firm dealing in American securities became an ordinary member. Other stockbrokers followed their lead. They included Kerkhoven & Co., a firm founded in 1812 which had traded in American securities since 1870, the Amsterdam Trustees Office, and H.G. Aikema & Co. and G.H. Voorhoeve, both of Rotterdam.

Besides being the financial center of the Netherlands, Amsterdam was also one of the principal European entrepôts for tropical products like coffee and tobacco, a large proportion of which was shipped to the United States. The membership of the Chamber included various firms and individuals dealing in tropical commodities, including the Amsterdam Trading Company (HVA), which despite its name traded exclusively in agricultural products from the Dutch East Indies where it owned the largest sugarcane plantation, as well as the tobacco merchant F. Lieftinck, a member of the Amsterdam Chamber of Commerce, and Willem Heybroek Jr., co-founder of the Coffee Trade Association. Though several of the Rotterdam members traded in the same sectors as their Amsterdam counterparts, Rotterdam was primarily a port of transit for central Europe and this meant that most Rotterdam members traded in grain, oil and raw materials instead. Prominent Rotterdam members included Wm. Müller & Co., Steenkolen Handelsvereniging (SHV), grain merchants like W. Bunge & Co. and Van Stolk Bros., and the shipbrokers and forwarding agents, Ph. van Ommeren Corp. of New York.

Shipping was represented by the Rotterdam-based Netherlands-America Steamship Company, known since 1896 as the Holland-America Line, which together with two Amsterdam shipping companies, the Royal Netherlands Steamship Company and the Royal Dutch West India Mail, controlled a considerable part of the Atlantic trade. In contrast to the stock market, whose representatives were drawn from both Amsterdam and Rotterdam, the shipping sector seems to have viewed The Netherland Chamber of Commerce in America as an exclusively Rotterdam affair. Although the Royal Netherlands Steamship Company never joined, the Royal Dutch West India Mail did so in 1912, after the two companies merged.

The New York agents of the Holland-America Line played an active part in the Chamber's activities. When Rypperda Wierdsma returned to the Netherlands in 1906, he was succeeded on the Chamber's Board of Directors by A. Gips, the newly appointed New York agent of the Holland-America Line. Gips had previously served on the Chamber's Committee on Import and Export Trade, which assisted the secretary in handling enquiries, and the Audit Committee, which approved the annual accounts. A third representative of the company in New York was a long-time member of the Committee on Nominations. Two of the major Dutch East Indies shipping companies joined later. The growth in sales of the colony's agricultural products on the North American market gave the shipping companies an indirect interest in exports to the U.S. The Royal Packet Navigation Company (KPM) had the largest fleet of ships sailing between the islands of the archipelago, while the Royal Netherlands Steamship Company and the Stoomvaart Maatschappij Rotterdam Lloyd shipped the bulk of the tobacco, bark, and coffee produced in the colony to the Netherlands.

"Statendam",
The Holland-America
Line, 1919

The prominent part played by the Holland-America Line in The Netherland Chamber of Commerce in America warrants a brief account of the history of Dutch shipping in the Atlantic trade. The first attempts to establish a scheduled service to New York were made by the Royal Netherlands Steamship Company between 1870 and 1883. Because the economic tide was against the venture, the company narrowly escaped bankruptcy. Though the smaller Royal Dutch West India Mail extended its service between Amsterdam, Suriname, the Netherlands Antilles and Haiti to New York in 1888, a direct service between Amsterdam and New York was not opened until 1895. The Holland-America Line fared much better. In 1883, when heavy losses forced the Royal Netherlands Steamship Company to suspend its service to America temporarily, the Holland-America Line made its first sailing to New York. Thanks to the growing stream of emigrants from central and eastern Europe, it soon proved to be a profitable venture. Shortly afterwards the burgeoning trade between the two countries made it necessary for the Holland-America Line to introduce additional sailings. A scheduled service to the important grain port of Newport News in Virginia, begun in 1899, proved to be unprofitable and was switched to Philadelphia in 1907. Grain shipments from the Midwest added Boston and Baltimore to the schedule, followed by Savannah in Georgia. Finally, in 1912 the Holland-America Line opened a scheduled service to New Orleans.

The company's interest in The Netherland Chamber of Commerce in America emerges yet more clearly from a brief glance at the composition of cargo traffic between 1901 and 1910. The cargo shipped from America to Europe in those years was roughly three times the amount carried from Europe to America. The profitability of the westward route was solely attributable to the transportation of emigrants. At the same time, the growing number of American tourists travelling to Europe provided an additional source of income. Probably for that reason the Chamber offered to assist Dutch travel agents with advertising, and the annual reports regularly devoted attention to the promotion of American tourism to the Netherlands.

Lastly, the membership roll of the Chamber included Dutch manufacturers and persons and institutions concerned with the promotion of exports for general economic reasons. The majority of Dutch manufacturers produced luxury commodities like chocolate, alcoholic beverages and ceramics. The membership included familiar names like the Weesp cocoa manufacturers C.J. van Houten & Son, "De Drie Fleschjes" distillery in Amsterdam which was later to become widely known under the name of its managing-director H. Bootz, and the Lucas Bols distillery, also in Amsterdam. Other members engaged in manufacturing were the Royal Brocades Pharmaceutical Company in Meppel, the Royal Rozenburg Porcelain and Stoneware Pottery in The Hague, and the Gouda Candle Co. in Gouda. Among engineering firms, the Chamber's membership included the Haarlem Engineering Works, the H.K. Jonker Engineering Co., also in Haarlem, and the Electrical Engineering Co. in Utrecht. Industry in the Zaan region was represented by Wessanen & Laan in Wormerveer, later The Royal Wessanen Co. Those registering with the Chamber for general economic reasons included Esquire C.F. van den Poll, president of the Netherlands Industrial Association, and Dr. H.F.R. Hubrecht, an influential member of Parliament for the Liberal Party and vice-president of the Amsterdam Chamber of Commerce. A number of regional Chambers of Commerce in the Netherlands and Dutch Chambers of Commerce abroad also became members over the years.

With regard to the American membership of The Netherland Chamber of Commerce in America, U.S. members domiciled almost exclusively in New York. It is striking how few American members were branches of Dutch companies. Apart from the Holland-America Line and the publisher Martinus Nijhoff, most Dutch exporters seem to have entrusted their U.S. operations to independent importers or agencies. Some of them are known to have been importers, like H. Duys & Co. and the Geo. F. Wiemann Co., trading respectively in tobacco from Sumatra and tea from Java. The bankers Goldman, Sachs & Co. represented the Amsterdam bankers Labouchère, Oyens & Co., while the Royal Bank of Canada handled the American accounts of the Amsterdamsche Bank and the Rotterdam-based Incasso Bank, and the Raymond Whitcomb Company handled the U.S. affairs of the KPM shipping company. Up to the first world war, branches of Dutch firms in the United States remained few in number, giving no indication of the rapidly increasing volume of direct investments that would follow later. The first major investment of a Dutch company in the United States occurred in 1910, when Royal Dutch Shell purchased Oklahoma oil fields through a subsidiary company and moved into the home territory of Standard Oil, its greatest competitor.

Several American members of the Chamber were household names in the United States. Edward W. Bok, journalist and publisher of *Ladies Home Journal*, was a well-known personality. Brown Brothers & Co. were influential New York bankers and the United States Steel Products Company was part of the conglomerate which had absorbed much of the U.S. steel industry. The names of firms like the Ohlemacher Brick Co. of Michigan City, Indiana, the United States Slicing Machine Co. of Chicago, the Atlantic Mutual Insurance Co., the East India Trading Company, and the General Provision Company of New York added their names to the membership roll of the Chamber. It may be deduced from addresses in Broad Street, Water Street, and Wall Street, in the financial heart of Manhattan, that the remaining members were bankers and stockbrokers or independent importers of Dutch goods.

[...Van Houten's Cocoa already started exporting to the United States in 1875. In 1889, a sales office was opened in New York and in 1890 in Chicago. In the 1890s, a packing and distribution center was established in Brooklyn to circumvent the steep U.S. tariffs on imports of prepackaged cocoa. In 1906, the U.S. Food and Drug Administration allowed Van Houten to import cocoa and chocolate into the United States without inspection.]

Invoice for shipment of Bols Liquor to the United States in 1821. Today, "Bols Royal Distilleries" is part of Koninklijke Bols Wessanen N.V., headquartered in Amstelveen, the Netherlands, has more than 9,000 employees worldwide. In the U.S. Bols Wessanen employs 4,700 people. Bols Wessanen markets a wide range of food and beverage products, including dairy and breakfast products, frozen foods, spirits and wines and non-alcoholic drinks.

The Promotion of Trade

The lack of sources makes it difficult to determine how the founders of The Netherland Chamber of Commerce in America proposed to promote Dutch trade with the United States. Only a few of the annual reports published between 1903 and 1916 have survived, and all correspondence files have vanished. Moreover, the fact that all business enquiries had to be treated in strict confidence implied that no details could be published in the annual reports. Therefore, little can be said with certainty about the number of enquiries received each year, the nature of the information requested, and the products concerned. Discussions between the government and the business sector in the Netherlands around the turn of the twentieth century shed some light on the way in which commercial information was provided and on the problems that were encountered.

Beyond the following reference in Article XIV, the Bylaws yield few clues on the actual activities of The Netherland Chamber of Commerce in America:

> "The Chamber is prohibited from engaging in any commercial transactions on its own account or in any transactions other than those necessary for the execution of its purposes."

This underscores one of the central elements of providing commercial information. Trade promotion stands or falls with the question of confidence. Can the persons or firms seeking information be sure that their enquiries will not be disclosed to others, misused or abused in any way? It appears from Article XIV that the Board of Directors were fully aware of the Chamber's position of trust. The Dutch envoy and the consul-general in New York were appointed as honorary members primarily to emphasize the Chamber's independence and integrity. A change in the method of handling enquiries in 1904 brought the Chamber's sensitive position even more to the fore. At first the secretary had dealt with all enquiries personally. Though he could count on the assistance of the Board and the consulate-general, it was clear by the end of the first fiscal year that he would soon be overwhelmed by the growing number of requests for information. So the first annual meeting on May 21, 1904 voted to set up a Committee on Import and Export Trade consisting of three ordinary members and two representatives of the Executive Committee, which thereafter met every Monday to deal with requests for information. Addressing the Committee at the meeting, Boissevain stated that the Chamber could only fulfil its function as an advisory body for Dutch and American trade and commerce if the conditions of impartiality and confidentiality were strictly observed.

It may in any event be deduced from the annual reports that providing information to Dutch and - albeit to a lesser extent - American firms constituted the bulk of the Chamber's activities. In addition, the Chamber acted as a spokesman for the business community by drawing the attention of the Dutch government to problems in Dutch trade relations with the United States. The Chamber advised the Washington legation in the negotiations on the trade agreement concluded in 1907 and on the tariff law of 1909 which were then before the U.S. Congress, and kept the relevant government departments in The Hague informed of amendments to U.S. customs and tariff legislation.

The number of enquiries, which probably amounted to no more than a few hundred each year between 1903 and the outbreak of the first world war, seems to have been largely determined by international economic developments. For instance, the short-lived 1907 recession caused a sharp downturn whose impact was still felt two years later. However, it did not stop the Chamber from moving to 136 Water Street in October, 1908, where it was adjacent to the offices of secretary-treasurer Greidanus and could consequently be reached by telephone and keep ordinary business hours.

Though the precise nature of trade enquires handled by the Chamber is unknown, several facts can be learned from the annual reports. Many firms seem to have approached the American market with little or no preparation. Few enquiries were to the point. To quote from the annual report for 1911-1912, unless "they take us more or less into their confidence and explain what they wish, either to buy or sell, and what special branch of business they are engaged in", it was practically impossible to provide useful advice. Another category of enquiries consisted of general requests for information on a wide diversity of products. As a reply more or less demanded a detailed description of the American business world, the writers were asked to reformulate their queries more precisely. Only a few bothered to do so. In many instances the writers were referred to the consular reports issued by the Netherlands Foreign Service. The last category of questions was related to the solvency and reliability of specific firms. Because of the "moral responsibility" involved, the Chamber, like its counterparts in other countries, did not provide such information but referred the enquirer to commercial trade information offices, whose extensive network of Dutch and foreign correspondents made them more competent to answer these queries. What the Chamber could and did do was supply the names and addresses of potential buyers, agents and importers, warn of the problems that could arise, and point out that business practices in the United States were different from those in the Netherlands in many respects.

In line with the aim of promoting Dutch exports to the United States in the widest possible sense, the Chamber's services were available to both members and non-members free of charge. In this respect, The Netherland Chamber of Commerce in America deviated from its counterpart organizations in other countries, which accorded priority to the interests of their members. The Chamber in London even went so far as to refuse to answer enquiries from non-members, while the Chamber in Paris responded to all inquiries but only if it was not likely to harm the interests of its members. In New York, the majority of Dutch firms wanted the names and addresses of potential customers or agents for a diverse range of commodities including cheese and other dairy products, cocoa butter, paintings, spices, wine and Haarlem oil. Dutch import firms sought contact with U.S. suppliers of products ranging from carpets, furniture, barbed wire and vaseline to apples and honey. Several inquiries requested information of a more general economic or political nature such as recent economic trends and tariff regulations. Others requested "education" in business practice and advertising in the United States. The broad demand for information on the U.S. market was based on the fact that Dutch exporters understood that nothing could be gained by trying to expand exports to the United States if the American economy was stagnating, if customs duties or restrictions ruled out all prospects of making a profit, or if U.S. firms were approached in a way that was bound to antagonize them.

The principal advice given by the Chamber to exporters looking for U.S. markets was to come to America themselves: "The journey pays when it is undertaken by wide-awake, capable men". For a Dutch exporter, sound financial reserves were a prerequisite for a reasonable chance of success in the United States. In contrast to agents in the Netherlands, American agents were not prepared to advertise new products without the financial backing of manufacturers. Because of the fierce competition among foreign firms for the services of reputable agents in the United States, the latter were in a position to demand a sizeable annual budget. Of course, it was possible to do business with smaller or newly established importers, but even in that case a solid investment was needed to build up a position on the U.S. market. For Dutch exporters who preferred to handle American sales themselves, opening a branch in New York was a good alternative. The initial costs for the Dutch exporter were higher, but experience showed it to be cost-effective in the long term.

A major stumbling block was the fact that many Dutch exporters were reluctant to trust a new business contact, notwithstanding the element of risk invariably attached to new business ventures. One of the main doubts of Dutch exporters was whether U.S. importers, however solvent and trustworthy, would have the resources needed to launch new products on the American market. Many Dutch exporters did not dare to take the risk. This point was raised in the annual report for 1909-1910:

Many firms, unknown in the market, are anxious to do business, but begin their demands with a request for bankers' letters of credit, cash against documents, etc., asking all possible faith and confidence for themselves but unwilling to demonstrate their worthiness by showing a little confidence in the honesty of the customers whose orders they are soliciting, and by giving the buyer at least an opportunity to examine the goods they are buying from a stranger before handing over the purchase price.

With this in mind the Chamber devoted a considerable amount of attention to trends in Dutch exports and U.S. tariff legislation, not only in the annual reports but, especially in the first few years, also in journals with a wide circulation in Dutch business circles, such as *Algemeen Nederlands Exportblad*, *Tijdschrift der Maatschappij van Nijverheid* and the businessman's newspaper *Nieuwe Courant*. After 1907 the Chamber made more use of *Handelsberichten*, a weekly published by the Ministry of Agriculture, Trade and Industry.

Enhancing the overall image of the Netherlands in the United States was regarded by the Chamber as an important part of its work. It was actively involved in the arrangements for the Dutch exhibition at the 1905 World's Fair in St. Louis, and in New York's celebration of the 1909 tricentenary of Henry Hudson's discovery of Manhattan. In 1913, on behalf of the Chamber, Cornelius Vanderbilt II chaired the organizing committee for the commemoration of the settlement of Manhattan by Dutch colonists three hundred years before.

Difficult though it is to determine how Dutch exporters regarded The Netherland Chamber of Commerce in America, it seems to have established itself as part of the trade pattern in the years between its establishment and the disruption of Dutch-American trade relations by the first world war. It was at all times assured of the cooperation of leading American businessmen and the Dutch community in New York, and after the first period of its existence, membership in both countries steadily increased. However important its services may have been for individual firms, as a small organization that was dependent on the gratuitous work of its directors, it was not in a position to exercise any major influence on either the volume or the composition of Dutch exports to the United States. The history of the private promotion of trade with the United States was in fact largely determined by trends in the Dutch and American economies.

The Netherlands and its Position on the American Market

As the membership records show, The Netherland Chamber of Commerce in America drew its members from a relatively small number of business sectors. A good number of members were engaged in commercial activities like shipping, banking and stockbroking, while a smaller group represented the manufacturing industry. Comparing this membership composition with the categories of Dutch exports to the United States, it is immediately apparent that the exporters of important products like diamonds, tobacco, and bulbs were conspicuous by their absence. Since it is impossible to account for each individual firm, the reasons behind this fact are to be found in the developments in the Dutch economy. After all, the rapid growth of foreign trade since the end of the nineteenth century, combined with exporters' inadequate knowledge of business practices in the United States, contributed to the growing interest in the American market in the years preceding and at the time of the Chamber's existence. Therefore, the majority of members came from industries that had emerged in the second half of the nineteenth century, when the Dutch economy was developing at a rapid pace and when the volume and diversity of Dutch exports were increasing accordingly.

The Dutch economy around the turn of the century was "a relatively small, highly diversified economy which thanks to a modern infrastructure, a strong tradition of free trade and an exceptionally favorable geographical location" occupied a position in international trade that was disproportionate to its size. Trade figures convey the rapid pace of development that had brought about radical changes in the Netherlands in the preceding thirty years. Though industrialization is the most important feature of the modernization of the Dutch economy after 1870, it was not confined to industry alone. The factors contributing to industrial growth had an equally modernizing effect on the agricultural and service sectors which had formed the basis of the Dutch economy in the first half of the nineteenth century.

While foreign trade had always been an important part of the Dutch economy, it acquired added significance in the closing decades of the nineteenth century. The scope of the international trade boom of the Netherlands is unknown. The official statistics of the Netherlands are notoriously unreliable, because they failed to distinguish properly between the real import, export, and transit figures. Between 1872 and 1895, when the world economy was mired in the "Great Depression", Dutch foreign trade showed a slow but steady growth, rising from Dfl. 550 million in 1872 to Dfl. 840 million in 1895. Through the growing Dutch demand for raw materials and manufacturing supplies in agriculture and industry, modernization still largely related to imports. The average annual growth rate of Dutch imports of 2.5 percent between 1872 and 1895 almost was almost double the rate of Dutch export growth. The volume of Dutch imports doubled from Dfl. 280 million in 1872 to Dfl. 500 million in 1895. The growth of exports in the same period rose by no more than 25 percent from Dfl. 260 million to Dfl. 330 million. It accelerated only when the international economy improved in the closing years of the nineteenth century and the foreign demand for Dutch goods rose accordingly. The average annual rate of growth for both imports and exports then increased by almost 4 percent up to 1913. In that year, Dutch imports amounted to Dfl. 975 million and exports to Dfl. 650 million. The accelerated growth of exports stabilized the import cover on the balance of trade, which had dropped from 85 percent in 1872 to 70 percent in 1895 because of the greater demand for raw materials and manufacturing supplies. Comparison of the composition of Dutch exports in 1913 with that in 1870 reveals that the share of manufactured goods doubled to 40 percent up to 1895 and remained at that level. Despite a partial shift from animal to agricultural products, the total share of the primary sector remained very much the same at about 35 percent. The sharpest drop in the composition of Dutch exports occurred in the tropical products sector, which fell from 25 to 16 percent between 1870 and 1913.

Though the value of Dutch exports to the United States showed a corresponding increase, the Dutch products sold on the American market differed markedly from the overall composition of Dutch exports. The figures on Dutch exports to the United States provide a rough estimate rather than a definite overview of the actual development of trade between the two countries.[3] Amounting to $ 14 million in 1872, total trade figures between the United States and the Netherlands rose to $ 46 million in 1895, and to $ 164 million in 1913. The doubling of Dutch exports to the U.S. from $ 15 million to $ 38 million between 1895 and 1913 was nonetheless modest compared to the growth of American exports to the Netherlands, which quadrupled from $ 31 million to $ 125 million in the same period. A substantial proportion of U.S. exports to the Netherlands was probably transshipped to Germany, as evidenced by the fact that large quantities of industrial raw materials were shipped from the United States to the Netherlands, although there was no Dutch processing industry of significance at that time. However, the United States played an important role in the rapid modernization of the Dutch economy as supplier of foodstuffs, animal feed, raw materials, manufacturing supplies and semi-finished products. This is reflected in the radical change in the Dutch balance of trade with the United States: whereas 50 to 70 percent of Dutch imports from the U.S. were covered by Dutch exports to the United States between 1872 and 1900, this figure was no higher than 35 percent in subsequent years.

In contrast to other Dutch exports, mostly within western Europe, the composition of exports to the United States remained relatively unchanged between 1895 and 1913. Tobacco and diamonds still occupied an important place, albeit with two major differences. First, their combined share of Dutch exports to the United States declined from 62 to 50 percent, and secondly, tobacco exports fell sharply after the introduction of high U.S. customs duties in 1895, while diamond exports showed a distinct rise.[4] Dutch exports to the United States of primary products like hides, fish, seeds, flax, plants and bulbs showed the greatest increase, rising from 10 to almost 20 percent. Dutch manufactured products, on the other hand, was struggling to maintain a foothold in the United States. Although exports of manufactured products accounted for 35 to 40 percent of total Dutch exports, its share of exports to the United States was no more than 14 percent. This is not surprising considering the strong competitive position of American industry and the high tariff barriers protecting the U.S. home market.[5] The far-reaching consequences of U.S. customs duties for Dutch exports of industrial products are clearly apparent from the effects of a new U.S. tariff law enacted in 1897. The Dingley Act of 1897 raised U.S. customs duties on imports of industrial products to unprecedented levels, reducing the share of manufactured products in total Dutch exports to the United States from 13 percent in 1895 to 8 percent in 1909. The Payne-Aldrich Act of 1909 introduced lower tariffs which resulted in a recovery of Dutch manufacturing exports to the United States. Over the next three years industry accounted for 14 percent of total Dutch exports to the United States, with products ranging from chocolate and cocoa butter to spirits, glass, glycerine, preserved vegetables, hardware, cheese, vegetable oils and starch.

The remaining category of goods exported to the United States in large quantities consisted of tropical products, several of which had been traded on the international staples market in Amsterdam since the seventeenth century. Tropical products included mostly agricultural products as cocoa, coffee, rice, rubber, spices, tobacco, and dried goods like cinchona bark imported from the Dutch East Indies. Between 1895 and 1912 the share of tropical products in overall Dutch exports to the United States declined from 12 percent to 10 percent.

Because the first official Dutch balance of payments figures were not published before 1926, it is impossible to measure the size of the Dutch trade deficit with the United States or the extent to which it was offset by earnings in the services sector and investments in American securities. Even the total outflow of capital from the Netherlands between 1870 and 1914 remains obscure. It is known that Dutch investors showed a growing interest in foreign securities in this time period. Interest rates in the Netherlands were lower than elsewhere, investment opportunities were limited, and investors were prepared to buy low-priced shares in the hope of selling them later at a good profit. The number of foreign securities listed on the Amsterdam Stock Exchange rose rapidly from 184 in 1875 to 531 in 1900 and to 840 in 1914. These foreign securities were in fact not exceeded by Dutch securities until after 1900. American stocks and bonds, most of which were issued by railroad companies and mortgage banks, comprised approximately one third of the Amsterdam Stock Exchange list. Earlier estimates of total Dutch investments in the United States are unreliable. It is not unlikely that Dutch investments in the United States rose from $ 240 million in 1899 to $ 600 million in 1907, and further to $ 650 million in 1914. Though the amount of Dutch capital invested in American railroads and land continued to grow, the interest of Dutch investors gradually shifted to heavy industry, and well-known corporations like the Studebaker Corporation, Rockefeller's Amalgamated Copper Company, U.S. Steel, and Bethlehem Steel listed a considerable number of their shares on the Amsterdam Stock Exchange. At the same time, direct U.S. investment in Dutch-controlled companies increased to $ 135 million in 1914. With a share of 10 percent, in 1914 the Netherlands ranked as the third greatest foreign investor in the United States after Britain and Germany.

Modernization of the Dutch Economy

The predominance of tobacco and diamonds in exports to the United States indicates a structural weakness in the position of Dutch industry in the American market. Generally speaking, industry was the most significant factor in the growth of foreign trade, but in exports to the United States it lagged behind other sectors, such as agriculture. There were various reasons for industry's poor performance in exporting to the United States. First, the high U.S. tariff barriers were specifically designed to impede the American import of foreign manufactured products. Secondly, the decline in the Dutch share of the world market after 1898, at a time when international trade was booming and economic growth in the Netherlands had reached a new high, points to a growing interest of Dutch manufacturers in the domestic market. While domestic demand rose, international penetration abated as competitors began to focus more on their home markets. Products with a relatively low added value, such as agricultural and staples market products, retained their large share of Dutch exports and tended to be the first to benefit from an upturn in the world economy. The industrial sector showed no improvement in competitiveness, and hence in its exports, until after 1910. In the interim years Dutch firms utilized growing domestic demand to strengthen their position on the home market and temporarily to withdraw from the heavy competition in foreign markets. It is debatable whether this tactic was an unqualified success. Complaints about foreign penetration of the Dutch market in journals like *Tijdschrift van de Maatschappij van Nijverheid* gradually dwindled after 1900, but it is uncertain to what extent Dutch companies managed to increase their share of the home market before the outbreak of the first world war put a halt to foreign imports.

A closer look at the composition of Dutch trade with the United States reveals that the most successful products had little competition on the American market. Besides diamonds and tropical products like the highly prized cigar wrappers from Sumatra, bulbs and plants grown by horticulturalists in the Netherlands were not produced in the United States. Few Dutch exporters of these products were members of The Netherland Chamber of Commerce in America, and the same is true of the representatives of Dutch cheese export cooperatives. The explanation is not hard to find. By and large, these Dutch companies traded in bulk goods which could be exported successfully to the United States through established trade channels. The diamond trade, for instance, was in the hands of merchants in Amsterdam and New York who were closely connected by family ties. Tropical products were handled by long-established firms, and the trade in bulbs was handled by exporters who dispatched hundreds of salesmen to the United States every year. So it would seem that the information provided by The Netherland Chamber of Commerce in America was largely concentrated on Dutch industrial products.

*Diamond factories
I.J. Asscher,
Amsterdam
(photo c. 1925)*

A combination of two factors may explain the failure of Dutch industry to penetrate the U.S. market. First, the United States entered a period of explosive industrial growth after the Civil War, culminating in a level of labor productivity that was infinitely higher than that of its two main competitors, Britain and Germany. Secondly, industrialization started later in the Netherlands than in other European countries. Dutch industrialization was first evident in the consumer goods sector, where it required no more than a moderate initial investment as the required skills could be acquired on the job or through cottage industry. Modernization began in the Netherlands around 1850 but did not evolve into a dynamic, self-reinforcing process until 1890. Mechanization got underway in the Dutch chemical engineering, paper, engineering, and ceramics industries between 1850 and 1870, followed by other sectors in the next phase, which roughly extended from 1870 to 1895. Mechanizing industries included the Twente mills producing cotton goods for the Dutch East Indies, the strawboard and potato flour factories in Groningen, and confectionery and canning factories. In most instances modernization was a gradual process that was completed in later years. Only a small number of companies adopted new production methods and full rationalization of production through technological improvements was not realized until after 1895. However, Dutch industry was not the only sector of the Dutch economy that underwent industrialization in the late nineteenth century. Older processing industries and trades which successfully switched to the steam engine included the geneva distilleries, the Amsterdam diamond-cutting factories and the oil mills concentrated in the Zaan region.

The industrialization process accelerated after the recovery of the world economy in the mid-1890s, when the earlier improvements in productivity and production capacity were at last reflected in profit margins. Modernization received a new impetus, spread to other branches of industry, and underwent a structural change. The introduction of labor-saving methods pushed down Dutch production costs. Most significantly of all, workshops employing fewer than five workers were replaced by large and medium-sized companies. This development laid the foundations for the growth of a modern capital goods industry in the Netherlands. Many new initiatives followed in the years up to 1914, notably in engineering, shipbuilding and vehicle production.

The number of incorporated companies, the financial form best suited to factory production, rose from 295 corporations with a total capital of Dfl. 60 million in 1890-1894 to 882 corporations with a collective capital of Dfl. 145 million in 1905-1908. But the rapid development of Dutch industry was still insignificant compared to American industry. After its listing on the New York Stock Exchange, U.S. Steel, for instance, was valued at $ 10.5 billion. In terms of total Dutch employment, despite the advances of manufacturing, agriculture had retained its prominent place in the Dutch economy. Between 1890 and 1910, the proportion of the Dutch working population employed in industry rose from 31 percent to 33.5 percent, a much lower percentage than in European countries where industrialization had started much earlier. For example, in 1910, half of the workforce in Belgium and Germany was employed in industry.

The modernization of agriculture led to similar extensive changes. Through innovations like the introduction of artificial fertilizers, dairy factories, the construction of roads and railways, and the emergence of production and marketing cooperatives, Dutch agriculture forged rapidly ahead in terms of production levels, labor productivity, and product specialization. Traditionally important crops as cereals and madder gave way to high-grade cash crops like potatoes and flax; and in Dutch stock farming, the emphasis shifted to dairy herds and pig-breeding. Though modernization had begun around 1880, it did not penetrate all sectors of Dutch agriculture until the economic recovery in the 1890s, when demand for agricultural products rose steeply in the Netherlands and its European neighbors, and when exports displayed the first signs of rapid growth they were to reach in the course of the twentieth century.

The United States was not viewed as a potential market for the majority of Dutch agricultural products. Not only was there sufficient demand for Dutch agricultural products in Germany, Belgium, and Britain, but Dutch exporters also foresaw difficulties competing with American producers on their home market. Virtually the only exception was the horticultural sector, which successfully shifted from perishable commodities like fruit, vegetables or cut flowers, to bulbs, plants and shrubs, products that were well-established on the U.S. market before the end of the nineteenth century. The recession affecting the world economy between 1872 and 1895, when agriculture was particularly hard hit, had relatively little effect on Dutch horticulture owing to the luxury nature of its products. Dutch horticultural exports had already doubled after 1870, and rose still further after the economic upturn in 1895. Though the pre-recession rate of growth, a ten-fold increase between 1850 and 1870, was never again attained, Dutch horticulturalists had nothing to complain about. Up to 1914, domestic sales of horticultural products rose by 60 percent and exports by 300 to 400 percent. In 1912, the total production of Dutch horticultural products is estimated to have been worth Dfl. 65 million, with annual exports amounting to one-third. The first exports of Dutch bulbs to the United States can be dated to around 1890, when U.S. customs tariffs were revised and bulbs were placed on the free list. Thereafter, exports continued to grow, even after customs tariffs were reintroduced in 1897. By 1903, the value of Dutch bulb exports to the United States probably exceeded Dfl. 2 million, making the United States the biggest export market after Britain and Germany. Between 1903 and 1913, Dutch bulb exports to the U.S. doubled again to Dfl. 4 million and the United States became the second most important export market.

The Competitiveness of the Netherlands

Competitive strength is not solely determined by productivity, but just as much by marketing methods. Reports which frequently appeared in publications like the journal of the Netherlands Industrial Association suggest that Dutch manufacturers were often deficient in marketing their products. Needless to say, this was bound to affect the image and sales of Dutch products, not least in the Netherlands itself, where government and consumers alike tended to be wary of home-produced goods and to prefer those of foreign origin. It is known that Dutch industry repeatedly complained about the government's preference for foreign capital goods. Indeed, such complaints related not just to the capital goods sector, but to consumer goods as well. Even chocolate manufacturers with an international reputation like Van Houten, Blooker, and Bensdorp lamented that a large part of the domestic market had been lost to their Swiss competitors. Some Dutch manufacturers did not shun trickery in their efforts to endow their products with greater appeal. Articles of clothing, for instance, were often given foreign labels or even dispatched on a short return journey across a nearby border to give them the official status of imported goods.

Despite producers' efforts, the Dutch public at times subscribed to the notion that foreign wares were of infinitely superior quality to anything produced at home. This was illustrated by two news items about Dutch and British jams appearing in the course of two years. In 1904, the Rotterdam Food Inspectorate tested the quality of Dutch and imported jams and reported that few home products could compare with the well-known British Crosse & Blackwell brand. Barely two years later a report issued by the British Factory Inspectorate revealed that British jam manufacturers, almost without exception, disregarded even the most elementary standards of hygiene. The Netherlands Industrial Association drily observed that British jam's famous aftertaste, whose absence in Dutch jam had been so greatly deplored, was possibly due to the "murky, foul-smelling water" used in Britain to wash the pots and jars and changed only once a week. Lower production costs nevertheless enabled British jam manufacturers to maintain their hold on the Dutch market up to 1914. The turnabout came during the first world war, when the British products disappeared from the shelves and Dutch jam consumption rose steeply in the Netherlands, Germany and Britain. The result was that by 1918, forty factories were processing and exporting much of the fruit grown in the Netherlands.

While the Dutch jam industry was saved by the unexpected opportunities offered by the first world war, Dutch geneva distillers had been engaged for years in such fierce warfare for a share of the U.S. market that this once thriving outlet had all but disappeared before 1914. In the mid-nineteenth century, geneva, or Holland gin, had been the principal commodity exported from the Netherlands to the United States, but sales later declined markedly through the growth of the American gin industry and the imposition of heavy customs duties. By the end of the nineteenth century, American products of similar quality like whisky and dry gin had replaced geneva as the most popular spirit amongst the lower income groups in the United States, and it was regarded as a luxury item ever since. The reputation of Dutch geneva was further eroded by a flood of American-made gin of inferior quality that was sold under a bogus Dutch label. The importers' efforts to stop this through legislation were defeated by the distillery lobby in the U.S. Senate. When the Dutch government proposed to open negotiations with the U.S. on a new trade agreement in 1912, it was informed by Dutch geneva distillers that the protectionist tariff introduced in 1897 was chiefly to blame for the loss of the American market. However, as Dutch geneva exports to the United States rose only marginally after 1907, when U.S. customs duties were lowered, this could not have been the sole reason. As the Dutch geneva distillers finally admitted, their American competitors had driven them out of the market largely through advertising. Instead of following the example of British

A 1931 advertisement of the Bensdorp Royal Dutch Cocoa factories.

Blookers original windmill, built in 1806 at Amsterdam, and transferred to the World's Columbian Exposition, Chicago, 1893

81

spirits manufacturers, who had financed successful advertising campaigns in the United States by keeping their prices high, Dutch distillers were undercutting each other's prices. This had a backlash effect, for it not only failed to increase their U.S. sales, but it damaged the reputation of geneva as well. Furthermore, the conservative Dutch distillers failed to take measures that could have boosted their U.S. sales, like exporting the product in labelled bottles instead of casks, which would have highlighted the brand name without extra advertising. They had also failed to respond to the changing tastes and drinking habits of the American public. The growing popularity of cocktails in the United States worked to the advantage of the sweeter British dry gin, and even though Dutch distillers were fully aware of this they did not change their products. A new U.S. tariff increase in 1910, raising customs duties to five times the value of the product shipped from the Netherlands, spelled the end of Dutch geneva exports to the United States. In 1912, when it was rumored that customs duties might be lowered after the U.S. presidential election, the Netherlands Ministry of Agriculture, Trade and Industry suggested that Dutch manufacturers and their American representatives launch a joint advertising campaign, but the idea was not greeted with much enthusiasm. Dutch distillers unanimously believed that exports to the United States could only be revived by a sharp tariff cut, and that the cost of an advertising campaign would be out of all proportion to the already narrow profit margin of geneva, especially as it would have to be handled by an expensive American advertising agency.

It was finally a survey conducted by the Netherlands Industrial Association among its members in 1903 that shed light on the question whether the numerous complaints in the Netherlands about the quality of Dutch products were justified. The published responses made it amply clear that Dutch industry had only itself to blame, as there were good reasons for the Dutch public's preference for the products of foreign competitors. Reliability was not one of the distinguishing characteristics of Dutch manufacturers. The efforts of Dutch manufacturers to cut production costs gave the edge in quality and packaging to foreign competitors. The range of products was often limited and the inventories small, so that deliveries were slow. Moreover, retailers regularly found that repeat orders were of inferior quality to the initial deliveries while the price remained the same. Because of the importance of the retailer in the chain from producer to consumer, this could have a serious effect on sales. Before the emergence of proprietary brands in the late nineteenth century, retailers were entirely free to order supplies where they wished. Though the growth in advertising later tended to restrict that freedom, if retailers were dissatisfied with the performance of one supplier, their customers' brand loyalty was

1. *The Foreign Commerce and Navigation of the United States*, Washington. The Dutch share of the total trade of the United States (imports and exports) was 4.54 percent in 1901, and 4.15 percent in 1902.
2. *Annual Report* 1912-1913, 17.

Membership	Abroad	USA	Life	Assoc.	Total
1903-1904	137	48	6	7	198
1904-1905	146	43	6	7	202
1905-1906	133	35	6	5	179
1906-1907	134	30	6	6	176
1907-1908	135	31	6	8	180
1908-1909	141	36	6	8	191
1909-1910	160	49	6	14	229
1910-1911	172	58	6	13	249
1911-1912	184	56	6	16	262
1912-1913	198	53	6	13	270

3. Annual Report 1905-1906, 25-27. According to the Bureau of Statistics of the U.S. Department of Commerce and Labor, a large proportion of American exports to the Netherlands was in transit to other destinations such as Belgium, Germany, and the Austro-Hungarian Empire. U.S. consular officials registering trade flows to and from the United States recorded the countries of origin and of destination.
4. B.J.M. Ammerlaan, *Praktische problemen uit de handelsstatistiek* (Practical Problems with Trade Statistics), Amsterdam, 1930, 33. The extent of the Dutch diamond trade with the United States is not precisely

known. The parcel post, which was the principal means of transporting diamonds, was not taken into account in Dutch foreign trade figures, and the U.S. figures are unreliable due to the widespread smuggling. The rapid growth of the diamond trade after 1897 is largely attributable to the lowering of U.S. customs duties from 25 to 10 percent. See G.J. Kloos, *De handelspolitieke betrekkingen tusschen Nederland en de Vereenigde Staten van Amerika 1814-1914* (Trade Relations between the Netherlands and the United States of America, 1814-1914), Amsterdam, 1923, 133. Gerlof D. Homan, "That 'Beautiful Tobacco': the Sumatra cigar wrapper and the American tariff, c. 1880-1941" in *ESHJ 50, Amsterdam 1987, 145-156.*

5. *Foreign Commerce and Navigation of the United States,* various years.

Dutch exports to the United States in various sectors, in percentages:					
	<u>1895</u>	<u>1903</u>	<u>1906</u>	<u>1909</u>	<u>1912</u>
Finished products	13	10	8	10	14
Staples	12	8	5	7	9
Primary sector	10	12	14	17	18
Tobacco	44	19	23	20	22
Diamonds	18	41	41	36	30

Banquet of Holland American Chamber of Commerce, San Francisco, April, 1914

[... By the late nineteenth century Amsterdam had become an international and cosmopolitan city. This change of status was felt at once by a Dutchman, Steinigeweg, when he returned to Amsterdam after having lived in the United States for many years. He decided that the Leidseplein, in Amsterdam, would be a perfect location for an American-style hotel, so in 1879 he started construction of what was to become the American Hotel.]

Petrus Stuyvesant, 1794
Painting by
Gilbert Stuart
(1755-1828)
The New-York Historical
Society
Gift of Robert van
Rensselaer Stuyvesant,
his great-grandson.

View of New York Harbor from Brooklyn Heights, c. 1860. Painting by unknown artist The New-York Historical Society

Gerardus Duyckinck was the first native born American painter in 1695.

His grandfather Evert Duyckinck emigrated to New Amsterdam on 1638. A small number of early New York limners painted mostly religious subjects and portraits on commission.

The work was uncovered in a Chicago warehouse in 1976, and it is the earliest painting known to exist, signed and dated.

Birth of the Virgin, 1713
Painting by
Gerardus Duyckinck
(1695-1746)
Private Collection
Photo courtesy R.H. Love
Gallery, Chicago

⇒
Suzanna Truax, 1730
Painting by
Pieter van der Lyn
National Gallery of Art,
Washington D.C.

⇒⇒
De Peyster Boy with
Fawn, 1787
Painting by
Gerardus Duyckinck
(1723-1797)
The New-York Historical
Society

Niagara Falls, 1803
Painting by
John van der Lyn
(1776-1852)
Courtesy of the Society
for the preservation of
New England
Antiquities,
Codman House, Lincoln,
Massachusetts

*Ariadne asleep on the
Island of Naxos, 1809
Painting by
John van der Lyn
(1776-1852)
The Pennsylvania
Academy of the Fine Arts
Gift of
Mrs Sarah Harrison*

CHAPTER III

1914 - 1940: CHANGING FORTUNES

Introduction

The Armistice signed at Compiègne in northern France on November 11, 1918, terminated a war that had ravaged Europe for four long years. The military defeat of Germany and the Austro-Hungarian Empire was sealed nine months later at the Peace Conference in Versailles, France.

But the *Nieuwe Rotterdamsche Courant* warned:

> Peace will be followed soon afterwards by an economic conflict which no country will escape and which will decide the future of the nations. The outcome of that struggle will be of greater significance for our national life than the outcome of the war now being waged.

As the war dragged on with no final victory in sight, this theme recurred ever more often in public debate and in the press. After the suspension of hostilities, so the reasoning went, the contest for the world markets that had been one of the causes of the war would finally be decided by economic means. The Netherlands, too, felt that no time should be lost in preparing for this economic conflict. Although the outcome of the war prevented a struggle for economic power and though the free flow of goods, services, and capital resumed in the summer of 1919, it soon became apparent that the pre-war liberal economic world order would not return. The war had irrevocably changed international economic relations. Through its loans to Britain, France and Italy, the United States had now become the world's greatest creditor, Europe was impoverished, and Germany's political stability was eroded. The world economy was accordingly dominated by economic crises, monetary instability, and ever higher trade barriers up to 1939. With the exception of the agricultural sector, which had languished worldwide since the war, the world economy grew rapidly in the second half of the 1920s, 'the roaring twenties'. Economic recession and stagnation followed in the troubled years of the 1930s.

This was the backdrop to the history of the Chamber of Commerce for America between 1919 and 1940. In the summer of 1919 the Dutch business community in New York together with the envoy to Washington and the consul-general in New York reestablished the New York Chamber of Commerce for the Netherlands and the Netherlands East and West Indies, Inc., which in 1921 changed its name to the Netherlands Chamber of Commerce in New York, Inc. In order to establish closer ties with businessmen in the Netherlands, a sister organization, the Netherlands-American Chamber of Commerce, was set up in Amsterdam in the following year. Over the next twenty years they worked closely together with another sister organization, the Holland-American Chamber of Commerce for the Pacific Coast States, Inc. in San Francisco to promote Dutch exports to the West Coast of the United States.

Their history in the course of those twenty years is described in the next two chapters. This chapter deals with the background to the Netherlands Chamber in New York and its sister organization in Amsterdam, their members and activities, and the economic context in which they operated. It devotes special attention to their relations with the Dutch government.

The issue of providing information on commercial matters was widely discussed in the 1920s, and the Dutch government was repeatedly urged to do more. These attempts failed, but so too did those of the opponents of a more active government policy to realize the privatization of the rudimentary information service run by the Trade Division of the Ministry of Agriculture, Trade and Industry. Action was finally taken after the onset of the Depression, when the Minister for Economic Affairs, T.J. Verschuur, set up an economic information service in 1933. Reorganized in 1936, it thereafter functioned as a central information service for government and private enterprise, and supervised the subsidized private trade information centers. For the Netherlands-American Chamber of Commerce in Amsterdam this meant the end of its role as an adviser to the Dutch government on trade relations with the United States. Closely involved as the Chamber was with the legal proceedings instituted by American companies to block imports, it was well-informed on all aspects of trade with the United States, and played an important part in the preparations for the trade agreement negotiations conducted in Washington in 1935. The liberalization of trade prompted the Chamber to open a Dutch center in New York in March, 1940, to organize commercial and general publicity for the Netherlands, an initiative which was cut short by the German invasion of the Netherlands two months later.

On the Brink of War

[... J.T. Cremer, a former Minister for the Colonies and an ex-president of the Netherlands Trading Society, presented his credentials as the new special envoy and minister plenipotentiary to President Woodrow Wilson on November 29, 1918.]
Archives ABN Amro

J.T. Cremer, a former Minister for the Colonies and an ex-president of the Netherlands Trading Society, presented his credentials as the new special envoy and minister plenipotentiary to President Woodrow Wilson on November 29, 1918, heralding the end of one of the most troubled periods in the history of Dutch-American relations. Since the outbreak of war in 1914, the interests of the two countries had progressively diverged. Whereas the Netherlands had sought to retain its neutrality in the war, the United States had to all intents and purposes taken the side of the Entente - Britain, France, and Russia - since 1915. That was no impediment to the maintenance of friendly relations, especially in view of the fact that before long the United States was the Netherlands' principal overseas supplier of raw materials and manufacturing supplies.

The situation changed abruptly when the United States declared war on Germany on April 6, 1917; within a year relations had deteriorated to the point that the Wilson administration recalled its envoy, John W. Garrett, from The Hague for consultations in the spring of 1918, severing contact with the Netherlands government at the highest diplomatic level. Relations were resumed at the end of the year when Garrett returned to The Hague and Cremer was received at the White House.

The United States was the only great power to remain neutral in August, 1914 when hostilities broke out in Europe. It soon became clear that the Wilson administration did not intend to act as the protector of neutral European states such as the Netherlands, Spain, and the Scandinavian countries. So the Netherlands was powerless to act when in 1915 and 1916 Britain and France extended the economic blockade of Germany and Austria to the adjoining neutral states. When the United States entered the war, its relations with the Netherlands rapidly deteriorated. This could not have come at a worse moment for the Netherlands. Since February, 1917, when Germany announced the policy of unrestricted submarine warfare that brought the United States into the war two months later, there had been an acute shortage in the Netherlands of many raw materials and manufacturing supplies, including coal, artificial fertilizers and foodstuffs like cereals and salt. Nevertheless, confident that the United States would not fail the Netherlands, the Dutch government made little attempt after April, 1917, to buy these commodities elsewhere or to introduce a system of rationing. All indications that measures were necessary were consistently ignored by the Dutch government. Despite the warnings of the Netherlands Overseas Trust Company, a private company importing supplies from overseas since the beginning of the war, the government saw no need to team up with other neutral countries in negotiating with Washington on new deliveries of raw materials, fuel, and foodstuffs. The Dutch government was soon rudely awakened. In July, 1917, an anti-Dutch press campaign began more or less simultaneously in the United States and in Britain. The Netherlands was accused of deliberately misleading the U.S. government about its domestic needs and about selling its surplus imports to Germany.[1]

The house of cards collapsed on July 15, 1917, when President Wilson extended the blockade to the neutral states bordering on Germany and banned the export of the raw materials and manufacturing supplies that were vital for Dutch industry and the population.[2] The bread ration in the Netherlands had to be cut by half barely six weeks later. Though the United States had acted entirely for its own reasons, the

94

Netherlands was convinced that Britain was the evil genius behind the negative press publications and that it had misinformed the U.S. government about the true extent of Dutch needs.

The Netherlands' ties with the United States were strained, and for the Dutch government it was vitally important to restore relations to their former friendly footing. Matters were made worse by the uncompromising attitude displayed by the Dutch envoy, W.L.F.C. van Rappard, since the beginning of the war. Taking no account of the changes which participation in the war had brought about in the U.S. government and in American public opinion, Van Rappard demanded strict observance of the Netherlands' rights as a neutral state under international law. Now that the United States was one of the belligerents, such a strictly legalistic stance met with little sympathy with the U.S. government or the American public, in whose view everyone must be on one side of the conflict or the other; no middle course was possible.

A top-level Dutch delegation sent to Washington in August, 1917, was unable to persuade the American government to change its mind. The Dutch merchant ships lying idle in American ports since Germany had embarked on its policy of unrestricted submarine warfare were the main point of contention. With the mounting Allied losses at sea, the Dutch ships were becoming ever more important. Since February, 1917, German submarines had taken a heavy toll on Allied shipping, so heavy in fact that for a time Britain's supplies of cereals and raw materials were in danger of being cut off. It being impossible for the Allied shipyards to replace the losses in the short term, the balance seemed to be shifting in Germany's favor. So it was of vital importance for Britain and the United States to gain the use of the neutral merchant ships laid up in their ports. In August, 1917, the American government was prepared to supply cereals to the Netherlands, but nothing more, in exchange for the Dutch ships, an offer which was unacceptable to the Dutch government. A solution seemed to be at hand in March, 1918, when Germany agreed that every ship carrying supplies from America to the Netherlands could be matched by a ship of equal tonnage sailing from Amsterdam or Rotterdam to the United States. But the crisis deepened a few days later when it appeared that in view of their continuing losses, the Allies wished to use the ships in European waters. The Netherlands, not wanting to endanger its neutral status with Germany, stipulated that no troops or war materials were to be carried on the ships. As a result, on March 18, 1918, 90 Dutch vessels were requisitioned in American ports, and 45 in British ports.

After that relations between the Netherlands and the United States rapidly worsened. On March 22, 1918, the Dutch Prime Minister, P.W.A. Cort van der Linden, voiced "a furious protest" in Parliament, and behind the scenes feelings about "the ship robbery" ran even higher. According to rumors still circulating years after the war, the Cabinet, with the backing of Queen Wilhelmina, resolved to present an ultimatum or to declare war - it is not clear which - to the United States and Britain. It was only with the utmost difficulty deterred from doing so by Finance Minister M.W.F. Treub, who argued that Germany's state of exhaustion must soon force it to plead for peace. So the Dutch government settled for a strongly worded diplomatic protest, underscored by termination of the passage through the Netherlands of food supplies destined for Belgium and northern France and indefinite deferment of the appointment of a new envoy to the United States. Van Rappard had been succeeded in December, 1917, by A. Philips, who however had returned to the Netherlands shortly afterwards due to ill health, leaving what Ernst Heldring, a prominent shipowner, termed "that vitally important post" in charge of the first secretary, W.H. de Beaufort. Pressure brought to bear by Britain and the United States soon resulted in the resumption of transit food shipments to German-occupied France and Belgium, but the Allies were left with the impression that the Netherlands took little or no account of the war and the critical phase it had entered in the spring of 1918. That impression was strengthened by the Dutch government's continued failure to appoint a new envoy to Washington, spurred on by Queen Wilhelmina who was "deeply offended by this affront to the House of Orange". The initial readiness in influential British and American circles if possible to sweeten the pill for the Netherlands was gone, and the American government recalled its envoy from The Hague for consultations. In the following months the Netherlands chose to remain in diplomatic isolation. Up to the end of the war American products were shipped to the Netherlands in mere dribs and drabs, and the Netherlands' reputation in the United States sank to rock bottom.

The policy pursued by the Dutch government was not universally supported, as is evident from Treub's opposition to the confrontation contemplated by the Cabinet and the Queen in March, 1918. Those most opposed to it was the business community, which was also the source of most proposals for ending the impasse in Dutch-American relations. The driving force was probably J.T. Cremer, who in any event was the person who organized a meeting of top figures in trade, shipping, and banking on September 12, 1918 to discuss the crisis of confidence. The moment for action had arrived on September 9, 1918, with the installation of a new Dutch government under Ruys de Beerenbrouck and the appointment of Esquire H.A. Karnebeek as Minister for Foreign Affairs.

The representatives of many leading corporations were among those who gathered in The Hague on September 12, 1918. The banks were represented by W. Westerman, president of the Rotterdamsche Bankvereeniging, and C.J.K. van Aalst, president of the Netherlands Trading Society and a prominent figure in the Netherlands Overseas Trust Company; the shipowners by L.P.D. op ten Noort, president of the KPM, and J.R. Wierdsma, president of the Holland-America Line; commercial interests by E.P. de Monchy, president of the Rotterdam Chamber of Commerce; and the Dutch East Indies business community by H. Colijn, director of the Bataafsche Petroleum Company (BPM).

Cremer produced two letters on the subject of the Netherlands' reputation in the United States which he had received in June, 1918 from the writer and historian Hendrik Willem van Loon, who was to become widely known in the United States after the publication of his popular study, *The Story of Mankind*, in 1921.[3] Several months before, in December, 1917, Van Loon had warned the Foreign Minister, John Loudon, about the deteriorating image of the Netherlands in the United States. Before the war the Netherlands had been known as the land of *Hans Brinker or the Silver Skates*, the land of polders, dams, windmills and clogs, and the land of the seventeenth-century republic described in *The Rise of the Dutch Republic* by the mid-nineteenth century American historian John L. Motley. It was virtually unknown that because of its neutrality and its support for the development of international law the Netherlands had been invited to host the peace conferences of 1899 and 1907, and practically no one knew that The Hague was the seat of the International Court of Justice funded by the steel magnate Andrew Carnegie. After six months of warfare, it was widely thought that the Netherlands was connected in some way with Germany and was denying the American government the use of its merchant ships lying idle in American ports.
Van Loon was against the idea of a publicity campaign presenting the Dutch viewpoint. It would be of no use in a country priding itself on fighting for "the hallowed cause" of peace, freedom, and democracy. It would be better to mount a campaign portraying the Dutch as a democratic, civilized nation with a rich past, highlighting the fact that the seventeenth-century Dutch Republic was the cradle of constitutional and parliamentary government, of practically all modern sciences, and above all of international law. It should be made clear to the public that the Netherlands had for centuries been "an inviolable bastion" safeguarding the rights of the individual, the nation, and the international community. Endowing a Grotius lectureship on Netherlands history at Harvard or Yale would be a step in the right direction. It is not known whether Loudon took these suggestions seriously, or discussed them with others. It was only after Van Loon wrote to Cremer in June, 1918, that things started moving.

At the end of June, 1918, Van Loon had more to report about the Netherlands' worsening reputation in the United States than six months earlier. Since Germany had launched an offensive in March, 1918, and because the Allies' position had become precarious, virulent anti-Dutch campaigns had been conducted in the United States and Britain. Van Loon wrote that most reports originated in the British tabloid newspapers and were "rubbish", but because American newspapers and magazines printed many of them unabridged with no further comment, they were not without effect. Switzerland, Norway, Sweden, and Denmark all sent their best diplomats to Washington and invested large sums in protecting their image, while van Loon struggled alone to save the Netherlands' reputation in the United States. Not that it made much difference. The British government had now branded him "a hired agent of the Dutch government" and he was under secret service surveillance. The Netherlands must act, or be known forever after as a country of war profiteers and "crypto-Germans". As a first step, he suggested following the example of Spain, Sweden, and Norway in setting up an institute for general cultural publicity in the United States.
Van Loon's anxieties were not only shared by Dutch businessmen in Europe and the United States, but they strongly believed that something should be done without delay. The change of government in the Netherlands on September 9, 1918, held out the prospect of ending the impasse in which foreign policy had been mired since the previous March. Though the blockade was felt ever more acutely in the summer

months, the Dutch Cabinet had been deeply divided on how to react to the requisitioning of the merchant ships. With a general election scheduled for July 3, 1918, little progress had been made in negotiations with the United States and Britain on the resumption of deliveries of raw materials and manufacturing supplies. The choice of a passive stance in the negotiations was influenced at least as much by developments on the war front. In March the Germans had at last broken through the Allied lines, but were repelled almost at the gates of Paris for the second time in four years. In July, 1918, the French, British, and American armies launched a massive offensive and the war came to an end on November 11, 1918.

When Cremer opened the meeting of top representatives of the business world on September 12, 1918, the armistice could not yet be foreseen. The German army had been in retreat for almost two months, but the war raged on and the defeat of the Central Powers seemed to be more a question of years than of months. The meeting was nevertheless unanimously of the opinion that active measures needed to be taken in the short term to further the Netherlands' commercial and political interests in the United States. Though no one disputed the merits of Van Loon's proposal, it was felt that a cultural organization should not take precedence over the appointment of a new envoy to Washington. The refusal to send a replacement for Philips had caused bad feelings in Washington. Furthermore, improving the commercial section of the legation was just as important. The fact that in the course of the war the United States had become one of the principal markets for the Dutch East Indies had greatly increased the legation's workload, while the coming international economic struggle made it imperative that the economic information service be expanded. Colijn was able to reassure the meeting. He had heard from Foreign Minister Van Karnebeek that the appointment of a new envoy and a commercial attaché could be expected within a few weeks.

Welcome as this was, it was felt that the changes required would need to go further than simply reorganizing the diplomatic mission. Dutch business interests in the United States were so important that the business community could not passively wait for the Ministry of Foreign Affairs to act. Instead of relying on the legation, they could join forces with Dutch colonial interest groups to establish a solidly-based permanent trade mission in the United States. Equipped with good archives, a publicity department and showrooms, and run by a properly qualified staff headed by the commercial attaché, this would be a valuable addition to the legation. One of the main arguments in its favor was the infinitely greater freedom of a non-governmental institution to present the Dutch view to the American public.

The meeting appointed a small committee representing the various sectors of industry and commerce with interests in the United States to elaborate the proposals put forward and to confer with Foreign Minister Van Karnebeek. Cremer, as chairman, was to act as coordinator. Before the new government took office he had discussed the question of improving relations with the American government with Van Karnebeek, who soon proved to be more dynamic than his predecessor. Within a few weeks he nominated Cremer as the new envoy to Washington, and began looking around for a suitable candidate for the job of commercial attaché. Neither appointment was a routine affair. When the Dutch ships had been requisitioned by the United States Cremer had spoken very sharply in the Upper House of Parliament and Washington had reservations about accepting his nomination. The Dutch government was obliged to wait three weeks before Washington let it be known that it approved the appointment.

Accompanied by C. van Vollenhoven, a Leiden University professor with an international reputation in constitutional law, Cremer sailed for the United States in November, 1918. Van Vollenhoven was seconded to the legation for six months to assist Cremer in explaining the Netherlands' rights as a neutral state to the U.S. government and to influential circles in general. They lost no time in setting about their mission. One of their most effective weapons was the freedom accorded to foreign investors in the Dutch East Indies. Though given a sympathetic hearing by Secretary of Commerce Redfield, it was soon clear that the United States was preoccupied with weightier matters than a small country like the Netherlands. Talks on the terms of peace and the founding of the League of Nations were in progress in Versailles, and the American troops were returning from France. The speeches both men gave in the winter of 1918 to audiences of politicians, businessmen, journalists, geographical societies, and others had little effect. It was not until the arrival of D.H. Andreae, the new commercial attaché, and K.F. van den Berg, director of the Java Bank, sent to assess the situation for the authorities in the Dutch East Indies, that a real start could be made with the dissemination of information on the Netherlands and the Dutch East Indies.

Reestablishment of the Chamber

With the mission to help Cremer advance the economic interests of the Netherlands and the Dutch East Indies, Andreae and Van den Berg were at first occupied with the task of improving the image of the Netherlands in the United States. One of the first projects was the establishment of a Netherlands-American institute "to foster greater contact between the United States and the Netherlands and its colonies in the fields of science, the arts and economics". The Dutch business community contributed Dfl. 50,000, part of which was to be used for a `Netherlands House' in New York accommodating the consulate-general, a Netherlands Chamber of Commerce, and a showroom. In consultation with Cremer, Andreae and Van den Berg set to work. Their first attempt, supported by New York businessmen, to set up an American-Netherlands Association to provide general information came to nothing as both the envoy and the Americans wanted to exercise full control.

While in the Netherlands the supervisory committee chaired by the banker W. Westerman deliberated on how the money was to be spent, Andreae and Van den Berg were seeking other ways of organizing Dutch interests in New York. They invited fifty representatives of Dutch and East Indies firms to a meeting at the Netherland Club in New York on Friday, June 13, 1919 to discuss the reestablishment of a Netherlands Chamber of Commerce in the United States. Virtually all firms connected with trade and shipping between the United States and the Netherlands and its East Indies colonies were represented at the meeting. It voted unanimously to set up a small organizing committee, which met five days later in the office of the chairman, D.J. Steyn Parvé, acting consul-general in New York. The other members were H.W. Van Loon, V. van der Hoeven of Lindeteves, Inc., and Walter G. Hathaway of Colgate & Co. After discussions with Andreae and Cremer, the committee decided on July 9, 1919, to reestablish the New York Chamber of Commerce for the Netherlands and the Netherlands East and West Indies, Inc. to further the bilateral trade between the Netherlands and the United States. The annual membership fee would be $ 50. In contrast to the earlier Netherland Chamber of Commerce in America, the secretary was to be an experienced person with a sound knowledge of economic developments in the Netherlands, its colonies, and the United States. He would be supported by one or two permanent committees composed of members of the Board of Directors. At the instigation of the legation, Van Loon's suggestion of cultural publicity to improve the image of the Netherlands was implemented with the formation of a special body, the Committee for Arts, Sciences and Friendly Relations. As stated in the statutes:

W. Westerman
Archives ABN Amro

> If the Chamber of Commerce is to do its full duty it will have to pay attention to the development
> of the non-direct commercial side of the relations between the United States and the Netherlands
> and her colonies.

Other committees were set up for specific areas including banking and currency, the customs service and revenue law, development and trade, and entertainment.

It was some months before the plan was put into effect. Many businessmen were absent from New York in the summer months, a secretary had to be found, and as the American-Netherlands Association had not materialized, the Westerman committee had to decide how the capital was now to be spent. So the organizing committee could not begin its work until the end of September. Westerman consented to Cremer's allocating the interest from the fund to the Committee for Arts, Sciences and Friendly Relations.[4] Other possibilities considered were a student exchange program, inviting guest lecturers from the Netherlands, preferably in conjunction with the Queen Wilhelmina Lectureship in Leiden, screening films about the Netherlands, commissioning translations of Dutch literature, and visits by American scientists and technologists to the Netherlands. The committee allocated Dfl. 13,500 to the Queen Wilhelmina Lectureship, Dfl. 1000 to an exhibition of modern Dutch art in America, and Dfl. 300 to a publication on Vincent Van Gogh. A secretary was found in the Netherlands and the statutes neared completion. On October 10, 1919, the organizing committee invited Dutch and American businessmen in the United States to become members of the New York Chamber of Commerce for the Netherlands and the Netherlands East and West Indies. The aim of the new organization was to further economic and cultural relations between the two countries.[5]

Dutch exports to the United States were slow to recover, and partly for that reason the recruitment of members made little headway, despite the solid backing of the Dutch government. Expectations were high, but there was also an underlying awareness of a possible economic recession. There was a heavy demand in Europe for goods that had been unavailable during the war and were now reappearing on the market. Wide fluctuations in the exchange rate of the Belgian and French franc and the German mark undermined confidence in the European economy. The major factor was probably the wage level in the Netherlands, the highest in Europe after Britain, which put Dutch exporters at a competitive disadvantage. It seemed to be almost with a feeling of relief that the weekly *Imports and Exports* announced in May, 1920, that "The recession has come". In 1919 Dutch exports were adversely affected by the strong guilder, and the exchange rate fluctuations together with the undervaluation of the French and Belgian franc and the German mark compounded the uncertainty. Dutch exports showed no sign of picking up until later in the year.

In late November, 1919, there were still only 56 members of the Chamber, all based in New York. In the same month, the newly-found secretary informed the committee that he had accepted another job. To infuse new life into the enterprise and to catch the interest of the business community, the organizing committee decided to organize a number of dinners. By inviting the press as well, attention could also be focused on the dispute with Belgium, which at the Peace Conference in Versailles was claiming part of Dutch territory. But the social season was in full swing, and the earliest possible date for a large-scale dinner was the following March. The plan had to be abandoned. To make matters worse, Cremer fell ill, forcing him to return to the Netherlands a few months later.

Despite these setbacks, the committee eventually succeeded in increasing the membership. There was an encouraging response to a press report released on December 6, 1919 by D.J. Steyn Parvé, the acting consul-general, and membership doubled before the charter meeting on January 20, 1920.[6] The executive committee elected at the meeting consisted of Nicolaas G.M. Luykx, vice-president of the Sinclair Consolidated Oil Company, chairman; T. Frederick Aspden, vice-president of the Park Union Foreign Banking Corporation, deputy chairman; Elias A. de Lima, president of the Battery Park National Bank, secretary; and the hitherto unknown Esquire L. Wittert van Hoogland. The eighteen-member Board of Directors represented both Dutch and American firms in the banking, trade, and shipping sectors. Two additional members were G.J.M. Simons, correspondent of *De Telegraaf* newspaper, and Adriaan J. Barnouw, the newly appointed Queen Wilhelmina Lecturer at Columbia University. Only one member, Stuyvesant Fish, had served on the Board of the former Netherland Chamber of Commerce in America. The offices of the Chamber were located at 44 Beaver Street, in the commercial center of Manhattan.

Besides electing the two governing bodies, the meeting resolved to set up a sister organization in order to strengthen the financial basis and to intensify relations with the business community in the Netherlands. The Amsterdam lawyer Eduard H. von Baumhauer, later a leading personality in the Chamber, contacted S.P. van Eeghen and E.P. de Monchy Rzn., the presidents of the Amsterdam and Rotterdam Chambers of Commerce, who organized preliminary meetings on March 23, 1920 in Amsterdam and on April 15, 1920 in Rotterdam. The charter meeting, at which Cremer was present, took place on July 1, 1920. The initial membership of the Chamber in Amsterdam was 107. To neutralize the traditional rivalry between Amsterdam and Rotterdam, the executive posts were divided equally between the two cities, and the Chamber was officially registered in The Hague. The secretariat was established at Von Baumhauer's office at 83 Damrak, Amsterdam, the commercial center of the city, opposite the Stock Exchange and a stone's throw from the Trade Information Center. Up to 1923, when a formal agreement was concluded, cooperation with the Chamber in New York was entirely in the nature of a gentleman's agreement. So Dutch trade and shipping again had a supportive base in the United States, this time with the assured backing and cooperation of the Dutch government and business community.

Whether and in what measure the two Chambers of Commerce could help to boost Dutch exports depended first and foremost on economic developments, and there was no guarantee that exports to the United States would be such as to warrant the existence of two full-time centers of information.

The Roaring Twenties and the Troubled Thirties

The hope cherished by Dutch private enterprise towards the end of 1918 that world trade would revive soon after the war was briefly fulfilled in the summer of 1919. The development of the world economy up to the end of 1920 foreshadowed the events of the next two decades. The gradual growth of the pre-war era was replaced by a rollercoaster economy hurtling from high to low in rapid successions.

Just how radically the world economy had changed over the past four years became evident when international trade was resumed in the summer of 1919. Europe, greatly impoverished, was faced with much stiffer competition from the United States and Japan. Trade relations with the Far East and Latin America in particular were severed, and in many cases could be restored only with the greatest of difficulty, for which reason it was often not attempted at all. Furthermore, tariff and other regulations proved to be

Grand Central Station, New York. c. 1920

Empire State Building, New York Postcard, the twenties

greater obstacles to international trade than before the war. The map of Europe had been redrawn with the emergence of the new states founded on the territory of Russia and the former Austro-Hungarian Empire, increasing the number of European states from twenty-five to thirty-eight. In addition, during the war many countries had established new industries to produce the goods no longer supplied from abroad. In the Netherlands these included the Royal Netherlands Iron and Steel Foundries at IJmuiden and the first chemical and pharmaceutical plants. Other Dutch factories were modernized and enlarged by the end of the war as to be practically entirely new. With the resumption of free trade, however, it was soon apparent that many Dutch companies would not survive international competition without protectionist measures. On the other hand, the readiness evinced by other countries to impose protectionist measures was unthinkable in the Netherlands, devoted as it was to the principle of free trade. So the commercial, shipping, manufacturing, and agricultural sectors had to contend with foreign competition more or less on their own up to 1931.

That is not to say that the Netherlands did not benefit from the brief spectacular upturn in the world economy following the lifting of the wartime trade barriers in the late spring of 1919. It was more than a matter of repairing the damage caused by the war: the heavy demand for consumer and capital goods accumulated in those years had now to be met without delay. Britain and the United States in particular, but also the Netherlands and Denmark, had emerged from the war with their industries and transport systems intact, and were now able to profit from the deferred demand. To restart production they only needed to import the necessary raw materials and manufacturing supplies.

In barely one year's time the world economy passed through the full cycle from boom to bust. The gloomy predictions of the war years made way for unbridled optimism in 1919, resulting in a boom which spread rapidly from the United States and the producers of raw materials to all parts of the industrialized world. The pendulum swung back just a year later, for wages failed to keep pace with the rising prices and consumption began to fall back. The decline began in the United States in January, 1920, and it was there that the economy began to recover two years later. But meanwhile millions were unemployed, wages fell dramatically, and production and imports followed suit. The turning point was reached after eighteen months or so, and except for two brief periods in 1924 and 1927, the American economy followed an upward curve until the latter part of 1929. If Wall Street was the most spectacular element of the Roaring Twenties, it was by no means the principal contributor to the prosperity of those years. Thanks to "the second industrial revolution", U.S. manufacturing rose by 45 percent between 1922 and 1929, and total exports by 48 percent. A multitude of new products, like the radio and refrigerator, appeared on the market, and Henry Ford's assembly line brought the automobile within the reach of the general public. In Manhattan, the reconstruction of the area around Grand Central Station created an entirely new skyline dominated by the Empire State Building, the tallest skyscraper in the world, and an equally remarkable office building complex, Rockefeller Center, was beginning to take shape. But not everyone shared in the new prosperity. While real wages went up by 11 percent, company profits showed an increase of 62 percent, and dividends 65 percent. Older industrial sectors such as mining and textiles profited less from the boom, and agriculture was chronically depressed throughout the whole of the decade owing to overproduction.

As foreign trade accounted for a large proportion of national income, the Netherlands also felt the effects of the fluctuations in the world economy in the inter-war years. The post-war economic upturn and the spirit of optimism prevailing in world trade were in evidence there as elsewhere, clouded only by the initially low volume of imports, which prevented production from moving into high gear. Imports of essential raw materials started again in the spring of 1919. The fuel shortage was more prolonged because of declining labor productivity in the Limburg mines and the halt in coal deliveries from Germany. The Netherlands nevertheless prospered, and in 1920 was the only European country other than Denmark whose production exceeded the pre-war level. But there were already signs of the coming recession. Exports had risen rapidly since the beginning of 1919, culminating in an outflow of goods worth Dfl. 225 million in October of that year. The downturn that followed was just as sharp, exports falling by Dfl. 75 million, or 30 percent, in December. Then prices began to fall, the traditional harbinger of economic decline.

In the recession lasting from 1920 to 1923 Dutch exports were affected for the first time by the currency fluctuations generated by the abandonment of the pre-war gold standard which were to exert a powerful influence on world trade over the next two decades. The German mark, in particular, and the French and Belgian franc were heavily undervalued. Though the guilder, following the pound sterling, was devalued in March, 1919, Dutch competitiveness was clearly waning. The consequences were not only perceptible on the home market where German goods were sold at prices lower than the cost of raw materials for the Dutch manufacturer, but on foreign markets as well. The Amsterdam diamond trade, for instance, suffered severely from Belgian competition. There were two aspects to the course of foreign trade: on the one hand volume increased throughout the recession, and on the other hand its value rapidly depreciated

⇐
George Washington Vanderbilt, one of the founders of the Netherlands Chamber, was the grandson of "Commodore" Cornelius Vanderbilt (1794-1877). The Vanderbilt family, of Dutch origin, contributed greatly to the economic growth of the United States. Commodore Vanderbilt made his fortune by running a ferry for passengers and produce between Staten Island and Manhattan. The ferry developed into a very succesful steamship company and the Commodore became one of the richest men in the United States. Commodore Vanderbilt sold his steamships in 1764 and invested the proceeds into the New York Central Railroad. The New Amsterdam gazette in 1885 made the following comment:

"Commodore Vanderbilt was to his country, in a business view, what Washington was in a military. Vanderbilt virtually gave us the steamship & coasting lines, and the railroads were torpid and paid but little until Vanderbilt took hold of Central and made what it has been and yet will be. I very much doubt if this nation has as yet, produced Vanderbilt's equal in all things as a business man."

because of falling prices on the world market. So while Dutch exports to the United States rose from 132,000 tons in 1920 to 160,000 tons, their value dropped from Dfl. 87 million to Dfl. 62 million.

The greater volume of exports was small comfort to the working population. Unemployment rose from 5.8 percent in 1920 to 11.2 percent in 1923, and the 45-hour working week introduced in 1919 was raised again to 48 hours in 1922. However, as industry did not have to switch over from wartime to peacetime production, and the army to be demobilized was small, the Netherlands fared better in the depression years than neighboring countries.

The worst effects of the recession were felt in the Netherlands in 1923, two years later than in the United States. The first signs of recovery appeared shortly afterwards, but it took until April, 1925 for the economic situation to be transformed from "unfavorable" to "relatively satisfactory". The return to the gold standard in that year accelerated the process of recovery. In the wake of world trends the Dutch economy expanded gradually if somewhat unexceptionally over the next four years, culminating in a moderate boom in the summer of 1929. The initiative shown by industry in the war years began to bear fruit in this period. Annual production rose by more than 10 percent in the chemical and pharmaceutical sectors and in the paper and printing industries. The key processes stimulating the changes taking place were rationalization, mechanization, and economies of scale. Research was an increasingly significant aspect of industry. Between 1923 and 1929 manufacturing was one of the major factors in the growth of Dutch exports. While the overall annual figure was 7 percent, manufacturing exports rose by 10 percent.

The deep recession in the 1930s affected manufacturing less acutely than other sectors of the Dutch economy. This was attributable less to government support, which was concentrated more on agriculture and shipping, than to its competitiveness. But there were significant differences within the manufacturing sector. Whereas the production of consumer goods had exceeded the 1929 level by 1936, the production of capital goods was considerably less successful, partly through the greatly reduced elasticity of demand for consumer goods in a period of economic recession, and partly through the introduction of a quota system allowing quantitative ceilings to be fixed for imports from individual countries. Labor productivity rose annually by 2.5 percent, a figure comparing favorably with the 2 percent recorded from 1925 to 1929. However, industry's strong competitive position could not prevent widespread unemployment in the 1930s, which rose precipitously by 400,000 between 1929 and 1936. Two factors were responsible: population growth in the Netherlands was the highest in Europe and, paradoxically, rising productivity meant fewer jobs. A smaller workforce was achieving higher production levels.

Agriculture was the weakest branch of the Dutch economy between 1919 and 1939. It was hard hit by the world slump stemming from the cultivation of vast areas of new land during the war; the resultant increase in the supply of agricultural products caused a sharp drop in world prices. Horticulture, including bulb-growing and plant breeding, was one of the few sectors to escape the recession, indeed doubling the acreage devoted to bulb-growing up to 1930 and employing more intensive and more specialized production methods. Horticulture was more dependent on exports than any other Dutch agricultural sector. This was no problem during the boom period in the second half of the 1920s, when exports amounted to more than Dfl. 40 million a year, reaching a peak of Dfl. 46.5 million in 1930.

In absolute figures, between the upturn in world trade in 1919 and the Wall Street Crash of 1929, Dutch exports made a strong recovery from the drop in 1922 to reach Dfl. 1.4 billion shortly afterwards, and the record figure of more than Dfl. 2 billion in 1929. Exports had accounted for about 30 percent of national revenue for several years. The vigorous growth of Dutch exports despite the growing number of trade barriers is mainly attributable to the steep rise in the productivity of the manufacturing and horticultural sectors, leaving wage rates far behind.[8]

Dutch exports to the United States were an integral part of this pattern. Partly as a result of the highly inflated prices during and after the war, they amounted to Dfl. 218 million in 1920, a figure that was not again attained in the inter-war years.[9] The recession and the falling world market prices caused exports to fall over the next two years to Dfl. 140 million, but they rallied again in response to the upward trend of the American economy. A level of Dfl. 180 million was achieved in 1925, though this was largely attributable to quarantine measures due to be imposed on bulbs as from January, 1926, which prompted many U.S. importers to order extra stocks. The 1928 figure of Dfl. 160 million would therefore seem to be a more accurate indicator of the opportunities offered by the U.S. market to Dutch industry in the second half of the 1920s.

The composition of Dutch exports was much the same as before the war. Diamonds and tobacco still accounted for some 60 percent, and primary products, principally cheese, fish, bulbs and plants, for approximately 18 percent. Though the share of manufactures, consisting of finished and semi-finished products, rose from 16 percent to 21 percent between 1920 and 1928, this was still far below its 39 percent share of total exports.[10] The sharp rise in the U.S. customs duties levied on imported industrial products in 1922 will no doubt have been a contributing factor.[11]

DINNER
tendered by
LLAND-AMERICAN CHAMBER OF COMMERCE
to Officials of JAVA-PACIFIC LINE
Fairmont Hotel, San Francisco
December 13, 1927

Dinner hosted by Holland-American Chamber of Commerce for Officials of Java-Pacific Line, San Francisco, 1927

Just as before the war, there was an adverse trade balance with the United States, but there were distinct signs of improvement, particularly after the U.S. economy had recovered from the 1920-1921 recession and the Dutch backlog demand for raw materials and manufacturing supplies had been met. Between 1920 and 1925 the import cover rose from 40 percent to 60 percent, and remained at that level over the next five years. As the recession hit the United States two years before it spread to the Netherlands, Dutch exports to the U.S. dropped sooner and faster than Dutch imports, causing the import cover to fall below 50 percent in a short amount of time. Exports to the United States as a proportion of total Dutch exports declined from 12.7 percent in 1920 to 8 percent in 1928.

The Great Depression of the 1930s originated in the United States in 1929. Black Thursday on Wall Street marked the beginning of the descent into the black hole of the recession years for the Netherlands as well; the Roaring Twenties made way for the Troubled Thirties. The recession took hold in the United States at an alarming rate. By 1932, 13 million were out of work, 2 million were homeless, and people were dying of hunger. The Netherlands managed to stave off the worst effects of the slump up to that year, but was hit doubly hard thereafter. In those first two years the sharp drop in world trade was offset by Dutch industry's strong competitive position, which enabled it to enlarge its share of practically all the major foreign export markets. Then both the Dutch government and trade and industry were engulfed in recession. In 1931 and 1932 international capital and trade flows were almost at a standstill, protectionism mounted, and Dutch exports withered away. The call for protection in the agricultural sector was so insistent by the end of 1930 that the Netherlands abandoned the principle of free trade, and proceeded in September, 1931 to raise customs duties on finished products from 8 percent to 10 percent, and to introduce a quota system to shield domestic industry and agriculture from "excessive" competition. No duties were imposed on imports of raw materials and manufacturing supplies.

But one important step was left until some years later. Major competitors like Britain devalued their currencies in 1931, and departure from the gold standard was one of the first measures decreed by Franklin D. Roosevelt after his inauguration as president; the Netherlands, however, upheld the gold standard until September, 1936. The statement "we are not counterfeiters", and the fact that the Netherlands was the last country in Europe to devalue, illustrate the tenacity with which it clung to the gold standard. To offset the country's deteriorating competitive position, an attempt was made to reduce domestic costs, but there was no remedy against the plunging world market prices. A slow recovery got underway in 1932, but it was partial at best because of the problems associated with adhering to the gold standard, which hampered Dutch competitiveness on the international markets. The figures speak for themselves. Between 1931 and 1935 the international value of the guilder rose by 80 percent, and the Netherlands' share of world trade fell by 20 percent. In absolute figures, this meant that exports dropped from more than Dfl. 2 billion in 1929 to about Dfl. 700 million in 1935.

Though the world economy was slowly recovering by 1933, the Dutch economy remained in recession up to 1936. While unemployment was abating elsewhere, approximately one-third of the Dutch labor force was jobless in the winter of that year. Prices did not regain the international level until the devaluation of the guilder in September 1936, whereupon export prices fell to the level of the world market in just a few days. Thanks to the upturn in the world economy, international rearmament, and the conclusion of numerous trade agreements, Dutch exports rose and the economy revived. In 1937 exports again exceeded Dfl. 1.2 billion. At the same time, Dutch industry was still not competitive enough to recover lost international markets or to win new ones, and when the world economy entered a new downward spiral in 1938 its success proved to be of short duration. Dutch exports rose no higher than Dfl. 1 billion in 1938 and 1939.

In view of the United States' dominant position in the world economy, it is not surprising that the volatility of Dutch trade in the depression years was yet more pronounced in the trade with North America. Whereas the total value of Dutch exports fell by almost two-thirds between 1929 and 1935, exports to the United States fell by 75 percent between 1928 and 1932, declining from more than Dfl. 160 million in 1928 to Dfl. 40 million in 1932. Describing developments in those years solely in terms of value does not however do full justice to the situation. In terms of volume, exports rose from 260,000 tons in 1928 to almost 330,000 tons in 1932. With the recovery in world market prices Dutch exports to the United States again rose in value from that year, but did not exceed Dfl. 47 million in 1935, and their actual volume had dropped to just over 240,000 tons. Dutch exports to the United States began to pick up again later in the year when a new trade agreement gave a large number of commodities access to the American market. In 1936 Dutch exports to the United States totalled 355,000 tons, or Dfl. 65 million, rising to Dfl. 74 million in 1937 following the devaluation of the guilder. As a result of the downturn in the U.S. economy in the following year, which was more severe than the recession of 1929-1930, Dutch sales in the United States fell by half in terms of both value and volume in the next two years.

Regarding the composition of Dutch exports, the proportion accounted for by diamonds and tobacco declined dramatically in the 1930s. The diamond trade was first to be hit, cut diamonds in particular falling from almost 37 percent in 1928 to 13.1 percent in 1932, or from Dfl. 59 million to Dfl. 5.3 million. Deli tobacco, in demand in the United States as a cigar wrapper of superior quality, fared almost as badly. Comprising 20 percent of total exports, to the value of Dfl. 33 million, in 1928, sales to the United States fell by 75 percent and amounted to no more than Dfl. 4.1 million in 1937. The proportion of finished and semi-finished products, on the other hand, doubled from 24 percent in 1930 to 48 percent in 1932, and primary sector products and raw materials remained at 18 percent and 5 percent respectively.[12]

Between 1922 and 1929 the value of exports to the United States was more than half that of imports; after the onset of the recession the balance of trade fluctuated wildly. The import cover first fell to about 45 percent, then rapidly rose again. Recovery began sooner in the United States than in the Netherlands, where the ongoing recession kept imports down. A cover of 80 to 90 percent in 1935-1936 was probably the highest ever recorded in the history of United States-Netherlands trade relations. It dropped again to 55 percent in 1937, when the Dutch economy at last began to revive and the demand for raw materials and manufacturing imports rapidly increased. The economic situation worsened once more as a result of the short but severe recession affecting the United States in 1938 and the adverse effects on foreign trade of the growing political tensions in Europe. In 1939 Dutch exports to the United States amounted to less than 30 percent of imports from that country. In 1930 they comprised 5 percent of total exports, rising to a maximum of 8 percent in 1936.

As before the first world war, a large but unknown part of the adverse balance of trade was offset by income from investments in the United States. The figures for the inter-war period are however so inconclusive as to allow no more than a rough estimate of the total amount and its distribution over the various forms of capital. During the war total Dutch investments in the United States appear to have diminished by one-third. Holdings in stocks and shares were liquidated. In 1919 they amounted to about $ 400 million, an estimated 10 percent of total European investments in the United States. More selling seems to have taken place as a result of the high exchange rate of the dollar and the stocks issued by companies in the Netherlands and the Dutch East Indies during the short post-war recession. Dutch investments thus dwindled to an estimated $ 300 million in 1927. Following the Wall Street boom in 1928 and 1929, Dutch investors increased their holdings in American securities to at least $ 450 million. In any case, according to detailed figures for 1934, investments that year totalled more than $ 700 million, which meant that the Netherlands accounted for almost one-sixth of foreign investments in the United States. As a legacy of the railroad era, approximately one-third was invested in U.S. railroad companies.[13] Direct investments amounting to $ 224 million were mainly concentrated in two companies, namely the Royal Dutch Shell Group with $ 159 million, and AKU (part of today's AKZO Nobel) with $ 55 million. Shortly before the first world war Unilever expanded its holdings in the United States. Shrinking incomes in Europe, which were not likely to improve in the short term because of the political uncertainty, had to be boosted elsewhere. To give one example, Dfl. 3.8 million was invested in Thomas J. Lipton, Inc., the biggest tea wholesalers in the United States. Shortly before the outbreak of the second world war the Federal Reserve Board estimated Dutch investments in the United States somewhere between $ 800 million and $ 1 billion, a figure representing more than one-third of total Dutch holdings abroad.

The Dutch Chambers of Commerce for America: 1920 - 1930

On January 6, 1921, J.B.D. Pennink of the KPM shipping company reported to the Board of Directors of the Chamber in Amsterdam on the first annual meeting of the New York Chamber of Commerce for the Netherlands and the Netherlands East and West Indies, Inc. As head of the agency of one of the seven shipping companies which each donated an annual $ 1,000 to the Chamber, Pennink was on its Board of Directors.[14] The president of the Chamber in New York was N.G.M. Luykx, the central figure in the formation and expansion of Royal Dutch Shell's investments in the United States. Although Luykx was about to resign due to a lack of time, it was likely that the growing pains of the Chamber were over. Moreover, the Dutch government had been asked for a subsidy of $ 15,000 for publicity purposes in 1921. Of the various committees, the Committee for Arts, Sciences and Friendly Relations had shown special initiative by organizing a reception in honor of Willem Mengelberg, guest conductor of the National Symphony Orchestra, to be held in the Ritz-Carlton Hotel in New York on January 17, 1921.

A few months later the Dutch government granted the subsidy and the publicity section booked its first accomplishments. The reception for Mengelberg had been a resounding success, as was the exhibition of modern Dutch paintings held from April 24 to May 7, 1921 in the Anderson Galleries on Park Avenue and 59th Street in New York. The artists represented at the exhibition included Kees van Dongen, Jan Toorop, and George Breitner, but the works with the greatest impact were Vincent van Gogh's *Irises* and *Pietà after Delacroix*.[15] Because the Committee for Arts, Sciences and Friendly Relations was so successful, the Chamber decided that the Committee was ready to become an independent organization under its new name of the Netherland-America Foundation. (See page 164 for illustration.)

Behind the Netherland-America Foundation were a number of leading members of the Dutch community in New York and prominent Americans of Dutch descent, the majority of whom were then associated with the Chamber. The American members of the organizing committee of the Foundation came from the publishing world. Hamilton Holt was editor of *The Independent*, and Edward W. Bok, who had emigrated as a schoolboy from Den Helder to the United States, was the celebrated publisher of *The Ladies' Home Journal*. The vice-president of the Foundation became Franklin Delano Roosevelt, governor of New York and the future President of the United States.

Pennink was not very optimistic about the immediate future of the Chamber. Membership of the Chamber was declining, and before the year was out it might be unable to meet its financial commitments, not least because the Dutch government's subsidy was for one year only. Pennink very much doubted that the Dutch business community in New York was large enough to support the organization.

The fact that the services of both the New York and Amsterdam offices were constantly available to Dutch exporters up to the outbreak of the second world war indicates that Pennink's assessment of the possibilities was too negative. Wittert van Hoogland soon proved to be an enterprising secretary and the existence of The Netherlands-American Chamber of Commerce in Amsterdam strengthened ties with firms in the Netherlands, and the business community and the government donated substantial sums in the course of the years. But in 1922 the two Chambers of Commerce were facing difficult times.

Notwithstanding the backing of prominent businessmen, the 150-strong membership of the Netherlands-American Chamber of Commerce in Amsterdam, and the establishment of a sister organization in the Dutch East Indies, the promotion of exports was beset with difficulties over the next few years. Indeed in 1925 shrinking incomes and stagnating membership figures were questioning the survival of the Chamber in New york.

As a form of voluntary cooperation between business firms that functioned in principle without government support, the two Chambers were primarily dependent on their members. The few surviving financial documents show that membership of the Chambers in New York, San Francisco, and Amsterdam rarely exceeded 200 between 1920 and 1925. When Dutch exports recovered from the worst effects of the recession, the figure rose from 231 in 1927 to approximately 300 in 1930. Amsterdam then had 231 members, the largest number in the inter-war period, which rapidly declined in the next recession. A recruiting campaign attracted 21 new members in 1932, but from 1935 onwards membership stayed at about 175. New York then probably had between 40 and 60 members. No figures are available for San Francisco.

With such a limited membership, it will be clear that the Chambers had little room to manoeuver. Annual membership fees in the United States, the Netherlands, and the Dutch East Indies amounted to $ 4,500 between 1920 and 1923, a quarter of which was paid in the United States. In addition, subsidies were received from the KPM and six other shipping companies, which donated $ 7,000 in three successive years, and from the Netherlands Ministry of Foreign Affairs, which between 1921 and 1924 provided funds that were intended for publicity but were primarily used for commercial information. Aware of the limited financial resources of the other Dutch Chambers of Commerce abroad, the Ministry was wary of creating a precedent. When the economy was buoyant in 1924 and 1925 contributions amounted to over $ 5,500, but the financial situation of the Chamber in New York nevertheless worsened in those years. The shipping companies reduced their annual contribution by half after 1923, and in 1924 the Netherlands government paid its last subsidy of $ 5,000.[16] The resulting deficits were financed at the Chamber in

Amsterdam its director Von Baumhauer, and at the Chamber in New York by some of the directors as well. The 1925 budget of $ 19,000 of the Chamber in New York showed a deficit of $ 2,700. The last reserves were used, and severe cutbacks were inevitable. Wittert van Hoogland was succeeded in 1926 by Neil van Aken, head of the recently closed publicity section.

Despite these cost-cutting measures, the financial situation deteriorated further in the course of 1926, and bankruptcy seemed imminent before the end of the year. A last-ditch effort was made to persuade the Dutch government and the business community in the Netherlands and the East Indies to come to the rescue. The authorities in both parts of the kingdom agreed to help, but whereas the Dfl. 10,000 pledged by the East Indies authorities was paid the following year, the subsidy approved by the government in the Netherlands came in the form of a guarantee against further deficits, so that the remainder of the Dfl. 10,000 intended for 1927 was not received until 1928. The business community also rallied round with substantial sums, but part of the money was meant to attract American tourists to the Netherlands. The KPM shipping company and the Rotterdam shipowner P. van Ommeren each agreed to contribute $ 1000 for three years, as did also the Holland Bulb Exporters Association, the Amsterdam Chamber of Commerce, and KLM Royal Dutch Airlines. In addition, G.H. Hintzen of the Rotterdam bank R. Mees & Sons pledged an annual $ 2000 to finance deficits, and various sums totalling $ 20,000 were contributed for the period 1927-1929 by the Bataafsche Petroleum Company (BPM), the Netherlands Railways, the Netherlands Tourist Association, other banks and shipping companies, the Netherlands Dairy Federation, Hotel des Indes in The Hague, and the Amstel Hotel and Artis Zoo in Amsterdam. Including the subsequent donations for the promotion of tourism, the 1927 budget amounted to almost $ 35,000. The sum of $ 2000 was allocated to the Chamber in San Francisco and thirty-five agents throughout the United States; the remainder was divided equally between the Netherlands Chamber of Commerce in New York, the Netherlands-American Chamber in Amsterdam, and the Netherlands Railways office which opened in New York in 1927.

*Mr A. von Baumhauer
and Esquire J.P. Six*

*Waldorf Astoria,
New York's tallest hotel,
c. 1920*

From a financial point of view, 1929 was a crucial year for the Chambers, not only because of the effects of the Wall Street Crash, but more specifically because in that year private subsidies came to an end. A campaign conducted in the summer yielded Dfl. 70,000 for each of the next three years. After the Dutch government and the authorities in the East Indies, the biggest donor was the Netherlands Tourist Association, which contributed $ 4,000. G.H. Hintzen, the Netherlands Railways, and the KPM each donated $ 2,000, the Netherlands Trading Society, the Holland-America Line, the Stoomvaart Maatschappij Rotterdam Lloyd, and the Stoomvaart Maatschappij Nederland promised an annual $ 500, the Rotterdam International Credit and Trading Company $ 250, and the Netherlands Bank $ 100. Smaller contributions came from the Hotel Americain in Amsterdam, various regional Chambers of Commerce in the Netherlands, and Heck's Lunchroom in Rotterdam. The list ends with the Oranje Nassau Hotel in Arnhem, which donated $ 4.

As many of the pledges made in 1929 were for a period of three years, the impact of the deepening economic recession was cushioned up to 1933. After 1932, both members and donors steadily diminished in number. The lowest point was reached in 1936, when the budget was between Dfl. 55,000 and Dfl. 60,000, just over half that of the top year of 1929. As many of the subsidies were paid in Dutch guilders, the 1933 devaluation of the dollar almost entirely offset the decline. Although no data have been found for the period 1937-1940, it may be assumed that the upturn in the Dutch economy and in trade with the United States prevented the budget from falling further; it may even have risen somewhat.

From the few data available it would seem that the members in the United States represented large commercial, banking, shipping, and manufacturing firms.[17] New York firms like Boissevain & Co., the Rotterdamsche Bankvereeniging, the Bank of America, Brown Brothers & Co., Kuhn, Loeb & Co. and the Equitable Trust Co. indicate the closeness of the economic ties between the Netherlands and the United States. Kuhn, Loeb & Co. and the Equitable Trust Co. had brokered the listing of the Shell Oil Company on the U.S. stock exchange. The Guaranty Trust Co., a subsidiary of J.P. Morgan & Co., brokered loans for the Dutch East Indies in 1922 and 1923 totalling $ 150 million; Dillon, Read & Co. acted for the Dutch government in the issue of bonds to the value of Dfl. 300 million.[18] The oil sector was represented by the Standard Oil Co. of New York and two subsidiary companies of Shell Oil, namely Shell Company of California and the Asiatic Petroleum Company. The Holland Food Corporation, Catz American Co. Inc. and Wm.H. Müller & Co. were all major importers of Dutch products before the war. Shipping interests were represented by the Ph. Van Ommeren Corp. and the Royal Dutch West India Mail, and the port of New York by the Morse Dry Dock & Repair Co., the Shipping & Coal Co. Inc., and the Texas Transport & Terminal Co. Inc.

Dutch manufacturing and trade in East Indies products, both of which had been fairly prominent before the first world war, were almost entirely absent in the 1920s. Amongst the few representatives of the former were Van Houten Inc. and Anthony Fokker, while the Sino Java Trading Company was the sole representative of the latter. The U.S. Rubber Plantations, Inc. and Standard Oil, on the other hand, were two of the principal American investors in the Dutch colony. Bulb exports were represented by the Holland Bulb Exporters Association. The same membership structure was to be found at the Chamber in Amsterdam, in which business, banking, and shipping were equally prominent. Dutch manufacturing companies that had been members of the Chamber in New York before the first world war were now members of the Amsterdam organization. Some were firms processing traditional imported commodities, such as cocoa and chocolate producers; others had grown rapidly during and after the first world war, including the Philips concern, the Royal Netherlands Iron and Steel Foundries, and the Dutch branch of the Ford Motor Company.

Trade Promotion

Between 1920 and 1940, most of the routine work concerning trade promotion was performed in Amsterdam. The Chamber in New York had fewer staff and resources at its disposal, so that there was often a delay in dealing with correspondence. The first priority was to take on more staff. In the initial period Wittert van Hoogland had a staff of four, but Van Aken had to manage with one assistant and at most two typists, with the sole exception of the years from 1929 to 1931, when he also had four employees, including an assistant secretary. The Amsterdam office, in contrast, often had the assistance of six or more of the staff of Von Baumhauer's legal practice. Esquire Pieter J. Six, who succeeded Von Baumhauer as secretary in 1927, likewise needed to spend only part of his time on the business of the Chamber in Amsterdam. He was also the secretary of the Netherlands-Italian Chamber.

The records and the few remaining annual reports of the Chamber in Amsterdam show that working methods had changed since 1914. One of the differences was the greater use of the telegraph, which facilitated closer cooperation and speedier communication with the Chamber in New York. They made no distinction between each other's members. Though many of the requests for information reaching New York were forwarded by the office in Amsterdam, some were sent directly by firms in the Netherlands. The Amsterdam office, with the aid of the commercial publications in the reading room, answered as many of the queries as possible. Those which it passed on to New York were mainly requests for the names and addresses of exporters, importers, and agents received from practically all sectors of industry and commerce.

The number of requests handled jointly each year by the Chambers in Amsterdam and New York is unknown. The sole figures available relate to New York in the first half of 1924. The 330 letters despatched dealt with products ranging from woollen blankets, dairy produce, vegetable oils, and electric lamps to works of art, medicines, and spices. Almost 90 inquiries concerned the settlement of disputes, and 276 were in the general category called "the extension of trade". It may be deduced from the secretary's report that the total figure for 1924 was roughly twice as high. It is not improbable that 1924 saw a marked increase in the Chamber's activities. In that year Dutch exports to the United States showed a steep rise, and the Netherlands Foreign Ministry had just decided to economize by instructing the consulates to refer all requests for commercial information to private organizations. In 1925 the New York office received about 500 such queries from the consulates, and the same number from the Trade Division responsible for contact between the Dutch government and industry and commerce.

In referring queries to the Chambers of Commerce in New York and Amsterdam, the Netherlands Foreign Ministry placed a heavy burden on their limited resources. In 1924 more than 60 percent of their work was devoted to trade promotion, 90 percent of which related to queries addressed to the consulates by individuals or firms that were not members of either the offices in New York or Amsterdam.

Publicity

In the first years of its existence, publicity for the Netherlands was one of the most important tasks of the Netherlands Chamber of Commerce in New York, Inc. The legation had already taken the first steps in 1919, using the funds contributed by the business community in 1918 to contract a public relations firm, the Pelman Institute of America, for a period of two months. The war and the anti-Dutch campaigns in the American and British press had ended, but the threat to the Netherlands' neutrality had not subsided altogether. At the Peace Conference of Versailles in 1919, Belgium demanded the cession of Dutch territory, including the southernmost part of the province of Limburg and Dutch Flanders, as a buffer against any future attack by Germany. Though rejected by Britain and the United States, Belgium persisted in pressing the claim for some time afterwards. Towards the end of that year a state visit by the Belgian King and Queen to the United States was accompanied by an intensive press campaign, reviving the need to focus public attention on the position of the Netherlands.[19] The negative effects were not wholly dispelled by articles in American newspapers by Cremer, the head of the Dutch legation, De Beaufort, the first secretary, and Simons, the Washington correspondent of *De Telegraaf*.

The Pelman Institute advised the legation early in 1919 that regular contact with the press was essential if the Netherlands' standpoint was to be appreciated in the United States. A course of action that would have been unacceptable to many of his predecessors, since even at the height of the anti-Dutch campaign Van Rappard had shunned contact with the press, seems to have been a mere matter of routine for the politician and businessman Cremer.[20] Copies or summaries of important articles published in the Dutch

Philips and Lamond, Corliss & Company in New York had established an American sales company for Philips light bulbs as early as 1912 under the name of Laco. This is an early advertisement for Laco, which also used the slogan "Laco quality increases and the price decreases". Chicago, 1893

LACO LAMPS LAST LONGEST

press were to be circulated in the United States. Foreign Minister Van Karnebeek could consider following the British and French example by holding a weekly press conference for American correspondents. And the Chamber in New York could function as a publicity agency, for instance by issuing an illustrated monthly publication and regularly disseminating information on the Dutch economy. The objective was "... that Americans may feel that Holland stands for the same free and democratic principles in international affairs as the United States". A dinner was planned by the Chamber as an excellent opportunity to generate understanding of Dutch interests among the American business community.[21]

Only some of these suggestions could be put into practice. As a result of the negative wartime press abroad, a press department was established at the Netherlands Ministry of Foreign Affairs in 1920. The Ministry had difficulty carrying out the new policy of openness. One or two press conferences yielded little in results, and the head of the new department was soon known to the press corps as "Mister I-don't-know". American newspapers and magazines did not send their best reporters to The Hague either. The legacy of the war was repeatedly apparent in such biased reports that De Beaufort, then chargé-d'affaires, called personally on *The New York Sun and Herald* and *The New York Times*. His protests made little difference in the case of the former, which reported that on the Queen's birthday holiday in 1920 the entire Dutch population - men, women and children - had lain drunk in the streets, and that the country had grown fat on the proceeds of its trade with the belligerents in the war.

Nor was the legation very successful with another of its projects. Cremer's forced return to the Netherlands due to illness in the spring of 1920 prevented the planned contact with the quality newspapers and the New York dinner to invite the American business community had to be cancelled.[22] So it was left to the Chamber of Commerce and the Committee for Arts, Sciences and Friendly Relations to do something about the tarnished image of the Netherlands in the United States. In March, 1920 Simons and the Pelham Institute drew up a plan for the dissemination of photographic material, the publication of a short commercial bulletin by the leading New York papers and the screening of documentary films.[23] It took time, but the project was eventually realized by the Chamber of Commerce rather than the Committee. It seemed a better idea to keep the purely commercial publications of the Chamber of Commerce separate from the Committee's cultural activities. The legation was asked to allocate $ 6,000 a year for three years from the Westerman fund for the publication of a weekly trade bulletin. Cremer would go no further than a single subsidy of $ 1,800, enough for a typist for one year.[24]

The Chamber took matters into its own hands and sent a representative of the Pelham Institute to the

110

Netherlands in May, 1920 to obtain the backing of the government and the Netherland-America Foundation for the Committee for Arts, Sciences and Friendly Relations. Led by Daniël J. von Balluseck, the young New York correspondent of the *Algemeen Handelsblad* who later became its editor in chief and, after the second world war, the Dutch envoy to Moscow, the committee's work was to cover a wide field ranging from the organization of art exhibitions, the translation and publication of Dutch literature, and the performance of plays and music to exchange programs for students and academics and the promotion of the Netherlands as a tourist attraction. In July of that year the Netherland-America Foundation made available the $ 25,000 still remaining in the Westerman fund, from which the reception for Mengelberg and the Dutch art exhibition were financed.

The Foundation had stipulated that these funds could not be used by the Chamber on publications. If, as was essential, the Chamber of Commerce was to be brought to the attention of the Dutch and American business community, however, a publication appearing at regular intervals was indispensable.[25] The funds needed were drawn from the government subsidy of $ 15,000. The commercial bulletin, which had already been issued for some months, was financed from its own budget. Besides general commercial information, this weekly press communiqué contained reports on the development of trade between the United States, the Netherlands and the Dutch East Indies, and on Dutch industry, shipping, and banking.

The illustrated monthly *Holland and Her Colonies* attracted the most attention. Edited by Van Aken under the supervision of the legation, it appeared from 1921 to 1923,[26] featuring articles on such diverse subjects as the international position of the Netherlands, some of which were written by the legation staff, economics, and the literature and history of the Netherlands. It was printed in an edition of 1500 and distributed to libraries, universities, Chambers of Commerce, banks and leading newspapers and magazines. The Dutch government was pleased with the results, but spending cuts in 1923 spelled the end of the subsidy, and the last issue appeared in October.[27] Even though it heightened the American business community's awareness of the Chamber in New York, the decisive factor was its limited circulation and its accordingly limited publicity value. Soon after his arrival in the United States, the new envoy, Esquire Andries C.D. de Graeff, reported that there was still a pressing need for information: "The ignorance here about the Netherlands verges on the unbelievable". The Netherlands Foreign Ministry was not prepared to reconsider its decision as government resources were severely depleted by the recession. A more important reason could have been that five years after the end of the first world war, the Netherlands was at last free of the odium attaching to its neutral stance and had resumed its place on the international political scene.

Tourism

With the Dutch government subsidy about to be withdrawn and the shipowners' contributions halved, 1925 threatened to be a disastrous year for the Chamber in New York. However, the Dutch shipowners came to the rescue and appointed Van Aken as their joint representative with a remit to bring the tourist attractions of the Netherlands to the attention of wealthy Americans. It was in fact a camouflaged subsidy for trade promotion since the promotion of tourism would not be a full-time job for Van Aken. This together with the last $ 5000 government subsidy gave the Chamber the scope it needed to prove its viability. It would then need to find new sources of finance for the second half of 1926. Van Aken's appointment followed on a meeting about the promotion of American tourism held in Amsterdam on August 21, 1923, attended by representatives of the KPM, the Holland-America Line, the Royal Netherlands Steamship Company, the Dutch and East Indies railways, and KLM Royal Dutch Airlines. Others present included representatives of the Netherlands Tourist Association, various industrial and commercial concerns, regional Chambers of Commerce, municipal authorities, hotel owners, and the Chambers in New York and Amsterdam. The government was represented by the envoy to the United States, Esquire de Graeff, and the deputy head of the Economic Affairs Department, and the United States by Frank Mahin, the American consul in Amsterdam. It was decided that tourist publicity in the United States would be handled by a special body, the Netherlands Committee for Traffic Propaganda in America, which at the suggestion of the Chamber was established at 292 Herengracht, Amsterdam. Von Baumhauer was secretary of the Executive Committee. In the hope of profiting from the growing stream of American tourists travelling to Europe, special folders, films, and slides would be produced for the American market. Up to 1937 the Traffic Committee was part of the Chamber in Amsterdam and their bookkeeping was combined in order to enhance the latter's status in the eyes of potential donors, although it was not always clear how the money was spent. At any event the disbursement policy grew ever more obscure to those in New York, and the issue almost caused the two Chambers of Commerce to end their association in 1929. In the Netherlands, too, there was little clarity on this point.

American tourists were an important factor in the flow of funds between Europe and the United States in the 1920s. Whereas before 1914 an adverse balance of payments with Europe had been the rule, the United States emerged from the war as the world's chief creditor. To service and repay the debts contracted during and after the war, Europe had to increase its earnings from the flow of goods and services to the United States, but in view of the tariff barrier impeding the growth of exports other sources of income had to be found; tourism was one. The number of Americans crossing the Atlantic rose from 15,000 in 1912 to

KLM,
Royal Dutch Air Lines
DC-2 ca 1932

251,000 in 1929. The problem of war debt did not affect the Netherlands. What was felt, however, was the rapid decline in immigration following the enactment of new U.S. laws in 1921, causing shipping companies like the Holland-America Line to lose a sizeable proportion of traffic and earnings.

With an annual budget of $ 15,000, which included a tentative $ 4000 subsidy not yet approved by the Dutch government, the Traffic Committee set to work in 1924. In collaboration with the U.S. railroad companies and the Holland-America Line, Van Aken published brochures in print runs of 50,000 carrying slogans like "It costs so little to see so much in Tulipland". The major Philadelphia travel agency Belber, Trunk & Bag Coy financed the printing of two million copies of a brochure advertising the Netherlands.[28] Van Aken gave talks in the New York area which were illustrated with slides, and was a regular guest on radio programs. Notwithstanding the strong guilder, the number of Americans visiting the Netherlands went up by 60 percent in 1924, and again by 40 percent in 1925.

Tourist publicity seems to have been a heavy financial burden for the Chamber in New York, especially after Van Aken succeeded Wittert van Hoogland as secretary at the end of 1925. The annual publicity costs were so high that only a meager $ 800 was left for trade promotion, ruling out the possibility of replenishing the dwindling income from fees and donations. Early in 1926 it was patently obvious that without an injection of capital, liquidation at the end of the year was inevitable. The ending of the government subsidy, the shrinking membership, and the further reduction in the contributions of large Dutch concerns had eroded the Chamber's financial basis. Conversely, 1924 and 1925 were quite good years for the Chamber in Amsterdam. Although allowing for a budget deficit of Dfl. 500 in 1924, some items of expenditure had little to do with the promotion of exports. For example, such as the costs of a princely welcome extended to a visiting U.S. naval squadron, the lavish entertainment of the U.S. envoy Richard M. Tobin, and an expensive present for the departing American commercial attaché, totalling in all about Dfl. 3200. While the deficit of the Chamber in New York was almost $ 5,600 in 1925, leaving a third of the expenditure uncovered, the expenditures of the Chamber in Amsterdam rose to Dfl. 16,800.

Why was there such a disparity in the financial situation of two organizations working so closely together as the Chambers in Amsterdam and New York, and that in such a short time? While Amsterdam had scope for expenditures beyond the promotion of trade, New York was forced to make ever greater spending cuts by dismissing the secretary and one of the two remaining typists, and scaling down its commercial publications. The explanation lies in the way the two Chambers worked together and in the organizational structure of most of the Dutch Chambers of Commerce abroad.

Relations between the Chambers in New York and Amsterdam

William C. Redfield, the former U.S. Secretary of Commerce, who succeeded N.G.M. Luykx in December, 1921 as president of the Chamber, had excellent qualifications for the position. As U.S. Secretary of Commerce in the Wilson administration he had shown to understand the interests and problems of trade and industry. He had personally intervened during the first world war when French competitors accused the Rotterdam firm of Stokvis & Sons of trading with the enemy. As president of the American Manufacturers Export Association in 1920 and 1921 Redfield was a leading authority on foreign trade. At the time of his appointment he was a stockbroker in Wall Street, and had also accepted the presidency of the American-Russian Chamber of Commerce.

In July, 1925, Redfield was succeeded by Willem W. van Doorn, general manager of the Holland-America Line in New York, who took over as acting president of the Chamber. Both Luykx and Redfield were typical presidents of the early Chamber. The president was responsible for the formulation of policy. For reasons of prestige, preference was given to the directors of high-profile Dutch or American firms. This had the advantage that the person concerned had wide business experience, but also the disadvantage that he could not spare the time needed to attend to the Chamber. At the same time, the secretary, who directed the Chamber's day-to-day activities, usually did not have a seat on the Board.

Relations between the Chambers in New York and Amsterdam in the years from 1925 to 1940 present a classic example of contrasting styles of management; of policy-making by a president with many commitments, and by a secretary who was conversant with all aspects of the work and who had wide decision-making powers. In contrast to Van Aken, whose decisions were largely dependent on the president, Von Baumhauer occupied a position of authority in Amsterdam. Where Wittert van Hoogland and Van Aken were constantly obliged to seek the approval of the Board, Von Baumhauer was free to act as he saw fit. Most Board members regarded their position as purely formal, requiring no more than a minimum of time and attention. Of perhaps twenty members, it was quite usual for no more than one or two to visit the office with any regularity. Von Baumhauer's expansionist tendencies coupled with the chronic shortage of funds in New York placed the continued association of the Chambers in Amsterdam and New York under heavy strain.

The Chamber in Amsterdam was originally set up for the purpose of cementing the relationship of the Chamber in New York with the Dutch government and the business community in the Netherlands. Much more than support for New York was not envisaged. Gradually, however, their teamwork extended to financial and organizational aspects. Financially the Chamber in New York was largely dependent on sources in the Netherlands, while from an organizational point of view it was hoped that the inclusion of tourist promotion in their joint activities would augment the financial resources of both Chambers. Financial collaboration went no further than procuring subsidies and donations. The offices of the Chambers in New York and Amsterdam, and the New York office of the Netherlands Railways were entirely free to make their own decisions on disbursement. The Board of Directors in New York was not subject to any form of supervision and received no instructions from the Netherlands or vice versa.

The first contract sealing the association between the two Chambers was signed in 1923. Both parties stated their intention to work harmoniously together to promote Dutch exports to the United States. Von Baumhauer, who at that time was embarking on his career as an international lawyer, expanded his practice to far beyond the Netherlands, with close contacts in the United States, Germany, Britain, Austria, and Italy. His clients included Standard Oil, I.G. Farben, the *Deutsche Bank* and the *Darmstädter Bank*.[29] In the promotion of exports to the United States, Von Baumhauer was an enterprising organizer who never hesitated to seek support for his ideas in the highest government and business circles. Though his lack of tact tended to cause irritation, especially amongst government officials, he was a member of the delegation sent to Washington in 1937 by the Netherlands Ministry of Finance to negotiate (unsuccessfully) a treaty on the prevention of double taxation and in 1934 and 1935 he and Six played a leading part in the preparations for negotiations with the United States on a new trade agreement.

Von Baumhauer's lack of tact more than once caused his projects to collapse. A striking example is the blueprint for the reorganization of economic information, complete with a detailed budget, which he presented unrequested to the economic affairs department of the Netherlands Foreign Ministry in 1922. On the premise that private enterprise was more flexible and more cost-effective than a government department, he proposed that government responsibility be transferred wherever possible to private organizations. He seems to have been oblivious of the fact that various earlier attempts had foundered on the rock of political interests. The officials of the Ministry of Foreign Affairs, were not amused. As Johan A. Nederbragt, head of the economic affairs department, commented:

> "To what do we owe the fact that a private person takes it upon himself to devise the reorganization of a government department, and what value should be attached to a proposal that is utterly superficial even in its radical elements, and is crowned by calculations based on fantasy. What is in fact at stake here is the honor of the Economic Affairs Department."

As the fund-raiser and business manager of the Chamber in Amsterdam, Von Baumhauer had a profound effect on its relations with the Chamber in New York, largely because he took too little account of New York's often precarious financial situation. Too often, he lost sight of the fact that the two organizations worked together on a voluntary basis, and that his authority was restricted to Amsterdam. He had no qualms about censuring New York if requests for information were not dealt with promptly or adequately, or if new projects were not undertaken. In his view, if a member was seeking a suitable business contact, then it was up to the secretary to see to it personally. He too easily overlooked the fact that Wittert van Hoogland and Van Aken were often without staff and had to do everything themselves. When Six and the president, Westermann, visited New York in 1929 they discovered that Amsterdam had greatly overestimated the Chamber's resources.

But as he experienced in 1927, Von Baumhauer also got his share of criticism. The point of contention was the division of the costs of his legal practice and those of the Chamber of Commerce. Furnishing no evidence of any kind, he charged certain costs to the Chamber. More seriously, he was suspected of using his position in the Chamber to procure clients for his legal practice. Neither the Dutch government nor the business community approved of the combined financial administration, and when the question of financial support was raised again in October, 1926, both the business community and the Ministry of Labor, Trade and Industry were willing to assist New York but explicitly excluded Amsterdam. In 1927 the

114

Board decided that all purely legal enquiries would henceforth be referred to Von Baumhauer's legal practice, which meant that in Amsterdam a charge was made for the general information that was provided free in New York. The Netherlands Ministry of Labor, Trade and Industry tried unsuccessfully to sever the links between the Chamber and the Von Baumhauer's legal practice.

The Board of Directors' scant interest in the Chamber in New York was to a large extent the decisive factor in the collaboration with the Amsterdam organization in the 1920s. The details of their financial and organizational collaboration were laid down in writing on November 8, 1923. The Amsterdam office was to deal with all matters in the Netherlands, including contacts with the government, fund-raising, and the registration of new members. In return for not recruiting members in the Netherlands, the Chamber in New York would receive from the Chamber in Amsterdam at least $ 4,000 a year. With the end of its government subsidy in sight, the Chamber in New York was thus able to shore up its finances. As it turned out, the agreement was more advantageous to the Chamber in Amsterdam. Although trade promotion was primarily conducted by the Chamber in New York, the Chamber in Amsterdam profited from its position in the Netherlands, the home base of the exporters and large corporations with branches in America and the financial bedrock of the two Chambers of Commerce with 90 percent of their work being performed on behalf of Dutch and East Indies companies. The Chamber in New York no longer needed to worry about raising funds, finding subsidies, and attracting new members, but at the same time the 1923 agreement had the disadvantage of isolating it from its grassroots support. This in itself need not have been a problem if Von Baumhauer had not regarded the Chamber in New York more and more as a branch office. Consultations were infrequent at best, and the allocation formula remained a mystery to all in New York.

In 1924 Von Baumhauer became seriously concerned about the situation in New York. Wittert van Hoogland's handling of business enquiries went rapidly downhill and through the close ties linking the two Chambers, the Chamber in Amsterdam then found itself under pressure as well. Certainly, with the aid of directories, the texts of tariff laws, and so on, the Chamber in Amsterdam could deal with many queries itself. Nevertheless, the distance between the two countries prevented Amsterdam from ever being more than an intermediary between Dutch exporters and the Chamber in New York, which alone was capable of putting them in touch with customers, suppliers or agents, investigating their financial and ethical standing, and advising on markets for specific products. There was little that Von Baumhauer could do beyond urging a speedy solution. Van Aken's appointment as successor to Wittert van Hoogland ended the management crisis, but the financial problems remained. At the next general meeting Van Aken announced that if no further funds were forthcoming the Chamber would be wound up at the end of the year. This would bring an end to the last institution to which Dutch businessmen could apply for commercial information on the United States. The spending cuts had forced the abolition of the post of commercial attaché at the Washington legation in 1922, followed later by the closure of the showroom and the Dutch East Indies Government Office in New York. Even the Dutch business community seemed to be pulling back. The KPM shipping company made use of Van Aken's appointment to the Traffic Committee to close its New York agency, and the Rotterdamsche Bankvereeniging, whose director W. Westerman was president of the Chamber in Amsterdam, was about to close its New York branch.[30]

Three years after the Chamber in New York was plunged into financial difficulties by the withdrawal of the government subsidy and the termination of the consulates' commercial information services, the Dutch government reconsidered its decision. If the Chamber were to close its doors, the business community would promptly demand alternative facilities from the Netherlands government, and subsidizing a non-governmental organization would at least ensure that the costs were shared by industry and commerce. Experience had shown that private organizations could usually be run less expensively than official ones, and that their staffs were experienced and efficient. Van Aken and Six both spent thirteen years as secretaries of their respective Chamber offices. But the main argument for the Netherlands government was the wide difference in business practices in the two countries. As Van Aken put it, "the psychology of the American business man is entirely different from that of the European business man, so that different tactics and different modes of approach prevail here from those in Europe". All the same, the New York office was on the brink of bankruptcy twice more before the Netherlands Ministry of Labor, Trade and Industry honored its promise in 1926.

A Dutch Treat

De Graeff, the Dutch envoy to Washington, was the first government official in 1926 who persistently advocated renewing the subsidy to the Chamber in New York. In his view it was all very well for the Chamber to be burdened with the queries addressed to the legation and the consulates, but it was not right that the Foreign Ministry should provide no financial compensation. After all, almost a quarter of its work was performed free of charge in the interests of the Netherlands. The Dutch government, and notably the Foreign Ministry, did not regard the provision of commercial information as part of its task; if private enterprise was not willing to supply the necessary funds then there was no reason why the Chamber of Commerce should continue to exist. The Ministry accordingly made no move to make more funds available.

Thus the question of the survival of the Chamber in New York was tied to the question of the role of government in the economy. Though prior to the onset of the recession in 1929 Dutch government policy was guided by the principle of liberalism, change was brewing in government circles. Despite opposition from the Netherlands Ministry of Foreign Affairs, De Graeff was backed up a short time later by Jan R. Slotemaker de Bruïne, the Minister of Labor, Trade and Industry. The Minister acted on the advice of the head of the Trade Division, Floris K.J. Heringa, who supported the liberal policy in theory but was more receptive to the new arguments than his counterpart in Foreign Affairs, Nederbragt, head of the Economic Affairs Department. Whereas Nederbragt refused even to consider granting a subsidy, Heringa came to the conclusion that the Netherlands Chamber of Commerce in New York, Inc. played such a vital part in exports to the United States that the subsidy should be renewed as from 1927. He was strengthened in his view by the fact that the Dutch East Indies authorities had pledged a Dfl. 10,000 subsidy, and business circles in the Netherlands and the East Indies had promised additional funds, significantly augmenting the combined budget for trade promotion and tourist publicity. Since the subsidy was to be paid by the Ministry of Labor, Trade and Industry, the Foreign Ministry dropped its objections. The payment of the subsidy was delayed for some time because the Dutch government, having no say in the budget and the organizational structure of the two Chambers of Commerce, wished to go no further than a guarantee against budget deficits.[31] Heringa tried to sidetrack the Chamber in Amsterdam, but met with resistance from the business community. Finally, with bankruptcy looming, Slotemaker de Bruïne agreed to pay the subsidy for 1926.

Although it had to wait for the subsidy to materialize, the campaign in itself gave the Netherlands Chamber of Commerce in New York, Inc. breathing space. The money was earmarked for the employment of a temporary assistant secretary and an extra typist and for moving into a larger office in a better location on May 1, 1927. The premises at 32 Broadway, beside the Standard Oil Building in downtown Manhattan, were shared with the *Journal of Commerce*, the North German Lloyd, and the Deutsche Bank. The office was rented jointly with the KPM and the Netherlands Railways with the object of attracting tourists to the Netherlands and the Dutch East Indies. With finances again in order, it was not difficult to find a suitable candidate for the presidency. Willis H. Booth agreed to take over from Elias A. De Lima, who had temporarily replaced Van Doorn. Booth, a widely respected banker, was vice-president of the Guaranty Trust and a former president of the International Chamber of Commerce.

Despite the success of the subsidy campaign in 1926, the financial troubles were not yet over. The financial basis of the two Chambers of Commerce remained precarious because of their limited membership base. The instability of the Chamber in New York became all too apparent just six months later. The Dutch government had not yet made a definite commitment, which had been deferred to the end of the year, and the Chamber in New York was close to bankruptcy. Furthermore, $ 4000 of the money promised failed to materialize. All in all, it seemed that the 1927 financial year would end with a deficit of $ 2,600. This was largely attributable to an arrangement made by Van Aken with Von Baumhauer shortly before the 1926 campaign. They had assumed that the new stream of capital would swell the budget to $ 30,000, apart from the money the Chamber in Amsterdam had reserved for itself. But Van Aken had overlooked the possibility of the campaign yielding less, and had agreed to specific sums for Amsterdam, San Francisco, the Netherlands Railways office, and the network of agents, though not for New York. When the funds raised fell short of the target by $ 6,000, the executive of the Chamber in Amsterdam took it upon itself to cut the budget of its New York counterpart.

Not surprisingly, the Board of Directors in New York was displeased by Van Aken's arrangements. He seems to have gone to Amsterdam with wide powers to conclude a cooperative agreement with the Netherlands-American Chamber of Commerce, and his failure to allow for a lower yield from the subsidy campaign left the Board with no choice but to honor the agreement. Defective communication between New York and Amsterdam troubled relations still further. The Chamber in New York regarded the network of agents who were largely recruited from the honorary consuls as less useful, but since it was the result of an initiative of the Chamber in Amsterdam they agreed to finance the network. The Chamber in New York felt the same about the funds for the Chamber in San Francisco, and other commitments made by Amsterdam without prior consultation. And lastly, the close organizational and financial connection between the promotion of trade and tourist publicity proved to have more disadvantages than advantages for the organization in New York. Without consultation, the Traffic Committee, on the advice of the Chamber in Amsterdam, decided to set up a separate New York office in partnership with the Netherlands Railways. That left Van Aken free to concentrate on promoting trade, but the Chamber's revenues were reduced by a third.

In May, 1927, the treasurer of the Chamber in New York, J.A. de Lanoy, sought to reach agreement with the Chamber in Amsterdam on one of his periodic visits to the head office of the Holland-America Line. Relations between the two organizations needed to be clarified from a financial, organizational, and management points of view. He argued that since New York was the scene of most trade promotion activities, the Chamber in New York rather than the Chamber in Amsterdam should be regarded as the head office, and should have the freedom of action and financial resources it needed. If these two conditions were not met, the Board of Directors would start liquidation proceedings. A new financial arrangement was to be reached with Amsterdam, and the Netherlands government was to pay the promised subsidy for 1926 which had not yet materialized. The Board members had too often been obliged to dip into their own pockets. Precisely what De Lanoy accomplished in Amsterdam is not clear. In any case some sort of agreement was reached and De Lanoy allowed himself to be persuaded of the need for a separate tourist office in New York with the argument that the Netherlands as a tourist destination would otherwise be overshadowed by its neighbors. The two organizations continued to work together, but not wholeheartedly. Another conflict broke out before the end of the year, again about financial matters.

Despite Heringa's assurance late in 1926 that the Chamber in New York could count on an annual subsidy of Dfl. 10,000 from the Ministry of Labor, Trade and Industry, the final decision had still not been taken. In October, 1927, Van Aken approached the Dutch envoy, Jan H. van Roijen, on behalf of the Board of Directors. He told him the situation was so grave that the promotion of trade would soon be at a virtual standstill, and that the first task to be abolished would be the work performed free of charge for the Dutch government, which accounted for 25 percent of the Chamber's activities. Two weeks later Van Aken sent out invitations to a luncheon in honor of Anthony Fokker, the Dutch aeronautical engineer who manufactured about 40 percent of the world's civil aircraft. It was to be a "Dutch treat", the guests being requested to pay for the meal themselves.

Logo Fokker Aircraft Corporation of America

Heringa declined at the last minute an invitation to handle trade promotion himself from then on. Liquidation plans were again considered when Van Roijen informed the Board of Directors that he had insisted to Heringa that the subsidy must be forthcoming, and that the head of the Trade Division was now convinced of its need. Bolstered by a new pledge of unspecified worth, and with a zero bank balance, the Board decided to engage an assistant secretary. Van Aken would then at last have time for lectures on the Netherlands and the Dutch East Indies that were popular with American travellers. And at the same time the publicity department would be reopened. The Netherlands News Bureau would publish three monthly bulletins for distribution to the American press: one dealing with recent economic trends, one with tourism, and one with the colonies. But once again the Chamber in New York rejoiced too soon. The subsidy had still not arrived by the end of November and salaries and rent were due on December 2, 1927. The funds of the Chamber in Amsterdam were also exhausted and a bank loan offered no structural solution, so liquidation was inevitable unless the government instantly transferred the necessary funds and undertook to allocate at least $ 1000 for 1928. The threat of liquidation finally moved the Ministry of Labor, Trade and Industry to action, and the sum of $ 1,000 was despatched on December 1, 1927. There was still no certainty about the 1928 subsidy, but the Board decided to carry on for the time being.

The financial crisis not only resulted in the restoration of Dutch government subsidies for trade promotion by private enterprise, but also in the restructuring of the collaboration between the Chambers in Amsterdam and New York. When the Board reviewed the arrangements made by Van Aken and De Lanoy with the Chamber in Amsterdam, it was particularly critical of the fact that the Chamber in Amsterdam was permitted to disburse funds collected for New York. At the suggestion of the president, it was resolved to draft a new agreement which was signed by both Chambers of Commerce on June 14, 1928, and peace at last prevailed. $ 12,000 was apportioned to the Chamber in New York, $ 5,000 to the Netherlands Railways office, and $ 6,605 to the Chamber in Amsterdam and its agents across the United States. This problem was solved, but regardless of all its promises the Ministry of Labor, Trade and Industry was still not convinced that the subsidy was "absolutely essential", as Van Roijen was told when he called on Heringa during his leave in The Hague. Payment was withheld pending the approval by Parliament, and time was running out for the Chamber in New York. Its funds would be exhausted by October, 1928, if not sooner. "Our directors", Van Aken wrote to Van Roijen in a personal letter, "generally are sorely tried in their patience about ever recurring financial troubles which we must face one year after another". Although prominent businessmen like Booth, Redfield, and Baron van Eck, president of the Shell-Union Oil Corporation, worked hard on behalf of Dutch exports without remuneration, as far as financial support was concerned, the Dutch and East Indies beneficiaries chose to look the other way. It was now amply clear that nothing more could be expected from the American business community. Van Aken and his one remaining secretary spent 90 percent of their time on the promotion of Dutch and East Indies exports, and the Board of Directors raised $ 3,700, or 30 percent of the total budget of $ 12,000, a generous amount for the 10 percent of time devoted to American interests. The Dutch government was presented with an ultimatum: either it agreed to a subsidy or it could do the work itself. As Van Aken wrote to Van Roijen on the Directors, "they do not like to lend the prestige of their names and of the Companies they represent to an organization always on the verge of bankruptcy or liquidation".

Even though the financial and organizational relationship between the Chambers in New York and Amsterdam was a mystery to the Ministry, Heringa decided that financial support could no longer be deferred. After requesting and receiving details of their cooperative agreement, he finally decided that funds must be sent at once, by telegraph if need be, even if it meant guaranteeing the payment personally. That however was not necessary. He and Van Roijen discussed the situation with Westerman and Von Baumhauer, and the envoy and the president each decided to advance the Chamber in New York a thousand dollars to bridge the months before the government subsidy and the 1929 membership fees were paid. Before Christmas, 1928, Minister Slotemaker de Bruïne approved payment of the remaining part of the 1927 subsidy.

Heringa was satisfied with what he was told by the Chamber in Amsterdam about the collaboration with the Chamber in New York. His satisfaction was not shared in New York. Dutch exports to the United States had reached the highest level since the short post-first world war recession, and Van Aken and the Board of Directors had set their sights on more than simply ensuring the survival of the Chamber. The time had come, they felt, for it to be expanded into a full-fledged source of information for Dutch private enterprise. First of all, it was to be freed from its ties with the Chamber in Amsterdam, and the opportunity came when the Chamber in Amsterdam proposed to show a deficit for 1927 and 1928 so as to ensure payment of the subsidy. The Board in New York unanimously rejected the proposal, annulled the recent cooperative agreement, and refused to authorize the Chamber in Amsterdam to collect the remaining $ 3,000 of the 1927 subsidy. The "internal dispute" was now such that no government official would risk burning his fingers. Separation would undoubtedly impair the promotion of trade, but neither Van Roijen nor Heringa intended to try to persuade the Board of Directors in New York to change its mind. Heringa still had his doubts about the developments, for even though criticism of the Amsterdam organization might be justified, the office in New York was essentially a one-man enterprise run by Van Aken and neglected by the majority of its Directors. But he eventually decided that it was better for the promotion of trade that the Chamber remain in the hands of private enterprise.

Early in 1929, the Chamber in New York severed its ties with the Chamber in Amsterdam. Both Chambers would still cooperate in promoting trade, but each would be fully autonomous in all other respects. To strengthen the bond with its members in the Netherlands, the Chamber in New York would produce a monthly Dutch-language bulletin and would mount a campaign to recruit new members. Meanwhile, the Netherlands Ministry for the Colonies, which administered the subsidy granted by the Dutch East Indies authorities, was requested to pay it directly to New York. Correspondence between New York and Amsterdam was increasingly acrimonious, with countercharges flying back and forth, and as the confusion mounted Heringa decided the time had arrived to intervene. Heringa realized that separation could lead to a loss of the Dutch identity of the Chamber New York, which in turn would bring back the discussion on the renewal of the government subsidy. After all, if the Chamber in New York were to disappear, the business community would turn to the Trade Division and the consulates for information. A privately-run organization was less expensive. Heringa and Van Roijen requested the president and secretary of the Chamber in Amsterdam, Westerman and Six, to go to New York in May, 1929 in an attempt to reach an amicable agreement.

Probably to everyone's surprise, the differences of opinion were settled in a relatively short time. Many of the problems were found to stem from misunderstandings. For instance, Six discovered that practically no one in New York understood the complicated relationship with the Chamber in Amsterdam or the position of the Netherlands Railways office into the organizational structure. It was generally thought that both the Netherlands Railways office and the KPM booking office were quite separate from the trade promotion activities and had no claim to the funds raised in the Netherlands on behalf of the Chamber in New York. Six explained the situation. Westerman's offer to personally contribute $ 1000 to $ 1500 if the budget was in danger of falling below the $ 15,000 limit acceptable to all parties was a welcome gesture of support for Six. The Chamber in New York would in turn redouble its efforts to increase its membership in the United States. Its reputation in the Netherlands had not been enhanced by the fact that it contributed barely 10 percent of the total funds available for trade promotion and tourist publicity.
Due to the recession that started a few months later this idea came to nothing. The financial scope afforded by the additional $ 3000 was used to engage an assistant secretary, so that finally full attention could be devoted to commercial enquiries.[32] By the time Westerman left on the next stage of a world trip and Six went on to Washington to follow the progress of the new tariff legislation through Congress, all difficulties had been resolved.

The clarification of the situation in New York was welcomed by all parties, first and foremost by the Chamber in New York, which at last felt assured of a sound financial foundation. The Chamber in Amsterdam was pleased that New York's more solid financial base and the appointment of an assistant secretary would substantially improve the quality of its trade promotion activities. Moreover, the Chamber in New York itself estimated that the Netherlands Railways office could not operate with much less than $ 12,000; Six had put the figure much lower. But the best result was that with the removal of all suspicions and conflicts, the financial situation had now become clear to everyone. The Dutch government authorities were equally relieved, and not least Van Roijen, who in the past few years had often been ashamed of the slender resources with which Van Aken had to manage. He had always been convinced that the available funds were sufficient to support the offices in Amsterdam and New York, and more so after the Dutch and East Indies governments renewed their subsidies in 1927. As he remarked, "The only difficulty was the money, and if that is now resolved I believe the Chamber will continue to fulfil its task very well." It was after all "absolutely essential", even if "but an imperfect means of compensating for the lack of an experienced, practical commercial attaché".
The fact that the Chamber in New York in the end did not sever all ties with the Chamber in Amsterdam implies that there were advantages to the relationship. Because of the geographical distance between the two offices, each needed the other for its trade promoting activities and for establishing and maintaining contact with the business community. If the Chamber in New York had broken away completely it would have had to seek clients in the Netherlands, a step that would have been fiercely resisted by the Chamber in Amsterdam, which would never have allowed itself to be pushed aside. The Chamber in Amsterdam would have met with the same response if it had tried a similar approach in the United States. The Chamber in New York was assured of the backing of the Dutch government, and because New York was the central point for the promotion of Dutch exports, it would have received substantial contributions from commercial interests in the Netherlands. Undoubtedly the most cogent reason, however, was that for the promotion of exports the two Chambers had no choice but to work together. Two captains on one ship was not an ideal situation, but the most bothersome side effects could be neutralized through personal

discussions, and nothing more stood in the way of further collaboration. New York was the acknowledged center for the promotion of Dutch exports to the United States; and Amsterdam's pivotal administrative and financial position was confirmed.

The agreement reached in May, 1929 put the relationship between the Chamber in New York and the Chamber in Amsterdam on a new footing. Though the depression precipitated by the Wall Street crash barely six months later placed it under severe strain, it proved durable enough to survive on half the budget up to 1935. The first signs of a reduced income were already perceptible before the government at last paid the 1928 and 1929 subsidies on July 23, 1929, after waiting for the problems to be cleared out of the way. The Netherlands Ministry for the Colonies and the Netherlands Tourist Association announced reductions in their contributions. The economic boom of the past few years had passed its peak in the Dutch East Indies in 1927; it was another year before it was echoed in the Netherlands and the United States. There was as yet no question of a recession, but some belt tightening was indicated. The Tourist Association had undertaken more commitments than its income permitted. Heringa had to take measures to safeguard the subsidies for the two Chambers of Commerce for America.

To underscore the value of the East Indies subsidy, the Chamber in New York produced at the request of the envoy a survey of the work it performed for the colony. The two or three requests received each day were usually for general commercial information, and only occasionally for specific information such as the addresses of importers, etc. because the trade in products like rubber, tobacco, and coffee was so well organized that their share of the market was assured. In addition, the majority of these bulk goods were traded on the basis of specific quality standards and fixed prices. Partly in recognition of the reports he wrote at the request of libraries, universities, research institutes, and business organizations, Van Aken was invited in 1927 to become a member of the American Academy of Social and Political Science. The Chamber of Commerce considered itself to be the best informed semi-official organization in the United States on all matters pertaining to the Dutch colonies in the East Indies and the Caribbean. In the opinion of Van Roijen, the Netherlands envoy in Washington, this claim was by no means exaggerated.

Fokker's C-2 "America"

It became speedily apparent in 1929 that the budget estimates for the next few years were far too optimistic. Many of the commitments made in 1926 were due to expire in that year. The gradual economic decline increased the likelihood that 1930 would begin with a deficit of $ 5000, as against an estimated expenditure of $ 41,500. This, after the staff additions, did not affect plans to join the KPM shipping line and the Netherlands Railways office in a move to the Chrysler Building. The Chamber in Amsterdam also hired a new assistant secretary, albeit on a part-time basis. In 1930 the two Chambers of Commerce felt the impact of the recession in a number of ways. While Europe's failing economies turned the attention of a growing number of firms to the American market, they were unable to improve their financial position.[33] In the following years their income dwindled as the number of commercial enquiries increased, and the New York Board of Directors saw no way out.

Final Remarks

The agreement which ended the problems in the 1920s offered no solution to the sharp global economic decline that followed, and made no change in the weak structural position of the private trade promotion agencies. The Chamber in New York was the only Chamber of Commerce abroad with a professional staff. After Van Aken took over from Wittert van Hoogland, there were sometimes long periods when he had to manage alone, lacking even the assistance of a secretary. The fact that the Netherlands and the Dutch East Indies together were the United States' fourth biggest trade partner was nowhere reflected in the support of Dutch industry and commerce for the organizations that were promoting their interests. The $ 15,500 budget of the Chamber in New York was miserable in comparison with the $ 60,000 that the British and French Chambers, the two richest foreign Chambers of Commerce in New York spent each year, and it was long uncertain if even that low budget level could be maintained. The contributions in the United States fell by $ 1,200 to $ 2,800 in 1930, and the Directors and Van Roijen had to step in to stave off bankruptcy.

These shaky financial foundations were mainly attributable to two factors. The economic recession actually increased the workload of the Chamber by half as more companies tried to export to compensate for the domestic stagnation, while at the same time a growing number of small and medium-sized businesses reduced or cancelled their payments. New members were few and far between. No payment was received for almost 90 percent of the work performed that year. The Chambers of Commerce were almost entirely dependent on large corporations for their income, none of which however were prepared to increase their contributions, even though they shared the government's appreciation of the Chambers' work. As ever more firms opted out, the burden of promoting exports fell increasingly on the Netherlands government.

The Dutch government's attitude had changed in the 1920s. The political motives for the Foreign Ministry's support of the foundation of the Netherlands Chamber of Commerce in New York in 1919-1920 were later replaced by the economic motives of the Ministry of Labor, Trade and Industry. By and large, the Trade Division was motivated by ad hoc considerations. Nothing in the nature of a structural policy made its appearance until the 1930s. Heringa kept his hand on the purse, opening it only when things grew desperate. The continued existence of the Chamber in New York owed much to him, but at the same time he was opposed to a more structural approach to trade promotion.

The effect of the establishment of the Chamber in Amsterdam on the financial situation of the Chamber in New York, beneficial or otherwise, is difficult to determine. On the one hand, it seems clear that given the physical separation by the Atlantic Ocean and the slowness of communications, a point of contact in the Netherlands was essential. The Amsterdam office was undoubtedly of considerable assistance to Van Aken by dealing directly with straightforward enquiries. Von Baumhauer was also extremely active in soliciting donations and recruiting new members. On the other hand, it must be wondered whether the Chamber in Amsterdam did not in fact monopolize too much of the organizations' joint income. It had originally been intended as a branch office maintaining contact with the business community in the Netherlands. If Von Baumhauer had not stepped beyond these bounds, the financial scope of the Chamber in New York would have been wider and it could have expanded its sphere of activities. Instead, the financial problems besetting the private trade-promoting organizations after 1925 seem to have thrown them off balance.

Notes

1. Kathleen Burke, *Britain, America and the Sinews of War, 1914-1918*. Winchester 1985, 136. The British press campaign was led by the newspaper proprietor Lord Northcliffe, who headed the various war missions sent to the United States since June, 1917.
2. In 1916, Dutch imports averaged about 500,000 tons a month. The volume fell to 120,000 tons in 1917, and to 50,000 tons in 1918, in which year food riots erupted in the major Dutch cities.
3. *The Story of Mankind* was inspired by H.G. Wells' bestselling *An Outline of History*. On friendly terms with Franklin D. Roosevelt, Van Loon was the best-known Dutchman in America between the two world wars. But in 1918 he was still far removed from such renown. While keeping the Netherlands informed of its waning popularity in the United States, he earned his living by writing easy-to-read books about Dutch history.
4. The committee consisted of Westerman, C. van Vollenhoven, Mrs. Laman Trip-De Beaufort, J. Bierens de Haan, director of the Netherlands Trading Company, D. Hudig, director of the Royal Netherlands Steamship Company, J.R. Wierdsma of the Holland-America Line, A.G.N. Swart and P. van Ommeren Jr. of the Rotterdam shipbrokers Phs. van Ommeren. A short time later it became the Netherland-America Foundation.
5. Circular letter dated October 10, 1919, signed by H.P. de Vries of the Royal Netherlands Steamship Company, John W. Greene, J.C.H. Heldring of the Curaçao Trading Co., Jules Kievits of the America-Holland Trading Association, and Guy van Amringe and Van der Hoeven of Lindeteves, Inc.
6. The charter meeting was held on January 21, 1920 in the sample room of the Merchants Association in the Woolworth Building in downtown Manhattan.
7. One of the few exceptions was the so-called Shoe Law prohibiting U.S. imports of shoes between May, 1923 and July, 1924.
8. From 1920-1930 Dutch labor productivity rose by an annual 3.5 percent, and from 1930-1939 by 2.5 percent.
9. The Dutch trade figures are based on the published imports, exports, and transit statistics (SIUD) *and Foreign Commerce and Navigation of the United States*, Washington, various years. The former's reorganization in 1917 greatly increased the reliability of the Dutch figures. It is uncertain to what extent American trade statistics included Dutch transit trade. The figures were calculated by adding the U.S. figures for tobacco and diamond imports, converted into guilders, to the *Dutch* export figures. The exchange rate of the dollar was calculated using the unweighted quarterly figures as given in F.A.G. Keesing, *De conjuncturele ontwikkeling van Nederland en de evolutie van de economische overheidspolitiek* (The Economic Development of the Netherlands and the Evolution of Government Economic Policy), Utrecht/Antwerp, 1947, 2nd edition Nijmegen, 1978, 20, 40, 212, 274.
10. Between 1920 and 1930, industry's share of Dutch exports remained constant at just under 40 percent.
11. *SIUD* and *Foreign Commerce and Navigation*. Author's calculations.

	1920	1922	1925	1928
Diamonds	41	32	40	37
Tobacco	19	23	20	21
Primary sector	14	18	19	16
Industry	11	7	11	14
Raw materials	5	3	2	5
Semi-manufactured products	5	15	7	7
Total	95	98	99	100

12. *SIUD*, various years.

	1930	1932	1935	1936	1937
Diamonds	27	13	18	18	18
Tobacco	17	15	12	14	6
Primary sector	25	19	19	18	18
Raw materials	5	3	4	5	5
Finished products	13	16	16	21	19
Semi-manufactureds products	10	11	27	20	29
Total	97	77	96	96	95

*1932: A number of items totalling Dfl. 8.8 million are not specified. They are saltpetre and artificial fertilisers, stearin, radio sets and their components, and lamps. The proportion of semi-manufactured and finished products must therefore be increased by 21.4 percent to 48 percent. In 1936 beer was added for that year only, as were rubber and tin in 1939. Such additions were made if the product in question was exported by only one firm, such as Heineken in 1936.

13. The nominal value of Dutch holdings in 1934 was estimated at $ 207 million.
14. The other $ 6,000 came from the Holland-America Line, the Netherlands Shipping Co., Rotterdam Lloyd, Royal Dutch West-India Mail, Royal Holland Lloyd, and the Ph. van Ommeren Corporation.
15. *The New York Herald*, April 25, 1921. The exhibition comprised some sixty works, including six by Van Gogh. The catalogue was compiled by Adriaan Barnouw. National Archives, RG 84, Netherlands, 1921, Vol.10, file 840.3: *Modern Art of Holland. An Exhibition. Paintings, Etchings, Wood Engravings, Sculpture, and Batik Work*, New York, 1921. Jan Hulsker, *Van Gogh en zijn weg. Het complete werk* (Van Gogh and His Path. Complete Works), Amsterdam 1978. *Vase with irises*, catalogue no. 1977 (yellow background) or 1978 (pink background); *Piëta after Delacroix*, no. 1775; *Road beside the Seine near Asnières, no.1253*; *The Montmartre hill, no.1176*. The reception was reported in various papers, including *The New York Evening Post*, April 30, 1921.
16. The subsidy was reduced from $ 15,000 in 1921 to $ 12,500 in 1922, and $ 10,000 in 1923.
17. The Dutch members of the Chamber in New York were categorized as follows:
    trade 20; banking 20; industry 13; shipping and related enterprises 8; agriculture 1; unknown 14.
18. The nominal value was Dfl. 7.4 million, the yield probably more than five times as much.
19. The Dutch community in New York was so alarmed by these events that the Netherland Club decided to set up a press office. Several "generous donations" were received, and Adriaan Barnouw was the projected candidate for the position of director.
20. The Pelman Institute was approached on the recommendation of George Creel, head of the U.S. government publicity service during the first world war.
21. Another suggestion was that the Netherlands Ministry of Foreign Affairs should invite the influential American newspaper correspondents in Paris to visit the Netherlands.
22. A press lunch on December 9, 1919 attended by W. Westerman of the Rotterdamsche Bankvereeniging and the prominent Catholic politician W.H. Nolens went ahead as planned. They were on their way to the International Labor Conference in Washington.
23. A photo press agency was to be used for the distribution of the photos.
24. With the prospect of financial support six months earlier, the Westerman group had founded the Netherland-America Foundation, which now administered the funds.
25. $ 5,000 was allocated for this purpose from the Foreign Affairs budget and the remaining $ 10,000 was supplied by the Dutch East Indies authorities. The Colonial Ministry's contribution was conditional on the founding of the Dutch East Indies-American Chamber of Commerce in Batavia (today's Jakarta) which duly came into being in November, 1921.
26. The publication was issued under the auspices of the Netherlands-America Affiliation, set up jointly by the Netherlands Chamber of Commerce in New York, Inc. and the Netherland-America Foundation.

27. The Dutch East Indies monthly *Interocean* served as the journal of the Chambers of Commerce for America up to January 1, 1925, when it was replaced by *Commercial Holland. A Journal of Foreign Trade for the Netherlands and the Colonies*. In 1926 *Holland's Import & Export Trade*, a monthly English-language supplement to the weekly *SIUD*, became the official journal of the Netherlands-American Chamber of Commerce in Amsterdam.

28. The cost of the brochure was $ 200,000.

29. State Institute for War Documentation, Doc I-67, list of persons: Letter from Von Baumhauer, September 27, 1942, stating that shortly before the outbreak of the second world war the annual income from his legal practice was at least Dfl. 25,000.

30. "The Past, Present and Future of the Netherlands Chamber of Commerce in New York, Inc." A report presented to the members' meeting on February 17, 1926.

31. Applications for subsidies from other Dutch Chambers of Commerce abroad would be refused, pointing out that living costs were much higher in New York and that the Netherlands government attached particular importance to trade relations with the United States.

32. The funds were to be divided as follows:

The Netherlands Chamber of Commerce in New York, Inc.	$ 15,000
The Netherlands Railways office	$ 12,000
The Netherlands-American Chamber of Commerce together with the Traffic Committee	$ 10,000
The Holland-American Chamber of Commerce for the Pacific Coast States, Inc.	$ 1,000
Agents	$ 955
Total	$ 39,055

After deduction of the fixed sums for San Francisco and the agents, the remaining resources were apportioned according to the following ratio: the Netherlands Chamber of Commerce in New York, Inc. 150/371; the Netherlands Railways 120/371; the Netherlands-American Chamber of Commerce 101/371.

33. The Netherlands-American Chamber of Commerce, "Elucidation of the plan to appoint a Dutch East Indies expert in New York", July, 1930. One proposal was to finance the appointment of an expert on the Dutch East Indies as assistant secretary, and a special committee was formed for the purpose, consisting of J.D. Brand of KPM, D.A. Delprat of the Netherlands Steamship Company, G.A. Voûte of Mirandolle Voûte & Co., and F.A. de Lanoy of the Asiatic Petroleum Corporation.

CHAPTER IV

1914 - 1940: Trade Agreements, Tariffs, and Trade Promotion

Introduction

The establishment of an economic information service in the Netherlands Ministry of Economic Affairs in 1933 formed the basis for a structural approach to the promotion of trade. Almost fifty years had passed since the business community first called for such an organization. At the end of the first world war it had seemed that fundamental changes were at last on the way, but a few years later the need to economize forced the Netherlands Ministry of Foreign Affairs to reverse the process. The Ministry of Labor, Trade and Industry took a different view of the situation, as evidenced by the 1927 renewal of the subsidy for the Chambers. F.K.J. Heringa, head of the Trade Division, was even more firmly convinced of the fact that a reliable i.ndependent information center was essential for exports. If no subsidy was forthcoming, it would not be long before business firms were knocking at the Ministry's door for commercial information. In addition, Dutch government authorities needed to be informed of economic trends, both domestic and foreign, for the effective formulation of policy.

The *laissez-faire* free trade spirit permeating official circles in the 1920s was no longer consistent with the economic realities of the time. The Netherlands had quickly become an industrialized country. And it was the new range of industries that exerted constant pressure on the Dutch political establishment to adopt a more interventionist policy. The question of providing commercial information was one of the main points of contention. The economic depression broke the long-standing deadlock. Economic administration was centralized in the new Netherlands Ministry of Economic Affairs, which established an Economic Information Division in 1933. But it was only after a reorganization three years later that it could become a truly central service providing information on economic trends in the Netherlands and abroad for both government and private enterprise.

The Chamber followed these events with great interest. Government subsidies were crucial to their financial viability, and they sometimes worked in close collaboration with government organizations. Moreover, the Chambers possessed knowledge of economic relations with the United States that the government lacked. Not only were they familiar with the many aspects of trade promotion and information, but also with the post-first world war protectionism which was particularly evident in the United States and which constituted a growing threat to Dutch exports. American competitors tried to block imports wherever they could, using both tariffs and other measures to establish trade barriers. The imposition of import restrictions on daffodil and other important bulb species, in the wake of the introduction in 1918 of the first regulations prohibiting imports of diseased and infected bulbs and plants, provoked furious reactions in the Netherlands. Though ostensibly based on health considerations, the decision of the U.S. Federal Horticultural Board was prompted largely if not entirely by the interests of American horticulturalists. The chorus of protest from the Netherlands and other countries was simply ignored. The modest part played by the Chamber in this affair presaged their later involvement in similar activities. When a number of trade agreements were to be concluded after 1932, the Ministry of Economic Affairs, to which responsibility for trade policy had devolved from the Ministry of Foreign Affairs, enlisted the assistance of the business community. The Chamber, as representative of the business community, played an important part in negotiations with the United States in 1935.

"A Leap in the Dark": 1915 - 1930

When the reorganization of the promotion of exports was discussed in 1915 for the first time after the outbreak of hostilities, the war had reached a stalemate, and the outcome was the subject of much speculation in the Netherlands and elsewhere. A truce seemed the most likely possibility at that moment, and the conflict would be continued with economic weapons involving "... an economic alliance of the Central Powers [pitted against] an economic alliance of the Entente nations, separated by high tariff barriers designed to inflict damage on all outside". It was believed that the weakened state of international competition would place Dutch commerce, industry, and agriculture in a good position to retain or even increase their share of world trade. Nevertheless, there could be no doubt that Dutch firms would be faced with immense problems after the war, and it was necessary for the Dutch government, industry, and commerce to take precautionary measures, starting with the reorganization of the economic information services.

To ascertain the views of its members, the Netherlands Industrial Association conducted a survey towards the end of 1915. As already noted, the reorganization that began in 1906 had left the working methods of the consular service and the structure of the information services virtually intact, and there was an acute need for a central information organization. Another source of frustration was the small number of career consuls and their deficient knowledge of the Dutch economy. At the end of 1915 the consular service consisted of 18 career officers and 664 honorary consuls, of whom three out of four were foreign nationals. Their commitment to Dutch industry and commerce and to Dutch interests in general was questionable; moreover, the majority of them did not read or speak any Dutch. This was not a problem for big corporations, since they could manage for themselves. But it meant that if the managements of small and medium-sized businesses were not proficient in other languages, as was generally the case, they did not have access to one of the few valuable sources of information on other countries.

None of this criticism was new, but this time - in contrast to the years before 1914 - it caused disquiet in the Foreign Ministry. In the summer of 1916, barely three months after the publication of the survey findings, a bill to update economic information had been drafted. It is clear, however, that the ad hoc committee appointed for that purpose, consisting of representatives of the relevant ministries (Foreign Affairs, Colonies, and Agriculture, Trade and Industry) and of the various commercial sectors, had not managed to resolve all difficulties. Presenting the draft bill to the Dutch Parliament, Foreign Minister John Loudon said "the hand must now be put to the plough", but the uncertainty shrouding the post-first world war situation ruled out the possibility of comprehensive measures. He was therefore prepared at most to allocate Dfl. 50,000 to further the mobility of consular officials and to increase the knowledge of economic affairs in the Ministry.

The Ministry's scant knowledge of and interest in commercial information was again highlighted in Parliament a few months later. As virtually no measures had been implemented, the provisions of the unamended draft bill appeared as a separate item in the budget because, it was explained, the war claimed the full attention of the Minister and his officials. There was even greater tumult in the House when practically no argument was put forward in explanation of the amount of money involved. The Minister had to admit that neither he nor his officials had the knowledge or experience needed to draw up properly detailed estimates. As he said himself, the result was "a leap in the dark" that could just as easily have been Dfl. 20,000 as the Dfl. 200,000 that Parliament was now asked to approve. He added that although the existing organization might be "totally inadequate", there was nothing wrong with its structure, and he therefore suggested that the House await the results of the budget proposals before voting on the question of reorganization. He was prepared to consider appointing an advisory committee on economic information drawn from the relevant ministries and industry and commerce, but nothing more. For the moment there was no question of increasing the number of career consuls, appointing commercial attachés or establishing a central office for foreign trade. All that could be expected was "one or two individual measures". Parliament was not satisfied with this, and approved the estimates only after Loudon had agreed to consider a fundamental reorganization at a later date. In 1917 many countries were taking steps "to be prepared to deal with the immense economic problems" anticipated in the transition from war to peace and the revival of the world economy, but in the Netherlands silence reigned on the subject of the projected reorganization of the structure to provide economic information. Though an advisory committee on the reorganization of providing foreign economic information was instituted in June, 1917, a year passed before it met for the first time. Six months later it produced a report shedding no new light on the subject and thereafter sank into oblivion.

Discussions later in 1917 between Dutch Foreign Minister Loudon and Folkert E. Posthuma, Minister of Agriculture, Trade and Industry, were more promising. The aim was to determine whether the provision of foreign economic information could be concentrated in one ministry, finally creating the much desired foreign trade center. However, the talks were more a ritual fulfillment of the promises made earlier to Parliament than a genuine attempt to find a mode of working together. That in any case was the impression given by the newspaper reports. One day the discussions focused on the fusion of the Trade Division and the Trade Policy and Consular Affairs Division; and the next day they were a total failure. A day later it was reported that they would work together, but would remain in their separate ministries. The end of the saga came with Loudon's retraction in Parliament of the whole idea of merger. The goal now was to determine "how a sound, practical link between the two divisions" could best be established. As far as Loudon and Posthuma were concerned that was the end of the matter. A full review of the provision of foreign economic information by the Foreign Ministry had to wait until a new government took office in the summer of 1918.

It would be wrong to assume that these discussions and schemes were without any result at all. The Netherlands Foreign Ministry was finally forced to face facts. As the shipowner and MP for the Free Liberal Union, Boudewijn Nierstrasz, said in Parliament in December, 1917, "Some years ago - before 1913 - Foreign Affairs didn't ask how they could assist those persons [who had requested information], but took the attitude: 'Let's answer them in such a way as to dispose of the matter once and for all'." He said he was pleased to note that matters had vastly improved since then. The Foreign Ministry's real challenge came with the resumption of international trade and shipping after the first world war.

Real preparations for improving the provision of foreign economic information were put in hand by the new Netherlands Foreign Minister, Esquire H.A. van Karnebeek, in September, 1918. He began by sweeping away traditional conservative attitudes, "...the dislike of everything new that was formerly so characteristic of the Ministry". In a comprehensive restructuring program, the Trade Policy and Consular Affairs Division was split in two, and foreign economic policy was placed under the Economic Affairs Department. Though this was one of its principal fields of activity, the Department focused most of its attention on negotiations with the Allies on the resumption of sea trade, in 1919 on the Versailles Peace Conference, and in the 1920s on the multiple trade agreements. It was assisted by an advisory council composed of businessmen who, like the Ministry itself, were ardent advocates of free trade. In the aftermath of the first world war, the council met practically every day. Its work more or less ended after the signing of the Treaty of Versailles and the removal of trade barriers. It continued for a few years to advise the Ministry on trade agreements, but by 1923 it was largely forgotten.

In the six months following the Armistice of November, 1918, the Ministry's attention was fixed on the negotiations with other countries, but at the same time it made a number of significant amendments to the provision of economic information. Because of the changes in international economic relations, information for industry and commerce had moved into the sphere of government. Van Karnebeek warned, however, that foreign service officers could not be expected to work miracles. Foreign service officers could give support and assistance, but the business community itself had to take the initiative, and for that reason the provision of economic information was kept strictly separate from the work of the Trade Division in the Netherlands.

The foreign service gathered economic information that was processed and made available to industry and commerce by the Trade Division, which in turn was kept informed of domestic economic developments by the business community. Queries which the Division was unable to answer were passed on to the consulates and legations. They were kept up to date by means of a monthly publication, *Economische Berichten* (Economic Reports), supplied by the Foreign Ministry. It also issued publications in English, French, and German for foreign businessmen. The Economic Affairs Department referred requests for information to the Trade Division, the Trade Information Center, the Rotterdam and Amsterdam Chambers of Commerce, and the Dutch Chambers of Commerce abroad.

Van Karnebeek also changed the way in which economic information was provided abroad. The first commercial attaché was posted to Berlin in 1916, and similar posts were opened in London, Brussels, Paris, and Washington between the end of 1918 and 1920. The object was not so much to gather information as to foster Dutch economic interests in a world still feeling the effects of the war.[1] So the appointment of D.H. Andreae as the commercial attaché in Washington was based less on a need to promote exports than to reanimate imports from the United States. In 1919 Andreae was mainly occupied with buying supplies of coal to relieve the acute fuel shortage in the Netherlands.

Almost immediately after his appointment as Netherlands Minister for Foreign Affairs in September, 1918, Van Karnebeek set about finding a suitable person to head the commercial section in the Washington legation and the consular services in the United States, Cuba, and Mexico. It was no easy task. In view of the importance of the post, it was not to be a hasty decision. The right person would be someone who was not too specialized; someone with wide experience who could deal with the most diverse aspects of trade and commerce. Unlike the consuls, whose task was limited to observing and reporting, the attaché would play a more active part: researching the market, facilitating publicity and acting in an advisory capacity. The person first considered for the post was Simon M.D. Valstar, secretary to the Board of the Netherlands Overseas Trust Company, but his work was of such vital importance that he could not be allowed to leave. After a further search, Van Karnebeek then appointed D.H. Andreae, a lawyer who had been closely involved in fishing rights negotiations with the Entente powers. His wife's friendship with President Wilson's daughters was an added advantage.

Andreae had spent two months preparing for his new job before his arrival in New York in February, 1919. At the special request of Hendrik A. van IJsselsteijn, Netherlands Minister of Agriculture, Trade and Industry, he had been fully briefed by bankers, shipowners, industrialists, and merchants, and he was to make an annual trip to the Netherlands to be informed of the latest developments in trade and industry. The high exchange rate of the dollar meant that he cost about Dfl. 30,000 a year. More shocks were in store for the thrifty officials in The Hague when the costs of promoting exports to the United States rose further.

Barely three months later Andreae submitted a reorganization plan for "the very poor services at present rendered in connection with the provision of information and the promotion of trade relations" by the consulates. He was astonished by the value placed by the American business community on personal contacts, reporting to The Hague, "it is a very strange country in many respects. People here are not as ready as we are to listen to every foreigner who arrives". He did not expect the honorary consuls to cooperate in any way, and the only career consul-general in the country, Van de Sande Bakhuyzen, had his hands more than full in New York, so he suggested appointing a trade advisor in every major city. These trade advisors should be experienced businessmen or bankers able to put visiting Dutch exporters in touch with the right circles and to keep the commercial attaché informed of the latest trends. Some twenty trade advisors would be needed to cover cities with more than 100,000 inhabitants, which on account of their infrastructure, wholesale warehouses, and factories would be classed as "chief distributing centers". The annual cost would be approximately $ 200 to $ 300 per advisor. Because John Venema, the honorary consul-general in Chicago, had good contacts in the surrounding midwestern states, Andreae proposed that he start putting the network together without delay. The Netherlands Ministry gave the go-ahead at the beginning of August, 1919, and made $ 5,000 available. Eight trade advisors were in place before the end of the year.[2] For the first time, the Foreign Ministry seemed willing to spare no effort in promoting Dutch exports. On September 15, 1919, B.J. Gratama was appointed temporary second commercial attaché at the Washington legation. Partly because of these innovations, the costs of economic information rose from Dfl. 100,000 in 1918-1919 to Dfl. 250,000 in 1919-1920, adding more than 20 percent to the Ministry's total budget in one year, even though not long before "an extra half million guilders for our foreign affairs would have had the same effect on the public and the legislature as the appearance of a mouse".

It is questionable whether the trade advisors met Andreae's expectations. He constantly complained about the lack of interest shown by them and by the honorary consuls, and no more were appointed after 1920. Both groups were too preoccupied with their own affairs to devote sufficient attention to Dutch exports. On his trips through the United States, Andreae also discovered that they knew next to nothing about the Netherlands - only a few had ever been there - and that they rarely read the publications sent to them. So in August, 1920 he suggested a total reorganization of the system. Annual conferences would be arranged at which the trade advisors and consuls would be informed about recent developments in the Dutch and the Dutch East Indies economies. They would receive a monthly bulletin,[3] and information on exporters and exported goods collated by the Dutch trade show center in Utrecht would be published weekly in American trade journals. The accompanying price lists and terms of delivery would be sent to the consuls and trade advisors.

Whether these proposals were implemented is uncertain. The economic decline starting in 1920 led to heavy spending cuts two years later, whereupon Andreae suggested replacing the trade advisors by the time-honored honorary consuls. J.C.A. Everwijn, a former head of the Trade Division who had succeeded Cremer as envoy to Washington in 1921, was against the idea on the grounds that even though the trade advisors had done little to promote exports, they were still in a position to provide businessmen with introductions that were beyond the reach of the average honorary consul. Everything points to the fact that up to 1926, when the system of trade advisors was abandoned, those who really promoted Dutch exports were the exception to the rule. One of the few firms known to have benefited was the trade and shipping company Wm. Müller & Co. Andreae resigned from the consular service in 1924 to run its New York agency, and he made regular use of the services of the trade advisors.

Andreae's move to private enterprise was a direct consequence of the cutbacks made by the Foreign Ministry since 1921 which were to lead, amongst other things, to the abolition of the position of commercial attaché in Washington. Not surprisingly, the Netherlands government attached greater value to a balanced budget than to the promotion of exports. Notwithstanding the protests of the Dutch Parliament, after 1920-1921 the trade promotion budget was cut by more than 80 percent, dwindling to Dfl. 63,850 in 1924-1925. The post of commercial attaché in Washington came to an end in 1922, when Andreae succeeded Steyn Parvé as consul-general in New York. Though various envoys asked for it to be reinstituted later when the economy started to pick up again, no new commercial attaché was sent to Washington until after the onset of the Depression in 1930.

The cutbacks in the years from 1920 onwards caused considerable dissatisfaction amongst Dutch parliamentarians and businessmen with the Foreign Ministry's policy, or more precisely the lack of it. Not only were they opposed to the cuts; they also deplored the foreign service officers' lack of interest in commercial matters. At a time when exports were largely at a standstill, foreign service officers did not seem to understand that providing industry and commerce with information was "a vitally important" part of their work. Van Karnebeek refuted most of the points raised, but did concede that the Ministry lacked the staff needed to function adequately in every way, saying it was being swamped with new tasks. He was very actively involved with the League of Nations, while moreover the profoundly changed world economic order made it necessary to conclude new trade agreements. Industry and commerce themselves should search for new outlets for their products.

The fact that foreign commercial information remained an issue over the next few years can be attributed to what was an ongoing debate on the place and role of government in the nation's economy. There were two conflicting schools of thought, the free trade faction in the Ministry of Foreign Affairs versus the supporters of the view of the Ministry of Labor, Trade and Industry that the pre-first world war policy of non-intervention in economic matters was out of touch with the times.

The failure of talks between Posthuma and Loudon in 1917 was by no means the end of the Netherlands Foreign Ministry's idea of creating a single body to provide foreign economic information. Indeed, in 1919 Loudon's successor, Van Karnebeek, seems to have contemplated turning the Ministry into the chief economic department. The refusal of J.A. van IJsselstein, Netherlands Minister of Agriculture, Trade and Industry, to acquiesce in the dismantling of his Ministry will however have caused little surprise. He would not go beyond a merger of the Trade Division and the Economic Affairs Department to form an interministerial body administered jointly by himself and his colleague at Foreign Affairs. Van Karnebeek and Nederbragt, determined not to be beaten, redoubled their efforts in the 1920s to strengthen the Foreign Ministry's hold on all aspects of foreign relations. The direct approach having failed, they concentrated on foreign economic information for government and private enterprise, the area in which the

Ministry worked in collaboration with the Trade Division and which, if the multitude of complaints was correct, could be made more efficient. Information from abroad often took a long time to reach exporters, and in trade talks official delegations repeatedly proved to be poorly informed about the interests of Dutch industry and commerce. All in all, there was a definite need for reorganization, as all concerned readily agreed. But that was the only point on which the parties in this issue saw eye to eye. The vehemence of the discussions from the outset shows clearly that all parties were well aware of how much more was at stake than simply deciding where savings could be made and how improvements could be effected. For some of the participants, indeed, the question of the Foreign Ministry's leading role in economic relations was of no more than of secondary importance. As they saw it, the proponents of no government interference had launched an attack on the expanding role of government in the nation's economy. If the Foreign Ministry and the business community were to succeed in their efforts to transform the Trade Division into a semi-government institution, the Dutch government would be deprived of its most effective instrument for taking a hand in the economy. The employers, in turn, would win back some or all of the influence they had exercised on government policy up to the end of the first world war.

When Posthuma, as president of the Netherlands Industrial Association, first raised the subject of reorganization in 1922, his main point was the lack of clarity surrounding the provision of foreign commercial information. The number of organizations active in this area had greatly increased since the first world war, which made it difficult to know where specific information could be found.[4] Many firms addressed their queries to several organizations at the same time. Industry and commerce as a whole may have taken a different view of the situation. Though one desk for all kinds of information would no doubt have been welcomed, the privately-run organizations declined to take part in the various integration plans. Did the problems lie with the Dutch government departments? This would have been emphatically denied by the Ministry of Labor, Trade and Industry. Admittedly, since more than one Ministry was involved, the information structure might have become a little more opaque, but given the available resources, the partnership between the Trade Division and the Economic Affairs Department left little to be desired. It would seem that the main problems could be traced to the Foreign Ministry.

Viewed in retrospect, the problems can be reduced to three factors: shortage of staff in the Trade Division and the consular service; insufficient coordination between the ministries; and the Foreign Ministry's lack of commercial information. Consequently, both the Netherlands government and private enterprise often knew little or nothing of developments abroad, and the press was usually faster and more reliable in reporting amendments to foreign tariff laws than the government. Though the Trade Division was also responsible, most of the difficulties arose at the Ministry of Foreign Affairs. Disregarding the fact that it was one of their principal tasks, many diplomats attached scant importance to commercial matters, preferring to leave such things to the consular service, which still had to cope with the same problems as before the first world war. Despite the repeated urging of Parliament, the Ministry did not instruct foreign service officers to adapt. For instance, a firm bypassing the rules and approaching a legation or consulate directly would be referred to the Ministry in The Hague. And anyone applying to the Economic Affairs Department for information could be referred to the Trade Division, the official government information agency. The legations were just as lax in the matter of economic reports. Many weeks sometimes passed before the Economic Affairs Department was informed of changes in tariff laws, if indeed it was informed at all. And it took more time for such information to be passed on to the Trade Division. The latter, in turn, was at times slow in informing interested parties because it was hit harder by the retrenchment measures than most other government departments and was understaffed. Complaints were also heard about the Ministry's inadequate preparation for international trade talks and its defense of the Dutch business community. The long-smoldering resentment on this score finally burst into flames after the conclusion of a new trade agreement with Germany in 1926, forcing the government in conjunction with the Netherlands Industrial Association to set up an advisory committee under Posthuma before the end of the year.

Much of the dissatisfaction with commercial information in the 1920s stemmed from the economic downturn after 1920, forcing the government to introduce heavy spending cuts which eroded the bulk of reforms effected by Van Karnebeek since 1918. Worse, the new austerity measures prevented the implementation of the most effective solution, namely expansion of both the Trade Division and the consular service. Political opposition moreover prevented the Foreign Ministry from giving consideration to two measures that could have remedied at least some of the ills. One was to correct the attitude of the foreign service to everything related to commerce. The other was to allow direct contact between the Trade Division and the business community in the Netherlands on the one hand, and the diplomatic representatives and consuls abroad on the other. A remarkable feature of these discussions is the fact that from the moment they started in 1922, no reference was ever made to these faults in the organizational structure of the Ministry of Foreign Affairs.

The opening shot in the battle over the reorganization of economic information was fired in October, 1922 by the president of the Netherlands Industrial Association. With the division of the Ministry of Agriculture, Trade and Industry about to be effected, Posthuma arranged a meeting of representatives of government and private information organizations to exchange ideas about improving the provision of economic information. In both form and content, the meeting set the tone for the discussions in the following years. Of the ministries represented, Foreign Affairs in the person of Nederbragt displayed the most enthusiasm. Not wishing to tie the hands of future ministers, Colonial Minister De Graaff and Prime Minister Ruys de Beerenbrouck, who had temporarily replaced Van IJsselsteijn, did not allow their senior officials to attend the meeting. In later discussions too, Nederbragt was the most forthcoming of the government officials. The solution proposed by the business community would not only have strengthened the Foreign Ministry's position, but would in fact have put a definite end to Trade and Industry's efforts to influence foreign economic relations. The discussions were not however dominated by Nederbragt, but by the two very different figures of Folkert Posthuma, who as chairman of various advisory committees was intent on steering the talks in the direction of the partial privatization of the trade division, and his principal opponent, F.K.H. Heringa, head of the Trade Division.

It was an unequal battle from the start. Posthuma was a leading spokesman for organized industry and commerce, while Heringa was a senior civil servant who knew he lacked the full backing of his Minister. Under Posthuma's direction the Industrial Association evolved in the second half of the 1920s into a bastion of the *laissez-faire* faction recently revived by the economic upturn and the prospect of a return to free trade.[5] Posthuma's influence in fact went much further. After resigning as Minister of Agriculture, Trade and Industry in 1918, he had accepted the chairmanship of a large number of organized interest groups, including several of particular prominence such as the Netherlands Dairy Producers Federation and the Industrial Council, a consultative body which advised the government in a semi-official capacity. Among the smaller organizations in which Posthuma was involved was the Federation of Dutch Chambers of Commerce Abroad, which he headed between 1920 and 1932.

His adversary Heringa was different in every way both from a personal and a professional point of view. On the insistence of the Dutch agricultural lobby, which claimed that the interests of agriculture were accorded lower priority than those of industry and commerce, the Ministry of Agriculture, Trade and Industry was split up on January 1, 1923. The Agriculture Department was transferred to the Ministry of Home Affairs, and the Trade and Industry Division to the Ministry of Labor. Until T.J. Verschuur took office in 1929, the Division functioned more or less as an appendage to the Ministry of Social Affairs. As every minister appointed in those years had distinguished himself in the field of social policy, economic policy tended to fade into the background. Through the heavy spending cuts, Heringa and his shrinking Division were on their own. A product of the pre-first world war civil service culture which gradually faded away in the 1920s, Heringa was not the man to advance the interests of his Division with the Minister. Unlike Nederbragt, who did not allow himself to be pushed aside and did not eschew bureaucratic trench warfare, Heringa was loyal, compliant, and above all punctilious in implementing ministerial decisions. At the committee meetings he was no match for Posthuma. The idea that, lacking the Minister's backing, he could have taken the initiative himself, did not occur to him. In the discussions, supported only by the representatives of the Colonial Ministry and the agriculture department, he lost practically every skirmish with the coalition of the Foreign Ministry and the business community. But he did block their path to the spoils of victory. Unable to steer the discussions in another direction, but backed by Theodoor J. Mansholt, the much more resolute head of the foreign agricultural information service, he managed to prevent J. Slotemaker de Bruïne, the Minister of Labor, Trade and Industry, from removing the trade division from the Ministry. Moreover, by endlessly protracting the discussions he was still holding on in 1930 when Verschuur abruptly put an end to all the plans. The spirit of *laissez-faire* survived the first world war, but in such a weakened state that the government could not be persuaded to share its most important instrument of economic policy with private enterprise.

The aim of the meeting called by the Netherlands Industrial Association in October, 1922 was for both parties to put forward suggestions for reducing expenditure on the provision of foreign economic information while at the same time rendering it more effective. The point of departure was a memorandum by Nederbragt describing the Foreign Ministry's efforts over many years to restrict government intervention and to place everything possible in the hands of private enterprise. There was "some sympathy" in the Ministry for his idea of combining the information activities of the Economic Affairs Department and the Trade Division in a bureau administered jointly by the government and private enterprise. He did not say precisely who was sympathetic, but he was undoubtedly referring to Van Karnebeek. His plan, he said, had two advantages. As private enterprise would be involved in the new organization, coordination would benefit, and after a few years the financial responsibility could be passed on to the business community.

But Nederbragt's plan was in fact misleading. Information being the principal task of the Trade Division, it would have to be transferred in its entirety to the new bureau. On the other hand, both the Economic Affairs Department and the consular service would remain under the authority of the Foreign Ministry because information was just a small part of their work. Nevertheless, the Ministry would provide a chairman for the steering committee in the person of the head of the Economic Affairs Department, while moreover in dealing with commercial enquiries outside the Netherlands, the bureau would be primarily dependent on the consulates, as Dutch Chambers of Commerce had been established in only a few countries. Sound coordination would be absolutely essential. Furthermore, in order to ensure that the consuls were not inundated with enquiries, all communication between the bureau and the consulates would be channelled through the Ministry.

Nederbragt himself admitted there were weak points in his proposal, which was based on purely personal reflections which the Trade Division did not share. The committee raised many objections, most of them financial. The organizational structure would be unnecessarily complicated because all contact with the consulates had to be through the Foreign Ministry. It was therefore debatable whether the new system would be cheaper. In addition, it was unlikely that the parties concerned would agree to bear all the costs. More importantly, there were few if any instances of industry and commerce voicing dissatisfaction with non-governmental economic information, including that provided by the Dutch Chambers of Commerce abroad. Quite possibly the division of tasks could be arranged more effectively, but there was no need to go beyond that, and Nederbragt's plan would only make matters worse. The non-governmental organizations greeted the plan with an equal lack of enthusiasm. Except for their participation in the central economic information service, Nederbragt's proposal was however to serve as the guideline for further discussions on the provision of commercial information in the 1920s.

The advocates of greater unity in Dutch information services and their transfer to private enterprise kept their hopes high. While the first chance had been missed with the reorganization on January 1, 1923, they were sure that there would be future opportunities. Once again it was Posthuma who made the next move, this time as president of the Federation of Dutch Chambers of Commerce Abroad.[6] In consultation with his fellow members of the executive committee, he informed the Economic Affairs Department that the Chambers of Commerce abroad were prepared to take over the handling of commercial enquiries from the consular service free of charge. Nederbragt accordingly informed the consulates and was then shocked to discover that the Chambers were fiercely opposed to the measure, which forced him to cancel the instructions. The Federation met only once a year, and Posthuma was empowered to consult with the government on its behalf, but an undertaking such as this required the prior agreement of all members. In not ascertaining their views, Posthuma had gone too far. He was greatly aggrieved by their opposition. One of the Chambers did however go along with the idea. As commercial information was provided free of charge in the United States, and the end of the subsidy period was drawing near, the Netherlands Chamber of Commerce in New York, Inc. took over the handling of commercial enquiries from the consulate-general in New York and the legation in Washington.

This early service station typified Shell's beginnings on the West Coast. Royal Dutch Shell started its operations in the United States in 1912, when the tanker S.S. Romany, carrying more than a million gallons of gasoline from Sumatra in the Netherlands East Indies, eased into Richmond Beach, a small port north of Seattle. Lured by America's burgeoning auto industry, the Royal Dutch Shell Group founded a marketing organization to sell gasoline in the Pacific Northwest and San Francisco Bay areas.

In 1912, a brand-new Shell tank car delivered 8,000 gallons of the shipment to Chehalis, Washington. Thus began the sale of Shell gasoline in the United States. The picture shows Roxana gasoline trucks in Ohio in 1926. By the early 1930s, Shell gasoline was sold in every U.S. state and territory. Shell is a wholly owned subsidiary of the Royal Dutch Shell Group.

Further discussions in the Federation revealed what Posthuma had wanted to achieve and where his reasoning had gone awry. By transferring the handling of enquiries from the consulates to the Chambers of Commerce abroad he had hoped to gain access to a new clientele. Firms that had formerly applied to the consulates for free information would be referred to the Chambers of Commerce. In Posthuma's proposal, companies would have to become a member of the Chamber if they wanted their queries answered. Posthuma had taken no account of whether this would be acceptable to the business community, especially firms wishing to do business in the many countries without a Dutch Chamber of Commerce, while the consular service was financed from public funds. He had also greatly overestimated the capacity of the Chambers to deal with such an increased demand for their services. Unlike the Chamber in New York, they had no staff of their own, their secretaries and other functionaries being employed full-time or part-time in other occupations. And it was amply clear after December, 1923 that it would stretch their resources beyond breaking point, the more so as they would be expected to provide information on matters traditionally dealt with by the government, such as trade agreements, tariff laws, customs regulations and more. The Chambers refused to accept this extra workload, and moreover had their doubts about the predicted financial advantages. While admittedly membership would rise, there was no guarantee that it would cover the rise in costs, also because it would be necessary to hire agents in other regions if the honorary consuls no longer provided commercial information. The annual costs for New York alone were put at $ 25,000. The project placed an onerous burden on an organizational form based solely on voluntary cooperation, and without financial support from the government it was out of the question.

Barely a year later, in the summer of 1925, Posthuma made another attempt to draw the Dutch Chambers of Commerce abroad into a merger of Dutch commercial information services. This time the plans were even more ambitious, the opposition was correspondingly greater, and it was obvious that the chairman of the Industrial Association knew little about the provision of commercial information. After talks with Nederbragt and Ernst Heldring, president of the Amsterdam Chamber of Commerce since 1922, he concluded that costs could be cut by transferring the work of the four government information divisions - in Foreign Affairs, Colonies, Labor, Trade and Industry, and Home Affairs - to a privately-run central office which would also include the existing private and semi-private organizations. He now cast the Dutch Chambers of Commerce abroad in a totally different role. In view of their scant resources, it would be best for them to confine their activities to the provision of general commercial information and to work in concert with the local consuls. All contact with industry and commerce in the Netherlands would be through the projected central office. He made a further distinction between commercial information and commercial intelligence, between information on matters of a more general nature and the fostering of a direct relationship between exporters and customers. With the exception of the Chambers in London and Brussels, which were large enough to cope with both areas, the Chambers should concentrate exclusively on information about local business practices. In order to avoid confusion, commercial intelligence should from now on be the exclusive responsibility of the consular service, and the central office in the Netherlands would be responsible for general commercial information.

Though Posthuma hinted that he was authorized from "higher up" to push through the reorganization of Dutch commercial information against all opposition, a storm of protest broke out at the annual meeting of the Federation on June 26, 1925. The Chambers of Commerce saw themselves as being pushed away to a side-track, not only because they would not be permitted to maintain contact with their supporters in the Netherlands, but more specifically because Posthuma wanted to stop them putting Dutch exporters in touch with foreign customers, which given their knowledge of local business conditions they were more qualified to do than any other organization. The crucial question was this: if they no longer had a direct link with the business community, how could they find new members? In short, Posthuma was threatening to sweep away the financial basis of the Federation of which he himself was president. The storm abated when Posthuma admitted that the budget for the new central office was no more than a rough estimate, that it was not the intention that the central office would supply addresses, and that his plan could have been formulated more felicitously. Once again, the plan was rejected.

Having failed to persuade the private organizations at home and abroad to join forces in a single commercial information service, its advocates turned their attention to the Netherlands government. When a new Cabinet was being formed in 1925-1926, Foreign Minister Van Karnebeek raised the subject with his col-

135

league at the Ministry of Labor, Trade and Industry, suggesting that a committee be set up under Nederbragt to study ways and means of coordinating the services provided in this area by their two Ministries and the private and semi-governmental organizations. The government's official advisory body, the Economic Policy Committee, which was chaired by D.A.P.N. Koolen, the outgoing Minister of Labor, Trade and Industry, would not be suitable as the study to be conducted would relate not to economic policy but to an organizational question affecting only the work of the Foreign Ministry. Koolen did not agree. According to Koolen, domestic and foreign commercial information were so interconnected that any study to be carried out should be entrusted to the advisory body. His successor, J. Slotemaker de Bruïne, was equally disinclined to act, but eventually yielded to pressure from his fellow cabinet members. The study was however to be restricted to foreign commercial information. He was also obliged to agree to cooperate with the Industrial Council, which he had opposed on the grounds that it would give the business community too much influence in the deliberations. Moreover, the Council represented only the large industrial corporations which made the least use of the official information services. Slotemaker de Bruïne feared that the interests of other branches of industry would be relegated to second place. It was for this reason that he opposed the proposal to appoint Posthuma as chairman. His uncompromising position on commercial information and his attempt to bully the Chambers of Commerce abroad did not recommend him as the ideal person to direct an objective study. At the insistence of Van Karnebeek and Finance Minister D.J. de Geer, Slotemaker de Bruïne had to concede this point as well and accept the head of the Industrial Council as the committee chairman.

Slotemaker de Bruïne's fears proved to be well-founded. A biased investigation into the existing official information services without an exploration of the various alternatives followed. One reason for this was that the committee worked under the auspices of the committee appointed by the government to look at ways of reducing public spending, so that cutting the costs of commercial information provision seemed to have been the primary objective. The findings of this study, which ignored the information activities of the Foreign Ministry altogether, must surely have been foreseen by the officials concerned. The committee concluded that "the present official organization fails to meet even the most modest demands", that the work of the various departments was uncoordinated, and that a comprehensive reorganization and centralization were urgently needed.

Not surprisingly, Heringa and Mansholt refused to sign the recommendations, and Mansholt sent a personal dissenting report to the government. Van Voorthuyzen signed on condition that the information provided by the Colonial Ministry was not to be affected. As the recommendations, like all earlier plans, left Foreign Affairs' Economic Affairs Department untouched, Nederbragt was the only civil servant who endorsed the committee's proposals without reservations.

In other words, decided differences of opinion existed between the representatives of industry and commerce led by Posthuma and the civil servants on the committee. Both sides were genuinely trying to improve the provision of commercial information, but their points of departure were so radically different as to preclude any possibility of agreement. Heldring, who as a member of the Consular Examinations Committee was regarded as one of the best informed businessmen on the committee, estimated that 75 percent of the Netherlands' foreign relations concerned economic matters. It was already the case, he said, that the Foreign Ministry was not up to its task, and it would become even further isolated from the economic life of the country if the entire commercial information system were to be placed under the Ministry of Labor, Trade and Industry. It was a choice between two evils. So long as the Foreign Ministry retained control of trade policy and there was no prospect of upgrading the Trade Division, the choice of the business community was clear.

Combining the different information services in a semi-official organization would have the added advantage of being able to influence policy. A central commercial information office would be a repository for all information collected by the government on the economy of the Netherlands and other countries, on agriculture, trade and industry, transport, expenditure on major projects abroad, tariff laws, customs regulations, import restrictions, and much more. In order to ensure that the ministries would not go back on the arrangement later on, all officials connected with the provision of information would be transferred to the new office.

Heringa and Mansholt forcefully reminded the businessmen on the committee that the government was in danger of finding itself severely handicapped in the performance of its tasks. The Dutch government had as great a need for information as private enterprise. In negotiating trade agreements the Netherlands government would surely not dare to depend on information supplied by a semi-autonomous organization. Tariffs were becoming increasingly detailed, one amendment followed swiftly on the heels of another, and a large number of agreements were concluded every year. Furthermore, foreign governments would not be prepared to give the same information to a privately-run office as to a governmental organization. The proposed strict separation of information from policy-making was utopian, even if only for the reason that both were often handled by the same person, who was also responsible for the accompanying technical information. The ministries' information services had come into being because the government needed information, and not because of the needs of industry and commerce. Without information, the ministries could no longer function properly and would lose all perception of the needs of the business community, a perception which according to many complaints was already inadequate. And finally, was it true that the work of the various services overlapped, as the committee alleged? Mansholt did not deny that they used the same information, like information on trade agreements and customs regulations, but their aims were very different.

Summarizing the views of Mansholt, the most outspoken civil servant on the committee, he found that preference should be given to strengthening the Trade and Industry Division, starting with a separate section to deal with tariffs. In his dissenting report he dissected the weak points in the concept of a semi-autonomous central office one by one. In contradiction to what the Posthuma group averred, the basic issue was not some form of privatization, but the question of whether it was permissible for the government to hand over to others the collection, processing, and interpretation of the information used for the formulation of policy. And if so, what categories of information could be handed over? Should the office be limited to providing information on trade agreements and tariffs obtained from the consulates and legations abroad, or should that information be interpreted in the light of all available economic data, including technical details, as was already the practice of the Trade Division? If the latter was preferred then the office could be charged with providing all the information required by the government, producing much greater integration than was originally intended. In that event there would be nothing more for the Trade Division to do, and it could be transposed in its entirety to the central office. That in turn would create difficulties regarding the special position occupied by the Foreign Ministry by virtue of the office's dependence on the information supplied by the foreign service. If the Foreign Minister, as part of his responsibility for foreign economic relations, were to be given special authority in respect of the office, the same privilege could hardly be denied to the Minister for Labor, Trade and Industry, who was responsible for domestic economic policy.

In Mansholt's view the government could not base its policy on information obtained from an office administered in partnership with third parties. The collection of information and the formulation of policy were inextricably interwoven, and that being so, each individual ministry should retain its own information facility. Allocating seats on the steering committee to the departmental officials concerned with policy-making was nothing more than a stop-gap, and it would certainly not result in the desired interdepartmental cooperation. It would remove one of the two basic premises of the Posthuma committee, i.e. the fusion of the official information services outside the aegis of the Ministry of Labor, Trade and Industry.

As Slotemaker de Bruïne stated in the Cabinet after the appearance of the report in April, 1928, the committee had not put forward a single argument that could warrant changing the existing organizational structure. The proposal was devoid of logic in other respects as well. The Trade Division had tried many times in the past to induce the Foreign Ministry to allow it to communicate directly with the consulates and diplomatic missions, and now suddenly, out of the blue, it was to be permitted to do so. Under pressure in the Cabinet, Slotemaker de Bruïne was finally obliged to agree to the institution of a central economic information service. The Posthuma committee could then start filling in the details of the work of the information service, which it promptly proceeded to do. The prospective director of the new organization, W. Graadt van Roggen, general secretary of the Dutch trade show center in Utrecht, was instructed to draft the terms of reference. When the committee issued its final report on November 14, 1929 it was obvious that it too had failed to disentangle all the knots. So Heringa and Mansholt were again not among the signatories, and the latter had written another dissenting report. He also urged his Minister to permit him to explain personally to the Cabinet why the committee's recommendations should not be implemented.

The business community was also highly critical of the report. The Amsterdam Chamber of Commerce accused the committee of ignorance and inaccuracy. However straightforward commercial information might seem to the outsider, "anyone unaware of the practical aspects of public information hasn't the slightest idea of how questions are usually phrased and of the experience needed to understand what is really meant". What was of primary importance was that queries should be answered with a minimum of delay. The deliberations should therefore be focused on decentralization rather than centralization, but only after the deficiencies of the present system had been properly catalogued, which the committee had failed to do. The existing private information services functioned efficiently and often provided more and better information, and more promptly, than the government services. Due to the organizational fragmentation since the first world war years, most of the problems were concentrated in the government services. In addition, the committee did not seem to realize that the government and private enterprise had very different needs in this respect. Where the government needed general information like trade statistics and the texts of trade agreements and laws, industry and commerce demanded first and foremost was to be put in touch with reliable business contacts. The Amsterdam Chamber of Commerce was also extremely doubtful about the semi-governmental structure favored by the committee. Government information was an essential component of government policy as laid down in the Constitution, and was therefore part of ministerial responsibility.[7] It wondered too whether the committee had tried to revive the pre-first world war system whereby practically the entire government economic information had been entrusted to the Ministry of Agriculture, Trade and Industry.

The Amsterdam Chamber's opinion of the proposed activities of the central office was even more negative. The concept of a catalogue filled with data on the nature, management, size, and products of all Dutch firms was considered to be either "pure humbug" as a means of winning the general public's support for reorganization, or proof of "abysmal ignorance". As the Rotterdam Chamber of Commerce had experienced some years before, this could only lead to total chaos. Even the business directories and the meticulous register of firms abounded with errors. The Posthuma committee would have been better advised to think in terms of the existing private commercial information organizations, which housed a great deal of information and expertise. The Amsterdam Chamber was equally unimpressed with the projected spending cuts, the more so since no budget had been produced. Even the cautious estimate of Dfl. 30,000 to Dfl. 40,000 mentioned by Mansholt in his report would cover only a fraction of the costs. All in all, the committee had been prompted by more motives than simply a desire to improve the system of foreign economic information.

Economic Information in the 1930's

In July, 1930, when the Posthuma committee report was circulating in the Amsterdam Chamber of Commerce, the prospects of a thorough reorganization of the government information services had grown much dimmer. A new Dutch government under Ruys de Beerenbrouck had taken office on August 10, 1929, and T.J. Verschuur was the new Minister of Labor, Trade and Industry. In the person of Verschuur, the Ministry was at last headed by someone who did not allow others to dictate the course he was to follow. Aware of the rapidly accumulating economic problems, he attached particular importance to the formulation of economic policy at home and abroad. Among the documents awaiting his attention when he took office were the reports of the Posthuma committee.

In light of the recession which began in the United States barely two months later, Verschuur soon decided that the committee's basic premise was right that the official economic information services indeed failed to meet "the most modest demands". But unlike the businessmen on the committee, he believed the solution was to expand the Trade and Industry Division, since the earlier reorganization in the end had resulted in nothing more than the detachment of the Trade Division to the detriment of the Ministry as a whole. What this implied is apparent from comparing the existing situation with the committee's recommendations. In the organizational structure for foreign economic information, the formal position of the Foreign Ministry had remained unchanged, but it had in fact grown stronger than the position of the other ministries. The Trade and Industry Department, in particular, had been side-tracked. This happened not only because it was to share responsibility for the Trade Division with other ministries and with private enterprise. A more important reason was that the same information and contacts with industry and commerce were now available to all ministries. For information on domestic commercial activities the Foreign Ministry was no longer dependent on other government agencies, and it was now free to appropriate foreign economic policy in its entirety.

This was unacceptable to Verschuur. The recession overtaking Europe's economies in the 1930s exposed the weaknesses in economic policy-making with increasing clarity, fuelling political pressure for reorganization to be undertaken at long last. The Foreign Minister, Esquire F. Beelaerts van Blokland, realized with a jolt that Verschuur had seized the initiative, and had to watch helplessly as Verschuur made it plain that neither the business community, Parliament nor the Cabinet would prevent him from reorganizing the information services on the foreign and domestic economy as he wished. The distribution of the information services over the various ministries remained as before, but before the year was out Verschuur set about the transformation of the Ministry of Labor, Trade and Industry into a central economic agency, to which end it had to be furnished with a fully official Economic Information Division. To get his way, Verschuur had threatened to resign, and the gamble paid off. Owing to the length of time it took to build up the Division, the question of whether or not it should be run by or in partnership with private enterprise was still being debated up to 1936, when it was settled once and for all by a new reorganization.

Verschuur had little difficulty in getting his bill providing for the reorganization of economic policy-making through Parliament in 1931. At the end of that year Heringa was succeeded by Hans M. Hirschfeld in the newly created post of Director-General of Trade and Industry. By way of fusion with the Agriculture Department, the Ministry of Labor and Economic Affairs came into existence on May 1, 1932, and on September 1, 1932 the consular officer Arnold T. Lamping was appointed first director of the Economic Information Division (EVD). In June, 1933 the new Ministry transferred some of its responsibilities to the Ministry of Social Affairs. Except for the period from August, 1935 to June, 1937, when there was a separate Ministry of Agriculture and Fisheries, it dominated economic policy up to the German invasion of the Netherlands in May, 1940. With the upgrading of the Trade and Industry Division to the status of a department, the shift in power relations was also perceptible to the outside world. The Foreign Ministry's Economic Affairs Department was downgraded to a Consular and Commercial Affairs Division, its status prior to the reorganization effected by Van Karnebeek in 1918.

Verschuur had at last provided the Dutch government with the means to obtain more and better information as a basis for economic policy. The Trade and Industry Department was expanded in 1933; Heringa's staff of 13 of three years before had grown to a staff of more than 30 in the Industry Section (later Division) alone by the end of 1936. When Heringa arrived in 1929, the one or two able officials in the Trade Division were reinforced by an increasing number of young economics graduates, earning the new department the nickname of "the economic youth center". The languishing existence of the Economic Information Division was out of tune with the rapid expansion of the other parts of the Ministry. This was largely due to the fact that Lamping, though head of the entire department, mostly concerned himself with trade policy, which the Council of Ministers had entrusted to Verschuur in 1933, and devoted too little time and attention to the economic information structure. It was Lamping who headed the delegation to the negotiations on a new trade agreement with the United States in 1935.[8] This situation lasted until Minister Gelissen reorganized and enlarged the Economic Information Division in April, 1936.

Once Verschuur had gained control of foreign economic policy, the information activities of the foreign service were the last of the thorny problems to be resolved with the Ministry of Foreign Affairs. The advent of a new government under Colijn in May-June, 1933 gave the signal for discussion to begin. Just a month later the failure of the World Economic Conference in London ended all prospect of a concerted international approach to the recession. The negative growth of exports, even though a 6 percent decline was less dramatic than the 18 percent decline in 1932, gave cause for great concern. It was attributable to a large extent to the pegging of the guilder to the gold standard, causing a marked depreciation in the Netherlands' competitive position on the world market.

The arrival of a new government infused new life into the promotion of Dutch exports. In addition to the trade agreements policy, exports were to be stimulated by indirect means. Export credit guarantees were made available on a wider scale, participation in foreign trade shows and expositions was encouraged, and the quality control of agricultural products was improved. Also, more attention was paid to the quality of the reports on economic trends and international markets. Partial agreement was reached on the question of direct communications between the foreign service and the EVD, but only after Verschuur, who objected to the length of time it took for the reports to reach the Netherlands, refused to accept all further responsibility for trade policy. Foreign service officers, who on the whole were well-disposed to the idea were now to send copies of all relevant reports to the Ministry of Labor, Trade and Industry. The innovations did not extend to stricter instructions regarding the quality and substance of the reports.

The issue was finally settled in 1937, in the wake of the reorganization of the economic information service in the Ministry of Trade, Industry and Shipping. In April, 1936 the Minister, Henri C.J.H. Gelissen, and Director-General Hirschfeld had carried out a fundamental reorganization of the provision of economic information. In the teeth of the opposition of the business community and virtually the entire Cabinet, they had decided it was to become part of their Ministry. It tripled the staff to 65, gave the economic research section full responsibility for the commercial information section and three other sections concerned with administrative, economic, and statistical documentation. With this reorganization the official information service was at last provided with the resources needed to rise above the level of simple commercial reports.

Tjalling P. van der Kooy was appointed as director of the Economic Information Division. Traversing the minefield of the problems and sensibilities which had plagued the discussions in the past, he personally called on the relevant private and semi-governmental organizations to solicit their cooperation. Like so many before him, he had an adequate fund of theoretical knowledge but was not versed in the practical aspects, as G.M. Greup, secretary of the Amsterdam Chamber of Commerce, remarked after their first meeting. Well aware of this himself, Van der Kooy introduced himself as an organizer and coordinator seeking to intensify cooperation between private enterprise and the government. For various reasons the expectations of the business community were not very high. As Ernst Heldring noted in his journal, Van der Kooy might be a first-rate financial analyst, but he knew nothing about other countries. That being so, the work of his Division would probably be focused primarily on the government, with industry and commerce taking second place.

The objective was no longer to try to concentrate all economic information under one roof. Overlapping was of course to be avoided, pressure on the foreign information channels was to be relieved, and maximum use was to be made of the information available in the Netherlands. Once this was achieved, the foreign service officers could spend more time and attention on finding new outlets for Dutch products. Despite a steady flow of publications pouring forth since the first reorganization in 1931, many Dutch exporters still had no idea of where to turn for information, and they often addressed the same query to several organizations. The Economic Information Division's files contained data of a general economic nature, particulars of markets and firms, business directories, and documentation on trade policy and management. Similar information was collected by most Chambers of Commerce and the so-called two-country organizations, depending on the regional economic activities and the interests of firms exporting to the countries in question. The Netherlands Employers Federation focused its attention on government measures; the regional Chambers of Commerce compiled information on terms of delivery and settlement, packaging requirements, etc. Those seeking names and addresses abroad could apply to the consulates or the Dutch Chambers of Commerce in the countries concerned, which also helped to settle disputes between Dutch exporters and local firms, acted as intermediaries in questions concerning tariff barriers and the related customs procedures, and gave advice on tax and currency regulations. Some Chambers abroad were active in the areas of general, economic, and tourist publicity as well. None of these organizations dared to risk supplying information on creditworthiness, and all such inquiries were referred to private commercial information offices.

In May, 1937 Minister Gelissen invited the Dutch Chambers of Commerce abroad to discuss ways and means of coordinating their work with that of the Ministry. Stating that their specialized knowledge and

their contacts in their respective countries would allow them to play a central part in the projected collaboration of governmental and non-governmental organizations, he suggested they could for instance advise on issues of special significance which were to be raised in consultations with the Dutch business community. The consultations he had in mind would for the most part be conducted with the Central Institute for the Promotion of Foreign Trade headed by Posthuma. Set up in 1933-1934 by the four major employers associations, it was the acknowledged consultative body for industry and commerce and hence for commercial information. Each individual Chamber of Commerce abroad could take part in the talks, provided it met the test of reliability in standards and autonomy, the criterion used by the Economic Information Division in passing on inquiries. In the opinion of the business community, the most eligible Chambers of Commerce were the Chambers in London and Paris, and the Netherlands-American Chamber of Commerce in Amsterdam.

To assist the Economic Information Division in assessing the qualities of the two-country organizations, as they were now called, the Federation of Dutch Chambers of Commerce Abroad embarked on a process of internal selection and assessment based on the Division's guidelines. The Division thereafter maintained more or less close contact with a number of the organizations, and held monthly meetings with the Netherlands-American Chamber of Commerce. The few remaining minutes of these meetings show that Van der Kooy and his officials regarded the Chamber's executive committee as a representation of the Dutch firms dealing with the United States, consulting it on matters relating both directly and indirectly to trade. Among the topics discussed were amendments to U.S. tariff laws, the influence of sound business practice on the reputation of sectors of industry, the participation of Dutch firms in the New York world exhibition scheduled for 1939, the planned Holland House in New York, fixed procedures for settling trade disputes, and the organization of joint sales campaigns in the United States.

To draw the consular service more closely into the combined efforts of government and private enterprise, a new consular manual was issued in 1937. Whereas in the past the Ministry of Foreign Affairs had been free to act as it pleased, it was now required to confer with the Ministry of Economic Affairs. This was complicated by two factors. First, economic information was just one of the tasks of the consular service; for its other tasks it was accountable to the Foreign Ministry. Understandably, the Consular Affairs and Trade Division was seriously concerned about the extra workload likely to result from the reorganization for career consuls and, more particularly, for the honorary consuls. Few improvements had been made to the unsatisfactory structure of the foreign service since the early 1930s. A more serious difficulty was the Division's antagonism to the innovators at the Ministry of Economic Affairs, to their concepts of economic information, and their efforts to remake the consular service in their own image. Remarks scrawled in the margins of documents show how aggrieved they felt. While not denying that "the officials are courteous and the Economic Information Division is well organized", one annotator sourly doubted that its information could be of any use: "At any event it meets a psychological need at a time when people enjoy throwing money away." Now that the balance of power had definitely shifted in favor of Economic Affairs, it could no longer be denied a voice in the organization and instructions of the consular service. The formal relationship between the Economic Information Division and the foreign service was the main issue in the talks on the 1937 consular manual. The Foreign Ministry managed with some success to fend off the Economic Information Division, shelving a proposal that Economic Affairs post representatives abroad. But it was a minor victory because it was forced to agree to direct correspondence between the diplomatic missions and the Economic Information Division. The Consular Affairs and Trade Division had by then been pushed so far to the sidelines that it gladly accepted being supplied with copies of all correspondence.

Van der Kooy also tried to change the structure of the consular service. The list of changes which he presented in August, 1937 to Minister Maximilien P.L. Steenberghe was long and - as he admitted himself - ambitious. He painted a gloomy picture of the consular service, pointing out that there were 36 career officers in 21 consulates, while of the more than 700 honorary consuls only 200 or so were Dutch nationals. With the sole exception of New York, all consuls in the United States were honorary. It had been suggested in 1936 that a young career officer be sent to assist the honorary consul-general in San Francisco, but nothing had yet been done. Though the situation was not universally bad, the differences in service were consistent with the degree of understaffing. Expansion of the consular service would consequently have the effect of raising standards. It was clear that since the beginning of the recession seven years before, the expansion of the foreign service had not kept pace with the demands made on commercial information by changing circumstances. Competition in foreign markets was heavier, foreign government measures were causing increasing difficulties, and the international economic structure had greatly changed. New markets that could have compensated for losses in traditional export markets like Germany were being neglected. And this certainly included the United States. New career consuls should therefore be stationed in Washington, New York, and New Orleans, and the honorary consul in Detroit replaced by a career officer. At the same time, the number of honorary consuls in the United States should be increased. Nor did the Foreign Ministry's sacrosanct diplomatic service escape Van der Kooy's attention. He wished to see it augmented by a few able commercial specialists to coordinate the work of consuls and diplomats. Knowing that the Foreign Ministry would be categorically opposed to his proposals and that the financial resources of the government were limited, he suggested first devoting a few months to gaining experience with the new consular manual while quietly pressing for reform.

Steenberghe's efforts to adapt the consular service to the needs of commercial information placed the Foreign Minister, Jacob A.N. Patijn, in a difficult position. Interdepartmental rivalry, awareness on both sides of the weak points in the new consular manual, exacerbated by petty intrigues and the tendency of Economic Affairs to monopolize trade policy, caused relations between the two ministries further to deteriorate. The rough edges of the conflict became manifest to the business community at a meeting of the Standing Committee of the Council for Economic Information on September 20, 1938, when Carel J.M. Schaepman, deputy head of the Foreign Ministry's Consular Affairs and Trade Division, expressed his personal opinion that "...economic information has no intrinsic value, but should rather be regarded as a fashionable whim, a phenomenon of the times or a superstition that yields not a farthing but costs an immense amount". Such an arrogant statement, a frontal attack on government policy, was not well received. Van der Kooy felt it was directed at him personally; nor was it appreciated by the business representatives on the committee. It took the combined efforts of Steenberghe, Patijn, and Prime Minister Colijn to calm the ruffled feathers.

These discussions brought the changing power relations between the two ministries to the political level. It was no longer the ministry responsible for the economy of the country that was seen as the interloper in the field of foreign trade, but the ministry that had traditionally dominated foreign relations. Thereafter the determining factor in the formulation of policy was not the hierarchical position in the machinery of government, but the knowledge and information accumulated by the individual ministries. Verschuur and his successors, backed by Hirschfeld, succeeded in persuading the Foreign Ministry, the Cabinet, and Parliament to go along with this revolutionary change. On the grounds that the Foreign Ministry took too little interest in the economic aspects of its work, and was not enterprising enough to qualify as a real alternative in the midst of a recession, the Ministry of Economic Affairs was offered the chance to effect the speedy transformation of what had been an extremely rudimentary system under Heringa in the 1920s, and which had a false start in 1933, into a full-fledged economic information service. The manner in which Van der Kooy set about, exploring all practical possibilities, was duplicated by the Ministry in the way it assumed responsibility for trade policy. Both compensated for their lack of knowledge so evident at the beginning of the crisis by utilizing the knowledge of the business community. And through the wide experience gained since 1920, the Chambers of Commerce for America emerged as valued discussion partners of the Netherlands government on the subject of Dutch trade with the United States.

Knowledge and Influence, but Power as Well?

Between the reestablishment of a private Dutch trade promotion organization in the United States in 1920 and the severance of trade relations between the two countries in May, 1940, U.S. tariff policy afforded the Chambers of Commerce for America with every opportunity to interpret the concept of trade policy in the widest possible sense. On the whole, it was more a question of protecting vested interests than of introducing new products or winning a larger share of the market. The trade barriers erected by American lobbyists in the 1920s had the effect of adding immeasurably to the Chamber's knowledge and experience of Dutch exports. This benefitted its role of advisor to the Dutch government when trade relations with the United States were placed on a new footing in the 1930s.

For reasons of both domestic and foreign relations, the Netherlands government decided in the 1920s not to intervene to assist Dutch exporters with problems arising from the campaigns mounted by American industry to restrict imports. Though its economic ties with other countries were closer than ever before, after 1918 the United States reverted in some respects to its pre-war protectionist policy. Foreign tariff increases, currency depreciation, and dumping practices, combined with a short but sharp international recession and a severe domestic agricultural crisis, led to a partial return to economic isolationism. But the American market was not so hermetically closed to foreign competitors as before. However imperfect, it was liberalization rather than protectionism that came to be the principle underlying the trade policy of successive Republican administrations. U.S. import restrictions, it was feared, would lead more or less automatically to discrimination against American exports, which would not only jeopardize the markets won during the first world war but would probably also exacerbate the existent imbalance in economic relations as well. If the United States were to export to Europe, so the reasoning went, it would first have to give the war-impoverished continent the opportunity to earn the money this would require. That would have the additional advantage of boosting the European currencies affected by the heavy fluctuations in exchange rates since the resumption of international trade.

While it is true that it introduced substantial increases, the tariff law passed by Congress in 1922 was a turning point in U.S. trade policy. Though the average level of duties on total imports - dutiable or not - rose from 8.8 percent to 13.9 percent, prohibiting the import of many goods, it was still far below the 20 percent level of the 1909 tariff law. The average tariff for listed commodities rose from 26 percent to 38 percent. More important, however, was the fact that the United States accepted for the first time the principle of unconditional most-favored-nation status, implying that the concessions offered in trade agreements applied in respect of all countries with which similar agreements were concluded.[9]

When the Republican Warren G. Harding became president of the United States in November, 1920, it was clear that the liberal tariff law of 1913 would shortly be replaced by more protectionist legislation. And indeed tariffs went up, but by less than predicted, and the president was empowered to authorize higher or lower tariffs in the interim. The 1922 Fordney-McCumber Act was based on the dual principle that tariffs were to be fixed on a systematic basis, and customs duties were to counterbalance the difference between production costs at home and abroad. The president could raise or lower duties up to 50 percent above or below existing tariffs, after examination by the Tariff Commission of company books. This measure was intended to facilitate interim tariff reductions, but in fact it led mostly to increases. Its significance for Dutch exports was not so much tariff increases but the threat of a Tariff Commission investigation. Between 1922 and 1929 the Commission completed barely 10 percent of the investigations it began, and the tariff was adjusted in only 38 cases, usually upward.[10] The greatest threat was that company secrets would be divulged to third parties. In addition, while the investigation was in progress and the president had not yet reached a decision, the company was required to deposit a sum to the value of the possible tariff increase for each consignment of goods. Instead, if they preferred, foreign firms could take out insurance covering the amount due. The additional costs were often so heavy, and the risk of a negative decision so great, that it was not unusual for exports to be halted altogether pending the outcome of an investigation. American competitors also made use of the opportunity to ask the Department of the Treasury to reclassify goods on the grounds that they deviated from the description in the tariff lists.

It is not known to what extent Dutch exports were investigated by the Tariff Commission or the Treasury, or how they were affected. In some cases American competitors tried for years to block foreign imports. Firms that attracted the attention of the Tariff Commission often denied it access to their books. They could count on nothing more than moral support from the Dutch government, and had to decide for themselves how they would act. In consultation with the Chamber and Von Baumhauer's legal office, some firms refused to cooperate with the Commission from the outset. The Dutch government took the view that tariff questions were an internal affair of the United States and did not wish to be involved. There was in fact not much that it could have done. The staff of the Tariff Commission and the Treasury did not have diplomatic status, and the Tariff Act did not specify that sanctions were to be imposed on firms denying access to their books. It was considered of greater importance in the early 1920s, when Europe was in economic and political disarray, that no offense was to be given to the American government.[11] But in 1925 the United States went too far in requesting diplomatic status for the staff of the Tariff Commission. After ascertaining the views of other European governments, the Netherlands Foreign Ministry refused.[12]

The Dutch government discounted the views of the Industrial Council, which was taking stock of the activities of American officials on Dutch soil: "Investigations by officials of foreign powers into Dutch firms established on Dutch territory must in principle ... be condemned in the strongest terms". Not only was it inconsistent with "the dignity" of Dutch industry, but above all it carried the risk of information "being used for ends other than those stated". On the whole, however, it advised adopting a cooperative attitude, especially in the early stages when the protectionist nature of the investigations was not yet certain and there was still hope of tariff reductions. It advised firms to provide the Tariff Commission with the information it requested. The cooperation of the Dutch business community came to an end when it became apparent that the work of the Commission impeded rather than facilitated access to the American market, and there was no longer any doubt that confidential information was being passed on to competitors. How the Commission came by its information, and whether or not the Treasury proceeded to reclassification in the event of non-cooperation, seemed to make little difference.

When the Dutch linseed oil industry was approached in 1922, it dared not refuse the U.S. Tariff Commission as its exports to the United States were of very recent date. Unhampered by customs duties, in the immediate years after the first world war, the industry, which had greatly expanded since 1914, had become strongly entrenched on the U.S. market. The 1922 Tariff Law had however introduced prohibitive duties on linseed oil. The Dutch producers protested vehemently and urged the Netherlands government to impose a ban on American linseed oil in retaliation, but without success. Exports then proved to be hit less hard than had been feared, and the manufacturers felt unable to refuse their cooperation when the Tariff Commission announced its intention of investigating the cost price. It was feared that if the Commission heard only the views of the American competitors, the tariff would be pushed up further.[13] It later appeared that this was the right decision. The investigation dragged on for years, but the Commission finally declared the accusations of dumping to be unfounded. Production costs in the Netherlands were in fact higher than in the United States. The American government nonetheless refused to lower the duties, and started a new investigation. This time the Netherlands Association of Oil Manufacturers refused to cooperate, but once again the charges were not found to warrant higher duties.

The investigation into production costs in the Dutch linseed oil industry was exceptional for the fact that the Netherlands Association of Oil Manufacturers defended its interests without seeking the aid of the Chamber. Moreover, it took seven years to complete. It also seems to be one of the few instances in which the U.S. Tariff Commission was active in the Netherlands.

The work of the Tariff Commission and the U.S. Customs Service of the Treasury Department, which checked the classification of goods in accordance with the tariff law, caused confusion in other European countries as well.[14] The Chamber had conducted regular dealings with Treasury agents in the 1920s. In contrast to the Tariff Commission, the Treasury was empowered to impose sanctions if information was withheld. It could ban or seize consignments of goods.

Early in 1926 the Dutch government was approached more or less simultaneously by the manufacturers of strawboard and stearic acid, used amongst other things in the manufacture of soap. There were reports of plans to raise U.S. customs duties on both commodities, and the two cases were very similar. They were both threatened with reclassification that could result in a much higher tariff if strawboard was classified as strawpaper, and stearic acid as palm oil. The first warning had come from the Chamber in New York.

Before the Tariff Commission had begun its investigation into strawboard, it was disclosed that stearic acid had already been reclassified, and the duties almost doubled, with retrospective effect from February 15, 1926. Tests in the laboratories of the New York Customs House had apparently shown that it was not animal stearic acid, but vegetable palmitic acid. Despite the importers' protests, the U.S. customs authorities refused to reconsider their decision. The importers argued that commercial palmitic acid did not exist, that stearic acid as such had been imported for years, and that the technical specifications in the Treasury Decision were purely theoretical. According to the Chamber, the Treasury Department's action had been undertaken at the behest of domestic producers, who had lost a large part of the market to foreign competitors owing to the high price of raw materials and high wage costs in the United States. The Dutch product, though of poorer quality, was a better buy in terms of its price-quality ratio, and exports to the

United States had risen from 18 tons in 1922 to 731 tons in 1925. This promising market was in danger of being lost because of the heavily increased customs duties.[15]

In consultation with Van Aken, the American importers decided to lodge a joint appeal against the decision, and engaged a lawyer to present their case at the hearing. Laboratory tests conducted towards the end of 1926 showed that the substance was indeed palmitic acid, and that stearic acid had for years been a generic term for all manner of products. Since the Fordney-McCumber Act distinguished between vegetable-based and animal-based acids, the American producers were insisting that customs duties be levied according to the letter of the law. It was more than a year before the Customs Court reached a decision, and it was a foregone conclusion that it would not settle the dispute once and for all. Both the importers and the American government announced in advance that they would appeal if the decision went against them. When the new classification was endorsed, Van Aken and the importers took their case to the Court of Customs Appeal, which however found against them in 1929. No exact figures are available for the effect of all this on the Dutch share of the market. But exports rose and 2,000 tons were shipped annually between 1931 and 1933.

The Chamber played a prominent part in this affair. Van Aken kept the importers and the legation informed of all developments, and Von Baumhauer acted as legal advisor to the Dutch manufacturers. When Six accompanied Westerman to New York in April, 1929, he went not just for talks with the Chamber, but also to defend the interests of the Dutch stearic acid manufacturers at the Congressional hearings on a proposed new tariff law.

Not reclassification but production methods were the issue in the case of the strawboard dispute. The manufacturers were not alarmed by the first reports reaching them from the Chamber in October, 1926. But they soon discovered there was good reason for the warnings. Strawboard exports had been affected in the past by price fixing on the part of their American competitors, who were now agitating for customs duties to be raised from 10 percent to 16 percent so as to eliminate the difference in production costs. Van Aken again organized the opposition, together with the representative of the W.A. Scholten Cardboard and Paper Company in Groningen.[16] The Tariff Commission declared the charge to be unfounded, whereupon the matter was taken to the Treasury Department in January, 1927. This time it was alleged that the product was not strawboard, but wrapping paper, on which customs duties were higher. Van Aken was optimistic about the outcome, but in June the duty was raised to 30 percent not, as the *Nieuwe Rotterdamsche Courant* wrote on the authority of the Chamber, because there was no market for strawboard, but because the outmoded U.S. industry was seeking protection from its more up-to-date foreign competitors. The Treasury Department based its verdict on the use made of the machines. Though theoretically they could produce both strawboard and wrapping paper, they were not used for this dual purpose because of the time it took to convert them. The Treasury considered the matter closed after one of its customs officers personally ascertained that the factory's machinery was suitable for the production of both paper and strawboard. Van Aken mobilized the American importers, and even though they felt sure of a favorable outcome, the reversal of the Treasury decision was hailed with relief. What counted was not the production method, but the thickness of strawboard and wrapping paper.

After these events the Dutch strawboard industry retained its place on the American market, not because of lower production costs but because sea transport cost a lot less than transporting goods by rail from Ohio, Indiana, and Illinois, where the main American manufacturers were located. The Dutch manufacturers, the only foreign competitors, had a 5 percent share of the American market in 1927. To show their appreciation of the support they had received from the Chamber, the ten manufacturers united in the Netherlands Association of Strawboard Manufacturers applied for membership.

The position of the Chamber as advisor to the Netherlands government and to the Dutch business community was highlighted again during the Congressional hearings on a new tariff law in 1929. A majority seemed at first to favor a limited tariff reduction, but pressure brought to bear by American agriculture, which had suffered a severe recession throughout the 1920s, and the growing instability of international trade helped protectionism to win the day. When it became apparent that the Hoover administration intended to abide by the Constitution and to refrain from interference in the legislative process, interest groups banded together and successfully pressed for increases in a large number of tariffs. Protectionism won more ground as a consequence of the Wall Street crash, the ailing economy and the tariff war waged in Europe at the end of 1929. With public opinion behind it, Congress was not swayed by the reactions to the Smoot-Hawley bill abroad. The average tariff for dutiable and hitherto exempt goods rose to 19 percent, and duties on some articles soared to an unprecedented 55 percent. Exemptions, on the other hand, were widened slightly. Higher duties were thus levied on fewer products.

With memories of the 1922 Fordney-McCumber Act still fresh, the Netherlands legation kept a close watch on developments from the start. Dr. J.H. Van Roijen, the head of the Netherlands legation in Washington, stayed in the background, and after discussions with Van Aken, left resistance to the business community. The United States regarded the fixing of tariffs as an internal matter, and Van Roijen felt that diplomatic steps could have the opposite effect to that intended. As Congressman Willis C. Hawley, one of the sponsors of the bill, stated in the *U.S. Daily*, "The protective tariff is a domestic question. Foreign interests have no inherent right to trade in our markets ... The admission of imports is an act of comity. We alone have a right to say what shall happen in this market and the conditions on which outsiders may enter the trade". The State Department had the impression that Van Roijen was intent on ensuring that he could not later be accused of having done too little for the interests of Dutch trade. In his discussions with American diplomats, his grasp of details left much to be desired. All in all, it was clear that it would be left to American importers to defend the Netherlands' interests.

It was obvious from the moment when the tariff law was first mentioned that Congress would take little account of foreign interests. The first hearing on oils and fats was arranged at such short notice that the Delft Glue and Gelatine Company was the sole foreign manufacturer that managed to be present on January 9, 1929. The other thirty witnesses, speaking on behalf of the American trade unions, urged the imposition of a uniform tariff of 45 percent on all edible and inedible oils and fats. The fact that, deprived of imports, the soap industry would be unable to meet the domestic demand, which would probably push prices up by 50 percent, was disregarded. The hearings were conducted with such haste that neither foreign firms nor their U.S. associates got the chance to adequately present their case. In addition, the term fixed for appeals was four weeks from the date of publication of the transcript of the hearings.

Though the four-week term had expired, Pieter Six utilized his visit to New York in April, 1929 to raise the question of Dutch exports in informal discussions with various authorities in Washington. Funds had been contributed by the strawboard and stearic acid manufacturers, the diamond trade, and the Amsterdam Trade Association. The plan was for Van Roijen to press for a counter-hearing to enable Six to put the case for Dutch interests through American connections. Given the speed with which the bill was passed by the House of Representatives, it is unlikely that Six could have achieved anything in Washington. The most important result was manifested later.

With undertakings from these sectors of industry in his pocket, Six retained a lawyer, Edward A. Brand, as tariff law advisor to the Chamber. Brand was to monitor events both during and after Congress's deliberations; more specifically, he was to prevent American competitors from repeating the tactics deployed after 1922, making improper use of the many new customs regulations to curb imports. Experience had shown that foreign exporters only took action after an irreversible decision was made. The sooner the dangers were detected, the better the chances of a successful defense. By the summer of 1929 Brand's work proved to entail much more than agreed with Six. The debates on the tariff bill were more protracted than expected, and Brand maintained regular contact with the legation, Van Aken, and the Chamber in Amsterdam, visited importers and agents of Dutch firms in New York, drew up briefs, and talked to members of Congress and foreign diplomats.

In August the Chamber suggested to the government and the business community in the Netherlands that he be offered a permanent contract. Fourteen firms subscribed more than $ 1,000 for the first half of 1930. But the hope of retaining his services ebbed with the economic tide. In 1931 the Chamber had to make two appeals to raise enough money for his fees for the whole of that year. The association with Brand came to an end the following year. He was prepared to lower his fee substantially, but the recession made it impossible to raise even $ 750.

Brand made extensive use of the possibilities for foreign manufacturers to lodge appeals. The main conditions were that production costs in the Netherlands must be no lower than those in the United States, and the products in question must be of superior quality to those of American competitors. Van Aken drew up a number of appeals for the Netherlands Rayon Company Ltd. in Breda, and some were sent directly from the Netherlands to Van Roijen for delivery to the State Department. Petitioners included Norit, Inc., the Netherlands Match Manufacturers Association, Leerdam Glassworks, Inc., and Groningen Brickworks, Inc. What further steps were taken is unknown. The envoy tried to persuade the diplomatic representatives of a few other countries to act in concert with the Netherlands, but Switzerland, Belgium, Norway, and Sweden were not in favor of synchronizing their protests. Though official protests were possible only after the bill had been passed by the House of Representatives and the Senate, many countries lodged an appeal after the first vote in the House in May, 1929. After conferring with the Netherlands government and Van Aken, Van Roijen dropped the idea of resistance. Public support for Congress was too great for any hope of success, as the Swiss envoy found to his dismay. His unequivocal condemnation of the bill prompted a group of senators to ask President Hoover to declare him *persona non grata*. So Van Roijen went no further than a "summarizing *démarche*" on May 29.[17] The Smoot-Hawley Tariff Act was passed by Congress on June 13, 1930. The Senate had proposed 1,253 amendments, with the result that it became the longest-debated and most amended tariff law in American history. It was signed by President Hoover on June 17, at the end of the last upsurge in the American economy before the Depression really set in.

An advertisement for Norit products in the late 1930's

Norit built a factory for charcoal filters in Jacksonville, Florida in 1934.

The new tariff law had serious consequences for international trade. The increases caused dismay in Europe, and some thirty countries delivered a diplomatic protest. Without ever officially confirming it, a number of European countries then proceeded to raise their own tariffs, or switched their trade to other countries by means of trade agreements. Partly for that reason, the United States was relatively hard hit by the decline in world trade.[18] Dutch exports to the United States declined between 1928 and 1930 from $ 83.6 million to $ 51.1 million. They reached their lowest ebb in 1934, when the figure was no higher than $ 22.3 million.

The rapidly deteriorating world trade situation compelled the Netherlands to abandon its free trade policy in 1931. All efforts to turn the protectionist tide by means of international cooperation had failed, and the disadvantages of possessing no trade policy weapons were becoming ever more apparent. After the relatively propitious development between 1929 and 1931, when the Netherlands increased its share of the world market, exports fell precipitously from 1932 on. Attempts to limit the damage by joint action with Belgium and the Scandinavian countries came to nothing. After the failure of the World Economic Conference in London in the summer of 1933, the Netherlands government was on its own. Faced with the fact that it was not a temporary decline, it exchanged the waiting attitude adopted at the beginning of the recession for a more active policy. In order to acquire a weapon for use in negotiations, import quotas were fixed for a large number of commodities. Lack of experience in pursuing a trade policy and an inadequate knowledge of economics stood in the way of a goal-oriented policy for quite some time. In 1932 economic policy was centralized in the new Ministry of Economic Affairs and Agriculture, which established immediate contact with business circles. In November of that year the employers organizations set up a central institute for the promotion of foreign trade. Headed by Folkert Posthuma, the former Minister for Agriculture, Trade and Industry, its mission was to advise the government on the many bilateral trade agreements under negotiation since the start of the recession. It acted in close collaboration with the Chamber during the Netherlands' negotiations with the United States on a new trade treaty in 1935.

The United States was one of the countries with which the Netherlands had conducted similar negotiations in the early 1920s, after the U.S. government had unilaterally terminated the former agreement in 1919. Trade policy had meanwhile changed considerably. Up to that time the United States had only been interested in agreements in which concessions applied solely to the other party. Europe's higher post-war tariffs however constituted a threat to American exports, so in 1922 it was decided that trade policy would henceforth be based on the principle of unconditional most-favored-nation status, allowing the United States to share in the concessions agreed by a treaty partner with other countries.

Negotiations with a number of countries, including the Netherlands, were opened in 1923.[19] The American commercial attaché in The Hague, Samuel H. Cross, had asked Nederbragt in October if the Netherlands would be interested in an agreement on an unconditional most-favored-nation basis. From the free trade point of view, the Netherlands welcomed all moves facilitating the liberalization of international trade, so Cross was able to report affirmatively to Washington.

Prior to the negotiations, the Trade Division set about listing the wishes and grievances of Dutch exporters. Not surprisingly, since the negative effects of the sharply increased American customs duties were apparent in the 1923 trade figures, they placed particular emphasis on lower tariffs. The manufacturers organizations stated through the Industrial Council that they would welcome an agreement "based on a mutual most-favored-nation status in its purest form". Dutch firms like Philips in Eindhoven, De Sphinx potteries in Maastricht, and the Delft Glue and Gelatine Company in Delft, which exported large quantities of goods to the United States, informed the Foreign Ministry of the damage they had suffered from the recent tariff increases. The Dutch business community stated their views most unequivocally in the Trade Agreements Review Committee, the consultative body in which the top officials of the relevant ministries regularly met with the Amsterdam and Rotterdam Chambers of Commerce and the Industrial Council. There was no place in these meetings for specific sectors of industry and commerce, as the Chamber discovered when it tried to approach the committee on behalf of the exporters of fats, oils, and oilseed.

Before the negotiations on the Friendship, Trade, and Consular Rights Treaty could get under way, there were two complications which almost made American proposals of whatever kind unacceptable in advance. While the United States had not revoked the 1852 Shipping Treaty shielding Dutch merchant ships from discriminatory American shipping legislation, goods transported on American ships were given a 10 percent reduction on railroad charges to protect the fast-growing American merchant fleet against foreign competition. Rather than sacrifice shipping interests, the Dutch government was prepared to opt for no agreement. The second difficulty arose from the United States' refusal to allow the unconditional most-favored-nation clause to be applicable to Cuba, Puerto Rico, the Canal Zone, and the Philippines, even though it would have to apply in respect of the Dutch colonies. Moreover, on closer scrutiny it appeared that most-favored-nation status was less unconditional than it seemed. The legation came into possession of a memorandum written by the Austrian chargé d'affaires about a similar draft agreement. The federal government had no say in how individual states chose to interpret international agreements, which was usually more according to the letter than the spirit of the law. Hence equal rights based on national legislation were virtually ruled out.

Tiffany
In the latter part of the 1920's , the American architect Frank Lloyd Wright was commissioned by a Dutch firm, The Leerdam Glasfabriek Company, to create a collection of glasware , dinner service and tabletop accesories. Although the architect completed sixteen designs, only one was actually produced. Based on octagonal and hexagonal patterns, the designs were too complicated for glass blowers to render with available technology.

149

So now the question for the government was what the United States in fact did have to offer. The answer was preciously little. The 1922 Act did not provide for the lower tariffs wanted by industry and commerce. Furthermore, a new agreement would not put an end to the discriminatory practices which Dutch agricultural products had endured since 1916. To guard against the introduction of plant diseases from Europe, U.S. imports of a growing list of plant and bulb species were restricted, and a practically complete ban on the main bulb varieties had been announced for 1926. The Dutch government and horticulturalists were basically right to think that these measures were largely designed to protect American growers. The Netherlands could furnish an almost absolute guarantee that its plants and bulbs were free of disease and other impurities. In the light of the large balance of trade deficit and the unrestricted entry of American agricultural products into the Netherlands, it was a politically sensitive issue, but as the low tariff level always made it possible to claim most-favored-nation status, a decision was soon reached.[20] The proposal would be rejected if the United States persisted in claiming privileges for its shipping and in discriminating against Dutch horticultural products.

The Dutch government felt it had made the right decision when it learned that other countries had also declared the U.S. proposals to be unacceptable. It suggested that a general most-favored-nation arrangement be affirmed in an Exchange of Notes.

U.S. Secretary of State Charles Evans Hughes agreed to the counterproposal without demur when De Graeff, the Dutch envoy, officially informed him of the Netherlands' objections to the draft agreement in May 1924. In February, in a debate on the agreement concluded with Germany, the Senate had undermined the U.S. position by adopting an amendment providing for preferential treatment for American merchant shipping. This move had endangered the entire agreement. With presidential elections approaching in November and the trade agreement with Germany in effect rejected by the Senate, Hughes took the hand extended to him by the Netherlands. Though a short agreement was unacceptable, he wrote to De Graeff that he understood the United States would now "apply most-favored-nation treatment to the commerce between the two countries. The United States, for its part, does not contemplate making any departure from that principle".

This declaration formed the basis for trade between the Netherlands and the United States up to the 1930s. Interest in a new agreement revived in 1933, when the Netherlands was in danger of losing its informal most-favored-nation status through far-reaching changes in U.S. trade policy. In the interim years the Netherlands Foreign Ministry was constantly aware of the lack of a legal foundation for trade relations, but had no wish to resume the talks in view of the unsatisfactory U.S. agreements policy. Small but proud, the Netherlands did not intend to join the ranks of the vanquished in the first world war. If others were prepared to negotiate on the basis of America's proposal, that was their affair, but as the Foreign Ministry stated, "... it may not be said that the model was accepted by the defeated countries plus the Netherlands."

Since the deadlock in the negotiations on a new agreement in 1924, trade between the two countries had proceeded on a general most-favored-nation basis. In 1929 the Hoover administration approached Nederbragt about the prospect of reopening the negotiations. The subsequent talks were broken off soon after they started because the United States still refused to concede preferential treatment for Dutch shipping. Negotiations were finally resumed when President Franklin D. Roosevelt decided to boost America's exports by lowering tariff rates and concluding bilateral trade agreements.

Barely four years after the enactment of the Smoot-Hawley tariff law, the Roosevelt administration abruptly changed course in 1934 with the introduction of the Reciprocal Trade Agreement Act. If it is not altogether rightly remembered for its highly protectionist nature, it is equally incorrect to regard it as an instrument used by the United States to assail international trade barriers. The American market was still shielded from foreign competition, and the 1930 tariffs remained largely intact. Just the same, the Reciprocal Trade Agreement Act marked a partial departure from the former tariff policy, ending the trend of ever higher tariffs and curbing the influence of lobbyists in Congress by delegating more negotiating powers to the executive branch of government. Negotiations on new trade agreements were opened with the first countries in 1934. Though also invited to begin talks in that year, the Netherlands waited until July, 1935.

150

The Netherlands Employers Federation and the Chamber had already alerted the Minister for Labor and Economic Affairs, T.J. Verschuur, to the change in trade policy in May, 1933. In 1934, soon after the passing of the Reciprocal Trade Agreement Act, representatives of Dutch industry and commerce met to discuss the question of negotiations. Talks on an agreement with Germany earlier that year had made it plain that the Ministry was heavily dependent on the business community for information. They met at the offices of the Chamber at 292-294 Herengracht, Amsterdam. The Chamber was represented by president Westerman, vice-president Everwijn, executive committee member Von Baumhauer, and secretary Six; the Institute for the Promotion of Foreign Trade by Folkert Posthuma; and the Netherlands Employers Federation by the former prime minister Pieter W.A. Cort van der Linden and the chairman, H.P. Gelderman, a textiles manufacturer. F.H. Fentener van Vlissingen attended as director of the Steenkolen Handels Vereniging (SHV) and president of the International Chamber of Commerce.

The aim of the meeting was to list the wishes of industry and commerce and to influence the composition of the Dutch delegation to the talks. A questionnaire was sent to the business community a few days later. Hearings began on May 8, 1934. Those taking part included the Royal Netherlands Iron and Steel Foundries of IJmuiden, the Glue and Gelatine Company Ltd. of Delft, the Droste Cocoa and Chocolate Company Ltd. of Haarlem, the Netherlands Association of Flour Manufacturers and the Holland Bulb Exporters Association. The Ministry of Economic Affairs was informed of the findings at the end of May.

Droste Cocoa tin,
c. 1935
Six Archives

The hearings revealed a number of facts: the 1930 tariff increase greatly exceeded the difference in cost price on which it should have been based; the depreciation of the dollar in 1933 had adversely affected the competitiveness of Dutch industry; and the sharp drop in world prices added to the burden of the fixed customs duties levied on specific products. Since the majority of Dutch and East Indies exports were not competitive with American home-produced goods, there was a good chance that the United States would be prepared to make concessions. At about the same time the attention of the U.S. State Department was drawn to the Netherlands' favorable treatment of American trade since the introduction of import restrictions in 1932. In addition, it was announced that countries with which bilateral trade agreements had recently been concluded could anticipate larger quotas, making negotiations more attractive for the United States as well.

In May, 1934, the new Dutch envoy, Esquire Hendrik M. van Haersma de With, asked the State Department if the United States still accorded most-favored-nation treatment to Dutch trade in accordance with the 1924 arrangements.[21] Under-Secretary of State William Philips made use of the opportunity to suggest regulating the existing situation in an agreement.[22]
The United States had little cause for complaint about the Netherlands' treatment of its exports, and there was no question of discrimination aimed specifically at the United States. Van Haersma de With replied that his government was not likely to refuse the proposal, and the State Department promptly set the wheels in motion. The envoy was handed a draft agreement on May 24, 1934, but with the prospect of Congress passing the Reciprocal Trade Agreement Act at the end of the month, the Netherlands' interest waned. In the hope that the Netherlands was intent on acquiring the status of most-favored-nation without delay, the United States suggested the inclusion of provisions on both tariffs and quantitative import restrictions in the agreement. The Roosevelt administration could practically guarantee that it would be passed by Congress before the start of the summer recess in June. Point by point negotiations could follow later.

The Ministry of Economic Affairs was less eager than Van Haersma de With because the Reciprocal Trade Agreement Act specified that every American concession must be matched by one of equal value. Since the Dutch tariffs were already fixed, a wider quota was the only possibility, and that could be waived if it was also covered by reciprocal most-favored-nation treatment. It was true that the agreement would only be valid for three years, but Economic Affairs had no intention of relinquishing one of its few bargaining chips. Negotiating in partnership with the Dutch East Indies, which had a balance of trade surplus, would put the Netherlands in a stronger position. The Ministry even envisaged the possibility of tackling some of the import restrictions based on hygiene considerations. Rather than rush into an agreement, it preferred to wait and observe the further development of U.S. trade policy.

The talks ended with the assurance that the Netherlands belonged to the small group of countries with which agreements would be concluded. The U.S. State Department wisely omitted to add that the Netherlands was the twenty-fourth and last on the list.

Though the talks were ended, the committee dealing with the questionnaire conferred with Netherlands Prime Minister Colijn and decided to go ahead with the listing of the business community's grievances and wishes. The Ministry turned down the idea of sending a delegation of businessmen to the United States as unofficial representatives of the government to gauge the mood of U.S. government and business circles, regarding it as an attempt by Von Baumhauer and others to have a hand in the negotiations. It did not object to the activities of the committee, but made it very clear that the formulation of policy was a matter for the Ministry alone. The committee completed its work at the end of October, in time to hand the report to Van Haersma de With, who was returning to Washington after home leave.

The American legation in The Hague noticed in the second half of 1934 that the Netherlands' attitude to the allocation of extra quotas was hardening. In anticipation of negotiations, it was manoeuvering to strengthen its position. The United States, in its turn, let it be known that it regarded the Netherlands and the East Indies as a single entity. That being the case, it considered its large trade surplus with the Netherlands to be offset by the colony's healthy balance of trade.

On December 12, 1934, it was announced in The Hague and Washington that talks would begin in a few months' time. The Ministry of Economic Affairs informed the Chamber that besides the representatives of the relevant ministries, there were places in the delegation for Westerman and Six. The invitation did not include Von Baumhauer. The risk of a conflict of interest was considered to be too great, for as the director of a subsidiary of the Standard Oil Company of California he was involved in its efforts to procure oil concessions in Dutch New Guinea.[23] Personal considerations probably played a role as well. Both Hirschfeld and Lamping, who was to head the delegation, had been irritated by Von Baumhauer's insistence on broad-based negotiations in the preparatory discussions in which everything would be on the table. He was deaf to the argument that by and large the Netherlands had few worthwhile concessions to make. Moreover, he had a personal stake in two points which he claimed would put the Netherlands in a stronger negotiating position. He repeatedly urged granting the New Guinea oil concession to Standard Oil, and kept raising the subject of the double taxation to which Dutch dividends from investments in the United States were liable. He had been retained by a number of firms and individuals to represent their interests with the Ministry of Finance.[24]

It was a great disappointment for Von Baumhauer. He had been involved with the issues from the first, and now felt deprived of his just reward. With Six's support, he threatened to leave the Chamber if the Board accepted the invitation. Westerman calmed things down by offering Von Baumhauer his own place. But he was passed over again, for the Economic Ministry then invited Fentener van Vlissingen to take Westerman's place in the delegation.

As the negotiations approached, the Dutch government grew ever more pessimistic. In presenting a list of their wishes, the business community in fact fixed their hopes on an overall tariff reduction of 50 percent. The Netherlands had little to offer in exchange. Tariffs were everywhere the same, and left no more than minimal scope for reductions. The quotas were set in accordance with each commodity's share in Dutch imports in 1931. The Netherlands was therefore largely dependent on incidental concessions of importance to the other party. To temper the expectations somewhat, one of the staff of the trade and industry department quietly contacted the American legation. In the end, the Ministry decided to compile a list of desiderata of such length that it might be able to extract a few concessions. The United States stated that it wished to discuss "everything constituting a barrier to international trade, such as quotas". It was agreed that the concessions required would be announced at the beginning of April, 1935. A delegation could be sent to Washington a few weeks beforehand.

However, as the U.S. State Department was also negotiating with a large number of other countries, and because there was growing internal dissatisfaction with the Reciprocal Trade Agreement Act, the preparations took much longer than foreseen, delaying the exchange of desiderata until May 15. The members of the questionnaire committee were deeply disappointed. Von Baumhauer, Fentener van Vlissingen and Everwijn had expected back in February that the negotiations would start at any moment and would take only a few weeks. When delay again seemed imminent at the end of May, this time caused by the Netherlands, Secretary of State Cordell Hull stated that he saw no reason why an agreement should not be completed within two weeks. One glance at the American list of desiderata was enough for the Ministry to know that this would be out of the question. In addition, the Roosevelt administration obviously knew little about the Netherlands' trade agreement policy, and had learned nothing from the 1934 negotiations, for it again proposed extending general most-favored-nation treatment to the quota policy. The Netherlands therefore suggested holding preliminary talks on the subject of trade policy in order to determine if there was a basis for more detailed negotiations. Only after Secretary of State Hull had given an explicit assurance that the difficulties were not insurmountable, and Emmett had reported a favorable climate for negotiations in Washington, did the Netherlands Ministry of Economic Affairs agree to go ahead. The Dutch delegation was to arrive in Washington no later than August 1. Fentener van Vlissingen withdrew from the delegation, and on Posthuma's recommendation Von Baumhauer was invited to take his place. As it happened, however, the progress made in the talks was such that neither he nor the other representatives of the business community went to the United States. So Lamping left alone at the end of July with the aim of concluding a trade agreement with the United States according to general most-favored-nation status.

A new Dutch body, the Study Group on Negotiations with the United States of America, met on July 29, 1935. Chaired by Posthuma and composed of government officials and representatives of industry and commerce, it examined the proposals put forward as the talks dragged on endlessly. It had seemed at first that Cordell Hull was right in thinking that the agreement could be concluded in a matter of weeks. For internal political reasons, the U.S. government badly needed a new trade policy success. It therefore wished to conclude the talks as soon as possible, and agreed to accept the existing U.S. share of Dutch imports. As the Reciprocal Trade Agreement Act was however designed first and foremost to create wider trade possibilities, the U.S. government needed reciprocal concessions to defend the agreement in Congress, and was prepared to concede a substantial number of points provided the Netherlands did the same.

To ensure that the talks moved forward at a good pace, the Cabinet had decided that Lamping would at first be accompanied by just a few officials. The rest of the delegation could follow once agreement was reached on the matter of general trade policy. They were meanwhile kept informed by the Study Group, on whose behalf Von Baumhauer, Six and E. Henny, secretary of the Central Institute, invited several businessmen to state their views on America's concessions on August 10 and 12. On August 13 Lamping presented the Netherlands' counterproposals, which were based in part on the businessmen's favorable assessment.

As the U.S. government could have known from experience, they largely related to formal acknowledgements of the existing tariffs and quotas. But the Americans were very disappointed. If the Netherlands Ministry of Economic Affairs had cherished the hope that the United States would accept concessions that were in fact little more than symbolic, that hope was now dashed. Contrary to what Fentener van Vlissingen, Von Baumhauer and others had assumed, President Roosevelt proved to be no "friendly Santa Claus whose greatest pleasure is handing out trade policy concessions", as Lamping reported. He was at a loss to understand why they had thought the talks would yield "mountains of gold", and had even expected America to adapt its customs legislation to Dutch demands. It had all been wishful thinking. The United States was the only declared opponent of the protectionist trend that suited the deed to the word in its trade policy. The political rhetoric used by the Roosevelt administration in defense of the Reciprocal Trade Agreement Act must have been music to the ears of the hard-pressed Dutch exporters. They should have realized sooner that it sounded too good to be true.

The United States seems to have fallen into the same rhetorical trap. The Dutch government had indeed adopted the stance of a firm advocate of free trade, but in thinking the Netherlands would relinquish one of its few real bargaining chips, the American government displayed a lack of political insight. Why it ignored the various warning signs and so greatly overestimated the Netherlands' readiness to make concessions remains a mystery.

Having arrived in Washington, and with the talks under way, Lamping thought agreement could be reached. Both sides would have to be prepared to compromise. As things turned out, he was right. Politically, the American government could not afford the failure of talks even with a small country like the Netherlands. When the bargaining stage was reached, the financial consequences of every concession had to be weighed one against the other. The Ministry asked Six to compile a list of the concessions that would most benefit Dutch industry and commerce, and to specify the U.S. tariffs comprising the greatest obstacles to trade. During the rest of the talks the Ministry kept the Chamber informed of all developments. The Study Group met again in mid-September. The concessions offered failed to meet America's demands, and the talks again seemed on the verge of collapse. Acting on the Study Group's recommendations, Lamping conceded a few extra points, but he was not at all optimistic about the outcome. It must have been one of the few occasions when the Ministry was in full agreement with Von Baumhauer. They considered the differences to be so great that it might be better to break off the negotiations, and to try again at a more auspicious time. But it did not come to this. The political pressure on both sides was too great to admit of failure. The United States at length agreed to the Netherlands' proposal that quotas be set for automobiles and spare parts. It was a minor victory for Von Baumhauer, for with the immense political influence of the automobile industry in mind, he had been hammering this point for months.

By late October, after four months, there seemed to be no further obstacles to the signing of the agreement. All that still remained was to complete the drafting of the text, to clear up a few details, and to await the signing of a trade agreement between the United States and Canada. Trade policy was coming under increasing pressure in the United States, and the Roosevelt administration decided to give public opinion a few weeks' rest before announcing the next agreement. It was signed on December 20, 1935 by Secretary of State Cordell Hull and Lamping, and was welcomed in both countries. Parliament noted with satisfaction that this was the first such agreement in years that liberalized rather than restricted trade. Apart from the most-favored-nation aspect, American tariffs for more than fifty Dutch and East Indies products were reduced, in twenty-six instances by 50 percent, the maximum permissible reduction. A solution had also been found to the quarantine question. Henceforth, in the event of the bulb trade being affected by new non-tariff regulations, a committee of experts would give a binding decision. The Netherlands and the East Indies for their part set tariffs for 52 products, halved customs duties on fruit and consolidated other duties on agricultural products. In addition, the Netherlands would import up to 5 percent of its wheat and wheat flour from the United States provided the price was competitive.

All in all, Dutch exports to the United States rose appreciably in 1936. The Netherlands cannot be held solely responsible for the length of time it took to reach agreement, and for the difficulties encountered on the way. Neither government had a free hand to act as it wished because of the pressure exerted on it to reserve the home market for home-produced goods. The Netherlands Ministry of Economic Affairs did not allow itself to be misled by the Reciprocal Trade Agreement Act, and insisted that tariff reductions could only be discussed in respect of goods of which the Netherlands was the principal foreign supplier, while the United States wished to confine the discussions to goods that were no threat to domestic production.

Both before and during the negotiations the relationship between the Chamber and the Ministry of Economic Affairs was very close. Even though neither Six nor Baumhauer was in the delegation, their specialized knowledge of Dutch exports to the United States made them valued members of the Study Group on Negotiations with the United States of America. They had no real influence in the matter of policy which, as it made quite plain, was the Ministry's exclusive domain. The Chamber's participation in the talks in the Netherlands proved in the following year to have other advantages besides earning the good opinion of H.C.J.H. Gelissen, Minister of Trade, Industry and Shipping. The growth of trade in 1936 facilitated new promotional activities which included the opening of a center for Dutch interests in the Rockefeller Center in New York.

The Holland House in New York

The 1935 trade agreement opened up new opportunities for Dutch trade and the Chamber. In combination with the revival of world trade and the currency devaluation which the Netherlands effected on September 26, 1936 - the last country in Europe to do so - it led to a marked growth in exports to the United States. Thanks to its greater competitiveness exports rose by 38 percent in 1936. The rise in imports was 11 percent.

During a short stopover in New York on the return journey to the Netherlands, some of the delegates conferred with representatives of the Netherlands Chamber of Commerce in New York and members of the Dutch business community on ways and means of capitalizing on the wider opportunities for exports. The J. Walter Thompson advertising agency was engaged to plan a collective advertising campaign for such commodities as cheese, herring, cocoa, bulbs, seed, and other agricultural products. Businessmen and officials of the relevant ministries met at the office of the Chamber in Amsterdam on March 25, 1936 to discuss the campaign plan. The sole point on which they agreed was the need for more advertising in the United States. In all other respects there were wide differences of opinion. Each individual sector wanted to conduct its own campaign, and was not interested in the idea of a joint presentation of Dutch products. And if advertising was to be focused on separate products, they saw little point in setting up a Holland House in New York, the proposal for which they had in fact met to discuss. The annual costs of such a center for government and business activities were estimated between $ 50,000 and $ 70,000.

Having rejected the scheme for a joint or closely coordinated advertising campaign, some industrial sectors enlisted the aid of American advertising agencies for campaigns of their own, and others decided to take no action at all. It was the devaluation of the guilder that breathed new life into the Holland House project.

The devaluation of the dollar in 1933 had nullified much of the effect of the declining income in guilders of the Chamber in New York. In 1936, however, a serious financial crisis seemed imminent. In the preceding years the gold bloc, i.e. the group of countries, including the Netherlands, which had continued to peg their respective currencies to the gold standard, had been crumbling. The question was no longer whether, but when the Netherlands would abandon the gold standard. This issue had precipitated a brief Cabinet crisis in 1935, when Lamping was on his way to Washington, and the anticipated devaluation of the guilder had been in the news ever since. Because the Chamber was heavily dependent on the exchange rate of the guilder, prudence dictated that the Chamber would seek new sources of income, especially when the revenues of the Chamber in New York dropped to $ 10,000 in 1936. The American contributions had shrunk to less than $ 2000. With such slender financial resources, the majority of the Board of Directors considered it to be impossible to deal properly with the enquiries that had been flooding in since the beginning of the recession. Weary of the constant financial uncertainty, they decided in 1937 to make a last appeal to the Dutch business community. If extra resources were not promptly forthcoming, the Chamber would have to close down. In the event, it was the Dutch government that came to the rescue.

The Chamber heard in August, 1936 that American bulb importers had raised $ 10,000 for general advertising purposes. The drive was initiated by John T. Scheepers, a bulb importer of Dutch descent. Part of the proceeds were earmarked for a Holland House. When it then became known that the Holland-America Line was contributing another $ 10,000, Von Baumhauer and Six swung into action. Up to the date of the opening of Holland House in the Rockefeller Center in March, 1940, they worked day and night to get it off the ground. They decided to find suitably prestigious premises to accommodate the largest possible number of Dutch firms and government organizations. Besides the consulate-general, the Netherlands Chamber of Commerce, and the office of the Netherlands Railways, they hoped the new premises would house the agents of the smaller exporters, the various shipping companies and KLM Royal Dutch Airlines. This would make it possible to follow the example of Britain and other countries by occupying premises in a prestigious building near the Rockefeller Center on 5th Avenue which would be in line with the status of the Netherlands as a leading economic power. Holland House would be an asset to Dutch exhibitors at the 1939 New York World Fair, and Von Baumhauer and Six also felt it would enhance the general image of the Netherlands.

D. A. HOOGENDIJK & Co.

640 KEIZERSGRACHT

AMSTERDAM

HIGH CLASS PAINTINGS BY OLD MASTERS

High class paintings by old masters were advertised to sell to the United States (c. 1930) Important Art Collections were formed during the beginning of the 20th century, like Getty, Mellon, Vanderbilt, Havemeyer, Frick and others.

155

First of all, the business community had to be drawn into the project. Even with firm pledges for $ 20,000, this was more difficult than expected. Most of the firms that were suitable candidates found it unnecessary and too expensive to move to 5th Avenue. By the beginning of 1937 the only commitments had come from the Holland-America Line, whose manager, W.H. de Monchy, had recently become president of the Chamber in Amsterdam, from the commercial representatives of the Dutch East Indies in the United States, from KLM Royal Dutch Airlines, and from the agents of Dutch cheese and bulb exporters. To get things moving, the Netherlands Minister of Trade, Industry and Shipping was asked for an annual subsidy of $ 12,500, a quarter of the $ 50,000 annual budget. Efforts were meanwhile still being made to interest private enterprise in the project. Gelissen approved the application sooner than expected, and at the same time increased the subsidy for the Chamber from Dfl. 8,000 to Dfl. 15,000, raising the government's contribution to the dissemination of general and commercial information on the Netherlands in the United States.

This gesture seems to have been motivated by economic and political developments in Europe. The Netherlands stood to gain from better relations with the United States. Economic revival was at last on the way, and the Netherlands together with other small European states was seeking to end international protectionism. World prices were no longer rising and exports benefited accordingly, displaying a growth of 19 percent in real terms in 1937. Partly owing to a sharp downturn in the U.S. economy in May, the tide had turned before the end of 1937. An attempt to liberalize trade with Belgium and the Scandinavian countries encountered opposition from Britain, while the German market, the Netherlands' main outlet, was becoming increasingly protectionist. As free trade lost ground in Europe, the Dutch government and industry and commerce became increasingly interested in the American market. Even in times of economic decline its dimensions were such as to offer almost boundless possibilities for the comparatively small Dutch export trade. For political reasons as well, closer relations with the United States were desirable. In contrast to the indecisive attitude of most European governments to Germany and Italy, President Roosevelt left no doubt about his anti-German and anti-fascist feelings. As the storm clouds gathered over Europe, the United States stood firm as a bastion of democracy.

In October, 1937, with the definite assurance that the subsidies would be paid in 1938, Von Baumhauer and Six could start looking for suitable premises for Holland House. Time was pressing. Office rents were soaring in anticipation of the World Fair in two years' time. Worried about the limited interest shown by the Chamber in New York in the Holland House, Von Baumhauer and Six went to New York in January, 1938 to look into the real estate situation and to raise more funds. They also wished to discuss the financial situation that had again become an issue. The arrangement reached in 1929 had been dropped in 1933, and New York was again in the dark on the allocation of resources.

The New York Board of Directors felt it had been pushed aside in the matter of Holland House, and it also felt that its share of the joint budget was too small. As Six and Von Baumhauer had included the Chamber's revenues in the financial estimates for Holland House, it even seemed to the Board that the intention was to outflank it altogether.

During Six and Von Baumhauer's stay in New York the differences between the two organizations were not settled. The psychological distance between Amsterdam and New York stood in the way. But New York was not entirely free from blame either. It transpired that Van Aken had told the Board little or nothing about the Holland House project, and it knew nothing at all about the $ 12,500 state subsidy. It may have been simply an oversight on his part, bearing in mind that he had to manage the Chamber's affairs practically single-handedly. The local business community's lack of enthusiasm for Holland House probably led him to underestimate its viability.

The first reaction in New York to the explanation of Six and Von Baumhauer was to try to curb the influence of the Chamber in Amsterdam and to set up Holland House themselves. How the busy Board members proposed to do this is unknown, but it would certainly have meant the end of the project before it was properly off the ground. However, Von Baumhauer refused to be outmaneuvered, and set off with Six in search of new donors and office premises. They were helped by Heineken's agent, Leo von Münching, and Scheepers, the flower bulb importer who had raised the first $ 10,000. The New York

Chamber was incensed by their activities. They kept it informed of their progress, but in the Board's view what it was told was too little and too late. The conflict did not enhance the reputation of the Chamber among local Dutch businessmen.

The personal animosity aroused by Von Baumhauer's conduct, which the Board considered to be wilful and uncooperative, cast its shadow over the later relationship between New York and Amsterdam, notwithstanding the success of Holland House and von Baumhauer's many earlier achievements in the promotion of trade.

Six and Von Baumhauer spent several months in the United States. Using the many contacts established through his legal practice, Von Baumhauer interested the Rockefeller Center in the idea of a Netherlands Building to accommodate Holland House, and procured donations from various firms including Standard Oil of California, Standard Oil of New Jersey, Standard Vacuum Oil Corporation, Shell Union Oil Corporation, the International Nickel Company and North American Philips.[25] The preparations were completed with the founding of the Holland House Corporation. Many prominent businessmen were invited to join the Board. In addition to the presidents of the above companies, those who accepted included Winthrop W. Aldrich, president of the Board of Directors of Chase National Bank, and Thomas J. Watson, the founder of IBM and president of the Netherland-America Foundation. When Von Baumhauer returned to the Netherlands in the summer of 1938, Six stayed on to round off the preparations. They had succeeded in establishing a financial basis for the project, assembling a distinguished Board of Directors, and obtaining a building in the most prestigious office complex in the world. They had accomplished what they set out to do. At the forthcoming World Fair, the Netherlands could take what they considered to be its rightful place among the major economic powers.

The Holland House was a major factor in the deterioration of the relationship between the Chamber in Amsterdam and the Chamber in New York. The feelings of mistrust greeting Six and Von Baumhauer on their arrival in New York were further heightened by their activities. By leaving Six behind in New York, Von Baumhauer temporarily removed the linchpin holding the two Chambers together since 1929. After his visit to New York that year with Westerman, Six had been the person responsible for maintaining contact with New York, and in that time there had been no serious communication problems which, augmented almost automatically by the distance separating them, could have disrupted the collaboration between the two Chambers. But even for him it proved to be impossible to keep New York fully informed about everything, largely because of their different bookkeeping systems and the secret reserve fund accumulated by speculation on the exchange rate of the dollar. It was sometimes extremely difficult to convince the Chamber in New York that it was receiving its fair share of the joint revenues. While Six was in the United States, Von Baumhauer conducted the correspondence with New York, and continued to do so after the secretary returned to the Netherlands at the end of 1938. The effects were soon felt.

Financial problems in New York were at the root of the final break between the two Chambers. Even though the Dutch state subsidy had been doubled, the Chamber in New York again had a sizeable deficit at the end of 1938. In November the Board appointed a committee to visit the Netherlands and demand clarification of the financial situation from the president of the Chamber in Amsterdam, W.H. de Monchy. As they saw it, it was the Chamber in New York where the trade promotion activities actually took place. So if adequate resources for the proper promotion of trade were needed anywhere, they were needed at the Chamber in New York and not in Amsterdam. In the Board's opinion, deficits should henceforth be financed by the Chamber in Amsterdam, which after all was supposed to act in a supportive capacity. If the Chamber in Amsterdam was unable to provide the resources needed at the Chamber in New York, there was no point in continuing the financial partnership. The Board of Directors of the Chamber in Amsterdam responded at once by asking the newly-appointed envoy to Washington to act as intermediary. All hope of repairing the rift seemed to be gone before Esquire Alexander Loudon could offer his services to the Chamber in New York. After conferring with the executive committee, Von Baumhauer proposed a partnership agreement that would have reduced the Chamber in New York to a mere branch office. The Chamber in New York, in consultation with the Economic Information Division, rejected this out of hand. Van der Kooy, head of the Economic Information Division, informed the Chamber in Amsterdam that the Dutch government would not allow the Chamber in New York to be dismantled. Greater coordination of the work of the two Chambers was obviously needed, but it was in the general interest that this task would be entrusted to the legation in Washington and the consulate-general in New York. It would seem that the objective of the Chamber in Amsterdam was to end the association while attributing the blame to the Chamber in New York. In that way it could retain the contributions of the business community in the Netherlands. This indeed proved to be the case.

The proposed partnership agreement not only exacerbated the conflict between the two Chambers, but also forced the government organizations in both countries to take sides. This time it was not a matter of an internal squabble between two private organizations; the issue at stake was control over two institutions, the Chamber of Commerce and the Holland House Corporation, representing the Netherlands. Because of the growing commercial and political tensions in Europe, the Netherlands government had come to appreciate their value. Van der Kooy had no doubt of the fact that "from the point of view of economic information ... a well-established, active Chamber of Commerce abroad is of greater importance than a financially sound Chamber in the Netherlands". The same was true for Holland House. The Netherlands government should help Holland House in every way for it to evolve into a central point for the greatest possible number of Dutch and East Indies interests, especially in a location as attractive as Rockefeller Center in New York. The coordination efforts of the Chamber in Amsterdam, whose Board of Directors was probably unaware of all the facts, should therefore be brought to a halt.

Advertisement of the Holland-America Line to visit the New York World Exhibition, c. 1935 Archives Holland-America Line

Assured of the support of the Netherlands government, the Board of the Chamber in New York began preparations for separating their finances from those of the organization in Amsterdam. They first tried to ascertain precisely in what financial situation the Chamber in New York found itself, which firms had explicitly stated that their donations were intended for the Chamber in New York, and whether there were reserve funds to which the Chamber in New York was entitled. The Chamber in New York had completely lost track of its revenues. An audit conducted by the accountant of the *Rotterdamsche Bankvereeniging* revealed that the reserve funds formed from the proceeds of dollar speculation had been used some time before to keep the Chamber in New York afloat. In the first six months of 1939 the two Chambers of Commerce drifted ever further apart, to the point where the Chamber in Amsterdam refused to collect subsidies and contributions for its counterpart in New York.

In April, 1939, the Chamber in Amsterdam again appealed to the Netherlands Minister for Economic Affairs to call a halt to "the excessive independence" displayed by the Chamber in New York, but the matter was already settled. Both Loudon and Van der Kooy had decided in favor of the Chamber in New York, even though "the quality of the activities of the Chamber in Amsterdam, looked at from the standpoint of Chamber of Commerce work, is many times superior to the work which is done in New York", and the Chamber in New York was "a very poor show". It could not be denied that "the poverty of the results ... has given to Mr. Von Baumhauer a certain right to criticize and to try to intervene". When Von Baumhauer's former partner Edward von Saher - in whose reports the above opinions were expressed - conducted a survey amongst the Dutch business community in New York at the request of the Netherlands government, he was taken aback by the reactions to any mention of Von Baumhauer. No one denied that he had achieved a great deal, or that the concept and establishment of Holland House were "without doubt remarkable", but he was intensely disliked. Von Saher reported, "It is considered by practically all the members of the Dutch colony here as a serious offense to have anything to do with Mr von Baumhauer".

Aware of the fact that the Chamber in New York was the focal point of Dutch trade promotion in the United States, the Dutch government had no choice but to back the Chamber in New York. The Board of Directors unanimously resolved at a special meeting on June 5, 1939 to sever all financial ties with the Chamber in Amsterdam; cooperation in the field of Dutch trade promotion would continue as before. The two Chambers were fated, as it were, to work together. The next step was to find new sources of income.[26] So a few weeks later the previous and incumbent presidents, Louis van Zelm and James G. Blaine, president of the Marine Midland Trust Company of New York, went to The Hague for consultations with the Netherlands Ministries of Foreign Affairs, Economic Affairs, and the Colonies. The latter agreed to pay the full 1940 subsidy of Dfl. 5000 to the Chamber in New York, and Van der Kooy would allocate half the subsidy of Dfl. 16,000 to the Chamber in Amsterdam just once more.

158

Unilever started its operations in the United States when Jurgens Margarine Works, part of today's Unilever conglomerate, participated in Kellogg Products of Buffalo, New York in 1917 to produce margarine products for the American market.

The separation between the two Chambers was complete by the end of 1939. Dutch trade promotion remained the only joint activity. The outbreak of the second world war on September 3, 1939 had an immediate impact on Dutch exports to the United States, and much of the ground recovered since 1935 was again lost in a short space of time. Having risen from over Dfl. 47 million in 1935 to Dfl. 65 million in 1936 and Dfl. 75 million in 1937, Dutch exports to the United States fell to Dfl. 54 million in 1939.[27]

The Holland House was opened at 10 Rockefeller Plaza on March 19, 1940. The war situation prevented Von Baumhauer and Six from attending the opening. Among the tenants were the Netherlands Chamber of Commerce in New York, the Netherlands Railways office, and the Netherland-America Foundation. The Netherlands government was represented by the consulate-general, but industry and commerce on only a small scale by KLM Royal Dutch Airlines, Lindetevis Stokvis and the Holland Bulb Industry. No expense had been spared in designing a handsome setting for exhibitions, concerts, and lectures, including a portrayal of Peter Stuyvesant in the central stairwell by the stained-glass artist Joep Nicolas.
But all further plans had to be abandoned when Germany invaded the Netherlands on May 10, 1940. Dutch exports to the United States came to a standstill on that day. It was to be five years before the free flow of trade between the two countries was restored. In July, 1940, the Chamber in Amsterdam suspended its operations. Edward von Saher, appointed president pro tempore of the Chamber in New York in May, had kept the Dutch government informed of the steps taken by the United States to freeze Dutch assets, the value of which was estimated at $ 1.2 billion. Trade between the United States and the Dutch East Indies went along as before, so the Netherlands Chamber of Commerce in New York continued to function until the colony was invaded by Japan in 1942. That meant the suspension of the Chamber's activities until trade between the Netherlands and the United States would be resumed after the war.

Notes

1. A commercial section headed by a career consul-general was set up at the Berlin legation in 1916. This example was followed in Washington and London in 1918, and in Brussels in 1920. Two commercial attachés were appointed by the Paris legation in 1919 to further Dutch economic interests at the Versailles Peace Conference.

2. They were stationed in Indianapoilis, Milwaukee, Cincinatti, Pittsburgh, Dallas, Detroit, Birmingham, and Cleveland. Four were lawyers, two were bankers, one was an importer, and one was a businessman.

3. The bulletin was compiled in collaboration with the publicity section of the Netherlands Chamber of Commerce in New York. The first issue of *Netherlands Commercial and Economic Bulletin for the Dutch Consular Officers and Trade Advisors* appeared in November, 1920.

4. Since the division of the Netherlands Ministry of Agriculture, Trade and Industry the Agriculture Department was also required to provide information. It was strictly limited to agricultural information, so that information on agriculture-related areas such as the potato flour industry was the responsibility of the Trade and Industry Division. In 1922 the Chambers of Commerce were placed on a different legal footing and were officially made responsible for providing information for industry and commerce. There were 36 regional Chambers of Commerce. Those in Amsterdam and Rotterdam had reading rooms which were used intensively. A more recent privately-run initiative was the Netherlands trade show center in Utrecht, founded in 1916.

5. The proponents of greater government involvement in the national economy were united in industrial employers' organizations such as the Netherlands Federation of Manufacturers, the Netherlands Employers Federation and the Roman Catholic Employers Association.

6. Membership: Germany 850, Belgium 550, France 350, Switzerland 250, Britain 200, and the Dutch Chambers of Commerce for America 490. The latter figure is double the figure appearing in the records of the Netherlands-American Chamber of Commerce in Amsterdam. The secretary-treasurer of the Federation was H. van Beeck Vollenhoven of the Netherlands Chamber of Commerce in South Africa. Founded in 1920, the Federation was the consultative body for the principal Chambers of Commerce abroad. In addition to the three in America, it represented the Chambers in Britain, Belgium, France, Germany, Italy, South Africa, and Switzerland, linking 2,700 of the 3,000 firms associated with the Dutch Chambers of Commerce abroad.

7. On the legal and administrative consequences of the establishment of a semi-governmental information service, the Amsterdam Chamber of Commerce stated: "The consequences may not be taken lightly, for anyone with any understanding of economic and statistical documentation knows the special importance of selecting, assorting and processing the facts and figures, and the demands that must be made in respect of capabilities and personal integrity. A methodological error can wreak havoc, and for that reason no Government may entrust this part of its task to others. Only government can guarantee that not the interests of groups, but solely the interests of the Netherlands will be the decisive factor in the preparations for policy."

8. The Economic Information Division consisted of six sections, concerned with trade policy, commercial information, Dutch industry, retail trades, shipping, and publications.

9. The United States interpretation of the principle of unconditional most-favored-nation status however allowed for significant limitations.

10. The majority of the approximately 600 requests for tariff reviews were submitted by American firms. In 33 cases the President, who had the final decision, ordained that the tariffs were to be raised, and in five cases that they were to be lowered.

11. If Germany or France had made such a request to industry, the Netherlands government would have objected. But as it was the United States, no objection was to be raised.

12. The countries consulted included Britain, Sweden, and Switzerland.

13. National Archives, RG 59, Dec. files 1910-1929, file 865.83: George E. Anderson, consul-general in Rotterdam, to Secretary of State Charles Evans Hughes, 8 January 1923, 199. Exports of vegetable oils rose from Dfl. 1.5 million in 1920 to Dfl. 9.1 million in 1922, but fell to Dfl. 3.1 million in 1925.

14. It was still unclear even to the Netherlands Economic Affairs Department whether the U.S. Tariff Commission, customs officials or treasury agents were active in the Netherlands.

15. The value of exports rose from Dfl. 10,000 to Dfl. 459,000. The share of the Apollo Candle Company, Schiedam, in 1925 was 80 percent, and that of the Royal Gouda Candle Company 20 percent.

16. An earlier attempt by American wholesalers to ban imports of Dutch strawboard had been abandoned for fear of running into difficulties with the U.S. government.

17. The *démarche* contained a number of traditional points. It emphasized the United States' very favorable balance of trade and the Netherlands' free trade policy and low customs duties. The new legislation would increase the already heavy duties on Dutch products by 100 percent or even more.

18. Between 1929 and 1932 world trade declined in value by 65 percent, and in volume by 30 percent. The comparable figures for the United States were 48 percent and 78 percent.

19. The other countries included Germany, Austria, Finland, Hungary, and Czechoslovakia. The first new agreement was concluded with Brazil in 1923.

20. The Fordney-McCumber Act allowed no scope for negotiations on lower tariffs, but provided only for raising or lowering tariffs up to a maximum of 50 percent on individual commodities if the country in question discriminated against American commodities.

21. Since the introduction of the 1932 Revenue Act Dutch coke exports were no longer exempt from customs duties, while exemption was granted to countries that had concluded agreements on an unconditional most-favoured-nation basis, such as Germany and Britain. Coke exports were not voluminous, but it was regarded by the Foreign Ministry as a matter of principle.

22. National Archives, RG 59, Dec. files 1930-1939, ADT 611.5631/107: Philips, `Memorandum of conversation with the Minister of the Netherlands', 1 May 1934.

23. Von Baumhauer had resigned in the summer of 1934.

24. Von Baumhauer seems to have acted as legal counsel on a number of occasions.

25. Six later found other important donors such as The Texas Company, the parent company of Texaco, the Dutch East Indies Commercial Bank, and Lever Brothers.

26. Van Aken was chiefly occupied with the Dutch exhibition at the New York World Fair, and an assistant secretary, Henry G. Wolff, had been appointed for trade promotion.

27. The exchange rate was approximately Dfl. 1.85 to the dollar.

Maasdam IV, 1993
Holland-America Line
Painting by
Stephen Card
(born 1952)

Holland-America Line was founded in 1873 as the Netherlands-America SteamshipCompany, a shipping and passenger line and it became one of the principal carriers of emigrants from Europe to the United States. The Holland-America Line carried several millions of immigrants to the New World. Today, Holland-America Line is part of the Carnival Cooperation, the largest cruise line in the world.

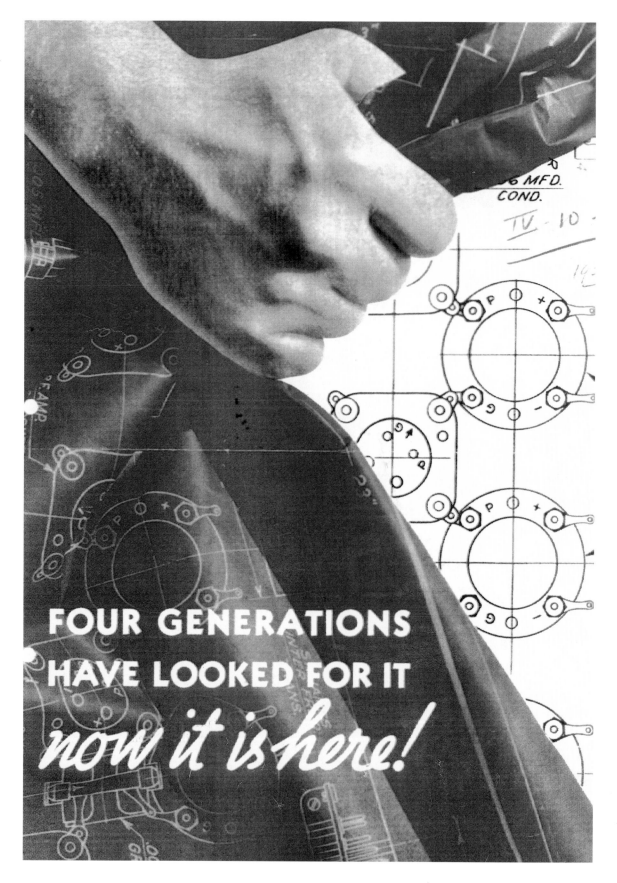

Océ-USA is the American subsidiary of Océ van der Grinten N.V., founded in the Netherlands in 1877. Océ-USA has been operating since the early 1920s and manufactures copiers, printers, and plotter systems as well as materials and other imaging supplies. Océ-USA is supported by 55 branch offices nationwide with more than 1,650 employees in the United States.

Heineken
Brewed in Holland

"Heineken's" was exported to the United States for the first time shortly after the repeal of prohibition in 1933. Represented by Leo Van Münching, a young Dutchman and a former crew member on the Holland-America Line who had convinced brewery representatives of the strong prospects for the brand in the U.S., Heineken was sold on six-pack at a time to New York area bars and restaurants. Heineken beer has since become the single largest commodity shipped in bulk from Europe to America each year. In 1988 the Chamber awarded the George Washington Vanderbilt Trophy to Leo Van Münching Jr. and Van Münching& Co. Today Van Münching is a wholly-owned subsidiary of Heineken Breweries in Amsterdam.
Heineken Museum Collection

"Irises", 1889
Painting by
Vincent van Gogh
(1853-1890)
Collection of the
J. Paul Getty Museum,
Malibu, California

The Cultural Committee of the Netherlands Chamber of Commerce in New York organized an exhibition of modern Dutch paintings from April 24 to May 7, 1921 in the Andersen Galleries on Park Avenue and 59th Street in New York. Exhibited were paintings by Kees van Dongen, Jan Toorop, George Breitner, and Vincent van Gogh. The painting with the greatest impact was Vincent van Gogh's "Irises". The Cultural Committee was so successful that in 1921 it became an independent organization under its new name: the Netherland-America Foundation, founded by leading members of the Dutch-American community, including Edward W. Bok, publisher of *Ladies Home Journal*, Thomas J. Watson, founder of IBM, and Franklin D. Roosevelt, Governor of the State of New York and future President of the United States.

"Man in Oriental
Costume", 1632
Painting by
Rembrandt van Rijn
(1606-1669)
The Metropolitan
Museum of Art
Bequest of William K.
Vanderbilt, 1920
William K. Vanderbilt
(1849-1920), was the
grandson of Commodore
Cornelius Vanderbilt and
the brother of George
Washington Vanderbilt,
one of the founders of the
Netherlands Chamber of
Commerce.

⇒
"Portrait of a Man",
1632
Painting by
Rembrandt van Rijn
The Metropolitan
Museum of Art
Bequest of Mrs H.O.
Havemeyer, 1929

⇒⇒
"Portrait of a Lady",
1632
Painting by
Rembrandt van Rijn
The Metropolitan
Museum of Art
Bequest of Mrs H.O.
Havemeyer, 1929

Henry Osborn
Havemeyer (1830-1907)
and his wife Louisine
Havemeyer (1832-1929)
were avid collectors of old
master paintings and
French impressionists,
respectively. Henry
Havemeyer, head of the
American Sugar Refining
Company in New York,
became one of the princi-
pal benefactors of New
York's Metropolitan
Museum.

The silver-plated American telephone used on January 30, 1926 in the opening of telephone communication between New York and Amsterdam. Mr. Willis H. Booth, president of the Netherlands Chamber of Commerce in New York spoke to Mr. W. Westerman, president of the Netherlands-American Chamber of Commerce.

CHAPTER V

1945-1964: SCARCE DOLLARS AND EXPORT PROMOTION

Introduction

Never before - or after - was the United States such an important part of the foreign economic relations of the Netherlands as in the first years after the second world war. Besides being the principal supplier of raw materials, manufacturing supplies, and capital goods which were essential for the reconstruction of the war-ravaged country, the United States also financed these Dutch imports. Partly owing to this aid, the Netherlands was quickly on the road to recovery, and the reconstruction period was officially declared at an end in 1949. The United States played a less prominent part in the changes in the Dutch economy over the next fifteen years, perhaps the most fundamental peacetime changes the Netherlands has ever experienced. In the approximately twenty years after 1950, a period of almost uninterrupted world economic growth, the Netherlands evolved into a modern economy based on industry, services, trade, and agriculture.

After the war the image of the United States in the Netherlands underwent a profound change. Together with Britain and the Soviet Union, it had emerged victorious from the war with Germany and Japan, and under the Marshall Plan put into effect in 1948 the United States contributed significantly to the economic recovery of Western Europe. Relations between the Soviet Union and its former allies were meanwhile deteriorating, so that from the political point of view as well the United States occupied a central position in the foreign policy of the Netherlands. A primary objective in those years was to improve the balance of payments with the United States, which had invariably been adverse in the past. The difference had been financed from the Dutch East Indies trade and from foreign investments. The war, however, had greatly reduced or suspended these sources of income. So the Netherlands government decided to encourage the promotion of exports and asked the private organizations active in this field for their cooperation. The growth of exports would help to reduce the balance of payments deficit with the United States.

Between 1945 and 1949 the Netherlands Chamber of Commerce in the United States, Inc. - as it was renamed in 1947 - was at the center of the promotion of Dutch exports to the United States. It assisted in the implementation of policy, provided information, and acted in an advisory capacity to the Netherlands government. However, in 1949 a sweeping change of policy took place. The private trade promotion organizations had to take second place to the government promotion of exports. No longer able to influence the formulation of policy or to take an active part in the promotion of exports, their role was confined to the traditional task of commercial mediation. Since it was not in a position to initiate new moves, the Chamber had no choice in the following years but to stand on the sidelines as government officials gradually lost contact with the Dutch business community. The official promotion of Dutch exports to the United States ended in 1964.

The leading actor in the promotion of Dutch exports to the United States between 1945 and 1949, the Chamber lost its preeminence on the American stage to the Netherlands Export Promotion Organization in the 1950s. With the waning of the Chamber's influence on policy-making after 1949, the interest of the various Dutch government organizations in the Chamber evaporated.

Exports

In the twenty years after 1949, when the war damage in the Netherlands had been repaired and the economy had recovered, Dutch exports developed at a rapid pace. This did not seem likely at first. Restrictions on international trade and the flow of funds kept Dutch exports between 1945 and 1949 at a low level, and it was not until the latter year that they again reached their 1938 volume. The composition of exports and their distribution over foreign markets underwent a far-reaching change over the next fifteen years. As the result of industrialization, manufactures accounted for a greater proportion of total exports. As their output rose, manufacturers focused increasingly on neighboring European countries at the expense of overseas markets.

Up to the early 1960s Netherlands government policy was aimed at the construction of a modern industrial sector and the promotion of international trade, accompanied by strict wage and price controls. Though emphasis was placed on the need to industrialize directly after the war, it was not until 1949 before industrialization was stimulated systematically, so by the 1950s Dutch exports underwent a significant change. In 1951, high-grade products earning badly needed dollars still comprised only 25 percent of Dutch exports; 20 percent consisted of products for which customers were difficult to find, and then only provided the vendor in turn agreed to buy goods that were neither easy to sell nor essential to the Netherlands' economic development. So more than half of Dutch exports consisted of products for which there was relatively little demand in the Netherlands. The concentration of Dutch industrialization in the chemical and engineering industries was reflected after 1950 in their increasing share of exports. The proportion of such traditional export commodities as textiles and food and beverages declined between 1950 and 1965 from 11.5 to 8.6 percent, and from 38.2 to 24.6 percent respectively. The chemical and engineering sectors, on the other hand, increased their exports from 7.6 to 10.2 percent, and from 7.8 to 15.8 percent in the same period.

The development of Dutch exports was determined not only by the composition of the package as a whole but equally by trends in the world economy and the competitiveness of the Netherlands. The growth of Dutch exports after 1949 went hand in hand with a considerable enlargement of the Netherlands' share of the international market. In 1949 the value of the guilder against the dollar declined by 30 percent. As a consequence of wage and price controls, the cost of living rose more slowly in the Netherlands than in other countries, an advantage which was retained even after a wage explosion in 1954. The Netherlands remained an island of low wages and prices up to the beginning of the 1960s. This provided the basis for its increased share of the world market, which by 1955 was 20 to 30 percent above the 1938 level and still expanding. Because of the country's strong competitive position, Dutch export earnings were highest in periods of recession.

The results may be termed spectacular. Annual growth percentages upwards of 8 percent were accompanied by a dramatic rise in the value of Dutch exports from Dfl. 2.7 billion in 1948 to Dfl. 23.1 billion in 1965. While developing somewhat less rapidly, Dutch exports to the United States increased likewise, rising from Dfl. 73 million in 1948 to Dfl. 724 million in 1965. Whereas total Dutch exports maintained a steady growth, Dutch exports to the United States fluctuated between years of stagnation or even decline and years of unexpectedly rapid growth. For instance, the peak years of the Korean War (1950-1953), resulting in part from an almost 50 percent increase in world market prices for raw materials within barely one year, were followed by a period of stagnation persisting up to 1964. From the mid-1950s the development of the European economies played an increasingly important role for the Dutch economy. The 1958-1959 recession in Europe directed the attention of Dutch exporters to the United States for a short time; 1959 remained the post-war record year for Dutch exports to the United States until 1964. Before long, the fast-growing European Economic Community that was established in 1958 absorbed almost the full production capacity for Dutch exports. For some years fourth on the list of Dutch export markets after West Germany, Belgium/Luxembourg, and Britain, after 1960 the United States was displaced, first by France and for a time by Italy.

The Netherlands' greater competitiveness was evident not only from its increasing share of world trade, but also from its gradually improving balance of trade. Having again reached the pre-war level of 65 percent in 1950, it rapidly improved in the following years and, except for 1956-1957, remained above the level of 80 percent. The balance of trade with the United States was at a lower level. Here too the pre-war level of 30 percent was regained in 1950, and although it rose to 77 percent in 1953, the improvement was short-lived because it stemmed from the outbreak of the Korean War and the subsequent spending cuts in the Netherlands, which sharply reduced imports. For the rest, the import cover hovered around 30 to 40 percent throughout the decade, with the sole exception of 1959, when it rose to 48 percent. The picture was much the same in the first half of the 1960s. The lowest point of barely 30 percent was reached in 1964.

In the twenty years from 1945 to 1965 there was a continuing deficit in the Dutch balance of trade with the United States partly due to the loss of dollar earnings from the Dutch East Indies. This was especially true in the reconstruction period after the war, when Europe was heavily dependent on supplies from the United States. The 1946 deficit in the Dutch balance of trade with the United States amounted to $ 700 million, even though the Netherlands government had borrowed $ 800 million and the Dutch business community liquidated $ 150 million in foreign investments. The worst year was 1947, when despite heavy cuts in imports from the dollar area the deficit increased by another $ 150 million. Dutch exports stagnated while imports of commodities essential for recovery continued to rise. The country managed to stay afloat by a new round of import restrictions and unexpectedly generous foreign credits. Marshall Aid got under way in the following year, and thereafter the scarcity of dollars was a less crucial point, a structural if partial improvement in the balance of trade with the United States was gradually effected. In this way, the Netherlands government could finally concentrate on industrialization and the promotion of Dutch exports. The deficit was halved in 1950, and was even converted into a surplus in 1953, though only in that year. The structural deficit per year was $ 125 to $ 150 million. The improved situation with regard to the dollar in the 1950s was however largely attributable to the liberalization of trade within Europe. The last remaining restrictions were lifted in 1958.

Little is known of the extent of Dutch direct investments in the United States and of their contribution to the balance of payments. American estimates put total Dutch investments at $ 330 million in 1950, or 10 percent of total foreign investment in the United States. In 1961 they amounted to $ 1 billion, and in 1965 to $ 1.3 billion, or almost 15 percent of total foreign direct investment in the United States. The oil sector accounted for approximately 50 percent of Dutch investments. Annual direct investment in industry increased after 1955, rising from $ 44 million in 1950 to more than $ 140 million in 1956, and to $ 330 million in 1965.

As the supplier of vital materials and foodstuffs, the United States played an important part in the Dutch economy in the immediate post-war years. Up to the introduction of the Marshall Plan in 1948, imports from the United States were heavily restricted owing to the scarcity of dollars. It was only in the mid-1950s, when the conversion of foreign currency was facilitated by the liberalization of inter-European trade, that this problem was finally overcome. Up to that time the promotion of exports to the dollar area was one of the major economic problems facing the Netherlands.

1945-1949: the Reconstruction Period

In the situation in which the Netherlands now finds itself it is certain that in nearly every instance there will be a fundamental imbalance. Our import needs are vast, as against the fact that our export capacities over the next few years will be utterly incommensurate with what is required to pay for imports with goods or services.

This is how Netherlands Finance Minister Pieter Lieftinck described the dilemma facing the Dutch government in September, 1945. The country had suffered heavy damage in the war. Dutch national assets had been reduced by 30 percent, and the national income by 45 percent. Half of the Dutch merchant marine was destroyed, industry had ground to a halt for lack of supplies, malnutrition was widespread, and 20 percent of housing was badly damaged or in ruins. The national debt had soared by Dfl. 19 billion to 23.6 billion. In May, 1945 the exhausted country was badly in need of raw materials, manufacturing supplies, and other basic commodities to feed and clothe the population, restart production, and repair the worst of the war damage.

Dutch trade and financial transactions with the United States were of crucial importance. In the immediate post-war years the United States was the principal supplier of raw materials, manufacturing supplies, and capital goods not only to the Netherlands but to the whole of Western Europe. Before the Marshall Plan brought relief, the Netherlands government had to struggle with an acute shortage of dollars. The main sources of Dutch income used to finance imports from the United States had dried up during the war. This in fact applied in respect of trade with all countries. It was one of the central themes in a radio address on June 27, 1945 in which Prime Minister W. Schermerhorn informed the country of the government's reconstruction policy. He stressed the immensity of change in the Netherlands' place in the world economy. Foreign investments were lost or liquidated; the East Indies, formerly such an important foreign currency earner, were still occupied by Japan; and with the defeat of Germany the Netherlands' principal pre-war export market was gone.[1] Nor were these the only impediments to the country's economic recovery. Its competitiveness in the world market had declined by some 15 percent as a result of the price rises over the preceding five years. In view of the accumulated demand, the lion's share of Dutch production would at first need to be reserved for the home market, and the composition of the Dutch exports package would not coincide with the demand on the world market. While Dutch exports consisted largely of raw materials, semi-manufactured products, and services, the international demand was for high-grade industrial products. To stimulate industrial growth and broaden the manufacturing base, the government proposed to take advantage of the growing world demand for manufactured products. This would in turn create the extra jobs needed for the thousands leaving the agricultural and service sectors and counterbalance the effects of the rise in population. Industrialization remained the central theme of Dutch economic policy up to 1963.

The promotion of Dutch exports therefore became a key factor in economic policy. Given the limited size of the home market, G. Brouwers, secretary-general in the Netherlands Ministry of Economic Affairs, stated unequivocally that the industrialization problem was primarily an outlets problem. The growth of Dutch exports was "a prerequisite" if the present and future needs of the nation were to be met. As with industrialization, however, a cohesive trade promotion policy was not formulated until J.R.M. van den Brink was appointed Minister for Economic Affairs in 1948. The ad-hoc policy pursued by the Ministry between 1945 and 1948 gave the Netherlands Chamber of Commerce in the United States, Inc. the chance to employ its expertise in influencing policy-making on the promotion of exports to the United States.

Anton Bestebreurtje, president of the Chamber between 1945 and 1954 seized every opportunity to inform the Ministry of the views of private enterprise, making good use of the reputation he had built up with the Netherlands' official organizations in the United States. The Ministry of Foreign Affairs described him as "an exceptional figure who devotes a vast amount of time and energy to the interests of the Netherlands", adding that unfortunately he was indeed exceptional amongst those concerned with the promotion of Dutch exports. Bestebreurtje moreover had the full cooperation of L. Smilde, deputy-director of the Economic Information Division. Up to 1949, when the new Dutch government policy relegated the Chamber to second place, they collaborated on many issues ranging from the practical aspects of Dutch trade promotion to policy recommendations and proposals presented to top government and business circles. They often simultaneously raised a particular point with the Ministry. Whereas Smilde was obliged to work through official channels, Bestebreurtje, as president of the Chamber, had much more latitude, and did not hesitate to approach cabinet ministers, Ambassadors and the president of the Netherlands Bank, or to use the press to influence political debates. During his term of office a meeting with the president and the executive committee of the Chamber in New York became a fixed part of the program of all Ministers for Economic Affairs visiting the United States.

Bestebreurtje's influence on Dutch government policy gradually waned after Van den Brink became Minister in 1948. When the Ministry, under American political pressure, took over virtually the entire field of export promotion in 1949, the Chamber could only take comfort in the fact that the new policy was based in part on the information and ideas it had supplied over the preceding years. It spelled the end of Bestebreurtje's hopes of concentrating all trade promotion activities in the United States in the Chamber.

172

Step by step, its work was reduced to the passive promotion of trade, while the more active components were entrusted to Dutch trade commissioners stationed around the United States whose task was to heighten Dutch exporters' awareness of the American market. This system was discontinued at the end of 1963.

Despite the rapidly growing balance of trade deficit, H. Vos, Netherlands Minister for Trade and Industry (1945-1946), and his successor G.W.M. Huysmans, Minister for Economic Affairs (1946-1948), took little direct action to foster Dutch exports. Vos, devoting special attention to rebuilding the industrial base, was preoccupied with the administrative aspects of foreign trade and wished first to meet the domestic demand accruing from the war years. He underestimated the gravity of the situation. Though barely off the ground in 1945, Dutch exports amounting to more than $ 450 million were projected for the following year. As the Ministry of Finance put it, "what other country would release foreign exchange for playing cards, children's books etc. to the tune of ten million?" Export earnings in 1946 were no higher than $ 400 million, less than 40 percent of the 1938 figure. Presumably with an eye to the general election scheduled for May, the Cabinet refused to cut back on goods for the home market. The promotion of exports was finally taken in hand a few months later by the new Minister for Economic Affairs, G.W.M. Huysmans.

Even though Vos failed to pursue a cohesive exports policy, he laid the foundation for the measures introduced by Huysmans to stimulate Dutch exports to the United States. So long as Europe was still recovering from the effects of the war, the wealthy American market was obviously the most important potential buyer of Dutch agricultural and industrial products. Western Europe as yet had no interest in such commodities as bulbs, plants or Heineken beer; its need was for capital goods, raw materials, and affordable food supplies. The Netherlands was also obliged to import many of these commodities from the United States. Towards the end of 1945 the Economic Information Division prepared to launch an export offensive - as it was called - in the United States. The Chamber was asked to assemble information on the changes that had occurred in the American economy during the war. Also available for this purpose was *The Economic, Financial and Social Development of the United States from 1940 to 1945*, a report produced in 1946 by the Netherlands Study Group chaired by P.F.S. Otten, a later executive director of Philips in Eindhoven. On the advice of the Netherlands Ambassador to the United States, Alexander Loudon, the Economic Information Division decided that all requests received for information in the United States would be referred to the Chamber. It was agreed at the same time that the Chamber would act as the unofficial representative of the Economic Information Division until such time as it had an agency of its own in the United States. The Chamber's subsidy was raised from $ 12,000 in 1945 to $ 50,000 in 1946.

Loudon's decision not to utilize the economic and financial expertise then available to the government in the United States stemmed from the aversion to government intervention displayed by the American public since the war. After the long years of economic recession and then of war, it was clear that Americans wished to return to the traditional system of private enterprise. A commercial section had been established in the Netherlands embassy before the war, and since then the number of government organizations concerned with information and economic affairs had grown considerably. They seemed to be just as well qualified as the Chamber to provide exporters with economic information about the United States. The Netherlands Information Bureau, with offices in New York, Washington, San Francisco, and Holland, Michigan, was the American branch of the Dutch government information service in London, set up during the war to disseminate general information on the occupied Netherlands. The Netherlands Purchasing Commission administered a large part of the U.S. assets of companies in the Dutch East Indies, and placed the orders for the first post-war deliveries to the Netherlands and the East Indies. The third Dutch government organization in the United States was a mission dealing with economic, financial and shipping matters. It had tried unsuccessfully to gain control of Dutch bank accounts in the United States, negotiated for the government a loan of $ 100 million advanced by the Chase National Bank, and superintended Dutch merchant shipping in the western hemisphere. In 1943 and 1944 it represented the Netherlands at Allied conferences on post-war monetary and economic questions.

The Netherlands Ministry of Economic Affairs abandoned its cautious attitude after the appointment of Huysmans as Minister in July, 1946. In view of the mounting balance of payments deficit, there was indeed no alternative. Almost a third of the deficit was accounted for by imports from the United States, which in 1946 amounted to Dfl. 536 million, compared to Dutch exports to the United States worth Dfl. 38 million. The total balance of trade deficit in that year was Dfl. 1.3 billion. Huysmans' export policy was based on the same principle as that underlying the 1949 industrialization policy. The Dutch government was to create a business climate stimulating private enterprise and technological renewal. An essential precondition was that the movement of goods and the transfer of payments were to be freed from all controls as soon as possible. Through the scarcity of goods and foreign exchange, most trade between European countries in the first years after the war was government-controlled. Trade was dominated by quantitative restrictions and government purchasing monopolies. As private enterprise was allocated a leading role in the new policy, it had the support of the Chamber. The Chamber was not so appreciative of the Ministry's appropriation of many of the activities involved in the promotion of Dutch exports a few years later.

In 1946 the Minister set up a new body, the Exports Promotion Committee, chaired by S.T.J. Teppema, head of the Foreign Economic Relations Directorate. In the following year the Economic Information Division was upgraded to a Directorate in recognition of the renewed political importance of the promotion of Dutch exports. The committee's task was to advise the Minister on the relaxation of administrative measures hampering exports and on the allocation of foreign exchange for imports of the additional raw materials and coal supplies required by exporters. In the same year Huysmans approved the institution of a trade information center, shortly afterwards renamed the Central Institute for the Promotion of Foreign Trade (CIHAN), to lighten the workload of the Economic Information Division and the foreign service and to coordinate the work of the private trade promotion organizations in the Netherlands. This enabled the Economic Information Division and the foreign service to focus more on general economic information. The Economic Information Division focused on information and research on the development of the economy and its structure, and on economic and political trends abroad. The embassies and consulates mainly concerned themselves with general economic developments. Bearing in mind the economic developments after the first world war, planners did not discount the possibility of a world recession, even a recurrence of the Great Depression of the 1930s. If that should occur, industry and commerce would be sorely in need of the Directorate's services. By allotting a greater share of export promotion to the private organizations, Huysmans also met the wishes of the business community, which accused the government of playing too dominant a role in the process of recovery.

Run by industry and commerce, CIHAN succeeded in coordinating much of the private trade promotion in the Netherlands. The chairman, Anton Bestebreurtje, president of the Netherlands Chamber of Commerce in the United States, Inc. was one of the founders, together with the presidents of the Amsterdam and Rotterdam Chambers of Commerce and T.P. van der Kooy, head of the Economic Information Division. In return for a subsidy amounting to half the annual budget, CIHAN took over a substantial part of the commercial information activities of the Economic Information Division and the foreign service. Just as the Chamber dealt with all queries addressed to government departments about trade between the Netherlands and the United States, CIHAN relieved the Economic Information Division of this task in the Netherlands. Foreign firms received information free of charge in the hope that it would stimulate Dutch exports; Dutch firms were charged a small fee. Besides acting in an intermediary capacity for contacts and addresses, the organization provided general information on export markets, conducted market research both in the Netherlands and abroad, and organized joint presentations at foreign trade shows. As one of the founders, the Chamber was more or less bound in 1947 to affiliate its new branch office to CIHAN. The Association of Netherlands Chambers of Commerce for America was established that year as a liaison body for government and industry and commerce. Although the secretary, Hendrik Zwarensteyn, was responsible to a steering committee, he received his instructions from New York, where policy and budgetary matters were decided. The steering committee mainly functioned as a consultative body for firms exporting on a large scale to the United States.

CIHAN also sought to achieve close collaboration with the Dutch Chambers of Commerce abroad, and to add to their number in consultation with local business communities. Where Dutch commercial interests were not such as to warrant a Chamber of Commerce, the solution would be to work in tandem with the embassies and consulates.[2] Local conditions were crucial in determining whether trade promotion could be conducted by private organizations. The Netherlands Chamber of Commerce in the United States, Inc., which according to Bestebreurtje was regarded by the Economic Information Division as "the foremost among Netherlands Chambers abroad", had been entrusted with all aspects of information on Dutch and American business since 1945. However, when the Economic Information Division included extensive market research in the promotion of exports, CIHAN was asked to assume this responsibility because it had the requisite expertise amongst its staff. The Chamber of Commerce in London, on the other hand, provided no more than the most elementary services. The commercial section of the embassy was responsible for information on the Netherlands and for basic market research, more ambitious projects being passed on to CIHAN. In Paris the division of tasks was the same, except for dealing with queries from foreign firms, which was the task of the Chamber. The Chamber in New York was the exception in being the only Dutch Chamber of Commerce abroad large enough to handle all aspects of commercial information.

The most important step taken by Huysmans to promote Dutch exports to the United States was to send L. Smilde, the deputy head of Economic Information Division, to New York. Though officially attached to CIHAN, to obviate any suspicion of government intervention he was seconded in 1946 to the Chamber in New York as director of trade promotion. The Economic Information Division was at first uncertain as to how it should set about promoting exports to a market so different from European markets. Smilde was given a free hand to investigate the situation, and proceeded with the aid of the Chamber to survey the overall marketing potential and to determine how Dutch exporters would need to adapt their business practice to the local market demands.

The assessments and suggestions drawn up by Smilde and the Chamber in New York between 1946 and 1949 formed the basis for the structure and working methods of the government and private organizations promoting exports to the United States up to 1964. They were confident that the American market offered wide opportunities. The U.S. market was so vast and so diverse that buyers could be found for virtually all products if the quality and price were right. The possibilities were indeed such that Dutch exporters were more likely to find themselves overstretched rather than lacking in buyers. Once a product found a customer base, the demand could outstrip the limited production capacities of the average Dutch exporter. So prospective Dutch exporters to the United States should be assisted from the moment they first ventured on to the American market. One of the problems connected with promotional activities was that many of the firms involved not only had no experience of exporting to the United States, but had no export experience at all. Information was therefore the key element in the plan presented by Smilde and the Chamber of Commerce to the Economic Information Division. They suggested that the Directorate and CIHAN assume responsibility in the Netherlands for the general economic information needed to prepare exporters for the intense competition they would meet in the United States. Their representatives arriving in New York would be informed of market conditions and supplied with the addresses and practical advice needed to make a solid start. But success would ultimately depend on the prior availability of information in the Netherlands.

Smilde's reports and the correspondence between the Chamber in New York and the Directorate in The Hague present a gloomy picture of the position of Dutch industry and commerce in the American market, and especially that of small and medium-sized businesses. Errors of judgment seem to have been more the rule than the exception. It is not clear to what extent the larger corporations made the same mistakes. The majority of firms seeking assistance in the United States belonged to branches of industry producing luxury consumer goods, such as food and beverages and articles in the gifts category. It was only in the course of the 1950s, with the growing prosperity in Europe demanding better products, that American complaints about the quality of Dutch exports were no longer heard.

Up-to-date, more expensive export and marketing methods were used on a limited scale in the Netherlands before the war, but the cheaper methods formerly employed by the traditional merchant houses to sell coffee, tobacco, and unlabeled commodities like cheese, fish, and cotton were still relied upon for exports to the United States in the post-war years. Merchant houses were not suitable for manufactured goods. A shortage of capital and what was only a passing interest in the U.S. market probably prompted many Dutch exporters to opt for the cheapest method. The Chamber concluded that there was "too often no willingness to make concessions, if necessary, to gain a firm foothold in a market". Relations with foreign buyers were poorly maintained, price changes were not passed on, and attention was given to correspondence only if an order seemed imminent. Many businessmen travelled to the United States with no prior preparation "to sell what they make and in the way they package it".

Dutch industry lagged behind its more productive and innovative American competitors, who had been able to forge further ahead during the war. Without precise specification, Smilde noted that U.S. markets for certain products had now become almost inaccessible to Dutch business. But in many cases the American price-quality ratio was much better. If Dutch manufacturers were to win back their pre-war share of the market, their products and packaging needed to be brought up to date. To make matters worse, Dutch exporters consistently underestimated the strict quality standards on the American market. The indirect pressure applied by the Netherlands government to stimulate exports frequently had the opposite effect. To be eligible for more raw materials, firms had to export. Whether they had for years successfully operated on the world market, or were now seeking for the first time to launch a new product abroad, made no difference. The concerted efforts of the Chamber in New York, Smilde, the Economic Information Division, and CIHAN failed to persuade the Foreign Economic Relations Directorate to rescind this measure. By 1949 exports of inferior products had so increased and were causing such damage to the Netherlands' reputation that the Economic Information Division and CIHAN urged the Foreign Economic Relations Directorate to introduce an official warrant of quality, but without success until later, when dollars were no longer in short supply.

The competitive position of the Netherlands in terms of packaging slipped further in the first post-war years. Other countries were increasingly using expensive high-grade packaging materials like plastics and aluminum foil. Dutch industry however lacked the vision, capital, and hard currency to buy the machinery needed. The situation changed when the period of acute dollar scarcity ended in 1949, and the information services had stressed the importance of modern packaging methods.

Even large corporations had no basic knowledge of trade with the United States, and broke the most elementary rules of commerce. Representatives with an inadequate command of English were sent off with little or no preparation, prices were inconsistent, and "exclusive" selling rights were sometimes accorded to two or more agents. Not infrequently the packaging and labelling of goods failed to comply with U.S. statutory regulations. Matters gradually improved, but it took years before mistakes were finally avoided. It was remarked as late as 1953 that Dutch exporters all too often had no notion of "proper service, attractive catalogues, samples collections and documentation". Agreements were not kept, and some switched repeatedly from one agent to another. The poor reputation of Dutch exporters began at last to improve in the 1950s, but meanwhile the Chamber was generally powerless to assist aggrieved American buyers. The Dutch firms concerned often did not take any notice. The United States was far away, and many of the goods sold were in any case remnants for which there was no market in Europe at that moment. All that the Chamber could do was warn the Dutch government, which seems to have shown little sign of concern.

Obsolescent technology and outdated management and marketing methods were not the only barriers with which export promoters had to cope. On the whole, Dutch manufacturers were not yet particularly interested in the United States. The Chamber could do nothing about the highly protectionist tariff laws shielding the American market from foreign competition up to the late 1950s. Reference was made to "the notorious impossibility" of selling large quantities of finished products in the United States.[3] What it could do, however, was suggest measures the Dutch government could take to make exports to the United States more attractive for individual firms. A difficulty here was that certainly up to 1949 the European demand for products of all kinds exceeded the supply, while the prices in the sellers' market in Europe were appreciably higher than in the United States. Manufacturers could thus be sure of selling their products in Europe, whatever the quality or price. Moreover, the price of Dutch products on the American market was 25 to 50 percent higher than that of comparable domestic products. This was largely attributable to higher production costs in the Netherlands and overvaluation of the guilder, but export regulations also contributed to the fact that many Dutch products were too expensive. While prices on the American market usually allowed for a reasonable margin of profit, the exporter often had to fix a higher price before the Ministry of Economic Affairs would issue an export permit. In these circumstances it was extremely difficult to arouse more interest in the U.S. market. If the Netherlands government would not reconsider, Smilde and the Chamber in New York decided that a special bonus might have the desired effect. They worked out a scheme whereby a proportion of the net dollar profit would be allotted to the Dutch exporter for him to spend freely in the United States. It was not at all easy to convince the Netherlands government of the advantages of the scheme.

In December, 1946, after consultation with the Chamber, Smilde presented a plan of action to the Economic Information Division. For the first time ever, all aspects of export promotion were to be tackled as one coherent whole: production and exports in the Netherlands; and imports, wholesaling, retailing, and advertising in the United States. A comprehensive survey of the American market would enable exporters to be provided with reliable information. The costs would be high, around $ 100,000 for 1947 alone. Smilde proposed to start by charting American import practices and marketing methods, using the fund of knowledge built up by the Chamber.

Next, the market openings and most suitable marketing methods would be determined for various commodities, such as cheese, fish, linen goods, glass, and ceramics, already available in sufficient quantity for export to the United States. Improved, more comprehensive documentation and publicity both in the Netherlands and the United States were of equal importance. On the assumption that a modern image was conducive to exports, the Netherlands was to be presented to the American businessman as more than "clogs, Volendam, and a finger in the dike". And in the Netherlands, the exporter was to be informed about business practices, market openings, price trends, new products, and production methods in the United States. Information collected by CIHAN on Dutch products available for export in the short term would be distributed among American importers, department stores, trade associations, and trade papers by the Chamber. The Economic Information Division approved the project almost without amendment, and made substantial funds available.[4]

Nothing is known of how the Chamber put the plan into operation. It is amply clear that Bestebreurtje and Smilde regarded their efforts as just one part of a greater whole. This is evidenced by the reaction of Bestebreurtje when he was informed of the Export Plan 1949 two years later. In his opinion the funds available for the new programs might have been better invested in activities to provide information in the Netherlands. He was presumably referring to the summarily rejected idea of expanding the official promotion of exports in the United States. In addition, he regarded providing information on the American market as a logical extension of publicity campaigns in the Netherlands, the center of promotional activities. The information obtained by the entrepreneur before exports were shipped abroad contributed at least as much to the country's export performance as the economic information provided on and in other countries.

The Free Dollar Program

When Smilde and the Chamber in New York set about guiding exporters on the American market in 1947, they knew it would be some time before the results were perceptible. In that year the Netherlands' dollar reserves were shrinking so fast that the Dutch government had at most not years or months, but only a few weeks to take measures. The scarcity of dollars could have precipitated an acute balance of payments crisis at any moment. Owing to industry's strong recovery and the attraction of investments, the demand for imported goods from the dollar area grew much faster than anticipated. A trade deficit of $ 700 million had originally been projected for 1947, more than half of which related to the dollar area. Therefore, the Netherlands government imposed severe restrictions on dollar imports at the end of 1946. The failure of new loans to materialize, the disappointing sales of securities in the United States, and the slow recovery of exports necessitated two more spending cuts in 1947. Finally, the government cut $ 400 million from imports of capital goods for agriculture and industry, reducing the figure to 40 percent of the original plan. Total imports from the dollar area amounted in that year to $ 600 million, and exports to barely $ 30 million. The announcement of the Marshall Plan in June, 1947 held out hope that the balance of payments crisis could finally be resolved, but as long as the Netherlands did not know how much aid it could count on, the need to increase exports to the United States remained.

It is not known precisely who suggested apportioning to exporters part of the dollar earnings of their products, or when the idea was first introduced. Bestebreurtje was one of its first and most staunch supporters. He had already advocated it early in 1947, a few months before the dollar scarcity reached its peak and before the announcement of the Marshall Plan. Nor was he the only one. Businessmen and government officials alike saw it as an extremely useful means of stimulating interest in the American market. With dollars to spend on American goods that were unobtainable elsewhere, Dutch exporters would be less interested in the European market, where prices were higher and competition less fierce. Though the scheme was repeatedly discussed, and other countries reported favorable results, its introduction was delayed until September, 1949. The Netherlands Minister for Economic Affairs first rejected it in April, 1947, when the acute currency shortage would not allow even a small percentage of dollar earnings to be retained by private industry and commerce. There would be political repercussions if in the midst of such scarcity a small section of the population were to be allowed to buy luxury products denied to the public at large. Finance Minister Lieftinck was undeterred however, and raised the subject again at a Cabinet meeting in May. He was unsuccessful because after temporarily suspending credits for Europe pending the announcement of the Marshall Plan, the United States had granted no new loans. In these circumstances no serious consideration was given to Bestebreurtje's argument that now was the time for Dutch exporters to gain a foothold on the American market, or otherwise they would be too late.

KLM poster, 1946

The president of the Chamber had no intention of leaving it at that. On a visit to the Netherlands in June, 1947 he tried to convince Huysmans and M.W. Holtrop, president of the Netherlands Bank, of the advantages of "the free dollar", and set out his arguments in the *Dagelijkse Beurscourant* of June 21. In the same month the Economic Information Division urged the Minister to release dollars for business costs in the United States, and for advertising in particular. Bestebreurtje was disheartened, the more so when the Cabinet decided later in the year that American firms requesting commercial information were to be charged a fee to cover the costs. Though in the short term it might bring in dollars, in the long term it would have a damaging effect on exports. He found it difficult to accept, and seriously considered scaling down the activities of the Chamber.

The government's rejection of the free dollar scheme was prompted not only by the acute dollar shortage but also by the prospect of American aid. Secretary of State George C. Marshall had outlined a proposal for what came to be known as Marshall Aid on June 5, 1947. The aid given to individual European countries since 1945, which included $ 737.5 million in credits to the Netherlands, was to be replaced by a program for all European nations. The point of departure was the balance of payments crisis threatening the West European economies at the beginning of 1947. Their lack of dollars was likely to block economic recovery in the long term. However, at first there was no indication of an approaching collapse, let alone of communism awaiting famine and waves of social unrest to get Western Europe in its grasp. Fast growing, somewhat overheated Western European economies seemed more in danger of faltering through lack of dollars.

The United States provided $ 12.5 billion in aid between 1948 and 1952. Its balance of payments deficit being comparatively large - the principal aid criterion - the Netherlands benefitted more than other countries. It was allocated a total of $ 1.3 billion, of which $ 1.1 billion was utilized. In effect, this amounted to more aid per head of population than was received by any other European country. After the first shipment of Marshall Aid goods arrived in April, 1948, the pressure on the dollar reserves quickly subsided, indeed so quickly that barely eighteen months later the aid seemed likely to exceed the need for dollars. The rapid economic recovery and the end of the fighting in Indonesia resolved all foreign exchange problems, with the result that the aid program could be terminated a year earlier than planned. The situation remained stable even after the disastrous floods that inundated the coastal areas of Zeeland in February, 1953.[5]

The shrinking dollar reserves and the subsequent initiation of Marshall Aid temporarily relieved the pressure on the Netherlands government to release more funds for the promotion of exports to the United States. The structural balance of trade deficit with the United States was however such as to make it highly improbable that it could ever be eliminated by exports alone. But as the Marshall Plan was designed to facilitate trade and the movement of funds within Europe, it gave the Netherlands the opportunity to earn dollars on the European market, its main export outlet. The Dutch government was therefore less concerned to promote exports to the United States. This was not at all to the liking of the Chamber, which proceeded in 1948 to make use of every opportunity to endorse the free dollar program.

When Van den Brink succeeded Huysmans at the beginning of 1948, the prospects for action seemed much brighter. He had been the main advocate of the free dollar program in the 1947 budget debate in the First Chamber of Dutch Parliament. A meeting of the Board, Dutch and American businessmen, Smilde, embassy officials, and representatives of the Netherlands Bank was held in the New York offices of the Chamber in May, 1948. They agreed unanimously that the allocation of 10 percent of their net dollar earnings to exporters would do much to awaken interest in the American market. Opinions were more divided on the desirability of spending restrictions. The businessmen were opposed to the idea; the government officials were in favor of specifying that the money was to be used solely for business purposes, and on no account for the purchase of luxury goods. The proposal was rejected by the Foreign Economic Relations Directorate in The Hague, which was only prepared to authorize barter trade. The American embassy described this in a report to the Department of State as "an important commercial policy development", but the results were disappointing.

Other proposals discussed at the New York meeting met with an equal lack of response from the Netherlands Ministry of Economic Affairs. It argued that only in exceptional cases were small and medium-sized businesses capable of financing the market research and advertising campaigns needed to build up a firm position on the American market. Moreover, their production capacity was usually too limited to supply even one of the smaller regional markets in the United States, and they devoted insufficient attention to the quality and packaging of their products. The Economic Information Division hoped to make them more competitive by integrating them into export cooperatives. Of the export cooperatives established since the founding of CIHAN in 1946, the cooperatives for herring, cigars, paint, linen, and confectionery had achieved reasonable results. The Netherlands government planned to help cooperatives by running publicity campaigns abroad and by backing the establishment of a private Dutch-American business enterprise, which together with the Chamber would handle marketing for individual firms that were unable or unwilling to join a cooperative. In addition, more and better information on the quality standards of the American market would be made available in the Netherlands. There was more enthusiasm for the projected business enterprise in New York than in the Netherlands, where it was opposed on the grounds that it would compete with existing exports, and the idea was eventually dropped. The public spending cuts in 1948 which prevented implementation of the other plans did nothing to increase the Dutch business community's confidence in the government.

In a personal discussion with Van der Brink and Foreign Minister D.U. Stikker in October, 1948, the president of the Chamber in The Hague, H.A. Quarles van Ufford, asked whether the government "was genuinely concerned with the promotion of exports to the United States of America". His question was prompted by the announcement that Smilde would be recalled from the United States prior to the following summer. However, before the government could actually do this, the situation changed. In August the new Netherlands Ambassador to the United States, E.N. van Kleffens, reported that spending cuts would not be welcomed by the American government, the International Bank for Reconstruction and Development, or the International Monetary Fund. Missions from the two latter institutions had visited the Netherlands shortly before, and had concluded that its efforts to promote exports lagged far behind those of other West European countries.[6] A relative disparity in this respect was acceptable, because the task of recovery had been more formidable for the Netherlands as the German occupation had lasted longer and the destruction had been comparatively more widespread.

Nonetheless, this fact has been noted here, and in discussion the authorities repeatedly stress the need for the Netherlands to redouble its efforts to increase its dollar earnings.

With talks on Marshall Aid for 1949-1950 due shortly, Van Kleffens said it would be unwise for the Netherlands to recall from the United States the only official who was specifically charged with the promotion of exports. Van den Brink was not swayed by this argument, even when called upon by Parliament to change his mind.

At the end of 1948 there was little hope that the government could be persuaded otherwise. The end of the sellers' market in Europe was in sight, and the government seemed prepared to leave exporters to their own devices in the sense that they would themselves have to seek outlets in the United States, even if it meant risking a loss. The Central Board for Foreign Economic Relations, though it did not agree, was powerless to act. Dutch industry and commerce already felt heavily burdened by all the economic restrictions in force. And now the Netherlands government seemed to expect that they would be willing to accept losses from exports to the United States, while there were sufficient opportunities to earn profits in Europe. The Central Board shared the view of the Chamber that if the national interest required loss-producing exports, then the national interest should also carry the risks.

The Economic Information Division and the Chamber in New York were able to capitalize on Smilde's approach to his work in their efforts to keep him longer in New York. The tepid interest of Dutch industry and commerce in exports to the United States had enabled him to build up a reserve fund of $ 40,000. They suggested that if the Directorate paid his salary and living expenses, and the Chamber the office costs, he could continue his work for another two years. Bestebreurtje made the sole condition that Smilde must then be officially attached to the Chamber. The idea was approved, and on March 1, 1949 Smilde entered the service of the Chamber as director of trade promotion. It was to be of only short duration. Under American pressure, a more radical change of policy with far-reaching implications for the Chamber in New York followed before the end of the year.

Marshall Aid, Industrialization, and Export Promotion

Opening the Netherlands Trade Show Center in Utrecht on September 6, 1949, the Minister for Economic Affairs stated that the Netherlands had now regained its pre-war share of world trade, but stressed the need for sustained growth. Exports to the United States remained far below the level to be expected now that dollars were in such short supply. It was true that in 1948 Dutch exports had risen by Dfl. 24 million to Dfl. 85 million, and that the balance of payments deficit had been reduced by Dfl. 300 million, but the total deficit still stood at more than Dfl. 1 billion. The Netherlands balance of payments position continued to improve in 1949, not so much because of increasing exports to the United States - a respectable Dfl. 130 million that year - but because more goods were being imported from elsewhere. The deficit fell further to Dfl. 574 million in 1949.

Economic Affairs Minister Van den Brink drafted an export plan in the spring of 1949, pressured by the Economic Cooperation Administration, the U.S. government organization which directed the Marshall Plan, and Max H. Hirschfeld, its coordinator in the Netherlands, and as a result of the warnings sounded by Van Kleffens, the IMF, and the World Bank. Hirschfeld underscored the advantages of a "well-considered economic policy" in light of the intention of the Economic Cooperation Administration (ECA), the U.S. agency responsible for the implementation of the Marshall Plan, to use the dollar position of a given country as a criterion for the allocation of aid. The Ministry then at last proceeded to expand the industrialization policy announced in 1945. Set out in a policy document produced in September, it accorded a central position to exports. As Van den Brink wrote later:

> The industrialization program for the years 1948-1952 was an export scenario ... Greater competitiveness and a better export performance were to be the foundations for a structure guaranteeing work and prosperity for our children.

Though a fundamental part of the industrialization policy, exports were not of special interest to the Ministry. Export Plan 1949 displayed various weak spots which the Cabinet glossed over, but which caused serious complications in practice. Produced hastily under political pressure to take immediate measures, the plan provided for the retention by exporters of 10 percent of their dollar earnings, more information services in the Netherlands and the United States for producers, merchants and consumers, and the establishment of an official organization which later proved to duplicate many of the activities of the private export promotion agencies.

During a visit to the Netherlands in the summer of 1949, Bestebreurtje was asked by the Economic Information Division what steps he thought were needed to give fresh impetus to Dutch exports. On his return to New York he could not say definitely how it would all work out, but he assured the Board that the government at last seemed prepared to make the necessary concessions. A committee of top-level officials from the Economic Information Division and the Foreign Economic Relations Directorate had come to the conclusion that one of the three plans under consideration was realistic. There was no question of devaluing the guilder.[7] In view of the 1947 tariff law amendments, the U.S. trade barriers were not likely to be lowered in the near future.[8] What remained was the free dollar program, which the committee regarded as promising. If it worked, Dutch exports to the United States could be doubled within a year. Their estimate was based on Smilde's market research and on the fact that the Netherlands had thus far devoted relatively little attention to fostering dollar exports. Supplementary measures could make the scheme still more successful. In the first two years CIHAN would pay half the start-up costs of new export cooperatives. A guarantee fund would make it possible to store stocks on the spot for quick delivery, price fluctuations in the past having caused heavy losses in this respect. CIHAN would also inform entrepreneurs in the Netherlands of new sales opportunities in the United States and of the standards to be met if their products were to have a reasonable chance of success.

The most significant practical measure was the establishment in the United States of the Netherlands Export Promotion Organization. Smilde, as chief trade commissioner, was to manage five offices, one in New York and four in regional commercial centers, the suggested locations being Chicago, New Orleans, Los Angeles, and Boston. The trade commissioners, to be drawn from the business community, were required to have wide experience of the American market and would work in close cooperation with the Chamber and CIHAN's market researchers. The overall coordination of the official and private organizations was in the hands of the Economic Information Division, which appointed Mr. Lolle Smit, a former Philips manager, as director of export promotion with the specific task of implementing the Export Plan on a strictly commercial basis. He was assisted by an advisory committee of businessmen chaired by Esquire H.A. Quarles van Ufford, a member of the steering committee of the Chamber in The Hague.[9]

The Export Plan 1949, with a budget of Dfl. 3.6 million, met with a mixed reception. The American authorities approved of it, although they had hoped for more than five trade commissioners.[10] Opinions in the Netherlands were divided. On the whole it was well received, with the exception of the free dollar scheme. Some queried it on the grounds that it was surely too late, since it already had been in operation in France and Italy for the past two years. Moreover, Marshall Aid had greatly improved the dollar position.

Philips Electronics N.V., founded in 1891 in Eindhoven, the Netherlands, build its first X-ray tube manufacturing plant in Mount Vernon, New York, in 1933.
This first plant, the Philips Metalix Company, started with 125 employees.

Others wondered whether ten percent was enough, and whether the restrictions regarding transfer to third parties and expenditure solely for production purposes would not affect the effectiveness of the program. The Ministries of Foreign Affairs and of Agriculture, Fisheries and Food were displeased that they had no part in drafting the plan. More importantly, the Netherlands Cabinet felt that the Ministry of Economic Affairs should have gone beyond general measures, that only experience would show how the money should be spent, and that the target group could have been wider than just small and medium-sized companies.[11] But because "no one doubts that this export drive is in the national interest', the plan was finally approved without too many objections".

The Chamber was probably the most disappointed of all parties concerned. Its complaints about trade promotion had never been taken seriously, and now it was suddenly confronted with an entirely new organization to be run by government officials. However, the Ministry of Economic Affairs was firmly opposed to the further expansion of private trade promotion organizations for various reasons. In the first place, the implementation of "a planned economic policy" could not be entrusted to an independent organization. A more compelling reason for setting up an official organization was the subsidy comprising a large part of the Chamber's budget. To add to that the budget for the new organization, which was twice

Certificate to memorise the flight, signed by A. Plesman, 1947

Dutch-Americans and Dutch immigrants in Holland, Michigan, welcome KLM's Holland-Michigan flight, in 1947

as high, would be inconsistent with subsidy guidelines. A sum so large could not be paid to an organization that was not fully responsible to the Netherlands government. But since the war the Chamber had been a semi-government organization in all but name. The consulate-general was represented at all meetings of the Executive Committee and the Board of Directors, and when important issues were on the agenda, the head of the embassy's commercial section was usually present. If he was unable to attend, he was always consulted in advance. The Chamber was also financially dependent on the Dutch government, its income from membership fees and payment for services in 1950, for instance, amounted barely to $ 21,000, as against a subsidy of $ 80,000. The existence of a private organization also had its advantages for the Ministry of Economic Affairs. The expenditure on trade mediation was partly reimbursed by the business community, and a private organization could more easily obtain information from American firms and government agencies.

The operations of the Netherlands Export Promotion Organization convinced the Chamber that it now had an official rival. The Chamber was involved only marginally in the execution of Export Plan 1949 in terms of providing information as it had always done, while the Export Promotion Organization clearly had the more active role. Moreover, as the Economic Information Division now had its own agency in place and had no need to consult others, the Chamber no longer had any say in policy-making. The failure of the official promotion organization might otherwise have been apparent sooner. Notwithstanding the fact that Export Plan 1949 was soon overtaken by economic, political, and organizational developments, it formed the basis for the promotion of exports to the United States up to 1964. This is illustrated by the Dutch export trend. The rise in Dutch exports to the United States from Dfl. 271 million in 1950 to Dfl. 736 million in 1963 was largely attributable to the fast-growing world economy. This is attested by the fact that the percentage of Dutch exports to the United States remained the same. The outbreak of the Korean War in 1950 produced a boom in the United States. Dutch exports reached Dfl. 688 million in 1953, an increase partly due however to price inflation on the raw materials markets. Exports to the United States doubled from 4.3 percent to 8 percent of total exports. They dropped to Dfl. 596 million in 1957, rising again to Dfl. 778 million two years later owing to negative developments in Europe. They stayed for a time at 5.7 percent, but declined to 4 percent in 1963.

In July, 1950, barely ten months after it was put into effect, the Economic Information Division had to admit that the plan had not met its expectations. Though the Export Promotion Organization was not supposed to concern itself with the operations of individual firms, it encroached ever more on the territory of the Chamber. Instead of investigating the market, assisting exports cooperatives, collecting data on import financing, advertising and price policies, and keeping up to date with export promotion policy, the trade commissioners were engaged in the passive promotion of trade. They were instructed to leave all initial contact with industry and commerce in the Netherlands to the Chamber of Commerce. The Directorate recommended that the "free dollar" percentage be raised, since exporters were not as interested as anticipated in 10 percent tied to strict disbursement rules. For the free dollar program to succeed, Dutch exporters should be allowed a greater share of their dollar earnings. Further incentives would be to exempt their share from taxation and for the government to reimburse part of the costs of unsuccessful export projects, covering market research, advertising costs, and the sizeable stockpiles required for the American market. The Netherlands government adopted some of these measures two years later. The free dollar program worked for only a short time because of the rapid liberalization of international trade and the reduced role of the United States as the major supplier of manufactures, raw materials, and manufacturing supplies. When the EVD concluded in 1950 that it was not functioning as expected, the exchange rate of the "free dollar" was 5 to 6 percent higher than the official rate; by 1953 this had dropped below 1 percent. The dollar position having greatly improved, the program was abolished in October.

Some of the measures suggested by the Economic Information Division in 1950 to make the American market more attractive were incorporated in the second export plan presented to Parliament by the Minister for Economic Affairs in 1952. The Netherlands' structural trade deficit with the United States was between $ 125 million and $ 150 million. Dollar imports could not be greatly reduced, and the restrictions governing European trade and the transfer of payments ruled out the possibility of higher dollar earnings from other sources in the short term. Exports must be both increased and more widely distributed, and the percentage of manufactures in the exports package was still too low. Almost 70 percent of exports went to other European countries; indeed the figure for agricultural products was 75 percent. The Ministry was confident of continuing liberalization in Europe, but felt that exports to other markets, including the United States, called for specific measures. A partial tax exemption on export earnings was expected to have a particularly positive effect. But both the Council of State and Parliament were opposed to the idea. Not only would its effect be minimal, but the further growth of exports was impeded by structural problems in the American market. American businessmen had no wish to be dependent on foreign suppliers, and tariff legislation was still rooted in protectionism. Practically no use had been made of other measures, such as an investment guarantee for market research. So long as no premium could be offered for switching from the European to the American market, exporters would not jeopardize the position they had established in Western Europe. This was especially true in the period of economic prosperity that lasted without interruption from 1950 to 1973, when the American market rapidly declined in importance.

The turnaround in the Dutch export offensive came in 1953. With the recovery of the world economy, growing demand in the Netherlands, and the reaccessibility of the German market - the Netherlands' principal pre-war outlet - the exports drive lost its impetus. The balance of payments with the dollar area had so improved by 1953 that shortly after the ending of the free dollar program, the majority of the restrictions on imports from the dollar area were lifted. In evaluating the results of the two export plans in 1956, the Economic Information Division found that the remaining measures had lost much of their purpose through the vastly improved economic situation. All that in fact still remained of the export promotion program, begun with such high hopes in 1949, were the offices of the Netherlands Export Promotion Organization scattered across the United States. Promotional activities there had been in the doldrums since the relationship between the official and the private organizations, and their division of tasks, was settled in 1953.

In 1954 the Ministers of Economic Affairs, Foreign Affairs, and Agriculture, Fisheries and Food asked a committee of government officials and businessmen to draw up a report on the basic elements of trade promotion, with special reference to the relationship between the government and the business community. The Oijevaar committee, named after its chairman, produced its report in 1958. A follow-up report compiled by an expanded committee appeared in 1961. It recommended that the private organizations be encouraged to play a greater part in the promotion of exports. In that same year an evaluation by H. van Blankenstein of the work being performed in the United States initiated the transfer of responsibilities of the official export promotion organization, which had lost all contact with the business community in the Netherlands and had to make strenuous efforts to find anyone interested in its services.

The establishment of the Netherlands Export Promotion Organization was more than a damper on the services rendered by the Chamber to the Dutch government and business community between 1945 and 1949. It was the first time that government had itself moved into the field of export promotion. The official and private agencies eventually reached a modus vivendi, but the price was high. The official organization worked in a vacuum, as it were, and the Chamber was cast in a passive role. The government thus financed two organizations that were unable to function adequately and were constantly in each other's way.

The Netherlands Chamber of Commerce in the United States, Inc.

Restoration of Trade Promotion

About a year before the end of the war in Europe, the Netherlands Chamber of Commerce in the United States, Inc. began preparations for the resumption of trade relations between the Netherlands and the United States. It was awakened from its years of hibernation by the Dutch government and the business community in the United States. Since 1942 the Chamber's activities had been confined to publicity for the Dutch cause. Membership had not significantly declined, and thanks to the sympathy felt for the Netherlands, the support of the government in exile in London, and the importance of the Dutch East Indies as a source of raw materials, the number of affiliated firms grew from 76 in 1939 to 261 in March, 1941. This was probably as many as had been registered with the combined Chambers at the time of their separation in 1939. After Japan occupied the Dutch East Indies at the beginning of 1942, membership gradually declined to 165 by March, 1944. With the end of the war in sight, the number of members rapidly increased towards the end of that year. They included corporations like RCA Communications, Inc. and the agricultural machinery manufacturers International Harvester Co. The annual income from membership fees rose accordingly from $ 8,000 in 1944 to $ 11,000 in January, 1945 and $ 15,000 in April, 1945. By November, 1945 the number of members had swelled to 380, and the fees to almost $ 20,000.

Though the Netherlands Chamber of Commerce in the United States, Inc. now had the largest budget in its history, there was still a substantial deficit. Following the advice of Ambassador Loudon, the Dutch government in exile approved a $ 10,000 subsidy for 1944, and $ 12,000 for the following year. For the same reasons that it was considered preferable to leave the promotion of exports to a private organization, outsiders better not know that the Dutch government could influence the Board's decisions. Even Board members who were not concerned with day-to-day activities were to have no knowledge of this.

Under Anton Bestebreurtje (1944-1954), who became president in January, 1944 on Loudon's recommendation, the Chamber in New York began preparations in the spring of 1945 for the resumption of international trade. Bestebreurtje, then aged 55, had begun his career with the Van den Bergh margarine concern in Rotterdam, managing its subsidiary company in Berlin from 1929 to 1935. For some years he was a financial advisor managing private investments in Switzerland, where Loudon got to know him as president of the Netherlands Chamber of Commerce in Berne. In 1941 he became manager of a chemicals plant in the United States, and in 1943 Loudon asked him to take over the presidency of the Chamber in New York.

In 1944 Bestebreurtje and the Board drafted a provisional management plan that could later be adapted to economic developments. Shortly afterwards the executive secretary, Philip J. Gomperts, and three assistants carried out market research projects for major exports commodities like bulbs, fisheries products, and spirits. Together with the Netherlands Study Group, Gomperts closely monitored economic developments in the United States. The Board appointed a committee from among its members to determine what products were likely to be in demand in the United States immediately after the war. Similar committees dealt with public relations, the recruitment of members, and representation. It was decided to open a branch office in Amsterdam or Rotterdam as soon as possible to maintain contact with the Netherlands government and private industry. With memories still fresh of the friction before the war, Von Baumhauer and the Netherlands-American Chamber of Commerce in Amsterdam were not to be involved. Local representatives would be appointed in such commercial centers outside New York as St. Louis, Philadelphia, Houston and New Orleans. The southern part of the Netherlands was liberated in 1944, and when the first queries reached New York in April, 1945, the preparations had just been completed. The stage was set for the resumption of international trade relations, the revival of the Netherlands' production capacity, and the reawakening of interest in the American market.

Members and Finances

The greater importance of the United States for the Netherlands after the war assured the Netherlands Chamber of Commerce in the United States, Inc. of the interest and support of the Dutch government and business community. The subsidy reached heights hitherto undreamt of, and membership increased five-fold. The turning point came with the full recovery of the European economies in the mid-1950s. The government subsidy was gradually reduced from 1953 onward, and was followed a year later by a decline in membership.

The membership figure rose fastest shortly after the war, especially in the Netherlands. The Economic Information Division organized a highly successful recruitment campaign in 1947, when the Netherlands Chamber of Commerce for America was opened in The Hague to maintain relations with the Dutch government and private industry. On July 1, 1946 there were 46 members of the Chamber of Commerce in the Netherlands; membership of the new Chamber was 258 in 1947, and 522 by the end of 1948. Together with the 359 members in the United States, total membership of the two Chambers was 881. The low-key sister organization in San Francisco had 108 members in 1950. After exports to the United States picked up after September, 1949, membership rose swiftly, peaking in 1952 at 1,190 members of the three Chambers. The figure dropped again after 1954, when exports rapidly declined in both relative and absolute terms, and was 916 as of November 1, 1959, and 867 in 1962.[12]

While partly due to economic trends, the decline in membership also stemmed from structural factors. The Chamber inspired less interest among businessmen in the United States and the Netherlands, and what interest there was waned further when the world economy picked up. American firms were not accustomed to paying for information that could help to boost imports, whether in the form of payment for services or membership fees. Also, as the average size of Dutch firms increased, their interest in the Chambers of Commerce abroad was reduced. The major corporations had long had their own sources of information, and now medium-sized firms were often large enough to manage without the private trade promotion agencies. The big companies usually joined as a matter of principle, sometimes prompted by personal relations between their managements and the secretaries or presidents of the private organizations. If spending cuts were necessary, their contributions to the Chamber were usually among the first items to be slashed. Moreover, the Dutch Chambers of Commerce abroad did not succeed in fostering a sense of commitment in their members, many of whom joined for a time, perhaps after one or two successful transactions, and then left again when they felt sufficiently secure in the new market. Chambers also faced greater competition from commercial sources of information like banks and company representatives. An added impediment to the establishment of lasting ties was the fact that by and large the services that Chambers offered were most in demand in the initial stages of export ventures. A Chamber of Commerce abroad had little to offer once the market had been explored and business relations were established. Efforts to strengthen the ties with members by means of bulletins and monthly journals came to little. In addition, the ongoing liberalization of international trade meant the Chambers' services were less in demand in connection with import restrictions. Before the war the Chambers had helped Dutch exporters to deal with all kinds of trade barriers, either tariff-based or otherwise. In 1956 there were few such matters claiming the attention of the Chamber. Almost 70 percent of its time was spent in furnishing addresses, some 20 percent in providing information on the creditworthiness and reliability of firms, and 10 percent in editing and publishing its bulletin and mediating in disputes.

With close to 1,000 members, the Chamber of Commerce in the United States was one of the larger organizations of its kind. Only those for Belgium and Germany were much bigger, but they were concerned with imports as well as exports. The Chamber for Belgium had some 4,000 members in 1949, and its equivalent for Germany a good 2,000 members. The Chamber for Italy, with 990 members in 1950, was comparable in size to that for America; fewer than 800 firms were affiliated to the Chamber for Britain.

The Chambers' income from membership fees depended on the number of members. A considerable part of the fees paid to the Chamber came from "sustaining members", most of whom were large corporations or their managements acting for reasons of principle. Their contributions of $ 250 and $ 100, respectively, amounted to 30 or 40 percent of the income raised by the Chamber itself. While sustaining members made use of the Chamber's services only very occasionally, they seldom demurred if the fees were increased. Small and medium-sized businesses were not so accommodating, and for that reason the Board of Directors long avoided any increase for fear of precipitating an exodus of smaller members. If new projects were planned or the income for whatever reason was insufficient, the Chamber looked first of all to the Netherlands government for aid. The disappointing development of trade with the Netherlands caused the income from fees to drop from $ 21,500 in 1947 to $ 18,350 in 1948. To compensate for the loss and at the same time to finance new activities, the government subsidy was increased from $ 50,000 in 1946 to $ 60,000 in 1948, which covered approximately two-thirds of the Chamber's expenses in 1947 and 1948. The fees collected in the United States stayed around $ 15,000 for years. It was only in the Netherlands that fees as a source of income increased, rising from under Dfl. 7,000 in 1946 to Dfl. 26,500 in 1947 and Dfl. 44,000 in 1948. From the early 1950s membership fees in the Netherlands totalled some Dfl. 60,000. When the office in The Hague was opened in 1946, it was assumed that it could help to finance the head office in New York. And indeed, in the first few years its income rose faster than its expenditures, but from 1952 on, when it also functioned as a link between Dutch industry and commerce and the Netherlands Export Promotion Organization, its workload rapidly increased. The surplus turned into a deficit, and before long the office in The Hague too was in need of a subsidy. In 1948 the subsidy for the Chamber was $ 70,000, rising to $ 100,000 in 1949 and 1950, and to $ 125,000 in 1951, of which the Chamber in New York received $ 105,000, and the Chamber in San Francisco $ 20,000. In subsequent years it was reduced substantially, first through spending cuts and then because of the expansion of the Netherlands Export Promotion Organization. The reduction mainly hurt the Chambers in New York and The Hague. The share of the Chamber in San Francisco was untouched, for even though its annual income from membership fees barely rose above $ 2,000, the Economic Information Division had high hopes of the economic potential of the West Coast and felt a $ 20,000 annual subsidy was warranted.

The recession following the Korean War forced the Netherlands government to make heavy spending cuts in 1951-1952. The Economic Information Division had already issued new subsidy guidelines in 1950 designed to reduce the government's contribution to Chambers. Instead of allocating funds to cover budget deficits, from now on only specifically designated activities would be eligible for funding. Although there is no indication that this regulation was actually implemented in the 1950s - quite possibly to avoid further complications in the relationship with the Chamber after the problems encountered with the Export Promotion Organization - it represented a principle that was to dominate the private promotion of trade in the 1970s.

Further difficulties with the subsidy arose in 1953. In June, 1952 the Minister for Economic Affairs had personally intervened to prevent that the subsidy would be reduced by half. Geveke, head of the Economic Information Division, had proposed that the work of the Chamber be limited to general public relations for the Netherlands. The Export Promotion Organization had now settled into its role, and could take over the remaining areas of trade promotion. The Minister, Van den Brink, thought it was going too far to cut out the private organizations altogether. After the change of policy in 1953, which included termination of the free dollar program, lower subsidies were inevitable. The fact that the total government contribution to the private promotion of trade was reduced by no more than $ 20,000 in 1954 is attributable to the lower exchange rate of the dollar and to the Economic Information Division having concluded that the Chamber formed a useful complement to the Export Promotion Organization. Further cuts were in the offing however. The final liberalization of trade in 1958 was preceded by another subsidy reduction in 1957, this time by $ 12,000. Two years later it was fixed at $ 60,000, or approximately 65 percent of the expenditure of the Chamber in New York. The government subsidy remained at this level until the work load of the official organizations was transferred to the Chamber in January, 1964.

The importance attached by the government to the growth of exports to the United States is clearly apparent from a comparison of the subsidies made available for this purpose with the financial support received by other Dutch Chambers of Commerce abroad. The sum of $ 50,000 was allocated to the Chamber in New York Chamber in 1948. The equivalent in Dutch currency, Dfl. 168,210, amounted to 55 percent of the funds made available for the private promotion of trade. By 1953 the scarcity of dollars had lost much of its political and economic significance, but the Dutch government subsidy to the Chamber nonetheless totalled Dfl. 305,000, or $ 80,000, five times as much as the equivalent for the Chamber of Commerce for

France (Dfl. 61,000). The amounts received by the other eight Netherlands Chambers of Commerce eligible for a subsidy that year were appreciably smaller. Together with those for France, Spain, and Mexico, the Chamber comprised a group whose costs were paid by the Dutch government up to a maximum of 60 or 70 percent of their respective budgets. In 1957, for instance, the Economic Information Division allocated Dfl. 266,000 of the Dfl. 700,000 budget to the Chamber in New York. The large subsidy received by the Chamber was also exceptional in comparison with that of other foreign Chambers of Commerce in New York.

As industrialization forged ahead in the Netherlands, the number of industrial corporations that were members of the Chamber gradually increased. According to the Chamber, at the beginning of 1949 over 42 percent of all members were manufacturing companies, a figure that rose to 50 percent a year later. No data are available for the years after 1950, but it may be assumed from the attention devoted by the Dutch government to the exports of small and medium-sized manufacturers that the trend continued throughout those years.

As in the pre-war years, the Chamber recruited the majority of their members from small and medium-sized businesses. The Board of Directors of the Chamber and the Steering Committee of the Chamber in The Hague included leading businessmen. They were recruited on the basis of two unwritten rules. Virtually all branches of industry were to be represented, and outgoing members were succeeded wherever possible by someone from the same firm, often nominated by the person to be replaced. With the continuing growth of exports, it became necessary to enlarge the Board of Directors to forty members. Besides multinationals like Westinghouse Electric International Company, International General Electric Company, and General Motors, they represented a conspicuous number of financial institutions including Irving Trust, Manufacturers Trust Company, the Central Hanover Bank and Trust Company, Brown Brothers Harriman and Company, the Chase National Bank of the City of New York, and the Guaranty Trust Company of New York. The Dutch business community was represented by directors of companies that had long operated in the United States, such as the Heineken importer L. van Munching, Frederick R. Wierdsma of the Holland-America Line, A.A. van der Poel of Lindetevis, Inc., and T.R. Barclay of Internatio-Rotterdam. Pieter van den Berg of North American Philips Co. Inc. and Jan van Laer of America Enka Corporation were the first Board members representing the growing number of Dutch direct investors in the United States.

Although the function of the office in The Hague was to be supportive, and that of the Steering Committee up to the early Sixties to be mainly representative, both were endowed with their own distinctive character and prestige. The Committee was composed of prominent members of the business community. The first president was Esquire H.G.A. Quarles van Ufford of the BPM oil company; other Committee members were K.P. van der Mandele, president of the Rotterdam Chamber of Commerce, W.H. de Monchy, executive president of the Holland-America Line, A. Plesman, founder of KLM Royal Dutch Airlines, P.F.S. Otten of Philips, W.G.F. Jongejan, president of the association representing Dutch East Indies business interests, F.H. Fentener van Vlissingen, director of the SHV, representing the trade fair center in Utrecht, and H. Albarda of the Netherlands Trading Society. D.U. Stikker, director of Heineken Breweries in 1947, was appointed Minister for Foreign Affairs and was succeeded on the Committee by Esquire P.R. Feith. Though the members changed in the course of the years, the same firms were represented on the Committee. The one exception was Esquire P.J. Six. After Von Baumhauer's death in 1950, the former secretary of the Netherlands-American Chamber of Commerce in Amsterdam was a key figure in the fusion with the Netherlands Chamber of Commerce for America in The Hague. As the representative of the smaller organization, which had barely fifty members in 1950, he was elected to the Steering Committee and the Executive Committee.

"A Total Blackout of Information"

In the first months after the liberation of the Netherlands in May, 1945, no Dutch trade promotion took place. The first transactions took place at the end of the year, but it was not until the second half of 1946 that Dutch exports reached any significant volume. In 1945 the export earnings of the bulb trade, the first

industry to reestablish contact with American buyers, amounted to Dfl. 8.6 million. The Chamber anticipated that exports over the next few years would mainly consist of labor-intensive luxury goods like
cheese, beer, preserved fish, and arts and crafts. Dutch exports to the United States had to be of a consistently high quality and to be available in large quantities, as American importers were only interested in
smaller consignments of "unique" goods like glassware and ceramics.

Trade information, on the other hand, was available immediately after the war. Even if the Chamber had
been able to collect information on the U.S. market during the war years, the emphasis would still have
been on the Netherlands. A growing stream of enquiries reached the Chamber from all parts of the United
States, but as long as reports from the Netherlands only arrived in a trickle, little could be done. It was
clear that American firms wanted to resume business in Europe as soon as possible. After nearly six years
of war, subsidiaries had to be rebuilt or modernized, and locations selected for new enterprises. If the
Netherlands was to attract American investors, the Chamber needed to be in possession of information
that was reliable and up to date. In 1944 the Netherlands Study Group had drawn up a report on the
Netherlands as a possible location for the European headquarters of American companies. In 1945 it was
more concerned with up-to-date information on the economic situation in the Netherlands. Having been
liberated later than for instance France and Belgium, the Netherlands lagged behind these countries,
which moreover had suffered less physical damage. It took time to reestablish contacts, and in June the
Netherlands embassy in Washington was asked to pass on information with the utmost speed. But the
embassy knew nothing more than what was being reported by the news agencies.

In the course of 1945 the staff of the Chamber was gradually expanded to thirteen. The number of enquiries grew month by month, and in July the Chamber took over the commercial information task of the

*Johnson & Johnson
started in the Netherlands
in 1961 through its
subsidiary Chicopee and
opened a new plant in
1965 to produce
non-wovens.*

Dutch government organizations in the United States. In combination with the publicity campaign
launched later in the year to attract American businesses to the Netherlands, this meant a much heavier
workload, 850 to 900 enquiries being handled in August, September, and October: 45 percent from the
Netherlands, 50 percent from the Dutch government organizations in the United States, and 5 percent

from other sources. So many enquiries came in throughout November that practically the entire staff was engaged full-time in answering all requests, including the assistant secretary for publicity and market research and the staff member responsible for recruiting members. After the years of war, there was "a total blackout of information" in both countries.

Despite the renewed flow of information between the two countries - or perhaps because of it - the number and complexity of the enquiries further increased in 1946. No longer general enquiries as in the first post-war months, the majority of new enquiries required individual attention. Most of the requests related to specific branches of industry or product lines. The dissemination of general economic information about the Netherlands, focused on the ongoing work of reconstruction, was mostly conducted by means of *Holland Rebuilds*, a monthly bulletin published in an edition of 10,000 copies which were sent to members and non-members alike in the Netherlands and the United States. The staff of the Chamber reached its maximum size in 1946, with a staff of twenty at the end of the year, some of whom also assisted Smilde, the deputy-director of the Economic Information Division.

The staff was reduced in 1947 to fourteen. Smilde then had a staff of his own, and the volume of Dutch exports to the United States had not grown as expected. The number of activities further diminished in 1947, when the Chamber introduced a service charge for non-members in an effort to increase its income and to erect a barrier against the foolhardy export ventures that were damaging the reputation of Dutch products in the United States. For the same reason it was decided in 1948 to restrict the provision of detailed information to firms of known repute, and to supply all others with nothing more than general information. Over the next few years, with the expansion of the Netherlands Export Promotion Organization, the staff was gradually reduced to the eleven employed as of January 1, 1953. In addition to the secretary, P.C.A.M. de Bruyn, The Hague office had a staff of four; the secretary in San Francisco, D. Koetser, employed two. This was the picture up to 1964. With regards to the Netherlands Export Promotion Organization, there were at least ten government officials in its New York headquarters, and a trade commissioner assisted by a secretary and, in some cases, an assistant trade commissioner in each of its regional branches.

During the period that the Netherlands Export Promotion Organization existed, the Chamber sent extensive reports to the Economic Information Division on the difficulties besetting Dutch exports to the United States. The reports did not discuss everyday business at the Chamber. The Chamber in New York was at the heart of the activities of the non-government organizations promoting trade with the United States. Trade promotion meant finding markets, and the commercial center of the United States was the obvious place to start. The Chamber in The Hague became a full partner in a relatively short time, surpassing in importance the Chamber in San Francisco, which in 1947 functioned with the support of the Shell concern and a small group of local businessmen with few contacts outside San Francisco. The staff consisted of one young lady who tried to keep things going "with praiseworthy energy and optimism". In 1948 a $ 15,000 subsidy made it possible to engage a secretary, but trade with the Netherlands was not as large as hoped. From 1950 the Chamber in San Francisco worked in close collaboration with the two other Chambers while retaining its autonomy. Its members automatically became members of the two other Chambers and were thus entitled to the use of their facilities. Having the fewest members and the smallest income from membership fees, the Chamber in San Francisco was very much a junior partner.

The Netherlands Export Promotion Organization

The establishment of the Netherlands Export Promotion Organization (NEPO) at the end of 1949 was the start of a new era in the promotion of exports to the United States. The Netherlands government had never before instituted an organization whose sole purpose was to foster Dutch exports. Before long, the initial dismay with which the Chamber greeted this new venture turned to utter disillusionment. Within a few months there were ruptures between the two organizations that could not be healed. Personal factors, the fact that NEPO had no clear directives, and lack of coordination between the various official institutions all took their toll. The Chamber felt thwarted by an interloper that profited from the experience it had accumulated and the reports it had compiled since 1945.

In December NEPO decided not to occupy premises adjoining the Chamber but to seek office space elsewhere. This was a sign of things to come. Bestebreurtje soon found the Chamber and himself relegated to second place. Having given all kinds of assistance in the early stages, he was now obliged to watch while others executed many of the plans he and Smilde had drawn up. For instance, NEPO was to open offices in Chicago and Houston or Dallas, locations which they had pinpointed for agencies at the beginning of the year.

In running NEPO, Smilde avoided cooperating with the Chamber wherever possible. A division of tasks was agreed in December, but within a few months the Chamber was objecting to NEPO's activities. Commercial information and mediation were reserved to the Chamber, but the trade commissioners claimed that passive mediation and the active promotion of exports were too closely interwoven to be regarded as separate areas of activity. Knowledge of the one was indispensable for the performance of the other. The approach of the trade commissioners, all drawn from industry and commerce, was more that of businessmen than of government officials. However, their wide experience with foreign trade did not extend to trade with the United States. While not necessarily a barrier to the promotion of Dutch exports, it did mean the trade commissioners had to start learning the nuances of the American import trade, which was structurally different from Europe. They then vigorously set about closing the gap between Dutch exports and those of other West European countries, most of which had begun export promotion at the beginning of 1949 and had meanwhile opened offices and mounted exhibitions to stimulate the sale of consumer goods. Owing to organizational defects, the results did not meet expectations, and the Economic Cooperation Administration was looking for a public relations success before the end of the year. For Smit and his trade commissioners this was the perfect opportunity to show what they could do for Dutch exports.

According to Ambassador Van Kleffens, the problems occurring after that were mainly due to Smilde's management. He had excellent qualifications for the post of head of NEPO. In the three years that he spent with the Chamber in New York there had been nothing but praise for his capacities, and particularly for the market research he had conducted. When CIHAN was looking for a new director at the beginning of 1949, it coincided with a period of spending cuts likely to mean Smilde's recall to the Netherlands, and his was the first name to be mentioned; the Economic Information Division indeed considered him to be "eminently suitable" for the post. Bestebreurtje went to great lengths to keep him in the United States, and persuaded the Economic Information Division to allow him to stay in New York. Van Kleffens described him as courteous, capable, and intelligent, and as a hard worker. In the event, however, he lacked the drive and the insight needed to run an organization covering the whole of the United States. When things threatened to get out of hand, he tended to retire from the fray rather than take decisive action.

L. Smit also possessed good qualifications to direct the promotion of exports and to implement the Exports Plan. He was personally recommended by the former secretary-general of the Ministry of Economic Affairs, Max H. Hirschfeld, whose word carried much weight in the Ministry. However, Smit was much occupied with the organization in the Netherlands, and did not get on with Smilde. In addition, he was unable to make the psychological transition from the business world to a structure in which autonomous organizations with their own tasks and responsibilities worked closely together. He found it difficult to be dependent on the approval and cooperation of others, whether the Chamber the embassy, or a government department in The Hague. Consequently, relations between the official and the private trade promotion organizations deteriorated so rapidly that the Chamber's president, Bestebreurtje, telegraphed to G. Brouwers, secretary-general of the Ministry, that the situation was spinning out of control.

The Economic Information Division itself was largely responsible for the difficulties. It could not be blamed for the appointment of the two directors, who seemed to be the right choice, but it should not have left the problems to fester for so long. The director, B.J. Geveke, delayed going to New York for talks until November, 1950. Action could have been taken sooner if the embassy had been given a coordinating or supervisory part in the proceedings, but the Economic Information Division was unwilling to cede any influence in decisions or their implementation to the Foreign Ministry. The memory of the pre-war tussles was still fresh. Smilde even objected to the trade commissioners' instructions to send copies of their reports to the embassy. So it was only via third parties that the embassy learned, but by no means everything, of structural matters and where the trade commissioners were to be stationed. The Foreign Service became involved when at a certain point some of the commissioners asked them for instructions because, as they said, Smilde had no time. All the embassy could do was to pass this on to the Economic Information Division and it was left to the Chamber to do deal with the problems regarding NEPO.

In July, 1950, Bestebreurtje wrote to Geveke asking for clarification of the situation. He had heard indirectly that NEPO was about to mount an exhibition in the building housing the Chamber's showroom of Dutch products in New York's Rockefeller Center. Moreover, there were reports that a trade commissioner was to be appointed in San Francisco, at the very moment when the local Chamber had just been revitalized through generous government funding to work under the auspices of the Chamber in New York. Bestebreurtje saw no point in the existence of two identical, heavily subsidized organizations. As the longer established and more experienced of the two, the Chamber should be entrusted with the task of coordinating the promotion of exports in the United States. If the Netherlands government did not agree, the Board of Directors would seriously consider resigning. After four years at the center of trade promotion, sacrificing whatever time they could from their demanding business lives to advise the Dutch government, they categorically refused to be relegated to second place. As a result of the conflict between the Chamber and NEPO, the Economic Information Division felt prompted to evaluate and modify the export drive.

Holland Fair

In January, 1950, the Economic Information Division announced that a Holland Fair was to be held in Gimbel Brothers department store in Philadelphia from May 5 to June 5, 1950, and urged as many Dutch manufacturers as possible to take part. The biggest exhibition of Dutch consumer goods organized under Export Plan 1949, it would allow the Economic Information Division to determine what products would sell in the United States, and how great the demand might be. A collection of thirty Old Masters was included as a crowd-puller. The exhibition was mounted by the celebrated architect Gerrit Rietveld, and the paintings were selected by A. van Schendel, curator of the *Rijksmuseum* in Amsterdam. It gained added luster from the fact that it was to be opened by Prince Bernhard of the Netherlands, Queen Juliana's husband.

From a publicity point of view, Holland Fair was a resounding success for Gimbel Brothers, Dutch exports, and the Economic Cooperation Administration. The arrival of the exhibition on the Holland-America Line's *Noordam*, attended by the governors of New Jersey and Delaware, was widely reported in the press. Nor did interest flag after that. Thousands visited on the first day, and the press coverage was extensive. The Dutch newspaper *Vrije Volk* reported:

What first strikes the visitor to Holland Fair, officially opened on Saturday morning, is the elegance of the exhibition as a whole. Architect Rietveld has transformed a prosaic department store floor into a charming Dutch square featuring small shops with gaily-colored awnings and a side street that I would christen Candy Lane because it is occupied by manufacturers of the most delicious Dutch cookies, chocolate and other delectables.

The wide variety of foods exhibited included cheese, canned ham, and herrings in tomato sauce. The arts and crafts section featured durable goods like ceramics, Leerdam glass, and silver and pewter ware. Sales were unexpectedly brisk, and KLM Royal Dutch Airlines had to fly in additional supplies. While some sections of the exhibition, like the collection of heavy oak furniture, were not so much to American tastes, the U.S. government, press and public were impressed by the wide range and the competitiveness of the goods on display. Of the Old Masters, Jan Steen and Ruysdael were special favorites with the public. The Economic Cooperation Administration's verdict was that through Holland Fair the Netherlands had made a worthwhile contribution to the campaign to bring foreign products to the attention of American consumers.

On the Dutch side there was less enthusiasm. In their first dealings with American commerce, Smit and Smilde encountered a businesslike attitude and the assumption that agreements would be honored. The Chamber felt that no use had been made of its expertise. The sales results of the Holland Fair fell short of expectations, and the Dutch press was critical of the quality of some of the goods exhibited. As an experiment, however, Holland Fair was regarded a success. Even before the opening it was clear that cooperation between the different Dutch institutions left much to be desired, and that a department store was not the ideal setting for an exhibition intended to attract the attention of wholesalers and importers. Smit had contacted Gimbel Brothers in October, 1949 at the suggestion of Paul Hoffmann, head of the Economic Cooperation Administration. At the very first meeting, he made promises that he was not authorized to make, promising for instance that the paintings would include works by Rembrandt and Frans Hals without first checking with the responsible Ministry in The Hague, which refused permission. Gimbel Brothers eventually accepted this in return for new commitments, including the pledge that the exhibition would be opened by Prince Bernhard of the Netherlands, the Queen's husband.

The preparations were inadequate in other ways as well. Four months' notice was too short to allow a representative exhibition to be put together. Since the initial response was disappointing, the Economic Information Division eased the conditions. Among those failing to react were the leading manufacturers in some branches of Dutch industry, including home appliances and luxury consumer goods. The price of many goods was too high, others were of inferior quality, and in many cases the presentation and packaging of the product were not up to American standards. Things went wrong in the United States as well. There were two days in which the Fair was open only to wholesalers and importers. But as the invitations were sent out only two days before, the turnout was disappointing. Nevertheless, some of the contacts established then resulted in orders later in the year. The number and value of the orders placed is not known, but the fact that orders were placed was one of the reasons for the Economic Information Division's decision to organize more exhibitions. Dutch industry welcomed the results, and was fairly unanimous in its opinion that Holland Fair could be repeated, even if only for the goodwill and the publicity it generated. So there were calls for more such shows and as soon as possible. Entries reached the Directorate before the date and place of the next exhibition had been fixed.

In consultation with the Netherlands Ministry of Agriculture, Fisheries and Food, it was decided to organize four smaller food shows in the winter of 1950 and the spring of 1951. They would be directed towards the consumer as well as the retail and wholesale trades. However, the shows never took place. The outbreak of the Korean War in June, 1950 and the recession that followed led to sharp cuts in public spending, allowing no financial support for the promotion of exports. Just the same, Holland Fair set the tone for the trade-oriented exhibitions program developed by the trade commissioners in following years.

The Netherlands Government in the Role of Export Promoter

After Holland Fair it was clear to Geveke that action had to be taken with regard to the structural relationship between the government organizations and the private trade promotion organizations. If Smit had first consulted the Chamber, he would for instance not have approached Gimbel Brothers, but a more upmarket department store like Macy's. Geveke insisted that while the division of tasks was to be maintained, the fullest possible use should be made of the knowledge and experience of the private organizations. The Exports Promotion Directorate was given the task of coordinating the work of the five different organizations which were active in New York, and which often put forward similar proposals. Besides the Chamber and NEPO, the consulate-general and the embassy were also involved with the promotion of trade, and CIHAN's market researchers worked regularly in New York as well. The trade commissioners were to spend more time on actively seeking outlets, setting up special projects, and assisting export cooperatives. It was explicitly stated that all activities were to be dependent on the interest shown by the business community in the form of financial support. The Chamber was allotted the task of passive commercial mediation, and the trade commissioners in the United States and the Trade Promotion Directorate in The Hague were instructed to refer all commercial enquiries to the Chamber. Only the trade commissioners in Chicago, Los Angeles, Houston, and Dallas were permitted to deal with such enquiries themselves. Geveke also issued instructions that the Chamber was to be involved wherever possible in the organization of joint campaigns and the group participation in exhibitions. He went himself to the United States in November, 1950 to try to mediate.

Bestebreurtje agreed to Geveke's proposals, but with reservations. In his view, active and passive trade promotion were so closely interrelated as to be inseparable. He finally yielded to Geveke's argument that for political reasons the Netherlands could not dissolve NEPO. The United States regarded it as the main channel through which the Netherlands was seeking to increase its exports to the dollar area. Geveke promised to return to New York in case new difficulties would arise.

While a certain amount of overlapping still remained, Geveke's intervention had established a basis for a modus vivendi. Bestebreurtje retired in 1954, and the succeeding presidents J.F. van Hengel (1954-1957) and L.M. Reuvers (1957-1962) adopted a more accommodating attitude. Bestebreurtje regarded the promotion of exports as principally a task for the business community itself, with financial and structural aid of the government where necessary. As he saw it, "the Chamber of Commerce is the permanent body... for the fostering of Dutch-American trade relations". Though at times under protest, his two successors accepted the primacy of the government. Thereafter, up to 1964, the Chamber confined its activities to dealing with commercial enquiries, most of which came from non-members.

Was the Economic Information Division correct in making private trade promotion subordinate to the Netherlands Export Promotion Organization? It is true that when it was dissolved in January, 1964, Dutch exports to the United States were much higher than in 1950, having risen from Dfl. 229 million to Dfl. 736 million. But the increase was due more to general economic factors than to the efforts of NEPO. At the beginning of the 1960s, H. van Blankenstein was appointed head of the commercial section of the embassy in Washington with instructions to wind up the official organization and to transfer its activities wherever possible to the private sector. This decision was based on the Oijevaar committee's report of 1958 and the follow-up report produced by the Advisory Council for Economic and Trade Information in 1961. The core of both reports was that the government should end its role in the promotion of exports.

Van Blankenstein's reports on the malfunctioning of the Netherlands Export Promotion Organization can have come as no surprise to the Economic Information Division. He was the first to record in writing how it had proceeded to lead a life of its own without direct contact with Dutch industry and commerce, and how it used subsidies and free access to facilities to "buy" participants for its various activities. In the early 1960s it functioned strictly according to a fixed routine, organizing every year individual and group participations in the same exhibitions and trade shows, and investing much time and money in special department store presentations and other events surrounded by what according to Dutch standards was a wave of publicity. Joint advertising campaigns and tailored articles for trade journals and periodicals were deemed the right way to enhance the image of the Netherlands in the eyes of American commerce and consumer alike. Van Blankenstein doubted whether all that *Holland Promotion* had in fact resulted in any extra sales of a single product. He also had his doubts about the value of trade shows and exhibitions. If success was booked one year, there was a good chance that the same trade show or exhibition would be on the agenda for the following years as well, however difficult it was to find participants. If there were not enough participants, subsidies were offered to attract the number of exhibitors required. Moreover, NEPO made the fundamental mistake of selecting trade shows on the advice of importers, when it was in fact the manufacturer who should decide whether there was a potential market in the United States for his products and whether he wished them to be displayed at a particular trade show. This however was a logical consequence of the fact that NEPO was not permitted to maintain direct contact with business in the Netherlands. Rather than depend on the private trade promotion sector, NEPO allowed itself to be led by the U.S. import trade, which on the whole was not prepared to make any financial commitments. Either the Dutch products that American importers carried were too small a proportion of the goods they imported to warrant a sizeable investment, or the importers themselves were too small. Dutch exporters were likewise unwilling to back the promotion of their wares on the American market financially.

Van Blankenstein therefore concluded that there sufficient reason to discontinue the Netherlands Export Promotion Organization. In the first round of reductions the local offices were annexed to the commercial sections of the consulates-general as from October 1, 1961, and the head office moved to the embassy in Washington. Its activities were gradually phased out, starting with the presentations at trade shows and exhibitions. Winding down the government organization proved to be a simpler matter than persuading the Chamber to take over its remaining responsibilities. The Chamber was already busy with the task of providing commercial information and mediation, while the new president, L.R.W. Soutendijk (1962-1969), felt it should have a more social and representative function, devoting more attention to the promotion of Dutch interests and publicity. He objected most of all to the fact that the government expected the Chamber ultimately to derive an income from the tasks which NEPO had only been able to perform with the assistance of a subsidy that would now be reduced. Van Blankenstein took the same view as Soutendijk, and agreed that the Economic Information Division would maintain the subsidy at a higher rate over the next few years.

The transfer of activities from the consulate-general in New York to the Chamber related primarily to mediation and trade promotion. As Bestebreurtje had argued in 1950, they were practically indistinguishable from the more active aspects of the promotion of trade. The core of all mediation activities, a card index system, containing up-to-date information on more than 1,100 Dutch manufacturers and approximately 980 American firms, including details of their products and trade marks, was moved to the Chamber. The Chamber also took over the work connected with trade shows and exhibitions, subject to the condition that only firms showing an active interest were to be represented, and "Holland promotion" in the form of advertising material for the retail trade. The consulate-general in New York retained responsibility for press releases advertising new products, but not the task of handling the resultant enquiries, which was the territory of the Chamber. The two consulate-general staff members responsible for the card index system and the display material moved to the Chamber. The official who arranged for participation in trade shows remained at the consulate-general and acted in an advisory capacity to the Chamber until his retirement a short time later.

Conclusions

In both financial and administrative terms, the Chamber was more dependent on the Dutch government between 1945 and 1964 than ever before. The reasons were partly economic but more political. The Netherlands government regarded the improvement of basic conditions - the liberalization of trade - as a more effective means of boosting exports than providing commercial information and specific trade promotion measures. In regard to exports to the United States, the minimal interest of Dutch producers in the American market was an additional factor that was a direct consequence of the government's failure to take stimulating measures, as evidenced by the protracted debates on the free dollar program. First there were no goods to export to the United States, and then Marshall Aid solved the problem of the dollar scarcity. The motivation behind Export Plan 1949 was political rather than economic.[13] It has been suggested that the impact of the eight policy documents on industrialization produced between 1949 and 1963 was more psychological than practical. Industrialization being by then under way, the documents were already behind the times when they appeared, so that they signified little more than encouragement for manufacturers to continue on the path they had already chosen for themselves. Similarly, the private and official information and export promotion services seem to have accomplished not so much the actual growth of Dutch exports but awareness among a new category of producers of the opportunities offered by foreign markets.

The greater importance of political factors prevented private institutions, whether the Chamber or the Central Board for Foreign Economic Relations, from having only a limited influence on policy. Suggestions were listened to, assessed on their merits, and sometimes accepted. As a pivotal element of economic policy, the course followed in respect of the dollar was determined solely by the government. Even the views of the Economic Information Division had no effect on the acceptance of the free dollar program.

It may be doubted whether the Chamber could have succeeded where the Netherlands Export Promotion Organization failed. The European market was considered to hold out infinitely greater prospects than those offered by the United States. Only a substantial bonus could have tempted Dutch exporters to abandon their existing outlets for an uncertain venture overseas. Given the Economic Information Division's firm finger on the financial pulse of the non-governmental information services, it may be assumed that it was well aware of the possibility of failure much sooner. If this was the case, why it waited so long to end the activities of the Netherlands Export Promotion Organization remains a mystery.

Notes

1. In 1939 Dutch income from foreign investments accounted for 18 percent of the balance of payments; in 1945 the figure was 6 percent.
2. The firms and organizations in CIHAN included the Trade Show Center in Utrecht, the Netherlands Tourist Association, the Netherlands Railways, the various industrial associations established since the war, and horticultural exports organizations such as the Bulb Growers Association and the Aalsmeer Horticulture Association.
3. This was a problem experienced by the all West European countries. No European manufactured products were among the twenty most imported goods in the United States.
4. Smilde was allocated $ 97,500 for trade promotion over 1946-1947 and 1948. The subsidy for the Netherlands Chamber of Commerce in the United States, Inc. was $ 50,000 in 1946 and 1947, and $ 60,000 in 1948.
5. The figure per head of population has been put at $ 109.
6. Britain had greatly expanded its export organization in New York and San Francisco just a short time before, and had set specific aims in consultation with the business community. The real value of British exports rose by 77 percent between 1946 and 1950.
7. The devaluation of the guilder and of other West European currencies in September, 1949 followed the devaluation of the English pound earlier in the month. The guilder was devalued by 30.5 percent against the value of gold and the dollar.
8. Foodstuffs, paper, and electrical appliances had benefited in particular. The effect was partly neutralized by the way the U.S. authorities enforced the regulations, which led repeatedly to problems and lengthy procedures. Among the casualties was the Holland Weavers Guild, one of the more successful Dutch export associations. U.S. customs duties on large shipments were not levied on the price per unit charged to the customer, but on the price for small shipments, thus nullifying price reductions for large quantities. The decentralized structure of the U.S. customs service allowed each individual office a large measure of freedom in determining the rate to be charged, which resulted in a of complaints from the business community. Moreover, in the case of food imports, the strict terms of the Food, Drug and Cosmetics Act needed to be fully met.
9. The 16 members of the committee included representatives of the Netherlands Trading Society (NHM), AKU, Philips, Heineken, Droste, and the *Internationale Crediet- en Handelsvereniging*

"Rotterdam" NV. Van der Kooy, director of CIHAN, and the chairmen of the Bulb Exporters Association and the Board for Industrial and Commercial Design were also on the committee.

10. Belgium appointed 12 trade commissioners and Britain 34.

11. The major trade and industry organizations had refused to cooperate, and the traders in agricultural products had their own sales channels.

12. The decline was partly due to the transition of the Dutch East Indies into the independent country of Indonesia in 1949. Why this was not reflected in the membership figures before 1954 is unknown.

13. In allowing the dollar shortage to become more acute in 1947, Europe seems to have gambled on American aid. This was less obvious in the case of the Netherlands.

William Merritt Chase in his studio on Tenth Street in New York with a copy of the painting "The Regents of the Old Men's Home" by Frans Hals (1580-1666).
c. 1895
The William Merritt Chase Archives,
The Parrish Art Museum,
Southampton
Gift of
Jackson Chase Storm

Many American painters analyzed and were influenced by the workmanship of the Dutch old masters. The American impressionists William Merrit Chase, John Singer Sargent, and Edmund C. Tarbell bridged the impressionism of Monet with selected techniques of Johannes Vermeer, Frans Hals, and Pieter de Hooch. Fortunately for the painters' continued study of the Dutch painters, American museums had an abundance of Dutch old masters.

*"View on Delft",
c. 1658-60
Painting by
Johannes Vermeer
(1632-1675)
Stichting Vrienden van
het Mauritshuis*

Many American painters frequently studied or painted in the Netherlands, among others John Singer Sargent, Theodore Robinson, George Hitchcock, Joseph Raphael, Frank Benson, John Twachtman, Frank Boggs, and James Carroll Beckwith.

James Augustus Suydam, an American of Dutch descent, was an avid landscape painter who befriended many fellow painters of the Hudson River School. During his life he acquired 92 of their works, which he bequeathed to the National Academy of Design in New York in 1865.

Paradise Rocks,
Painting by
James Augustus Suydam
(1819-1865)
National Academy of
Design, New York

⇒
Spring Blossoms
Painting by
George Hitchcock
(1850-1913)
Private collection
Courtesy of R.H. Love
Galleries, Chicago

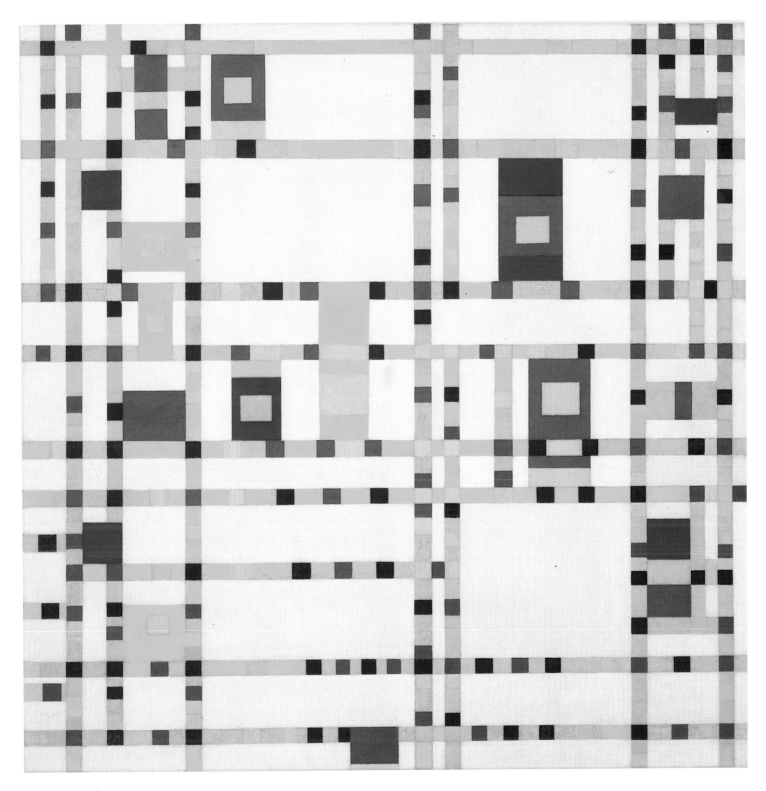

Born and raised in the Netherlands, Piet Mondriaan participated in "De Stijl" movement which emerged during World War I when an unprecedented global conflict seemd likely to destroy civilization, indeed reason itself. The clarity of design, the sharp-edged geometric forms and simple colors of De Stijl affirmed reason and order in a world gone mad. After moving to Paris in 1930, Mondriaan escaped from World War II in 1941 to New York where he worked until his death in 1944. "Broadway Boogie Woogie", one of Mondriaan's last paintings, is a reflection of the rational principles of De Stijl and typical New York elements like the ordered network of city streets and the staccato rhythms of street lights.

Broadway Boogie Woogie,
1942-43
Piet Mondriaan
(1872-1944)
The Museum of Modern
Art, New York

201

Fokker's F-100 of Midway Airlines

The Dutch aircraft pioneer Anthony Fokker first explored the American market in October 1920. The first Fokker III, named "Half Moon" after Henry Hudson's Dutch exploration ship in the seventeenth century, was being demonstrated in America as early as 1921. Soon thereafter landed a contract to build airplanes for the U.S. army and in 1924 an empty aircraft factory was acquired in Hasbrouck Heights, New Jersey. Fokker became a well-known name in the United States in 1925 as a result of the historic first flight across the North Pole by Lieutenant Commander Richard Buret's in a Fokker VIIa-3m. In 1927, Fokker's name in its association with epoch-making flights reached its peak with Maitland and Hegenberger's first flight across the Pacific from America to Hawaii in a Fokker C-2 and that same month the record-breaking flight of Buret, Balchen, Acosta, and Neville from New York to Europe, landing their Fokker C-2 in the water just off the beaches of France. Today, Fokker 100 and Fokker 70 aircraft fly throughout the American skies in the colors of American Airlines, US Air, Midway Airlines, and Mesa Airlines.

KLM Royal Dutch Airlines, the recipient of the 1994 George Washington Vanderbilt Trophy, is the oldest commercial airline in the world. On may 21st, 1946, KLM was the first continental European airline to start scheduled services to the USA. A pioneer in transatlantic flight, KLM Royal Dutch Airlines has confirmed its commitment to the United States market by forming a strategic partnership with Northwest Airlines. Together, KLM and Northwest constitute the world's first Airline Alliance with a route network of over 350 cities in more than 80 countries on 6 continents.

KLM-Boeing 747

⇒
*Tulip fields near
Hillegom,
the Netherlands,
Six Archives*

CHAPTER VI

1964 - 1976: COORDINATION AND CENTRALIZATION

Between 1964 and 1976 radical changes occurred in the Dutch economy, in the promotion of exports, and in providing commercial information. The buoyant economy of the 1950s and 1960s came to an abrupt end in 1973. The Yom Kippur War between Israel and the Arab states in 1967 precipitated a 35 percent rise in the price of oil and a worldwide recession. Growth stagnated and the watchword for the Dutch economy was retrenchment. The United States was still a secondary market for Dutch exporters. Though Dutch exports to the United States doubled between 1965 and 1970, industry focused increasingly on markets closer to home. Owing to the growing differences in trade policy between the Europe and the United States, and the devaluation of the dollar in 1971, exports to the United States comprised a smaller share of total Dutch exports. The prosperous 1960s gave way to the years of oil crises, spending cuts, and slower economic growth in the 1970s.

Similar to the developments in the world economy, the changes in the official promotion of Dutch trade with the United States had consequences for the Chamber. Its activities were expanded and professionalized, and the ties uniting the various offices were strengthened. The reasons behind the termination of the official promotion of Dutch exports to the United States had other repercussions in the Netherlands as well. A new institution, the Central Chamber for the Promotion of Trade (CKH), was set up to relieve the Netherlands government of the burden of trade promotion and to take over and extend the work of the Central Institute for the Promotion of Foreign Trade (CIHAN). It became a divisive element in the world of non-governmental trade promotion organizations. Instead of coordinating the Chambers' activities, as it was intended to do, the CKH aimed at centralization. The result was a ten-year battle in the field of export promotion in which the Chamber played a prominent part. The CKH lost this battle in 1974. Both costly and ineffective, it failed to attract additional funds from private industry, and its government subsidy was reduced when the Netherlands economy went into recession.

The growing importance of regional U.S. markets for Dutch exports led in 1972 to the establishment of an office in Chicago and the reopening of the Chamber in San Francisco. In 1975 it was transferred to Los Angeles, which had replaced San Francisco as the commercial center for the West Coast. The fragmented structure of the privately-run trade promotion organizations were no match for the pressure of the spending cuts enforced by the government since 1972. With the addition of an office in Chicago, the Netherlands Chamber of Commerce in the United States, Inc. consisted of four formally autonomous organizations, making a uniform policy and decisive action difficult to achieve.

The consequences were soon apparent. Attempts by the Economic Information Division to reduce the Chamber's dependence on subsidies by advocating a more businesslike, market-oriented approach did not coincide with the Chamber's view of trade promotion as primarily assistance for financially weaker small and medium-sized companies. If the Netherlands government wished to promote exports to the United States, then it should bear the costs itself. The Chamber managed to avoid reorganization and changes in their activities for quite some time. But as from January, 1975, when a new subsidy policy was introduced, it was forced to face the facts. Radical changes followed before the end of 1976. The management of the Netherlands Chamber of Commerce in the United States, Inc. was centered in New York, the Chambers in Chicago and Los Angeles were closed, and the activities in the Netherlands were transferred to the Netherlands Trade Promotion Center (NCH), which had succeeded the CKH. The Chamber was now obliged to bring its operations in line with the demands of a new era.

Dutch Exports

The first signs of approaching economic problems appeared towards the end of the 1960s, while the Dutch economy was still expanding. Rising wage costs eroded the Netherlands' competitiveness on the world market. Its 20 percent share of world trade between 1965 and 1974 had been based on a willingness to accept smaller profit margins in order to capitalize on the fast growing demand in other countries, and to consolidate the country's strong trading position in the European Community. The same was true of exports to the United States. Between 1973 and 1977 the relative price level of the products exported to the United States rose by only 2 percent.

Overall Dutch export earnings fell by 10 percent, a 'loss' that was offset by the relatively steep rise in prices on the domestic market. This however had the effect of eroding the home market position of Dutch producers, who were pushed on to the defensive by imports from cheap-labor countries. From 1970 onward, import penetration in all sectors of the Dutch economy grew by 2 percent per year. Industry had to watch foreign competitors increase their share of the market from some 39 percent in 1970 to 45 percent in 1978. By the end of the 1970s, imports accounted for more than half the consumer goods sold in the Netherlands.

Passing on the rising production costs to the domestic market had the effect of fuelling inflation in the Netherlands, partly because higher prices automatically led to wage rises. In 1971 and 1972 inflation was higher in the Netherlands than in any other industrialized country. Between 1963 and 1974 it averaged 5.6 percent, in 1975-1976 as much as 9.5 percent. The competitiveness of Dutch industry and commerce was further undermined by the strong guilder, which rose in value against the dollar by 30 to 40 percent up to 1979.

The growth of the Dutch economy slowed significantly after 1973. In the previous decade GDP rose by an annual 5.5 percent in response to the upward trend of the world economy. In 1974, when recession set in, GDP growth dropped to 2.7 percent. An overheated world economy caused problems in the labor and raw materials markets, culminating in inflation on an international scale. The collapse of the dollar in 1971 ended the system of fixed exchange rates that had played such a large part in the rapid growth of world trade since 1945. The 1973 oil crisis triggered an abrupt rise of more than 30 percent in the price of oil imports.

Internal factors played an equally important part in the relatively slow economic development of the Netherlands between 1965 and 1974. Industry underwent radical and structural changes. Labor-intensive industries like textiles, clothing, and leather manufacturing lost ground to the capital-intensive chemical, oil refining, transport equipment, and electrotechnical industries. The growth of other major industrial sectors also slowed after 1965. Generally speaking, boundless success was confined to industrial sectors dominated by corporations like Philips, Shell, Unilever, and AKZO. Food and beverage manufacturing, traditionally a mainstay of Dutch exports, remained the principal export sector. After 1974, following the energy crisis, natural gas accounted for a significant proportion of Dutch exports. In the boom years the composition of Dutch exports was a positive element in the country's competitiveness, but after the downturn in the world economy demand shifted to less energy-consuming products. Post-war industrialization had been based to a large extent on the consumption of large quantities of cheap energy. When oil prices soared in 1973, a sizeable share of the export market was lost.

Dutch export earnings rose steadily from Dfl. 21.7 billion in 1965 to Dfl. 42.6 billion in 1970, Dfl. 61 billion in 1973, and almost Dfl. 96 billion in 1976. The index of Dutch exports according to volume (1975=100) showed an increase from 40 in 1965 to 71 in 1970, 101 in 1973, and 113 in 1976. This trend was clearly perceptible in exports to the United States. Between 1958 and 1964 the rapidly growing demand in the Netherlands and the other E.C. member states absorbed virtually the entire production capacity and deflected the attention of exporters from the more difficult U.S. market. The stagnation of economic growth in Western Europe after 1965 then forced Dutch firms to seek new outlets for their products. Fortunately, this development coincided with the search of American corporations for foreign suppliers to supplement inadequate domestic production capacity. Partly owing to the booming U.S. economy, the value of Dutch exports to the United States doubled over the next five years, rising from Dfl. 880 million in 1965 to Dfl. 1.8 billion in 1970. The United States accounted for 3.9 percent of Dutch exports in 1965, and 5.2 percent in 1968. Like all European countries, the Netherlands was dependent for its exports on a comparatively small number of products largely specific to the country. Home-produced agricultural products such as ham, bulbs, and cheese, and staples market commodities like tobacco, tea, and cocoa, accounted for almost one-third of Dutch exports to the United States. The manufacturing sector was dominated by Philips products (30%), machinery (14%), chemical products (10%), and iron and steel (7%). Durable consumer goods like carpets and office equipment gradually won a place on the American market. Much of the growth was attributable to Dutch subsidiaries of American firms, which had ready access to the United States.

In contrast to the rest of the European Community, only a small proportion of Dutch exports went to the United States. The American market was capable of absorbing such large quantities of specific products that only very large corporations or industrial sectors could produce to meet demand. Dutch industry, with its much smaller production units and wide range of products, was consequently at a disadvantage as compared with countries with large domestic markets.

After 1970 there were few Dutch manufacturers with the commercial allure, high-grade products, and production and investment capacity needed to succeed on the American market, which was primarily regarded as a secondary outlet. Dutch exports to the United States declined rapidly after 1970, first due to the buoyant West European economies, then to the recession in the United States, the devaluation of the dollar in 1971 and again in 1973, and the high level of inflation in the Netherlands. The competitiveness of Dutch industry was affected most by the fall in the dollar's exchange rate from Dfl. 3.60 to Dfl. 2.70, and the precipitate rise in domestic costs. Whereas in 1970 the United States accounted for 4.3 percent of Dutch exports, this figure was 2.8 percent by 1975.

The import cover improved considerably between 1967 and 1974. Following the trend of other E.C. countries' trade with the United States, Dutch exports expanded at a faster rate than imports, rising from around 30 percent in the early 1960s to more than 40 percent. The concentration of Dutch exporters on neighboring markets combined with the low exchange rate of the dollar partly accounts for the drop to 30 percent import cover in 1975-1976. Throughout the 1960s and 1970s, the European Community had an effective monopoly of lower technology products in its own market. Even though labor productivity averaged no more than 30 to 50 percent of that in the United States, production could focus on the goods for which demand was heaviest in the E.C. Trade between the member states grew at almost three times the rate of trade with other countries. Dutch trade was almost regional in character, approximately half being confined to an area reaching no further than one hundred miles from the national borders. Owing largely to the thriving trade with West Germany, the share of the E.C. in Dutch exports increased from 67 percent in 1964 to 72 percent in 1976.

Throughout this period the Netherlands retained its position as one of the principal investors in the United States. Between 1965 and 1970 the value of Dutch direct investments in the United States rose from $ 1.3 billion to more than $ 2.1 billion. Shell Oil, with a share of $ 1.3 billion, was at the top of the list. The volume of industrial investments doubled in barely five years from $ 328 million to $ 652 million. At the end of 1974 Dutch assets in the United States amounted to Dfl. 6.6 billion, almost a quarter of the Dfl. 49.6 billion of foreign direct investment.

The interest of Dutch exporters in the United States showed an increase in the second half of the 1960s, which however evaporated with the 1973 downturn in the world economy. Economic developments had an impact both on the Chambers and on the organization of private promotion of trade in the Netherlands.

Centralization, the User-Pays Principle, and the Non-Conformists

The private and official promotion of Dutch trade underwent far-reaching changes between 1963 and 1976. The decision of the Netherlands government in 1961 to introduce the User-Pays Principle was supported by some representatives of private industry as an instrument to integrate all trade promotion organizations in the Netherlands into a central institution. They believed that centralization would curb duplication of effort, increase efficiency, and foster greater readiness on the part of government and private enterprise to allocate funds. The leadership of the Centrale Kamer van Handelsbevordering (CKH), the Central Chamber of Trade Promotion, regarded duplication inevitable in the existing system of private and official trade promotion, and disregarding all other options, it saw centralization as the only solution. The CKH considered it unnecessary to present any evidence in support of its case, but for quite some time political pressure was brought to bear to prevent the opponents of centralization from examining the facts on which it was said to be based.

In the early years of its existence the CKH primarily concentrated on integrating the various private organizations. Agreement was reached with the majority of those in the Netherlands in 1967 and in 1970 with the Dutch Chambers of Commerce abroad. The Netherlands Ministry of Economic Affairs was at first not actively involved in the issue, but when the CKH tried to capitalize on the appointment of a new Minister for Economic Affairs in 1967 to obtain official trade promotion responsibilities, the situation changed.

The Minister involved, L. de Block (1967-1970), lent a willing ear to the supporters of the CKH view. He was the last Minister for Economic Affairs to endorse the prevailing post-war principle that government should play an active part in the promotion of exports. It was during his term of office that the first signs of the policy principle elaborated in 1971-1972 by his successor, H.J. Langman, became perceptible, namely that the promotion of exports was primarily a matter for industry and commerce itself. Taking it as axiomatic that a privately-run central institution would function more efficiently, De Block was of the

With an annual total of nearly 300 million tons of cargo being handled and visits by over 30,000 seagoing vessels and 125,000 inland vessels, the Port of Rotterdam is by far the world's greatest hub of shipping activity. Over 80 percent of the total cargo handled in Rotterdam is forwarded to other major destinations within Europe, making Rotterdam the true Gateway to Europe. Adding to its prime location at the mouth of the Rhine river and the free access ships enjoy without locks or tidal restrictions, the Port of Rotterdam is continuing its major investment programs in infrastructure and automation in order to extend its lead in the 21st century.

opinion that export-promoting activities should be transferred to the partly state-financed CKH wherever possible. He took no account of the growing opposition in the Dutch business community and the top ranks of his Ministry, where there were serious doubts about the advantages offered by centralization. The senior Ministry officials who were opposed to the plan wielded considerable influence and were instrumental in its eventual defeat. The plan was based on the fact that economic information was required both by government and by private enterprise, and that it was already efficiently supplied by the Economic Information Division. De Block's policy was faithfully implemented and his officials assisted him to the best of their ability, but their heart was not in it. According to rumors, officials in the Ministry were responsible for the change of policy immediately following De Block's resignation in February, 1970. A general election was scheduled for 1971, and the responsible Junior Minister, L. van Son, felt the decision should be left to the next Cabinet. While economic growth gradually slowed, and the Ministry came under increasing pressure to start the reorganization, the Economic Information Division under Van Son carried out a policy evaluation. The conclusion was that the policy formulated in the 1950s was out of step with the changes that had meanwhile occurred in the structure of international trade, and that future policy should be based on systematic appraisal of the effectiveness of the information services.

It was not until 1972, when Minister Langman took office, that the views of Ministry officials were sympathetically received at political level. Like De Block, Langman felt that trade promotion was principally a matter for industry and commerce itself, but took it a step further than his predecessor by insisting that this applied to the financial side as well. His policy announced in September, 1972 imposed both organizational and financial restrictions on the role of the Netherlands government in the promotion of Dutch exports. Van der Torn & Buningh, a Utrecht firm of management consultants, was commissioned to work out the practical details of the new policy, and specifically to determine what financial advantages would accrue from "the full or partial integration of the departments and institutions concerned with the promotion of trade and of exports". A quantitative input and output analysis produced by the Economic Information Division, the CKH and its associated institutions, and the Dutch Chambers of Commerce

abroad showed that there was indeed a certain amount of overlap, but chiefly in the work of the CKH. Given the high overhead costs, centralization would not result in significant savings. Decentralization and cost-effectiveness were thereafter the key-words for providing commercial information and promoting Dutch exports.

Recommendations (1958-1962)

Officials at the Netherlands Ministry of Economic Affairs and the private trade promotion organizations were extremely concerned about the course that would be followed by the CKH even before it replaced CIHAN in 1963. On July 14, 1954 the Ministers for Economic Affairs, Foreign Affairs, and Agriculture, Fisheries and Food set up the Advisory Committee on Economic and Trade Information to look at the viability and subsidization of the organizations in the Netherlands and abroad, and to coordinate initiatives taken by the government and private enterprise. Chaired by Jan J. Oijevaar, it was composed of representatives of the three relevant ministries and four members representing the Central Board for Foreign Economic Relations.

Over the next ten years Oijevaar was a dominant figure in the discussions on the substance and, more specifically, the organizational structure of Dutch trade promotion and commercial information. Since joining the Economic Information Division in 1936, he had risen rapidly in the ranks of the civil service. In 1939 he was appointed deputy director of the State Maritime Shipping Office, and during the second world war he was a senior assistant to secretary-general Hirschfeld of Economic Affairs. As director-general of the Ministry of Transport and Public Works after the second world war, Oijevaar played an important part in rebuilding the Dutch merchant marine, and represented the Netherlands on a number of intergovernmental shipping organizations. In 1952 he joined the Board of Directors of the Rotterdam shipping company Phs. van Ommeren NV, and was thereafter closely involved in consultations between the Netherlands government and private industry. Oijevaar was one of the initiators of the regular consultations between the Chambers of Commerce in Dutch sea ports that began in the 1950s, was a member of the Central Board for Foreign Economic Relations, represented the Netherlands as chairman of the OECD Maritime Transport Committee, and was intimately acquainted with many officials and politicians. He was determined to push through the centralization of trade promotion, despite the vehement protests of the Ministry of Economic Affairs up to the level of the Minister. The Oijevaar committee's recommendations to the Netherlands government were contained in a report issued on March 6, 1958. Without having evaluated either the working methods or the structure of the various government and private export promotion organizations, the committee concluded that their work was fragmented and overlapping, and that centralization was the only way ahead. CIHAN should be radically reorganized and expanded. In addition, the subsidy guidelines should be tightened up in order to guarantee the continued existence of the private organizations. Integration would moreover strengthen their bargaining position with the Netherlands government. The committee also expressed the hope that the private organizations would be drawn more closely into the managing and supervising the government economic information services, and would in time become the principal advisors to the government on the promotion of exports.

After the publication of the report, the Minister for Economic Affairs, J. Zijlstra, asked the Central Board to nominate the members of a new body, the Advisory Council for Economic and Trade Information. Oijevaar was chairman. His assignment this time was to evaluate the activities of the information sector, after which "a healthy structure" for the entire sector could be established. B.J. Geveke, head of the Economic Information Division, emphasized the Council's task of "retaining what was good" and eliminating excesses and duplication. It was soon evident that Oijevaar had the support of the main employers' organizations, which wished to see all commercial information and export promotion activities concentrated in the hands of private enterprise.

The report produced on March 28, 1961 was on much the same lines as the 1958 report. Evaluation was again cursory at most. The Council members were representatives of large corporations which had little experience with export promotion. It was nonetheless decided not to hold hearings to give various organizations the opportunity to present their views. The Council saw no need of hard facts to validate the argument that the work of the private and government organizations should be coordinated. The Economic Information Division and the private organizations were not opposed to coordination as such. A certain measure of supervision and professional management would benefit the smaller Chambers abroad. According to Abeln, head of the Economic Information Division, many of them were run by lackluster managements. Moreover, as the Dutch Chambers of Commerce abroad often lacked the right contacts in the Netherlands, it was virtually impossible for them to find adequate support for even the best designed market research and marketing plans.

The main problem was to know exactly what Oijevaar actually had in mind. Would he stop at coordination, or was centralization his goal? The Ministry was adamantly opposed to centralization. The government needed economic information, and could not relinquish this responsibility to an institution not under its full authority. The financing and maintenance of contacts with the foreign service, in particular, were an "inalienable" responsibility. It was inconceivable that a semi-private organization could be authorized to issue instructions on economic information to embassies and consulates. Nor was Abeln prepared to countenance sharing responsibility for policy-making with private enterprise in return for more financial support.

The Ministry was not alone in rejecting the recommendations of the Advisory Council. Opposition was growing within the Council itself as the concept of centralization loomed ever larger. The opponents included prominent businessmen like D.A. Delprat, a representative of shipping interests and president of the Amsterdam Chamber of Commerce, W.H. de Monchy, former president of the Netherlands Chamber of Commerce in the United States in The Hague, and H.C.J.H. Gelissen, a former Minister for Economic Affairs. They supported the Ministry by advocating greater coordination through CIHAN, but retention of the existing institutions' independence. The importance of the Chambers of Commerce abroad for exports was based first and foremost on the composition of their boards, and restricting their freedom of action could result in the exodus of many of their members. Such a loss of local contacts and expertise could not be compensated from the Netherlands. It was for that reason that the Netherlands Chamber of Commerce in the United States rejected the proposed close collaboration with the CKH in 1964, arguing that it was precisely because of the personal contacts of the secretary that prominent businessmen were prepared to accept a seat on the Board. Integration with the CKH would assuredly cause the "extremely representative" New York Board of Directors to lose all interest in the Chamber. Lack of interest on the part of some Council members and the failure of the opposition to unite, believing that Oijevaar had the support of the government, enabled him to ensure that the Council's final report reflected his views. The Minister for Economic Affairs, J.W. de Pous, lost no time in announcing that the Council could claim no right to participate in the formulation of government policy. Since there was enough private enterprise support for the proposal, he had no objection to the reorganization of CIHAN. Oijevaar seized on the establishment of the CKH to expedite his plans for non-governmental promotion of exports.

The reason for establishing the CKH was the widespread dissatisfaction in government and business circles with the functioning of CIHAN. Since its inception in 1946, CIHAN had remained a semi-official body, remote in some respects from the business community. This was now to change with the advent of the CKH, which was envisaged as a broad-based organization not only coordinating the private promotion of trade but also providing administrative services and support for the smaller trade promotion organizations. CKH would also promote exports to countries not covered by private organizations and, in general, fill the gaps in the system. Government and private enterprise agreed to put up a joint starting capital of Dfl. 1.5 million; thereafter CKH was to be self-supporting through donations and service charges. The Netherlands Ministry of Economic Affairs agreed to pay an annual subsidy equal to the amount of the other revenues. To facilitate cooperation between private and government organizations, the Advisory Council suggested that each be allocated specific spheres of activity. The government organizations could assume responsibility for macro-information, i.e. the dissemination of general economic information, official publicity, and the reception of foreign missions, while the private organizations would concern themselves with micro-information, i.e. information for individual firms plus such activities as training courses, advising on exhibits for trade fairs, market research, and trade missions to other countries. Finally, the Council recommended that the Netherlands be the focal point for information relating to exports, it being after all the exporters themselves who decided where to send their products.

The organizational structure of the CKH displayed serious shortcomings from the start. The Council's report made no mention of how it was to be incorporated into the existing system of private organizations. The gaps in the system proved in practice to be smaller than had been thought, and the necessary work was already being performed by private or official organizations. The private trade promotion organizations, though covering a comparatively small number of countries owing to the geographical concentration of Dutch exports, included the five most important Netherlands Chambers of Commerce abroad, namely in West Germany, Belgium, France, Britain, and the United States. The countries accounting for three-quarters of Dutch exports. There was a private trade promotion organization for practically every country with which the Netherlands maintained trade relations of any significance. Even before the Advisory Council had produced its report, the Netherlands Ministry of Economic Affairs stated unequivocally that there would be no question of transferring any of its responsibilities. The private organizations expressed themselves in the same vein. The CKH was obliged to deploy all its powers of persuasion to get cooperation with the private sector off the ground. Meanwhile it had expanded into an institution with a staff of approximately 120, and before long, in search of employment, it encroached on the terrain of the private organizations. The overlap that the CKH later used as a reason for integration was thus largely of its own making. Before an association agreement was concluded with the Netherlands Chambers of Commerce abroad in 1968, its 11-strong West European section duplicated a considerable part of their work.

The tone of the Council's report, a compilation of clichés, was that everything should be bigger and better. Once a sound organizational structure was in place and the right people were found, new methods and activities would automatically follow. Instead, the result was friction with all organizations.

Private Trade Promotion: for and against Integration

The CKH was founded in 1963. The chairman, nominated by Oijevaar, was Sidney J. van den Bergh, an ex-Minister of Defense for the Liberal Party; the director was B.J. Udink, head of the information department of the Rotterdam Chamber of Commerce. It was soon apparent that both men supported Oijevaar's views. Van den Bergh was to be the principal spokesman for the CKH up to its dissolution in 1974, assisted first by Udink until his appointment in 1967 as Minister for Development Cooperation, and then by P.H. Noordwal, former secretary of the Netherlands Employers Federation. There were five regional directors, of whom H. Bloemendaal was responsible for the United States and Canada. Before an association agreement was concluded with the Federation of Chambers of Commerce for Foreign Trade in 1968, Bloemendaal was active in other areas, such as the GATT negotiations in 1967-1968.

The CKH was handicapped from the outset by the fact that Oijevaar had more or less ignored the wishes of the private organizations in his expansionist drive. Although the Economic Information Division repeatedly avowed that it was prepared to cooperate and indeed to make concessions, relations between the private organizations and the CKH showed little sign of improvement in the first two years. Notwithstanding all expressions of good will, the private organizations were highly suspicious of the CKH and its true intentions. Oijevaar did not help matters by repeatedly urging for more centralization. And Van den Bergh and Udink were sometimes less than diplomatic. Van den Bergh approached the promotion of exports as a businessman. He chose his goal and headed for it regardless of all opposition. Abeln, who suggested that he would accomplish more by a less abrasive approach, was advised by Van den Bergh to follow his example.

However, Van den Bergh was firmly convinced that once he had silenced his main critics, the end results would prove him right. According to Abeln, Udink was also extremely difficult to work with, and in planning the CKH's work program he was overly inclined to judge all earlier activities with a severely critical eye.

The storm broke in October, 1963. Just when Van den Bergh had said he wanted to achieve closer collaboration, Oijevaar proposed that all private organizations be fully integrated into the CKH, which would take over their administration and finances, and leave them with the sole task of implementation. Oijevaar's proposal caused utter consternation. Abeln, who attended the meetings between the Advisory

212

Council and the private organizations as an observer for the Netherlands Ministry of Economic Affairs, felt it necessary for the first time to intervene. He warned that Dutch exporters would lose vital contacts and a fund of specialized knowledge if the CKH continued on this course. The managements of the private institutions would resign rather than be absorbed into the CKH. He advised a six-month cooling-off period. On the instructions of G. Brouwers, secretary-general of the Ministry of Economic Affairs, Abeln thereafter abstained from participating in the dispute. The Ministry attached great importance to the systematized collaboration of the information institutions, but felt it should be initiated by the private trade promotion organizations themselves. On the other hand, the influential export lobby was in no way to be antagonized. So the Ministry adopted a non-partisan stance, leaving it to the business community itself to find a way out of the crisis. But when in the course of 1967 the CKH extended its empire-building ambitions to the Economic Information Division, the Ministry refused, as it had done before, to change its subsidies policy in order to force the private organizations to cooperate.

The CKH and the private organizations met again in April, 1964. Abeln was not hopeful of the outcome. Through their tactlessness and their equivocal attitude to the question of integration, Oijevaar, Van den Bergh, and Udink seemed to rule out all possibility of reaching agreement. To be sure, Udink was in a difficult position. The private organizations' suspicions of his motives had deepened after Oijevaar's last integration proposal. No one believed his statements that he had no prior knowledge. Before the meeting, Abeln told Minister Andriessen that he expected the directors of some of the organizations to resign if the integration plan was forced through. He was thinking in particular of the Netherlands Chamber of Commerce in the United States in The Hague. And it did indeed follow the example of the Africa Institute and the Netherlands-Israel Chamber of Commerce in refusing to work in association with the CKH. Five more organizations made the same decision in July, including the important Netherlands-German Chamber of Commerce. The CKH was forced to moderate its demands.

The CKH and twenty-three smaller organizations in the Netherlands were finally associated in 1965, becoming the CKH-Associated Institutions. No agreement was reached with the Netherlands Chambers of Commerce for America and Germany, the only two with offices both in the Netherlands and abroad. To avoid the risk of being played off one against the other, the "nonconformists", as they came to be known, united in the Federation of Chambers of Commerce for Foreign Trade, with which the similar organizations for France, Belgium-Luxembourg, and Switzerland also affiliated. The president was Esquire W. van Andringa de Kempenaer, president of the Netherlands Chamber of Commerce for Germany and director of the Haarlem publishers Joh. Enschede & Son NV.

Conciliation and Association

The Federation and the CKH spent almost three years in negotiations. No headway could be made until the latter at length renounced the idea of centralization and adapted the recruitment of members to the wishes of the Netherlands Chambers of Commerce abroad. Shortly after its inception the CKH had set out to raise more money by increasing its membership. This complicated the individual Chambers' own recruitment efforts, the more so since the CKH presented itself as an institution that could assist businessmen in all parts of the world. As the business community knew little about the structure of the private commercial information organizations, CKH members thought they were entitled to the services of the nonconformists. The nonconformists refused an offer of collective CKH membership in return for making their services available to their members. The CKH then threatened to acquire the influence it sought by other means.

The CKH turned down a mediation offer from the Central Board for Foreign Economic Relations in 1966, but in June, 1967 the situation came into motion when, at the request of the Federation, the CKH drew up a proposal designed to serve as a basis for further discussion between the CKH directors F.A.F. Scheurleer and H. Bloemendaal, and L.F. van der Zee and R.H. Marius for the Federation. A draft association agreement was signed by Van den Bergh and Van Andringa de Kempenaer in February, 1968. While retaining their autonomy, the Federation and the CKH would work together in a new body, the National Council for the Promotion of Foreign Trade (NRH). The CKH committee was converted into a joint steering committee, with the addition of five members representing the Federation and five representing the Associated Institutions. The Council's task was to draw up guidelines for the export drive to be organized each year, to suggest ways of achieving greater efficiency, to establish priorities, and to raise, administer, and allocate the necessary funds. The members representing the Federation had voting rights only in respect of projects relating to their respective countries or regions. The implementation of policy was in the hands of a coordinating committee chaired by P.H. Noordwal, the newly appointed CKH director. The committee members were drawn from the board of the CKH and the directors and secretaries of the non-conformists. The CKH set out to draw up and implement all future plans in close consultation with the Chambers of Commerce abroad, to which the CKH would refer all queries relating to the areas of activity of non-associated Chambers. Collective CKH membership was replaced by country-related contributions. The non-associated Chambers of Commerce retained the right to initiate policy for their own areas of activity, the reversal of which required a two-thirds majority in the Council.

The National Council for the Promotion of Foreign Trade was installed on September 18, 1968. Van den Bergh was appointed president, and Van Andringa de Kempenaer, representing the Federation, first vice-president. The Council met for consultations prior to its meetings with the Economic Information Division to decide on the allocation of funds for the export drive in the following year. The coordinating committee drew up annual proposals based on comprehensive reviews of world market trends and the Netherlands' export prospects carried out by the CKH and the Economic Information Division. A new initiative could be supported for a maximum of three years, and was then transferred to the budget of the organization concerned. Projects eligible for support included market research programs, joint presentations at foreign trade shows, and the despatch of fact-finding teams and trade missions. The teams consisted of a small number of experts who explored the possibilities for Dutch exports, joint ventures, and participation in large-scale projects. Trade missions, headed by Van den Bergh as president of the CKH or by the Netherlands Minister for Economic Affairs, covered both collective representation and the promotion of individual business interests.

For a project to be eligible for inclusion in the export drive, it needed the support of the business community in the form of a sizeable financial contribution. The export drive budget rose from Dfl. 2.9 million in 1966 to Dfl. 5.7 million in 1968, but dropped to Dfl. 3.3 million in 1970. In that year the government subsidy of 25 to 35 percent of the budget was cut, probably because in the favorable economic climate of that time Dutch industry was working to full production capacity. In 1972 the Minister for Economic Affairs announced that the program would end as from January 1, 1975. Dfl. 400,000 was still available for 1973, and Dfl. 200,000 for 1974.

The first joint export promotion program following the establishment of the National Council was drawn up in 1969. The system of annual budgets was replaced by a three-year plan for the period 1970-1972. More than Dfl. 1 million was reserved for the United States, of which Dfl. 402,000 was intended for the projected establishment of an office outside New York. A further Dfl. 316,500 was earmarked for two fact-finding missions composed of businessmen to the United States. Van den Bergh and Noordwal, accompanied by Van der Zee and Esquire P.R. Feith, president of the Netherlands Chamber of Commerce for America in The Hague, went to New York in November, 1969 to discuss sending a trade mission, aid for the Chamber in San Francisco, and the opening of new offices in Chicago and Houston. In accordance with Van den Bergh's wishes, it was first agreed to draw up a five-year plan, but after consulting the embassy, the Chamber in New York decided it was better to wait and see how exports developed before thinking in terms of expansion. The new office in Chicago was financed from the 1972 and 1973 export drive budgets, but as both the CKH and the National Council expected to be disbanded after 1972, no further projects were initiated. The CKH's pursuit of centralization had turned out to work to its disadvantage.

CKH versus the Netherlands Ministry of Economic Affairs

The CKH's attempts to dominate the export sector were a latent threat not only to the Netherlands Chambers of Commerce abroad, but to the Netherlands Ministry of Economic Affairs as well. The consequences were multiple. Van den Bergh's efforts to enforce the integration concept on to the Ministry by mobilizing advisory bodies failed, and were in fact the prime reason for the subsequent sweeping changes in export promotion under the Langman doctrine.

Even though Minister De Pous had stated when the Advisory Council's report was published that there would be no question of transferring the Economic Information Division's responsibilities, the CKH remained obsessed with the idea. Up to its dissolution in 1974, this was the guiding principle of all CKH's dealings with the Ministry. In the first few years Van den Bergh had the support of a powerful lobby opposed to spending cuts in the promotion of Dutch exports. According to the Economic Information Division, the lobby was led by such prominent figures as Hendrik J. Kruls, member of KLM's board of directors, and Van Andringa de Kempenaer, president of the Netherlands-German Chamber of Commerce and of the Federation of Chambers of Commerce for Foreign Trade. It was reported that a number of unnamed ambassadors had given their backing to the campaign to wind up the Economic Information Division. The CKH waged an active press campaign to convince the public that prosperity

Industries along the river Zaan, north of Amsterdam

215

and economic growth were dependent on exports, and organized biannual "export fairs" at the RAI exhibition center in Amsterdam. Together with the Central Board for Foreign Economic Relations and the principal employers' organizations, the CKH presented a memorandum on exports to the *politician* responsible for forming the new Dutch government in 1967. The central element of the document was the request for an additional annual 30 to 45 million guilders to be made available from the national budget for the promotion of Dutch exports. This would amount to between 1 and 1.5 percent of the estimated annual growth of exports.

To increase its resources, the CKH resorted to an old ploy, applying in two successive years for much higher subsidies without specifying why the additional funds were needed. Success would mean that virtually nothing would be left for the other private organizations. The Economic Information Division, rightly convinced - as it later turned out - that the money was intended for the unwarranted expansion of the CKH's administrative network and not for constructive new projects, blocked the applications. In 1967 the CKH tried to break through the 50/50 budget ratio, but was again foiled by Abeln. The Economic Information Division soon began to doubt whether the CKH's method of promoting exports was in fact all that effective.

Like the trade commissioners in the 1950s, the CKH made the mistake of financing a considerable part of the costs of participation in trade shows with the sole object of attracting as many "clients" as possible. The Economic Information Division wanted to break with this system of mass collective participation, and instead to focus subsidies on individual producers. This would save the CKH huge overheads, and established exporters would no longer qualify for financial assistance. As it was, only participation in trade shows in East bloc countries functioned to everyone's satisfaction.

The new Netherlands government which took office in the summer of 1967 was faced with a huge deficit in the national budget. Ministerial committees were appointed to review their ministries' expenditures and to identify areas where savings could be made. The Minister for Economic Affairs, L. de Block, made use of the opportunity to investigate CKH's claim that the promotion of exports was bedeviled by duplication of effort, defective coordination, and inefficiency. Though a believer in a fundamental approach to export promotion, Abeln advised the Minister to limit the study to the areas covered by the various organizations. De Block's reputation for ineffectiveness is bound to have influenced Abeln's advice. The business community, too, had been dissatisfied with the situation since the publication of Oijevaar's report in 1961. But the time was not yet right for a truly fundamental approach. As Abeln wrote to De Block, "It means criticizing the work of Oijevaar, Van den Bergh and others who are still very much to the fore. The numerous other voices are unfortunately still muffled." He suggested setting up an official working party chaired by a representative of his Ministry, but he had no illusions about the outcome. "The committee will propose a new division of tasks to which the government organizations will strictly adhere. For the rest, the power struggle at the root of the problem will go on as before."

Bound by its limited terms of reference, the committee chaired by F.W. Rutten, a general advisor to the Minister, was indeed unable to produce a report offering a solution to the conflict. For the Economic Information Division, it was confirmation of its view that the overlap was mainly attributable to the CKH. In general terms, the Directorate supplied the bulk of commercial information, specifically relating to the access to foreign markets and their dimensions, while the private organizations provided addresses and business contacts. While this division of tasks was fairly straightforward in theory, it proved in practice to be fraught with difficulties which the business community considered to amount to fragmentation. Though often contiguous, commercial information and mediation were treated separately, to the annoyance of the exporters that were obliged to enlist the aid of two organizations for one particular project. It was especially irritating that the private organizations found it necessary to keep themselves fully informed of developments in the markets concerned and were thus in possession of some of the same information as the Economic Information Division. Individual firms with little interest in the structure of trade mediation and commercial information failed to see the rationale behind this division. The committee concluded that this "somewhat vague and infelicitous situation" could not be improved without integrating the two kinds of information in one organization. It was clear that although all concerned were in favor of integration, the CKH and the Economic Information Division were light years apart in the search for a solution. The committee saw no immediate prospect of solving the problem, but thought that the National Council for the Promotion of Foreign Trade, which was being formed at that time, might provide the answer. It could work in tandem with the Committee on Economic and Commercial Information to be instituted shortly by the Socio-Economic Council (SER). The only concrete recommendation which the committee ventured to make was that the Economic Information Division should support the CKH in the conflict between the private organizations. Its standards had risen appreciably over the past few years, and ever since the agreement with the Federation it could now validate its claim to be at the center of the private promotion of trade. The report strengthened the hand of the proponents of integration. The final decision was left to the SER committee.

The committee was chaired by the former prime minister J.E. de Quay, president of the CKH Chamber for Japan, and consisted further of Oijevaar and Rutten. De Quay could be considered to be non-partisan, and as prime minister had proved himself to be adept in crisis management.
The committee's mission was to ascertain the form of cooperation between the National Council and the Economic Information Division which would be of maximum benefit for commercial information and the promotion of exports.

Very soon the committee's discussions focused on relations between the Economic Information Division and the internally divided National Council. The point of contention was the CKH's claim that it was the cornerstone of the entire trade promotion structure, which was fiercely contested by the Economic Information Division and the business community. The conflict between the CKH and the Federation was rekindled when Van den Bergh tried to impose his views on the National Council. The Federation again openly chose the side of the Economic Information Division, and censured the CKH's export promotion methods. As the committee's investigations proceeded, the business community also expressed its growing dissatisfaction with the CKH and rejected the idea of the Economic Information Division being integrated into the CKH. Van den Bergh and his chief supporter, CKH director Noordwal, found themselves increasingly isolated in the National Council. After Van den Bergh unsuccessfully attempted to persuade the Economic Information Division to join forces with the CKH in answering the committee's questions on the most appropriate organizational structure, in a personal discussion he tried to coerce Abeln into saying that integration was necessary. The discussion took place at his home on February 17, 1969, and when this attempt also failed he was pessimistic about the chances of working out a modus vivendi. If it was not possible to integrate the Economic Information Division into the CKH, he felt it should in any case not work in direct contact with industry and commerce. On further inquiry, Abeln found that only a few directors had expressed the view that it would simplify matters for industry and commerce if there were only one information service. He summed up Van den Bergh's attitude in just a few words: "There must and there shall be one single organization. The dogma of one entity, based above all on 'one's own' organization, ... renders all reasonable discussion impossible." In his report to the Minister, Abeln pointed out that the government already bore 70 to 80 percent of the costs of the CKH.

Not surprisingly, the SER Committee on Economic and Commercial Information finally concluded that the private and government organizations should not be integrated. Given the obscurity of the structure of the information services, however, it felt that reorganization was to be recommended. The government and the business community would work together in a statutory body uniting the Economic Information Division, sections of the Foreign Agricultural Information Department of the Ministry of Agriculture and Fisheries, and the CKH and Associated Institutions. Association agreements could be concluded with the Netherlands Chambers of Commerce abroad; the Economic Information Division's authority to issue instructions to the diplomatic and consular missions would be transferred to the director of the new institute; the latter would be supervised by a board of ten members - seven businessmen and three representatives of the Ministries of Economic Affairs, Agriculture and Fisheries, and Foreign Affairs - whose authority would be that of a board of governors and who would not be involved in the day-to-day management of the institute. Attention was also given to the financial aspects. Not only would such a reorganization yield considerable savings, but it would also be an excellent opportunity to reintroduce the user-pays principle in the promotion of exports. Should the Ministry of Foreign Affairs require payment for the work of the embassies and consulates, the Netherlands Chambers of Commerce abroad would be able to add significantly to their revenues from the services they provided. Meanwhile De Quay let it be known that a prerequisite for the merger was Van den Bergh's departure from the CKH and the National Council for the Promotion of Foreign Trade.

With the resignation of De Block in the spring of 1970, Van den Bergh lost his political support. The Socio-Economic Council's report thereafter became irrelevant. Shortly afterwards Abeln resigned for health reasons and the appointment of Minister Langman in July, 1971 finally brought the radical reorganization of Dutch export promotion.

Subsidies, the User-Pays Principle, and the Langman Doctrine

The dependence of the private trade promotion organizations on government subsidies had been a thorn in the side of the Ministry of Economic Affairs since the end of the 1950s. The two Oijevaar reports of 1958 and 1961 and the institution of the CKH in 1963 had in part stemmed from the need to cut public spending. This had resulted in the transfer of responsibility from the trade commissioners to the Netherlands Chamber of Commerce in the United States, Inc. as from January 1, 1964. In the following years the Economic Information Division constantly strove to persuade the private organizations to adopt more up-to-date methods of trade promotion and to expand their sources of income. The first attempt, undertaken during J.M. den Uyl's brief period as Minister in 1965-1966, came to nothing. Because of the friction between the private organizations and De Block's personal views, the status quo was maintained while he was in office and for eighteen months afterwards. The problem was finally tackled in 1972.
The Economic Information Division had decided in 1965 that the United States was an exceptional case. It was the only overseas market where the local Netherlands Chambers of Commerce - albeit with substantial government support - performed the bulk of the work connected with commercial assistance and information. Those in other countries received too little support from industry and commerce and their function was mostly a social one, with the result that the provision of information was left to the embassies and consulates. As in the past, the Netherlands government played a central part both at home and abroad in the promotion of exports, and public funds were the main source of income. The introduction of some form of reimbursement seemed to be the only way of reducing this dependence. A solution widely favored was to leave trade promotion wherever possible to industry and commerce itself, first because it would reduce government expenditure, and secondly because civil servants usually lacked the creative approach required for promotional activities. In finding business contacts, private organizations could moreover apply stricter standards than the government, which was apt to be accused of discrimination. A precondition, however, was modernization of their trade promotion methods. The wholesale, fairly straightforward services provided in the 1940s and 1950s would have to make way for a more market-oriented approach.

The Rutten committee's, named after the secretary-general of the Netherlands Ministry of Economic Affairs who headed the committee, concentration on the division of tasks impeded a more fundamental evaluation of methods. It was clear that ad hoc considerations determined policy, and that the amount of the government contribution depended on local costs and the size and location of markets. The weakness of this structural basis made it impossible for many private organizations to adopt a modern marketing approach or to attempt anything beyond peripheral market research. Their managements usually lacked both time and interest, and their office staffs, owing to the chronic shortage of funds, lacked the proper qualifications. The result was a vicious circle of sub-standard services and inadequate financial resources. Suggestions of raising fees or introducing a reimbursement system, which seemed feasible because most of the work related to one-time activities, met with objections. In the view of the private organizations, though it was true that exports accounted for a certain part of their profits, small and medium-sized businesses were neither prepared nor in a position to pay for commercial mediation. The Rutten committee nevertheless recommended gradually reducing the subsidies from the current level of more than half the budget to a maximum of one quarter. With regard to the quality of the services, it had found widespread support for more centralized management, possibly by the National Council for the Promotion of Foreign Trade which was shortly to be instituted.

But this too found no wider currency than the committee's other recommendations. Before the De Quay committee had completed its work, the Economic Information Division tried in various ways to spur the private organizations to be more enterprising and to bring their working methods up to date. Practically none of the Chambers of Commerce abroad had an in-depth knowledge of the market or of the needs of modern business. Rational considerations played little part in the services they provided. As they clung fiercely to their independence and because the Economic Information Division had no political backing, the results of its efforts were negligible. The introduction of a reimbursement program had to await the arrival of Minister Langman in July, 1971.

Taking note of the recent economic downturn and the fast rising level of public spending, Langman proceeded to reorganization without delay. He pruned Dfl. 600,000 from the budget for the private promotion of exports in 1972, reducing it from Dfl. 10.5 million to Dfl. 9.9 million. This first spending cut primarily affected the export drive projects, many of which were experimental, and the participation in trade shows and exhibitions organized by the CKH. The subsidies for the organizations in the Netherlands were raised by 10.6 percent, and for those abroad by 6 percent. Knowing that more cuts and a fundamental change of policy would almost certainly follow in the next financial year, the National Council for the Promotion of Foreign Trade appealed to Dutch Parliament at the end of 1971, stressing the vital importance of promoting exports when the balance of trade and the balance of payments were deteriorating. It was to no avail. The Langman doctrine was announced at the opening of the fourth National Exports Convention on September 28, 1972. Exports would now be regarded as just one sector of routine marketing activities, as demonstrated by the large number of organizations providing services on a commercial basis. The costs of commercial information would therefore be charged to the user as of January 1, 1975. Only the costs of information provided to foreign companies would be financed from public funds. In addition, a consultancy firm would be commissioned to give quantitative substance to the conclusions of the De Quay committee. Its report could be expected to settle the conflict about the integration of export promotion once and for all.

The report of Van der Torn & Buningh management consultants indeed gave a definitive answer regarding the alleged merits of centralizing the private and government organizations. The savings would be negligible, and the administrative changes entailed underscored the advantages of decentralization. The promotion of foreign trade was characterized by a diversity of activities that centralization would render virtually impossible. Mediation beyond the furnishing of addresses required an active and resourceful approach: in other words, a business mentality. The provision of information, on the other hand, was based on a painstakingly methodical approach followed by government departments. The integration of two such contrasting cultures in a single organization would inevitably lead to difficulties and complicate the application of the user-pays principle. Inevitably, large organizations would react less decisively to disappointing results than smaller ones. The report sealed the fate of the CKH as a champion of government subsidies, a center of traditional, partially obsolete activities, and a prospective coordinator of the large-scale, more or less straightforward services provided by the Netherlands Chambers of Commerce abroad.

The recommendations of the Van der Torn & Buningh report were put into practice by R.F.M. Lubbers, who became Minister for Economic Affairs in May, 1973, supported by the proponents of a federative form of association. The reorganization took place in 1974. With a starting grant from the Ministry, the Netherlands Trade Promotion Center took over regional commercial information and mediation. Activities considered unsuitable for a commercial approach were phased out, and new services were offered only if private industry showed a decided interest.

The insecure financial position of the Netherlands Trade Promotion Center in the first period of its existence revealed the weakness in the new subsidy policy. As compensation for the free handling of foreign companies' enquiries, it received a government contribution of fifty percent of its earnings. The profits of industry and commerce and the related interest in trade promotion declined however after the economic downturn in 1973. The Netherlands Ministry of Economic Affairs had created a new vicious circle for export promotion in periods of stagnating economic growth.

The Netherlands Chamber of Commerce in the United States

Centralization, coordination, and commercialization were key concepts in the development of the Chamber between 1964 and 1976. Having assumed responsibility for the work of the defunct Netherlands

Export Promotion Organization, the Chamber was once more in a position to monopolize the promotion of trade with the United States as of January 1, 1964. A new rival appeared on the horizon shortly afterwards. In order to safeguard their independence, the Chamber was among the most resolute opponents of the CKH's centralization efforts. Together with the Economic Information Division, the Chamber forestalled every attempt of the CKH to branch out to the United States. But whereas the Chamber in The Hague saw advantages in coordination, the Chamber in New York long persisted in rejecting the idea for fear of endangering its freedom. It was not prepared to discuss either the subject of closer coordination with the Chamber in The Hague or the Economic Information Division's regular suggestions for a more businesslike approach until 1969, when a new president took over. Actual change followed only under pressure from the 1972 amendments to the government's subsidy policy and the slowing down of the world economy in 1973. But this too was tardy and incomplete, and severe cutbacks were needed in 1976 to prevent the collapse of the private commercial information services for the United States. In consultation with the Economic Information Division, two of the three Chamber offices were closed. They were the office in Chicago, which had been opened by the Chamber in New York in Chicago in 1971 in response to the growing importance of the Midwest, and the office in Los Angeles. Their work was taken over by the Netherlands consulates-general in the two cities and in San Francisco. In the Netherlands, the work of the Chamber was subcontracted to the Netherlands Trade Promotion Center.

Members and Finances

As evidenced by the development of trade between the Netherlands and the United States, the American market was only of genuine interest to Dutch exporters in the period of economic expansion between 1965 and 1970. This is reflected in the membership figures of the Chamber, whose membership in the late 1960s was approximately 850, of whom the majority were based in the Netherlands. In 1972 this number had fallen to 750. In the same year the Chambers for Britain, Belgium, Italy and Germany had from 2000 to 2800 members. Despite a successful recruitment campaign for the new Chamber office in Chicago, the recession year of 1974 ended with 650 members.

Since primarily small and medium-sized businesses turned away from the American market and the Chamber, the quality of the membership does not seem to have been greatly affected by the decline in numbers. Membership lists are only available for the Chamber in New York. Financial institutions occupied a prominent place. In addition to the Algemene Bank Nederland and the Amsterdam-Rotterdam Bank, the membership included the Bank of America, the Bank of New York, the Chase Manhattan Bank, the Chemical Bank New York Company, the First National City Bank of New York, Brown Brothers Harriman & Co., and the Morgan Guaranty Trust Co. of New York. Dutch multinationals were strongly represented with the Asiatic Petroleum Company, the American Enka Corporation, and North American Philips Co., Inc. Large American corporations included the Standard Oil Co., Gulf Oil, Mobil Oil, Coca-Cola, General Motors, IBM, ITT and RCA, and three of the five leading international grain dealers: the originally Dutch Bunge Corporation, the Continental Grain Company, and Cargill Inc. The names of other members can be traced to the early days of the Chamber, such as the Erven Lucas Bols Distilling Co. of Kentucky, the W.L.M. Bensdorp Company of Massachusetts, the Holland-America Line, Wm. H. Müller & Co., Inc. and Phs. van Ommeren (USA) Inc. of New York. Companies that had joined between the two world wars included the Royal Netherlands Aircraft Factories Fokker, KLM Royal Dutch Airlines, and the Royal Netherlands Steamship Company. Another member, the Van Itallie Corporation, a firm of diamond merchants, was founded shortly after the first world war by Dorus van Itallie, who was secretary of the Chamber for a number of years. Companies like the publishers Spaarnestad International, Inc., the engineering firm Stork America, and the Verolme United Shipyards, Inc. had been established in the United States since the early 1950s.

Economic developments were responsible for the downward trend in membership. During the economic boom in Western Europe in the second half of the 1960s, exporters' attention was focused on the European rather than the American market. When the growth of the European economies had passed its peak and more production capacity was available for overseas exports, the American market had however become less enticing. To counter the fast-growing balance of trade deficit, the U.S. government introduced a temporary additional customs duty of 10 percent on imports. The exchange rate of the dollar had been pegged to the gold price since 1944, and abandoning this system meant devaluation of the overvalued dollar. A second devaluation followed in early 1973. The lower exchange rate, the relatively high rate of inflation in the Netherlands, and the first major recession in the world economy since the second world war made the American market less attractive to Dutch exporters.

The Chamber was adversely affected by the recruitment campaigns of the CKH, which enticed new members with the assurance that they would be entitled to the services of all private organizations. This was far from the truth. Some companies that are not identified in the relevant documents cancelled their Chamber membership to join the CKH. Though the CKH campaign was not an aggressive one, the Chambers feared a further loss of members. In addition, they were faced with a more structural problem. Most of their members were small and medium-sized businesses. If they joined to show their appreciation of services rendered, it was almost always in the Netherlands. Others who made use of the Chambers' services just once saw no reason to apply for membership. This came down to the fact that businesses in the past had not been required to pay for information obtained from the government services and the heavily subsidized private trade promotion organizations. Researching a foreign market had never been considered part of ordinary business costs, and this being so, the Chamber did not succeed in their half-hearted attempts to charge for their services.

American companies were even less inclined to pay for the services they received. It was only in exceptional cases that they could be assisted, while U.S. government agencies supplied a wide range of information designed to boost American exports free of charge. Most of the work performed by the Chamber in

Fokker F27
"Golden Knights" U.S.
Parachute Team

New York was for firms in the Netherlands. The explanation is partly to be found in the buoyant economy of the late 1960s. Increasing numbers of American companies were in search of foreign suppliers, in the Netherlands and elsewhere. It often transpired that manufacturers of the kind they were seeking were already active in the American market, especially those in the food and beverages sector or in more recent branches of industry like electrical appliances, chemical products, or machinery. When charges were introduced in 1964, some American firms protested to the Netherlands embassy. Except for banks, American businesses tended not to join anything which did not yield immediate tangible results.

Private source membership fees and revenues from the services provided by the Chamber in New York increased only slightly between 1965 and 1976, rising from about $ 17,000 in 1965-1967 to $ 22,000 between 1970 and 1976. The same income of the Chamber in The Hague rose from Dfl. 77,000 in 1966 to Dfl. 104,000 in 1971, and then levelled off. Before and after 1970 new initiatives like the opening of the Chicago office in 1971 had to be funded by government subsidy. As a consequence of the policy pursued by De Block, a supporter of active private trade promotion, the subsidy for the Chamber was increased from Dfl. 385,000 in 1967 to Dfl. 832,000 in 1971. This amount covered 70 to 80 percent of their annual expenditure between 1964 and 1976.

Between Coordination and Centralization

Distrust of the true intentions of the CKH clouded its relations with the Chamber for several years. Its activities certainly warranted suspicion. Given the close collaboration between the Chambers in The Hague and New York, however, the coordination envisaged by the CKH could never have succeeded. Relations improved somewhat after cooperation between the CKH and the country organizations was formally regulated in the National Council for the Promotion of Foreign Trade. The reason was not so much a desire for cooperation as dissatisfaction at the Chamber in The Hague with the conservative management of the Chamber in New York. Time had caught up with the mediation and information provided by the Chamber in New York. The government's repeated requests to adopt a more commercial approach were ignored. To be sure, the collaboration between the Chamber in The Hague and the CKH never went very far, but indirectly it influenced the change of management in 1969 that marked the adoption of more up-to-date working methods at the Chamber in New York.

When the first talks with the five major Netherlands Chambers of Commerce abroad came to nothing in 1964, the CKH pressed on with its coordination and centralization efforts throughout the next two years. Its sights were fixed first of all on the Chambers for America and Germany, the two organizations with offices both in the Netherlands and abroad. As far as the Chamber in the United States was concerned, the CKH's persistent attempts since 1963 to impose collaboration on the private organizations rendered each of its proposals unacceptable in advance. It was accused of "an increasing propensity to take over the day-to-day management ..., obviously aimed at full integration". The board members of the Chamber in New York, in particular, viewed this with distrust, and threatened to resign if the Chambers in New York or The Hague were absorbed, as they feared, into the highly bureaucratic CKH as anonymous "desks". They were swayed not just by business considerations, but as much by the wish to retain the club-like atmosphere of the Chamber. Whatever the reasons may have been, the resignation of the majority of the board of the Chamber in New York would have had serious implications, for the effectiveness of the Chamber's trade mediation was to a large extent dependent on its ties with the New York business community.

Undeterred, the CKH tried to confront the Chamber with a *fait accompli* at the end of 1966. The threat that it would take over their trade promotion activities, preferably with their cooperation but otherwise without it, seemed very real. The American market had a tremendous potential for the future, and could therefore not be viewed in isolation from the overall export strategy of Dutch industry and commerce. In December, 1966 Udink approached Esquire P.R. Feith, president of the Chamber in The Hague, with the proposal that they initiate joint activities in the United States. What precisely this would entail was to be decided by the Chambers themselves. Collaboration with the CKH would have the advantage of the availability of extra resources and manpower for special projects. Udink made it quite plain that the CKH would not accept a refusal on what it considered to be inadequate grounds. It was a general trade promotion organization, and if its members were interested in the American market it would itself embark on mediation activities. While the discussion was still in progress, a number of projects in the United States were incorporated in the export drive for the following year, including a trade mission led by Van den Bergh.

One glance at the proposal will have been enough for Feith to see that it was unacceptable. Notwithstanding the earlier pledge to respect the collaboration between the three Chamber offices, Udink now wanted the Chamber in The Hague to gear its policy and finances to those of the CKH. Their association was to acquire an administrative structure through an interchange of board members. This was out of the question for the Chamber in The Hague. The focal point of its work was in the United States, and if that work and the financial aspects had to be geared then it could only be to the Netherlands Chamber of Commerce in the United States, Inc., as had been the case since 1964. Coordination with the CKH would damage that cooperation. With the support of the Federation of Chambers of Commerce for Foreign Trade, the Chamber in The Hague rejected the proposal. The major Netherlands Chambers of Commerce abroad unanimously agreed that collaboration aimed at one export market was infinitely more effective than collaboration between similar organizations.

As was soon apparent, the CKH had already considered the possibility of rejection. Before the discussions with Feith were ended, its vice-president, S. Joor, suggested to the Chamber in San Francisco that it act as the CKH's local representative. In the eyes of the Chambers in New York and The Hague, this exceeded all bounds of decency; for the Chamber in New York it meant the definite end of any kind of interest in collaboration. The president, L.R.W. Soutendijk (1962-1969), a partner in the firm of Brown Brothers Harriman & Co., and the secretary, Philip J. Gomperts, thereafter watched every move of the CKH with the deepest mistrust. With the discussions at a dead end, Udink tried to gain access to the U.S. market by an indirect route. In preparation for the trade mission, he contacted H. van Blankenstein, head of the commercial section of the Netherlands embassy in Washington. But Van Blankenstein had no wish to be embroiled in the "appalling squabbles" of the CKH and the Chamber, and in correspondence with Udink and Abeln he came to the conclusion that the CKH was largely to blame for the situation. The CKH's low popularity among the business community made the fight easier for the Chamber. Abeln refused outright to finance CKH activities aimed at the United States. He was not alone in taking a dim view of its actions, as evidenced by the negligible support it received from industry and commerce. Abeln also wanted to avoid overlapping, so he decided that if the CKH wanted to organize a trade mission it would have to find the funds itself.

Rebuffed on all sides, the CKH had no choice but to accept the situation. Any move in the direction of collaboration would now have to come from the Chamber itself. Two years passed before this point was reached. By the end of 1967 the Chamber in The Hague, the Economic Information Division and the embassy were all so exasperated by the Chamber in New York's tardiness in bringing its working methods up to date that the Chamber in The Hague moved towards conciliation with the CKH in the recently established National Council for the Promotion of Foreign Trade. At the time of the transfer of activities in 1964 the Economic Information Division had stated explicitly to president Soutendijk that the Chamber would itself have to shoulder a greater share of the budget. Possessing no real influence in how the Chamber in New York managed its affairs, the Economic Information Division and the Chamber in The Hague could only register the fact that the Chamber in New York seemed unaware of how greatly trade and commerce had changed over the past ten to fifteen years. The Chamber lacked the vision and enterprising spirit needed to strike out in a new direction, and was increasingly dependent on the government subsidy. It had been only with the greatest difficulty that the Economic Information Division managed to persuade the Chamber in 1963 to take over the official promotion of trade. The Chamber's reluctance can be explained by the fact that it had witnessed the government's appropriation of authority in 1949, and later, the Netherlands Export Promotion Organization's unsuccessful efforts to interest Dutch exporters in the American market using the same instruments that were now to be commercialized.

Cooperation in the National Council for the Promotion of Foreign Trade between the CKH and Van der Zee, the secretary of the Chamber in The Hague, opened the way to a revitalization of the promotion of exports to the United States in 1969. That year's export drive budget included an item providing for participation in trade shows and exhibitions, an area in which the CKH, in contrast to the Chamber in New York, was highly active. Until the financial consequences of the Langman doctrine became perceptible in 1973, the two organizations gradually came to work more closely together in the National Council. In 1970 the sum of Dfl. 70,000 was made available for the appointment of a full-time secretary to the Chamber in San Francisco for the West Coast and for participation in two trade shows.

The closer relationship between the CKH and the Chamber in The Hague compelled the Chamber in New York to change tactics and adopt a more businesslike attitude. J.C. Severiens, president of Nedlloyd Inc. in New York, succeeded Soutendijk as president in 1969, and Gomperts retired in 1970. The deputy secretary, J.M. Bakels, was appointed executive secretary and instructed to set about placing the promotion of trade on a commercial footing. He did not entirely succeed. The image of the Netherlands Chambers of Commerce abroad as non-profit institutions was difficult to dispel, as had been clear since the private trade promotion organizations had regained their monopoly of the American market in 1964. Like their predecessors, Severiens and Bakels were unable to change course dramatically and boost the Chamber's revenues in accordance with the wishes of the Ministry of Economic Affairs.

Commercial and Non-Commercial Services

The aim of the 1964 reorganization was to reduce government expenditure on the promotion of trade with the United States while at the same time improving the quality of the services, which were to be brought more into line with the needs of private industry. The first goal was reached quite easily by transferring the work of the commercial sections of the consulates-general in New York and San Francisco to the Chamber. Improving the quality and market-orientation of the services demanded considerably more time and effort. Taking the income from services to non-members as a criterion, the Economic Information Division was not satisfied with the performance of the private organizations. It was especially critical of the Chamber in New York as the organization that put exporters in touch with American business representatives. The Economic Information Division also seems to have taken too little account of the structural factors impeding a break with the past, such as the reaction of Dutch and American businessmen to the alien notion of non-profit institutions charging for their services.

The tide turned with the downturn in the Dutch economy at the beginning of the 1970s and the announcement of the Langman doctrine. The Economic Information Division unsuccessfully urged the Chamber to base its policy on a higher proportion of earned income. The situation became critical when the new subsidy policy came into effect on January 1, 1975. The Netherlands government no longer financed budget deficits, but limited subsidies to a maximum of 50 percent of the income earned from the provision of services. By 1976, unable adequately to increase their income from membership fees, donations, and services, the Chamber was heading for bankruptcy. It could only be averted by drastic action. The duties of the offices in Los Angeles, Chicago, and The Hague were transferred to the office in New York and the Netherlands Trade Promotion Center, respectively.

The Economic Information Division was itself partly to blame for the fact that so few of the changes it envisaged were actually realized. The 1964 subsidy policy contained too few incentives for the private organizations to seek ways to increase their incomes. Before the Chamber would agree to accept the additional tasks, the Directorate had to increase the subsidy and to state through Van Blankenstein that "the Netherlands Government realizes its responsibility and will not take any drastic action on short notice against the now required higher subsidy". In a period of economic growth, when the increasing volume of exports to the United States was accompanied by a growing number of commercial enquiries, this implied that as long as spending was kept within reasonable bounds, subsidy applications would be approved virtually unamended. The subsidy for the Chamber in New York rose from $ 67,000 in 1963 to more than $ 103,000 in 1967, while its income from services to non-members rose only marginally. In 1965 the Chamber in New York earned $ 543, $ 2,500 in 1967, and $ 4,000 in 1971. The collective expenditure of all Chamber offices in 1971 was close to $ 400,000. Up to 1967 the subsidy was mainly of benefit to the Chamber in New York. The Chamber in The Hague financed its higher expenditure by raising its fees. The slight decline affecting the Dutch economy in 1967 marked the end of the period in which the

Economic Information Division approved subsidies almost without question. In that year the Chamber in New York applied for a subsidy of $ 121,000, a $ 16,000 increase on the previous year, which the national budget could not sustain. The Chamber in New York reluctantly accepted a much lower amount. When the conflict with the CKH flared up, the Economic Information Division was preoccupied in The Hague, and it was not the moment to place the relationship with the Chamber in New York under further strain. The Chamber could accordingly disregard the efforts of both the Chamber in The Hague and the Netherlands government to commercialize its activities. In any case, the Chamber in New York believed that ever since it became burdened with the additional workload, it had been given too little time to make it pay.

Did the Economic Information Division overestimate the capacity of the private trade promotion organizations to generate more income themselves? Soutendijk and Gomperts certainly thought it did, and so, judging by their actions, did their successors. Although they never explicitly said so, the fact that no similar non-profit organizations in the United States or elsewhere charged for their services must surely have strengthened their conviction that it could not be a significant alternative source of income. The American government, for instance, provided comprehensive economic and commercial information on Europe entirely free of charge. In 1966 the Economic Information Division surveyed the promotion of trade in an international context for the first time. A more in-depth evaluation ten years later produced much the same results. It was the accepted practice in Europe to boost exports by means of free services. It made no difference whether public and private services existed side by side, as in the Netherlands, West Germany, and Denmark; or whether the promotion of trade was entirely in private hands, as in Switzerland, or in the hands of government or semi-government institutions. Whatever the structure, it was fully financed by the government and by private industry.[1] The activities of the Chambers of Commerce in New York representing countries where trade promotion was a task of government were almost entirely of a social nature. Only the Chambers for Germany and Switzerland were in any way comparable, and the financial support they received from their governments or business communities was greatly in excess of the funds allocated to the Chamber.[2] Outside New York, trade promotion was almost wholly government-supported, as Gomperts noted when he attended the opening of the Chicago office in 1972. Of the ten local foreign Chambers of Commerce, only those of Germany and Israel were engaged in such activities.

By the end of 1968 criticism of the financial situation and general management of the Chamber had reached such a pitch that it could no longer be ignored by the board. The institution of the National Council for the Promotion of Foreign Trade gave the Chamber in The Hague the opportunity to branch out on its own. At about the same time Van Blankenstein evaluated the work of the Chamber, concluding that the Chambers in New York and San Francisco were "reasonably effective" in providing commercial information and in the facilities they offered for furthering Dutch-American trade relations. He thought it unlikely that Soutendijk and Gomperts would themselves attempt to generate more income. The Chamber in New York clearly lacked the organizational capacities needed for renewal. Trade promotion, still geographically concentrated on Greater New York and San Francisco, ignored the fast-growing markets in the Midwest and Southwest. In addition, San Francisco had long been overtaken as a commercial center by Los Angeles. After consultation with the Netherlands, the Economic Information Division decided to follow up on Van Blankenstein's conclusions. The Chamber in New York was to become more enterprising. An assessment of Dutch exports could identify the best products to launch on the American market with the assistance of the Chambers of Commerce. The working methods were to be brought up to date, and local research would single out the most promising location for a branch office.

New Departures

Dutch exports to the United States surged ahead in the years 1965-1968. The downward economic trend in Western Europe prompted exporters to seek new outlets just as faster and cheaper communication media were making distant markets more accessible. Old trade patterns disintegrated, and the traditional import channels in the United States lost their importance, with the consequence that both Dutch and American firms increasingly called on the services of the Chambers of Commerce for America. American importers no longer waited to be approached, but themselves went in search of foreign suppliers. Turning to the

Chamber for information, they frequently found that firms involved in food and beverages, electrical appliances, chemical and engineering branches already had business contacts in the United States. The path was smoother for American exporters and manufacturers seeking access to the Dutch market. After the closure of the Institute for Netherlands-American Industrial Cooperation in January, 1964, they turned increasingly to the Netherlands Chamber of Commerce in the United States, Inc. The Hague office did the initial sifting of firms interested in trade partnerships and joint ventures.[3]

The Economic Information Division expected the activities formerly carried out by the Netherlands Export Promotion Organization to provide a source of income for the Chamber. However, organizing joint presentations at trade shows and exhibitions, arranging publicity for new products, providing advertising material for retailers, and keeping a card index system on Dutch exporters and their American contacts did not attract many new clients. Greater impetus came from the burgeoning trade between the two countries. Whereas in the past the Chamber had experienced great difficulty in recruiting new members, this was no longer the case after 1965. Nevertheless, their claim that they were consulted by practically every firm thinking of exporting to the United States was somewhat exaggerated. Much of the growth was accounted for by the hundred firms already responsible for almost 80 percent of Dutch exports, while the majority of firms enlisting the aid of the Chambers of Commerce were small and medium-sized companies. Moreover, they were traditionally focused on exports of consumer goods, not the capital goods that exhibited the fastest rate of growth and whose markets were located beyond Greater New York and San Francisco.

The task of the Chamber became both simpler and more complicated through the changing pattern of exports. It was simpler in the sense that many firms, notably those in the food and gift sectors, had tried earlier to sell their products in the United States, and were now making a more solidly based second attempt. They did not need to be told again that success required patience and a substantial financial investment, or that Americans preferred to negotiate face to face. Trade promotion was at the same time more complicated because firms made greater demands on the Chamber's sources of information. Not only were they were better informed about general economic matters than in the past, but through the modern communication they could now assess for themselves the opportunities offered by the American market. It was usually specialized information about the methods and structure of the American import trade that the Chamber was asked to provide.

The Chamber responded by concentrating more on market research. It had been active in this area before accepting the additional workload in 1964, but in a less intensive way. It had been agreed with the Netherlands Export Promotion Organization that it would conduct straightforward literature research, while the other organization would handle the more demanding research that required visits to business firms. It was originally the idea that the Chamber would continue these time-consuming activities, but the growing number of commercial enquiries made it impossible. Publications were still the main source of information, supplemented by details obtained from experts and firms in the sector in question. Through their many connections in the New York business community, the board members were also able to provide much valuable information. The substance and geographical scope of the Chamber's reports were limited. In addition to customs duties and regulations, its reports dealt with such matters as the import and distribution of competitors' products. Geographically, they were restricted to the commercial area of New York.

Dealing with enquiries about the high-technology products of Dutch industry took more time and attention. The Chamber was first confronted with regular queries of this kind in the 1960s. The more technical the product, the more time it took to deal with the enquiry. Many manufacturers were new to the American market and were poorly informed about local conditions, and it was often very difficult to convince them of the need to get in touch with a distributor. This in fact was essential, for it was only with the aid of an experienced distributor that the product could be packaged and advertised in the right way. These were usually the firms that expected the market reports to provide them with all the details they needed. Besides the information contained in the average report, they expected a detailed specification of technical standards in the United States, the fullest possible advice about bringing their products to the attention of wholesalers, retailers, and the general public, and particulars about the most suitable locations for service and spare parts depots. Lack of technical knowledge may have limited the value of the reports, but on the other hand businessmen visiting New York were generally accompanied to all meetings by a representative of the Chamber. After 1969, more attention was devoted to the sale and contents of market reports. From the fact that no more than four such reports were sold for Dfl. 2,000 each in 1970, it was concluded that exporters were unfamiliar with information of this kind and because of the attitude of their export managers: "He goes abroad to sell, not to investigate the market. His mind is fixed on his company's products instead of the market's demands". It was often difficult to convince exporters that the one could not go with the other.

No exact information is available on the Chamber's charges for other services. In view of the few thousand dollars and guilders earned per year by the Chamber at that time, it cannot have been very much. Knowing the situation in other Chambers of Commerce abroad, the Economic Information Division assumed that their charges by no means always covered the full costs.

After the 1964 reorganization, the Chamber was responsible for arranging the participation of Dutch firms in trade shows and the distribution of so-called product releases. Dutch exporters showed little interest in commercial exhibitions, and left the decision to the American importer. In 1967 the Chamber in New York tried unsuccessfully to arouse more interest by distributing detailed information on some twenty trade shows among industries in the Netherlands. The response was minimal. Dutch firms were represented on average at no more than three per year, and even then they were usually part of a collection of products presented by an existing importer or the Chamber. For the food sector it was different. In December, 1966 the Chamber had a booth at the National Food Sales Conference in New York featuring the products of thirty different manufacturers. Interest gradually increased, and in 1970, with the aid of the embassy and the consulate-general, the Chamber arranged for Dutch participation in seven shows, six of them in New York. They included the New York Boat Show, the Fancy Food Confectionery Show and the National Hardware Show. The Supermarket Institute Convention in Houston, Texas had been a fixture for some years. Until the reorganization at the end of 1976 four to seven trade shows and exhibitions were on the program every year.

The greatest financial success for the Chamber between 1965 and 1976 was the monthly publication *Netherlands-American Trade*. The layout of the earlier *US-Holland* bulletin needed to be brought up to date, so in 1962 it was given a new design and printed in color. Of the 6000 copies printed, 4,500 were distributed in the United States, and 1,500 in the Netherlands. Some 2000 were sent to members, and the remainder to firms likely to be interested in the articles, advertisements, and trade information. *Netherlands-American Trade* took its place in 1964. The approach this time was different, since the Chamber aimed to make the publication profitable as well as to enhance the prestige of the Netherlands. Practically all other foreign Chambers of Commerce in New York published journals of this kind. Making a profit, or indeed breaking even, proved harder than expected. The publication yielded a return after H.A.H. Sijthoff, owner of the *Financieel Dagblad*, helped to organize a campaign to recruit advertisers in 1965. About half of its 20 to 52 pages were advertisements. A modest profit of $ 6440 was booked in 1966, and $ 7400 in 1967. More support came from the United States than from the Netherlands, for American agents and importers attached much more importance to publicity than their Dutch suppliers, who were extremely slow about sending photos, technical and commercial information, and advertising texts. Though it yielded less after 1968, the journal made a sizeable contribution to the income of the Chamber.

Another successful initiative was the hosting of three to five lunches a year, at which eminent people were invited to speak on a wide variety of subjects of current interest. Many of the Chamber's members were prominent figures in the Dutch and American business communities, and the guest speakers were often visiting Dutch dignitaries such as Ambassador C.W.A. Schuurmann, who spoke in October, 1964 on the Netherlands' view of the GATT talks, and R.F.M. Lubbers, Minister for Economic Affairs, who in March, 1974 talked about recent economic trends in the Netherlands and trade relations with the United States. In 1974 William H. Shaw, Assistant Secretary of Commerce for Economic Affairs, spoke on the balance of payments and the business outlook in the United States; another speaker that year was European Commissioner Jean Rey. The guest speaker in January, 1968 was Dr S. Aldewereld, vice-president of the World Bank, whose subject was the rationale of certain world bank policies.

Reorganization, Coordination and, Deficits

The Chamber made few policy changes in the period between the retirement of Soutendijk in April, 1969 and Gomperts in September, 1971, and the subsidy cuts beginning in 1972. From then until the 1976 reorganization, the board felt that there was little point in its continued existence without substantial financial backing from the Netherlands government. The Chamber in The Hague, on the other hand, saw definite possibilities for improving the promotion of trade in a way that would increase its income. From 1969, the Economic Information Division focused more on improving the organizational structure than on the

After World War II, KLM was the first European airline to start services to the United States, May 21, 1946. This photo shows the transport of the Madurodam Exhibition to New York, 1965.

methods used in promoting trade. The area of activities of the Chamber was to extend beyond New York and San Francisco, and the ailing Chamber in the latter city was to be revitalized. At New York's suggestion, Van der Zee was commissioned to effect the closer coordination of the two Chambers. Although the Chambers had known since 1972 that the subsidy for 1975 would be reduced to Dfl. 500,000, they were unable to formulate an adequate plan of action. The main stumbling block was the fragmented structure of three separate institutions, each with its own management.

With the arrival of Severiens as president in the spring of 1969, the Chamber seized the opportunity to improve cooperation. Except for Sijthoff, the board showed little interest, but Severiens encouraged the secretariat to take new initiatives. On the insistence of the Economic Information Division, a list of priorities was drawn up based on the available resources, the existing supply of Dutch products, and the poten-

228

tial of the American market. The Chamber in New York was to deal only with products that were likely to sell. As an incentive for reorganization, the subsidy was raised, and Dfl. 70,000 was provided for a secretary in San Francisco. The Chamber in New York concluded an agreement with the Dutch trade show center in Utrecht to act as its official representative in the United States, and set about widening its sphere of activities. New modes of transport like containers facilitated direct links between local markets and foreign suppliers. Gomperts visited cities like Cleveland, Pittsburgh, Buffalo, and Rochester to investigate the possibilities for direct imports from the Netherlands, but found few importers and distributors of the right standing that were prepared to invest in new products. An attempt through the Holland-America Line's agent, the Texas Transport & Terminal Company, Inc., to find contacts in the Midwest and South foundered for lack of interest on the part of local managements. Because of the rapid economic growth of the nine Sunbelt states, it was decided to look at Dallas, Houston, and Atlanta as possible cities for a branch office outside Chicago. As the center for the commercially significant Midwest and the second most important stock market in the country, Chicago was an obvious choice, the more so as KLM Royal Dutch Airlines had recently acquired landing rights in Chicago and would benefit from the establishment of a Chamber. The Economic Information Division raised the subsidy from Dfl. 615,000 to Dfl. 685,000 in support of these various initiatives.

In January, 1971 Jan J. de Kam was seconded by the Chamber to Chicago, its first move beyond its traditional area of activity. The local KLM representative headed a provisional executive committee, members were enlisted among the local business community, and the Chicago office of the Netherlands Chamber of Commerce in the United States, Inc. was opened by the Dutch ambassador, Baron R.B. van Lynden, on February 15, 1972.

At about the same time the terms of association of the three Dutch Chambers of Commerce for America were formally laid down in a Memorandum of Understanding. The Chamber in San Francisco was placed under the financial and organizational aegis of New York, whose president, Severiens, and vice-president, Sijthoff, joined its Board of Directors. To further coordination, Sijthoff also took a seat on the board of the Chamber in The Hague.

Cooperation was however less smooth than the Economic Information Division had hoped. The fact that each Chamber had its own directors, secretary, and institutional position gave their collaboration an artificial quality that ruled out any effective coordination. With management at the Chamber in New York in the hands of the secretary, and coordination the responsibility of Van der Zee, the secretary in The Hague, responsibilities were fragmented. Driven by the financial crisis, the Chambers drifted further apart until at length, foreseeing their eventual liquidation, they were forced by the Economic Information Division to work together.

The first problems were encountered in 1973, shortly after it was announced that the private trade promotion organizations would have to reckon with heavy cutbacks as from January 1, 1975. The first subsidy reduction of Dfl. 60,000 was cushioned by the devaluation of the dollar in 1973, but the Chamber in New York made it very plain that if its own existence was threatened, the offices in San Francisco and Chicago would be closed. Because New York was the center of trade promotion in the United States, the Chamber in New York was of vital importance for Dutch exports. The Economic Information Division saw the point of this argument, but as the Chambers functioned independently of each other, all it could do was watch and wait, encouraging the Chambers to work more closely together while hoping that the collaboration between the Chambers in New York and The Hague would not be too badly affected by the financial problems. As the Chamber in New York saw it, the Chamber in The Hague did not understand how trade was promoted in the United States; the Chamber in The Hague, in turn, was convinced that the Chamber in New York was unenterprising and lacking in self-confidence. The distance separating them was an added obstacle to mutual understanding. Sijthoff, a member of both boards, could only agree that they were poorly informed about each other's activities.

The Economic Information Division arranged a meeting of the three presidents and secretaries on November 15, 1973 in New York in an attempt to clear up the misunderstandings, but it did not have the desired effect. True, it was agreed that policy would be formulated by the Chamber in The Hague, which after all was in touch with Dutch government and business circles, but this agreement was instantly eroded by the decision that the finances of the Chambers would be kept separate wherever possible: each office's income was now to be entirely its own responsibility. In 1974 the office in The Hague made a move that disturbed the relationship for some time to come. Without prior consultation with the Chamber in New York, the accountants Klynveld, Kraayenhof & Co. were asked to devise a new administrative structure. The idea of integrating the offices to form one organization was unacceptable to the Chamber in New York, which saw it as a threat to the administrative autonomy it had defended so resolutely against the CKH some years before. At the same time, it was clear that communication between the two offices was in need of improvement, so Sijthoff and L. van Münching, a fellow board member, went to The Hague in September to propose a new arrangement whereby the secretaries would meet twice a year and there would be closer contact between the boards. When A.T. Knoppers succeeded Severiens as president on November 13, 1974, the differences seemed to have been resolved.

In practice, however, the growing financial problems the Chamber was facing were caused by the failure to adjust to the amended subsidy policy and made cooperation more difficult than Knoppers had first assumed. The fact that the Economic Information Division allowed the Chamber considerably more lee-way than other comparable institutions made little difference. The basic principle of the Langman doctrine was that promotional activities for industry and commerce were no longer to be eligible for government support. Subsidies were to be granted only for the handling of foreign enquiries about Dutch products and services. The criterion applied to such subsidies was a maximum of 50 percent of the income from membership fees and services provided for Dutch firms. As the American market was known to be more difficult, the Chamber was accorded a subsidy doubling their income on the condition that their working methods were objective and professional. The amount pledged for 1975 was Dfl. 683,000.

The Chamber could not react adequately to the subsidy reduction. The first action they took was to move the Chamber in San Francisco to Los Angeles early in 1975. More than 70 percent of all income came from southern California. It was arranged that the Chamber in The Hague would handle the general enquiries from Dutch firms, and it was decided to keep the finances strictly separate, which meant that the individual Chambers would need to redouble their efforts to earn more money. The Chamber in The Hague was the first to feel the pressure. Since it had the closest ties with Dutch industry and commerce, it was thought to be in the best position to increase its earned income, also because the offices in the United States had to contend with heavy competition from the U.S. government agencies that provided information free of charge. The Economic Information Division objected to the arrangement, insisting that a joint task required uniform management and a common approach. Separating the Chambers' finances was at variance with the efforts to achieve greater coordination. And indeed the fragmented organizational structure was by far the greatest impediment to the higher standards needed to earn significantly more income. The Chambers knew too little about each other's activities, to which they accorded varying priorities. The secretaries' meetings made practically no difference in this respect. The international image of a Chamber of Commerce as a non-profit organization meant that firms did not appreciate having to pay for the costs of the Chambers' services. Commercialization also caused internal problems, as appears from a question posed to the Economic Information Division by the Chamber at a meeting in The Hague: "Can full justice be done to either free services or a commercial approach when they exist side by side?"

Unable to opt for either free services or commercialization, and confronted with a diminishing interest in the American market and shrinking advertising revenues from *Netherlands-American Trade*, the Chamber saw its budget deficit increase from Dfl. 88,000 in 1975, which exhausted practically all their reserves, to Dfl. 316,000 in 1976. The Chamber in New York had no hope of relief from the Netherlands Ministry of Economic Affairs, after Knoppers had made it abundantly clear to the Economic Information Division that under the present circumstances the Chamber could not survive. The Netherlands Chambers of Commerce throughout Europe were sufficiently viable because Dutch industry and commerce was largely orientated towards Europe. The volume and composition of exports to the United States limited the possibility of commercializing the promotion of trade, and the Chamber there could at most play only a very small part in exports of bulk goods and costly capital goods, and in the transactions of multinationals and other large corporations. The Economic Information Division found this unacceptable. The difficulties were attributable to structural rather than cyclical factors, and the Economic Information Division agreed with Ambassador A.R. Tammenons Bakker that on no account was the Chamber to be dissolved. Not only would that create a heavier workload for the foreign service but, more seriously, it would mean the irreparable loss of expertise, experience, and contacts. The problem was not the work performed by the offices in New York, Chicago, and The Hague, but the organizational structure, which stood in the way of working methods that were coordinated, efficient, and truly professional. The Directorate had always been prepared to finance any reorganization likely to produce an integrated policy and uniform methods of execution. The depleted reserves of the Chambers ruled out any further delay, but the precarious state of the Dutch national finances left no scope for an additional subsidy. Since the boards were unable to resolve the problem, the Economic Information Division requested that consultants to be called in.

Referring to industry's lack of interest in the Chamber's package of services, Golightly & Co. International advised that their managements be integrated. This constituted the basis for the subsequent reorganization of the Chamber. In May, 1976 the three boards agreed to concentrate the management of the organization in New York. Its principal tasks would be to deal with the commercial enquiries from American corporations, formerly handled by the embassy and the consulates, to supply Dutch industry and commerce with straightforward general information, and to actively foster trade with the United States on the basis of a program to be drawn up each year. The Economic Information Division stressed the priority of the first two tasks; the third would be contingent on demand, and was to be cost-effective. New York was promoted to head office, and Chicago, like Los Angeles, was closed and its work transferred to the New York office and the local consulate-general. The office in The Hague turned over its responsibilities to the Netherlands Trade Promotion Center on December 1, 1976, and the board, like that in Chicago, continued to function in an advisory capacity. At the request of the Economic Information Division, the Chamber in New York appointed Kersen J. de Jong, former manager of the Chicago office, as travelling representative for the Midwest. The 1976 subsidy was raised by Dfl. 130,000 to Dfl. 880,000 to get the new system off to a good start. Despite the priority accorded by the Economic Information Division to the passive promotion of trade, it was clear that financial viability would be wholly dependent on the active steps taken by the Chamber to increase trade with the United States.

Conclusions

After responsibility for the promotion of trade was transferred from the consulate-general in New York to the Chamber in 1964, the Economic Information Division had two interrelated goals: the work was to be adapted to the wishes and needs of private industry, and the Chamber was to function as cost-effectively as possible. Modernization of their services would boost their market value and their revenues, and the subsidy could be reduced accordingly. In the case of the CKH, it was the Netherlands Ministry of Economic Affairs that released the genie from the bottle. Dutch private enterprise acquired a voice in the promotion of trade but made no correspondingly greater contribution, while the Netherlands Ministry could exert no direct influence on the conduct of affairs and was moreover confronted with ever greater financial demands. In regard to both the CKH and the Chamber, the Economic Information Division had enormous difficulty in keeping the subsidies within limits. The grandiose scale on which Van den Bergh and his supporters proposed to stimulate exports did not impress the Directorate and eventually, through the replacement of the CKH by the Netherlands Trade Promotion Center, it put an end to its plans.

The necessary conditions for application of the user-pays principle were almost entirely absent. Economic developments played an important part here. Up to 1971 a substantial subsidy was essential in view of the much higher cost of living. In the ensuing years the dwindling interest in the American market caused by the falling exchange rate nullified the advantage of the devalued dollar. The key factor seems however to have been the lack of interest displayed by Dutch exporters, for whom the United States took second place after Europe. Save for a short period of rapid growth between 1965 and 1969, the scope for the promotion of Dutch trade with the United States was limited. This was especially true after 1970, when the Chamber was under mounting pressure to follow a more commercial approach.

For the Chamber, it was a foregone conclusion that given the economic environment, they could not operate without substantial government support. A non-profit institution offering its services on a commercial basis was unknown in the United States. As the Chamber regarded itself first and foremost a service organization, it did not make the mental transition to thinking in terms of a more commercial, market-oriented approach, with the result that its modus operandi remained much the same as before.

In the early 1960s the Netherlands government decreed that trade promotion was primarily a matter for private enterprise, which must itself bear more of the financial burden. It was soon apparent that this was easier said than done. The businessmen who shared this view were mainly representatives of large corporations that made little or no use of the Chambers' services. The administrative autonomy of the Chamber made it impossible for the Economic Information Division to enforce the new policy. In addition, lacking knowledge of the practical aspects of trade promotion, the Economic Information Division was unable to put forward suggestions of its own. It was therefore obliged to leave it to the organizations themselves to decide how they could best respond to market demands. This was the situation until the proclamation of the Langman doctrine in 1972, which acknowledged that only some trade promotional activities were suited to the new approach.

The Economic Information Division finally gained some measure of influence over the Chambers of Commerce for America when their prospects and their economic situation were seriously affected by the enforcement of the Langman doctrine. Since the Chamber's work standards met the Economic Information Division's criteria, there was no reason for it to intervene sooner. What these criteria amounted to in practice was the prevention of dissatisfaction in the business community.

In view of the amended subsidy policy due to take effect from January, 1975, the Chamber lived beyond its means after 1972. By establishing an office in Chicago and revitalizing the Chamber in California they improved and expanded their services, but at the same time increased their expenditures, which was not matched by higher revenues, especially in California. The reorganization in 1976 forced the Chamber to fall back on the office in New York. The Economic Information Division temporarily reinstituted the system of tailoring the subsidy to the size of the deficit. This gave the newly united Chamber a chance to straighten out its affairs, but whether it would be utilized by private enterprise would largely depend on its management.

Notes

1. The embassies and consulates of Belgium, France, Britain, and Italy were responsible for trade promotion, and in Norway and Sweden it was entrusted to semi-government institutions.
2. There was a close correlation between the nature of the work of the Chambers and the extent of government involvement in the promotion of trade. For example, the British American Chamber of Commerce, which had five hundred members, devoted itself entirely to social activities. The Chambers for Italy, France, Belgium, Sweden, and Denmark carried relatively little weight because trade promotion was conducted by their repective governments.
3. The closure of the Institute made an unfortunate impression on American investors, who no longer felt welcome in the Netherlands, and it was reopened four years later.

CHAPTER VII

1976-1987: SUBSIDIES, TRADE SHOWS, AND THE MARKET

Introduction

Following the reorganization in 1977, the Chamber was faced with the need to earn more income without delay. The higher subsidy was due to expire at the end of 1978, and the Economic Information Division had made it clear that there would be no going back. The subsidy for the Chamber could not be more than half its total income. But it did not reach such a point. As the Netherlands became less competitive on the international market, Dutch exporters began to look with renewed interest at the largest and richest market in the world, and Dutch government policy on the promotion of exports underwent a similar metamorphosis. The basic tenet of the Langman doctrine, namely that the private trade promotion organizations were to aim to generate more income themselves, remained unchanged. The business community however called for adjustments to the subsidy regulations which would assist small and medium-sized businesses to cope with intensifying international competition. Responding to the appeal, the Economic Information Division financed the reopening of the Chicago branch office at the end of 1978. An enhanced subsidy policy in the 1980s ensured the survival and ultimately the expansion of the promotion of trade with the United States.

At the end of 1980, the Chamber was facing a financial crisis. The subsidy policy introduced in 1975 demanded a more inventive approach to trade promotion, while at the same time inflation was causing expenditure to rise faster than income and the falling exchange rate of the dollar was dampening Dutch interest in the American market. The new management which took over in 1981 not only utilized the opportunities presented by the Langman doctrine but also succeeded in profiting from the renewed interest in the American market in the wake of the improving dollar exchange rate. Over the next few years the Chamber rapidly expanded its sphere of activities: a trade show program designed to acquaint small and medium-sized businesses with the American market, seminars highlighting the Netherlands as the gateway to Europe, and general publicity to strengthen the ties between the Dutch and American business communities. More importantly, the Chamber at last succeeded in placing the traditional forms of trade promotion on a commercial footing. The Chamber itself also expanded. A branch office was opened in Atlanta, Georgia, in 1986, and in 1987 the office in The Hague severed its ties with the Netherlands Trade Promotion Center to become a separate organization once again.

Cyclical factors contributed to the fluctuations in Dutch interest in the American market between 1976 and 1987. The following section outlines the export and direct investment trends in that period, the overall Dutch export promotion policy, and the use made by the Netherlands Chamber of Commerce in the United States, Inc. of the possibilities offered by the government subsidy policy and the Dutch export boom to the United States.

Exports and Investments

The key factor in the development of Dutch exports to the United States between 1976 and 1987 was the competitiveness of Dutch private enterprise. After a rapid decline up to 1979, the Netherlands' share of the world market increased substantially as the result of a drop in relative prices and wage costs stemming from the strong recovery of the dollar, which since 1976 had fallen against the guilder from Dfl. 2.64

The crew of the earth
orbiting Space Shuttle
Chalenger, among them is
the Dutchman Wubbo
Ockels.
Oct. 30 - Nov. 6, 1985
Nasa Archive

Akzo's fibers are used in
the uniforms of Space
Shuttle astronauts.

to Dfl. 1.99. The recovery was however of short duration. The U.S. dollar, peaking at Dfl. 3.82 in 1985, dropped again to Dfl. 2.03 in 1987. Following this trend, Dutch exports to the United States reached their highest point, tripling from Dfl. 3.6 billion in 1980 to Dfl. 11.8 billion in 1985, before falling by 31 percent to Dfl. 8.1 billion in 1987, primarily due to the dollar's decline in value. The United States was still the Netherlands' principal market after the European Community. The U.S. share of Dutch exports increased from 3.2 percent in 1980 to 6.2 percent in 1985, and thereafter fluctuated around 4.5 percent. And many Dutch firms had taken advantage of the boom years to establish permanent contacts in the United States.

With regard to direct investment in the United States, the Netherlands retained its position as the second largest foreign investor after Britain. The growth of Dutch assets kept pace with the upward surge of foreign direct investment in the United States between 1976 and 1987. Small and medium-sized business-es, the traditional target group of the Chamber, then moved for the first time into this area of investment. Yields were relatively low on the traditional European markets, which were saturated, and Dutch firms exhibited an increasing interest in foreign investment in general, and investment in the United States in particular. There was considerable demand on the large, homogeneous American market for high-grade products and services. The emphasis on product and management innovation formed an additional rea-son for Dutch companies to keep in touch with developments in the United States. A 1983 survey of Dutch investors that had established operations in the United States, conducted by the Chamber and Arthur Young International, showed that the economic freedom practiced in the United States guaranteed that foreign investors could operate under the same conditions as American corporations. Dutch foreign investments in 1983 amounted to Dfl. 120 billion, elevating the Netherlands to third place on the world list after the United States and Britain, and increased by more than Dfl. 20 billion a year throughout the 1980s. More than half of the 750 branches of Dutch firms in the United States in 1989 were established after 1980.

Although the available figures are not entirely consistent and, in view of their confidential nature, are pre-sumably not complete, they give a good indication of the rapid growth of Dutch economic interests in the United States. The Netherlands Bank noted a five-fold rise from Dfl. 6.6 billion to Dfl. 33.5 billion between 1973 and 1983. American sources put the figure much higher. The U.S. Department of Commerce estima-ted total Dutch direct investment in 1980 at $ 17 billion, and in 1981 at $ 20.2 billion. The low exchange rate of the dollar, which reduced the cost of investment in American corporations, and the stagnation of European economies undoubtedly acted as an additional stimulus. The dollar's recovery in the following year seems however to have made little difference to the growth of Dutch direct investment in the United States, which brought the total of actual investments to an estimated $ 37 billion in 1985, and $ 47 billion by 1987. A 1989 survey on Dutch enterprise in the United States, conducted by the Chamber and Arthur Young International, showed that as in the past, Dutch investment in the U.S. was largely concentrated in the oil, food-processing and chemical industries. After 1981 the relative share of Dutch investments de-clined when the Netherlands lost its place as the foremost foreign investor in the United States to Britain.

Foreign Investment in the United States		
	1987	
	$ billion	%
Netherlands	47.0	17.9
Britain	74.9	28.6
Japan	33.4	12.7
Canada	21.7	8.3
West Germany	19.6	7.5
France	10.2	3.9
Switzerland	14.3	5.5
Other	40.8	15.6
Total	261.9	100

In the following years Dutch and British investments remained much higher than those of Japan, Canada, West Germany and Switzerland.

While the oil-producing states and Japan were high-profile buyers of American corporations, Dutch direct investments went quietly ahead. Almost half of Dutch investments in the United States, 45 percent, yielded less than $ 5 million in 1989; 15 percent turned over more than $ 100 million a year. The more notable transactions included the takeover of Belridge Oil Fields by Royal Dutch/Shell for $ 3.7 billion in 1979, and Royal Dutch's purchase of all remaining Shell Oil shares for $ 5.7 billion in 1985, and the procurement by Unilever of Cheseborough-Ponds for $ 3.1 billion in 1987. Dutch corporations in the United States employed a workforce of 255,000, nearly 9 percent of the employees working for foreign companies in the United States in 1987.

Towards A New Policy on Export Promotion

Economic developments had to a large extent overtaken the basic premises of the Langman doctrine before it was put into practice in January, 1975. Formulated at the end of a boom period when Dutch exports rose every year, its purpose was to reduce the role of government in the promotion of exports. The distinct deterioration in the Netherlands' competitiveness on the world market after 1973 and pressure exerted by the Dutch business community forced the Netherlands government to reconsider its policy. The Netherlands Central Board for Foreign Economic Relations was the first body to raise the red flag in 1974. Thereafter, together with the employers organizations, it urged both officially and unofficially that the conditions for Dutch exports be improved, basing its arguments on the fact that export facilities in the Netherlands compared unfavorably with those in neighboring European countries.

The need to achieve greater competitiveness was crucial for consultations between Dutch private enterprise and the Netherlands government in this first serious economic crisis since the second world war. Wage costs soared and the guilder became stronger as a result of the balance of payments surplus recorded annually up to 1977. The relatively low Dutch rate of inflation after 1973 contributed to the guilder's 30 to 40 percent rise in value against the dollar up to 1979. It was clear from a 1976 policy document on balanced growth that the Netherlands government was receptive to the arguments of the business community. Adopting the industrialization policy of the 1950s as a model, the Netherlands government stated that competitiveness would be improved by restructuring the manufacturing sector. Firms in difficulties would be provided with subsidies to help them through the recession. In view of its worsening competitive position and its contracting share of the world market, Dutch industry was not content with these measures, and exerted pressure on the government to pursue an active export policy.

The renewed interest in the structure of the manufacturing sector displayed by the center-left Den Uyl administration did not suddenly appear. In 1971 the previous government had considered the restructuring of industry as necessary. Wage rises had gradually eroded the country's competitiveness since the early 1960s, and the only way to increase its share of the world market was to narrow profit margins. In 1976 the Minister for Economic Affairs, R.F.M. Lubbers, announced a new balanced growth policy - the so-called structure plan - which was partly based on the principles underlying the industrialization policy of the 1950s. By influencing private investment the Netherlands government would have a say in the direction to be followed by the economy. The outcome however was that support was given to weak branches of industry and loss-making companies. It did not halt the process of deindustrialization which reduced industry's share of total production from 33 percent in 1970 to 30 percent in 1978. It was not until 1979 that Dutch policy was geared more to technological renewal, innovation, and support for industries and branches of industry offering the prospect of growth. The weaknesses of Dutch industry were analyzed by two advisory bodies, both of which advocated a sector-oriented structural policy and concentration on innovative branches of industry likely to accelerate economic growth. The Netherlands government followed their advice, but because the fourteen areas selected for special attention covered practically all industrial activity in the Netherlands, there was no question of a sector-related policy. After 1980 virtually nothing remained of the control envisaged in the 1976 structure plan. The Netherlands government again turned its attention to improving the overall conditions needed for better utilization of existing technological potential.

236

Industry and the Promotion of Exports

In November, 1974 the Central Board for Foreign Economic Relations asked the Netherlands government for the first time since the late 1960s to take steps to promote exports. Both at that time and during the crisis at the beginning of the 1980s, special emphasis was placed on strengthening the competitive position of the large-scale industries which accounted for the bulk of Dutch exports. Only a few measures were taken to facilitate the entry of small and medium-sized businesses to new markets.

The reason for the Central Board's appeal to the government was the high interest rates which Dutch industries were forced to charge for credits extended to foreign firms, resulting in the loss of many orders. The limited facilities available since 1967 for financing exports of capital goods were minor compared with the support received by foreign competitors. Dutch firms that were fully competitive and booked orders on a cash payment basis found themselves excluded when it came to delivery on credit. The annual difference in interest rates sometimes exceeded 3 percent. As in the past, however, the Netherlands government was not prepared to subsidize export credits, arguing that in the long term the disadvantages of fewer outlets were outweighed by the short-term advantages. The situation changed with the stagnation of the world economy and the increase in competition distorting measures taken by other countries. The Central Board asked the government to establish export credits at the level agreed by the G-7 Group of industrialized countries. To prevent further distortion of competition, the United States, Japan, Canada, West Germany, France, Italy, and Britain had agreed not to allow the costs of financing export credits to fall below 7.5 percent, a figure much lower than the Dutch interest rate of 9.15 percent. As the economy deteriorated in 1975, Dutch industry increased pressure on the Ministry of Economic Affairs to bring its competitiveness up to the international level. In the following year the costs of financing exports of capital goods were lowered and the annual ceiling was raised from Dfl. 800 million to Dfl. 1.5 billion. Exporters of other goods were eligible for similar assistance as from 1978.

The Dutch business community made it plain to the Ministry at the end of 1975 that it also wished to see policy on the promotion of exports adapt to the changing circumstances. Foreign governments were increasingly supporting industries other than those in the capital goods sector, and many countries provided subsidies for participation in trade shows, advertising, market research and so on. In November, C. van Veen, president of the Netherlands Federation of Industry and Commerce, asked the government to raise export facilities to the same level as in neighboring countries, and to make structural adjustments to counter the ever worsening international competitiveness of Dutch industry. The free trade principle might be admirable in itself, but in the present circumstances it did nothing to strengthen industry's competitive position. In the Federation's view, what was needed was expansion of the established package of export promotion measures.

The 1976 structure plan partially met these demands. The new policy was aimed at opening up new outlets for entire industrial sectors through technological innovation and improved marketing tactics. Higher output and a greater return were not sufficient to qualify for support. Although small and medium-sized businesses were covered by the new arrangement, it was primarily directed towards large corporations. Besides the combination of export promotion measures for small and medium-sized businesses dating from the 1950s, it also provided for subsidies for large-scale projects such as the delivery of complete factories (turn-key projects) and hydraulic engineering projects. All subsidies were project-specific, which ruled out activities like recurrent participation in trade shows and ongoing market research.

In July, 1976 a large delegation of Dutch manufacturers again raised the subject of expanding the existing export promotion system at a meeting with the Netherlands Minister for Economic Affairs. The Minister merely acknowledged that more needed to be done to promote exports and that the relevant organizations should work more closely together. He rejected the idea of making extra funds available and of abandoning the Langman doctrine. These talks were followed by the Export Plan 1976 which the Central Board presented to Prime Minister Den Uyl on October 4, 1976 on behalf of the industrial organizations whose representatives had been present at the meeting. In the interests of employment, the Board urged "a switch to a more aggressive and inventive exports and export promotion policy", and wider export facilities for small and medium-sized businesses. It recommended increasing the number of export consultants attached to the regional Chambers of Commerce in the Netherlands as of the end of the 1960s, who functioned as the initial point of contact for firms interested in exports. In view of the depressed West European economies, the Board was concerned about the heavy concentration of Dutch exports on the European Community, which had accounted for more than 72 percent of Dutch exports in 1975. What was needed was systematic research into potential new markets in non-European countries with which the Netherlands had a large trade deficit, such as the United States, Canada, Japan, and Brazil. The United States, as the largest and richest consumer market, merited special attention in this respect. Knowing the financial difficulties under which the Chamber and other trade promotion agencies were operating, the Board urged that they be allowed wider scope. In addition, the embassies and consulates should be more active in economic matters, and economics should feature in the training of future foreign service officers.

After studying the plan, the Netherlands Bank and seven ministries headed by the Ministry of General Affairs concluded that there were few points on which the government could take direct action. Many of the aspects of the plan could only be dealt with by the European Community or GATT, and some were already being implemented or would require further study. The promotion of exports was one of the few exceptions. The study group shared the view of the Central Board that more should be done to promote trade. Market exploration and research, and assistance with joint participation in trade shows would help boost exports, provided they were undertaken in a group context. Providing information in the Netherlands was a different issue. The number of export consultants could not be increased, but representatives of the Netherlands Chambers of Commerce abroad could devote more time to regional consultations.

Before a meeting arranged between Minister Lubbers and representatives of industry headed by the chairman of the Central Board, J.H. de Koster, took place on February 2, 1977, the Economic Information Division had already made the first adjustments to the promotion of exports, including a review of the Langman doctrine. Rising inflation was progressively widening the gap between the income and expenditure of the Netherlands Chambers of Commerce abroad, in some cases posing a threat to their continued existence. The financial problems of the Chamber in the United States was however the main reason for relaxing the regulations. A fixed sum was to be made available for handling enquiries - often by telephone - from the Netherlands, for regional consultancy services in the Netherlands, and for travelling in the countries in which the Chambers were established. For the Netherlands Chamber of Commerce in the United States, Inc. this amounted to two man-years for 1978, raising the renumeration by Dfl. 240,000. The Economic Information Division also made available extra funds for special promotional activities. Despite these measures, the basic principles of the Langman doctrine remained intact, and there was no question of deficit financing. Renumerations were allocated only to industries displaying sufficient interest. The aim was to stimulate the demand for Dutch goods and services by means of joint presentations in promising new markets. Funds were reserved for expanding the trade show program, assisting visiting foreign trade missions, and printing and distributing publicity material. All such support was still on a once-only basis. As the global economic crisis deepened, the conditions were eased and the budget was enlarged.

On the whole, however, not too many plans were put into effect while Lubbers was Minister for Economic Affairs. After an early general election in 1977, the business community presented to the outgoing Cabinet a number of suggestions for improving the Netherlands' export position. Lowering the level of domestic costs was at the top of the list, followed by wider facilities for export credits and political revaluation of foreign trade. A minister responsible for foreign trade should be appointed to the Ministry, which should be renamed the Ministry for Economic Affairs and Foreign Trade, and the senior officials of the Foreign Economic Relations Directorate who headed delegations to international meetings should now have the rank of ambassador. Meanwhile the interests of industry and commerce were discussed "behind closed doors" as before, chiefly at the monthly meetings of the Central Board and the Foreign Economic Relations Directorate. In October 1977, the Board went public at a press conference, calling for a real "emergency export plan". As a result, more export credits were made available and a separate department for foreign trade was set up under the Minister for Foreign Trade.

The new government which took office in 1978 included K.H. Beyen, Minister for Foreign Trade and the promotion of exports. The plans he unfolded were consistent in practically all respects with those of the previous government. The business community was disappointed. After the center-left Den Uyl administration which had not been popular with businessmen, they had fixed their hopes on the center-right Van Agt administration. The Central Board let it be known via the press that the government's measures fell far short of what was required to rescue industry from its difficult position. The main problem was the hard guilder. The present credit facilities were inadequate as it was, and if the guilder should become even harder Dutch industry's international competitiveness would suffer still further. This negative perception was not entirely justified. Beyen's policies created more financial scope for the private promotion of trade and offered wider opportunities for small and medium-sized businesses to explore foreign markets. In just a few years the budget for export promotion doubled to Dfl. 21 million. The allocation of subsidies to small and medium-sized businesses was preceded by evaluation of their export strategies.

[...the hard guilder...]

Even though the 1974 crisis led to the creation of more instruments for the promotion of Dutch exports, the Langman doctrine remained applicable to small and medium-sized businesses. While their financial scope was enlarged, only the big corporations were in a position to deploy new initiatives. As the Netherlands government did not wish to take industry's place, it could not pursue a specific export policy, but opted instead for widening the possibilities for investigating foreign markets.

Export by Mail

A questionnaire sent to seventeen embassies at the beginning of 1979 yielded sufficient data to give the Netherlands Ministry of Economic Affairs a general idea of how small and medium-sized businesses tried to establish themselves in foreign markets. Whether and to what extent it was equally valid for firms that tried to export without aid is uncertain. With the exception of multinationals, Dutch firms usually made no systematic effort either quantitatively or qualitatively to explore foreign markets. Research was sporadic and unstructured. Their approach, lacking drive and imagination, left ample room for branch-oriented promotion through trade shows and trade missions. Many managers tried "to organize exports by mail", only to discover on going abroad that they were not properly prepared. In European markets Dutch products were generally unadapted to local customs, tastes, and quality standards for packaging and design.[1] At Beyen's insistence, as a result of the growing foreign competition on the home market, in 1978 the Ministry introduced a few new regulations designed to aid small and medium-sized businesses seeking outlets abroad. The export potential in this sector was large, but needed to be activated. A mere 866 of the 6,500 firms with fewer than 50 employees had earned between Dfl. 500,000 and Dfl. 5 million through exports in 1977; only 120 earned more, and the rest less. Like the large corporations, approximately 80 percent of their exports went to European countries. The majority of firms with a workforce under 200 were too small to employ an export manager, so that their managements, unaware of the demands of other markets, failed to measure up to the required standard. Lacking a structural approach to foreign markets, many firms obtained orders from abroad more or less by chance.[2]

PTT, Dutch stamps celebrating 200 years of friendly and uninterrupted diplomatic and trade relations between the Netherlands and the United States

To stimulate a more methodical approach, the Ministry issued new subsidy regulations intended to fill the gap in awareness of export strategies and to bring smaller-scale manufacturers into contact with foreign markets. Shortly after taking office, the new Netherlands government allocated an extra Dfl. 2.5 million for 1978 and 1979 for the expansion of the Economic Information Division. The budget was increased by a further Dfl. 8.9 million for trade shows, general publicity, market research, and trade mediation over the period 1979-1983. An additional Dfl. 750,000 was reserved for direct subsidies for the Netherlands Chambers of Commerce abroad. In the parliamentary debate on the 1979 budget, specific reference was made to the reopening of the Chicago office of the Chamber. The Netherlands Trade Promotion Center and the Chambers of Commerce abroad were made responsible for the organization of trade show participations. The Ministry also allocated Dfl. 3.5 million for the temporary appointment of export managers, and Dfl. 750,000 for the establishment of export cooperatives. The latter achieved the desired effect in that a hundred such cooperatives were in existence shortly afterwards. But some years later only a few were still active, the others having disbanded after the expiration of the subsidy.

To avoid spreading the funds too thinly, the Economic Information Division selected a number of so-called target countries: promising markets in which Dutch industry had as yet made little impact. Selection was based on investment conditions and the political and economic climate, the growth of prosperity in the preceding years and the indicators for the coming years, the development of foreign trade and the size of the country's financial reserves. As the largest and most prosperous market, the United States headed the list of 17, and later 20 target countries. But the main emphasis was on traditional European outlets like West Germany and France, whose regional markets were still largely unexplored by Dutch exporters. Separate action programs were drawn up for 11 countries, entailing participation in trade shows, orientation and follow-up visits to industrial centers and regional markets, business meetings, conventions, and so on. There was usually a fixed sequence of activities, starting with market research, followed by an official visit by the junior minister for foreign trade, a trade mission, and participation in a trade show or a similar event. There were 72 such action programs in 1980, of which 6 were focused on North America. This was the full extent of the instruments used by the Ministry in the 1980s to promote the exports by small and medium-sized businesses. These instruments were primarily aimed at the highly developed European markets. The only other initiative was taken in 1980 by the Ministry of Foreign Affairs, which decided in consultation with the Foreign Economic Relations Directorate and the Economic Information Division to reinforce five embassies and consulates outside Europe with experienced trade promoters drawn from the business community. The "Beyen five", as they came to be known because of Beyen's strong support for the idea, were posted for three years to Abidjan, Ivory Coast, to Manila, the Philippines, to Kuwait City, Kuwait, to Sydney, Australia, and to Los Angeles, California. The results were disappointing, and the experiment was discontinued at the end of the trial period.

"An Indispensable Link"

Finances

Barely three years after the fundamental reorganization of the Netherlands Chamber of Commerce in the United States, Inc. in 1976, the Ministry of Economic Affairs raised the budget for the promotion of exports and introduced a number of new measures to be implemented with the aid of the Chamber. The financial scope of the Chambers was broadened both directly and indirectly. They received the resources needed to move beyond their original territories, which in the case of the Netherlands Chamber of Commerce in the United States, Inc. resulted in the reopening of the branch office in Chicago at the end of 1978. There was also more money available for financing the participation in events like trade shows, depending on the number of participants. In order to benefit from these wider opportunities, the Chamber of Commerce in New York had to obtain the cooperation of the business community. The new government policy came just in time to save the Chamber from the financial consequences of the rapid decline in Dutch exports to the United States triggered by the second oil crisis in 1979, which threw the world economy into the greatest disarray since the second world war.

Contrary to the expectations of the Economic Information Division, the 1976 reorganization brought little improvement in the financial position of the Netherlands Chamber of Commerce in the United States, Inc. Its income from fees, donations, and services could not keep pace with the rapid rise in expenditures that came with the high rate of inflation in the United States. Salaries had to be raised by 18 percent during the period 1979-1980. It was due solely to the severe depreciation of the dollar between 1976 and 1980 (from Dfl. 2.64 to Dfl. 1.99) that the Chamber managed to cushion the effects of the reduced subsidy. To finance the reorganization, the Economic Information Division had agreed to reinstitute deficit-based subsidies over the period 1976-1978, so that the payment for 1976 amounted to Dfl. 820,000. In 1979 the Economic Information Division returned to the system of a subsidy equal to the amount of the Chamber's own income plus separate allocations for the offices in Chicago and New York. For 1979 this amount totalled Dfl. 795,000, covering 80 percent of the Chamber's costs. It was reduced to Dfl. 640,500 in 1980, largely because of Dutch exporters' dwindling interest in the American market. Owing to the steady fall in the value of the dollar against the guilder, the subsidy in dollars still remained the same, at $ 320,000. The Chamber's other income in 1980 was $ 208,000, almost 42 percent more than in 1978. Membership in the Netherlands dropped from 410 to 320 between 1976 and 1987, showing only a slight improvement when the combined membership of 750 was distributed equally over the United States and the Netherlands. Driven by inflation, expenditure rose so much faster than revenues that the accounts showed a loss of Dfl. 145,270, or $ 72,000, in 1980, and the financial reserves were close to exhaustion. At the end of 1978 the reserve funds had amounted to $ 193,000. At the beginning of 1981 it was clear that without a change of policy the deficit would be twice as high by the end of the year, and the Chamber would be bankrupt. In the event, the deficit that year was just above $ 87,000, leaving a reserve of slightly above zero.

The wider subsidy facilities available at the end of 1979 combined with more market-oriented management produced a higher income in the following years. A subsidy scheme for special export promotional projects covered 40 percent of the costs of new activities that were beyond the scope of the non-governmental trade promotion organizations. No financial ceiling was fixed for large export markets such as the United States, and consequently the subsidy increased in proportion to the initiatives taken by the Chamber. This was in addition to the fixed subsidy for handling foreign commercial enquiries, for minor services for which no charge could be made, and for the branch offices, which constituted a sizeable part of the budget. Revenues were higher on all fronts. Higher membership fees yielded an increase from $ 83,000 in 1979 to $ 257,000 in 1987. Income from the program for special promotional projects rose from $ 1,645 in 1979 to approximately $ 49,000 in 1983 and $ 79,000 in 1986. The greatest increase came from the routine services provided by the Chamber: commercial information for Dutch firms, which in 1977 had yielded only $ 53,000, generated $ 138,000 in 1981 and as much as $ 577,500 in 1987. The increase in the Chamber's income was matched by a corresponding increase in the subsidy, doubling from $ 393,000 in 1984 to $ 793,000 in 1986. Thus from 1982 onward subsidies covered about half the Chamber's costs, and the Chamber complied with the very intent of the Langman doctrine, a fact that was largely attributable to its market-oriented approach.

1977-1981: Towards a Second Reorganization

In 1977 the offices in The Hague, Chicago, and Los Angeles were closed as a result of the financial crisis affecting the Chambers of Commerce for America after the Chamber could not anticipate the consequences of the Langman doctrine. Since all aspects of trade promotion were concentrated thereafter in New York, it had to take action to ensure that a similar crisis would not recur in the future. The combination of soaring costs and Dutch exporters' declining interest in the United States brought the Chamber to the brink of financial disaster in 1980-1981.

The Netherlands Trade Promotion Center had taken over the work of the Chamber in The Hague in 1976, when Pieter G. Huser had been responsible for the liaison between the Chamber in New York and the business community in the Netherlands. The promotion of trade with Canada was also part of his job. At the suggestion of the Economic Information Division, which raised the subsidy for this purpose, the Chamber appointed the former manager of the Chicago office, Kersen J. de Jong, as its travelling representative for the Midwest and the West Coast based in New York. Unfortunately, while accompanying a trade mission from the Netherlands he was hit by a car and lost both his legs. He subsequently left the Chamber.

In the following years the Chamber's income doubled and, since some services were provided free of charge, the Economic Information Division allocated extra funds for the salaries of two more full-time employees. This additional support was needed because the Dfl. 125,000 deficit in 1976, the loss of half the West Coast members, and the reorganization costs had reduced the Chamber's reserves to less than Dfl. 60,000.

Notwithstanding these efforts, the reorganization had a negative impact on quality standards in 1977. After the closure of the offices in Chicago and Los Angeles the Chamber's sphere of activities was once again mainly confined to New York and its environs. The consulate-general in Chicago forwarded all commercial enquiries to New York, but was not satisfied with the situation. In the consul-general's view, Chicago, as a commercial center second only to New York in importance, was entitled to a trade promotion agency of its own, governmental or non-governmental. With the establishment of the Chamber's branch office in 1971 the consulate's commercial section had been closed, with the result that in 1976 there were no commercial specialists in Chicago. The consul-general, S.C. van Nispen, therefore wanted either the commercial section or the branch office to be reopened. He favored the latter option because the Chamber had in the past functioned more economically and with greater flexibility than foreign service officers. Van Nispen and the Chamber joined forces in 1978 to investigate the situation. They found that there was still sufficient interest among the Dutch business community to warrant the reopening of the branch office, whereupon the Economic Information Division extended the period covered by the transition subsidy to the end of 1979. Thereafter it would revert to 100 percent of the Chamber's income plus the equivalent of two man-years as compensation for the services that could not be commercialized. Kersen J. de Jong returned to the Chamber as manager of the Chicago office, where he resumed his activities in the fall of 1978.

At the beginning of 1979 the Economic Information Division noted with satisfaction that the reorganization of the Netherlands Chamber of Commerce in the United States, Inc. had been a success. It appeared to have a good relationship with the Netherlands Trade Promotion Center, and the Chamber in New York now employed a staff of ten under the direction of the president, Anthony T. Knoppers. The only concern was that the small two-man Chicago office seemed in danger of becoming over-extended with all kinds of new initiatives. Barely a year later the Chamber in The Hague was extremely worried by the operational results of the Chamber in general, and by troubled relations between the head office in New York and the branch office in Chicago. Collaboration at all levels was deficient. The Chamber in New York displayed a lack of initiative and rejected every suggestion made by the Chicago office. De Jong's jurisdiction was ill-defined and subject to constant change. The consulate-general in Chicago feared that the Chamber in New York would try to mitigate the effects of its deteriorating financial position by scaling down or even closing the branch office if the Netherlands government was not forthcoming with additional funds. Supported by the consulate-general and the Economic Information Division, Chicago successfully resisted a move in that direction. On a visit to the Netherlands in June, 1980, Knoppers sought the approval of the Economic Information Division for expanding the staff of both the Trade Promotion Center and the Chicago office, and for the establishment of an office in Atlanta.

Under Knoppers, who acted as president of the Chamber between 1974 and 1980, the two Chambers in New York and The Hague were merged and uniform policies and management were implemented. He was the last president in the long history of the Chamber who also acted as chief executive officer of the organization. By 1980, the Chamber was increasingly unable to react adequately to the worsening financial situation, despite efforts to put its services to a more commercial footing. The Chamber had to contend with a deficit of Dfl. 158,500, which threatened continued operations. To find a solution, H. IJssel de Schepper became interim president to review the organization of the Chamber. After the initial exploratory talks, he was succeeded on February 6, 1981 by J.J. van Steenbergen, president of Nedlloyd in New York. Bakels was succeeded as executive secretary by De Jong as of July 1, 1981 and became managing director. With a new Board and a new manager, the reorganization of the Chamber could now be completed. Staff were laid off, office premises were scaled down, new projects were launched, and the financial situation improved. By utilizing all reserves, 1982 ended with a balanced budget. An amendment to the statutes in 1983 transferred the title of chief executive officer, and thus responsibility for the Chamber's commercial operations, from the president to the managing director. Over the next years the situation of the Chamber steadily improved.

Close attention was devoted to the question of branch offices in other parts of the United States. The work of the former Chamber in Los Angeles had devolved to the various West Coast consulates. This gradually changed after the reopening of the Chicago office in 1978. After 1980, by which time it was firmly established, the more complicated enquiries that at first had been passed on to New York or the Trade Promotion Center were sent directly to Chicago. If this was the case for the West Coast, there had long been no alternative in the South but to entrust all commercial activities to the consulate-general in Houston, which complained in 1980 that the Chamber in New York showed no interest in the nine Southern States. The Netherlands was the only West European country without any form of commercial infrastructure in the rapidly evolving Sunbelt region extending from Florida and Georgia to Texas. The consulate-general's staff was barely large enough to perform the most essential tasks, many of which entailed a great deal of administrative work, leaving practically no time for promoting trade or providing commercial information.

A change seemed to be impending early in 1979, when Beyen, the Netherlands Minister for Foreign Trade, suggested to open a branch office of the Chamber in Atlanta. As in the case of the reopening of the Chicago office the year before he argued that an Atlanta office would relieve the pressure on the consulates and open the way for Dutch companies to a fast growing and promising market with scheduled services of KLM Royal Dutch Airlines. Beyen however took no account of the arguments of the consulate-general in Houston for locating trade promotional activities for the Sunbelt in "the world capital" of the offshore oil industry. He expressed his preference for Atlanta when it was clear that the establishment of a Chamber would be actively supported by the local Dutch business community. In contrast to the Dutch businessmen in Houston, most of whom were connected with large corporations, the majority in Atlanta represented small and medium-sized businesses. The honorary consul in Atlanta, Hans Beerkens, arranged a luncheon on January 9, 1980 where Knoppers and Bakels heard the views of the local business community. The general opinion was that Atlanta was a better gateway to the Sunbelt than Houston. It had recently acquired the status of a free port where goods could be temporarily stored without being liable for customs duties, and was the venue for important trade shows of home furnishings that offered promising opportunities for Dutch exports. In October the Economic Information Division invited the Chamber to draw up a proposal for the establishment of a branch office in Atlanta, but before it could do so the Chamber found itself confronted with serious financial problems. Under the chairmanship of Ton J. de Boer, Vice Chairman of ABN North America Inc., between 1984 and 1987, the Chamber continued to improve its position and realized a new branch office that could meet the Ministry's conditions for joint financing, comprising financial guarantees, the guaranteed support of the business community, and the availability of qualified staff. The Atlanta branch office was opened on April 17, 1986.

The Netherlands Trade Promotion Center functioned as the home base of the Chamber prior to the establishment of its own office in The Hague in 1987. The Chamber in New York had found that there were drawbacks to the cooperation with the Center. The more the Center moved away from regular trade promotion, the more importance it assumed. The Economic Information Division's contribution was enough to cover the appointment at the Center of a trade promoter and an assistant, but more staff were needed for adequate attention to be given to each individual request for information. As all newly generated income went to the Chamber in New York, there was not the same incentive at the Center as in a Chamber office to make an extra effort to obtain more commissions and attract new members.

Participation in trade shows was organized by both the Chamber and the Trade Promotion Center. The Chamber arranged for exhibits in New York and Chicago, and the Center for the traditional joint presentation at the Offshore Technology Conference in Houston; they worked together on the organization of subsidized presentations elsewhere in the United States. As the trade shows program and its own organization expanded, the Chamber gradually assumed more responsibility in this area. Their cooperation was on the same ad hoc basis for other promotional activities such as seminars and trade missions. Their association ended when the Center demanded a greater role in 1987. The Chamber had operated within the Center under its own identifiable flag since 1976, but the latter, finding this unsatisfactory, wanted full control of all projects commissioned by private enterprise. This was unacceptable to the Chamber so that a separate office was opened in The Hague in September, 1987 and ties with the Trade Promotion Center were severed.

1981-1987: Bicentennial, Target Market, and Action Plans

The Economic Information Division, the main source of the Chamber's income, was not in a position to influence the Chamber's policies in any significant way. The Chambers abroad were autonomous organizations with their own specific responsibilities. Both the Economic Information Division and the local foreign service officers, who exercised a kind of indirect supervision, therefore avoided intruding in their affairs wherever possible, and confined their role to suggestions and advice. Direct intervention was permissible only if the Chambers ceased to observe the conditions governing subsidization.

This had been a problem when the Langman doctrine was put into effect. The Netherlands government could devise policies, but if these policies involved autonomous organizations the government had little influence on how they were elaborated and implemented. It could of course threaten to reduce or withdraw the subsidy, but that would have been counterproductive in the case of the Chambers, for their subsequent liquidation would then have burdened the Netherlands government with the task of commercial information and trade promotion. Furthermore, non-governmental organizations were generally more economical and more flexible, they had closer connections with local industry and commerce, and they constituted a forum for the exchange of ideas between government and local commercial and industrial corporations. When the subsidy program for specific promotional projects was announced in September, 1979, the Economic Information Division had to wait and see what use would be made of it by the Chambers abroad. Only in the case of acute financial difficulties like those experienced by the Chamber in 1980-1981, when the Economic Information Division declined to finance the deficit, could the Chambers abroad be pressured into using the new program.

H.M. Queen Beatrix and President Bush during Presidents Bush visit of Leiden, the Netherlands Nationaal Foto Persburo b.v.

The new program was aimed at the collective presentation of Dutch goods and services on foreign markets. The Chambers abroad were expected to draw up and calculate the costs of an appropriate plan in joint consultation with the organizations representing the various branches of industry. Government contributed approximately 40 percent of the costs entailed. Chambers lacking the manpower needed to organize special events could engage the services of outside consultants or free-lance specialists. Although the Economic Information Division compiled a list of suggested activities including symposia, seminars, regular consultation and orientation missions that were aimed at leading industrial concerns, the Chambers were explicitly encouraged to put forward their own proposals. Sales campaigns in department stores and other publicity events designed to attract the general public did not qualify for support. An exception could be made if the target group was a limited one with substantial financial resources, as in the case of yacht-building. The Netherlands embassies and consulates were to provide support in their capacity of the country's official representatives. A special subsidy arrangement for participation in trade shows and exhibitions had been in force for some time.

It was not until the 1980s that the Chamber got a new president and executive secretary that it utilized the new program on an extensive scale. Prior to that, in 1979, De Jong and the consulate-general in Chicago had organized the first of three seminars in Minneapolis, Minnesota on "The Netherlands: A Trading Gateway to the World", dealing with the significance of the Netherlands for the transshipment of goods to and from other European countries and East Asia. In 1980 a delegation from Rotterdam attended four other seminars, one of which was held in Baltimore.

In March, 1981 De Jong suggested to organize four seminars each year in states like Iowa, Indiana, Missouri, Wisconsin, and Michigan, plus an unspecified number in industrial centers like Los Angeles, Dallas, New Orleans, and Atlanta. The seminars would be financed partly by manufacturers hoping to find buyers in this way, and partly by the Economic Information Division. After consultation with the Chambers, the Economic Information Division liberalized the subsidy regulations for specific promotional activities, placing greater emphasis on support for the institutions organizing such activities. Participants would be required to pay their own travelling and accommodation expenses, while the Economic Information Division would bear the greater part of the organizational costs and would also pay the full costs of groups of businessmen on short trade missions to the United States. The rules governing subsidies for providing information and services to foreign firms, such as mediation, finding business contacts, investigating the market for specific products, and trade missions, remained unchanged. The Netherlands Chamber of Commerce in the United States, Inc. received a subsidy equal to its previous year's income from services rendered to Dutch companies.

The new program was put into practice in 1982, the year of the Bicentennial celebrations commemorating two hundred years of uninterrupted diplomatic relations between the United States and the Netherlands. The Netherlands government regarded the various cultural manifestations planned for that year as an excellent opportunity to publicize Dutch products. The Netherlands Chamber of Commerce in the United States, Inc. organized joint participation in four trade shows, six seminars, and three trade missions, and adjusted and expanded its program in light of the experience thus gained. In the following years the number of events and participants increased appreciably through the upward turn in the American economy after 1982, the doubling of Dutch exports to the United States between 1981 and 1985, and the publicity surrounding the program. The seminars and trade shows formed the basis of the program, under which more than 100 firms were represented at 21 trade shows in 1987 alone. The majority of the trade shows took place in New York, Chicago, Atlanta, Los Angeles, and Dallas. They included the Builder's Show, the International Cycle Show, the International Gourmet Products Show, and the Graph Expo. Together with Holland International Distribution Center and Rotterdam Distriport, the Chamber also organized sixteen seminars on the Netherlands as a transit country in all parts of the United States.

To assist exporters with selecting and preparing for trade shows, the Chamber compiled a checklist of important issues. Though participation did not guarantee sales, it enabled small and medium-sized companies to gain first-hand knowledge of the American market, the conditions to be met by their products and managements, and the support available from government and non-governmental trade promotion organizations. On the whole, it was not productive until regular sales channels had been established and manufacturers had exhibited at the same trade shows for several consecutive years.

The way in which the Chamber organized collective participation in trade shows gave rise to a difference of opinion with the consulate-general in Chicago. The Chamber and the Economic Information Division felt that personal experience was the best basis for a manufacturer to assess the opportunities offered by the American market, which was so extensive and so diverse that there were bound to be outlets for all Dutch products. The subsidies were intended to remove the smaller manufacturer's inhibitions about displaying his products at trade shows. Van Nispen disagreed with this on two counts. First, he preferred a structural approach to the Economic Information Division's more opportunistic policy, believing that a longer-term policy requiring interested companies to meet certain criteria would provide a firmer basis for exports. This was diametrically opposed to the view of the Economic Information Division that it was not competent to conduct such a policy. Its efforts were focused on lowering the threshold of the American market in the hope that the largest possible number of Dutch manufacturers would be encouraged to export.

The consul-general's other objection was what he saw as the Chicago branch office's imperfect organization of participation in trade shows. This was however a temporary situation. Owing to the financial losses in 1980 and 1981 the staff were largely young and inexperienced, but as Van Nispen admitted, this difficulty was overcome after a few years and work standards vastly improved. As a result of the experience gained in the Bicentennial year, starting in 1983 the Chamber worked in close cooperation with the New York-based Springer Group to give greater publicity to Dutch participation in trade shows. Firms exhibiting for the first time sometimes mistakenly thought that their presence would in itself be of interest to newspapers, television, trade journals, and other publications. Gustave Springer was retained to advise and assist exhibitors at trade shows. Performing much of the work himself, the aid and assistance he provided covered many more shows. Springer or a locally-engaged public relations firm wrote and distributed press reports, alerted the trade press and advised exhibitors on how best to approach American buyers.

There was a variety of special export promotional activities after 1982. Although in retrospect the Bicentennial program had been too comprehensive, it had attracted a lot of publicity. Provided certain conditions were met, there was every reason to continue in the same way. On the recommendation of the Netherlands Advisory Committee on Industrial Policy, better known as the Wagner committee, named after its chairman, former Royal Dutch/Shell chairman G. Wagner, the promotion of exports was to focus more on the strong points of Dutch industry in general, and its competitiveness in the United States in particular. However, the response of individual firms to the opportunities offered was and remained the decisive factor. The Economic Information Division commissioned the Netherlands Chamber of Commerce in the United States, Inc. to conduct a survey of the competitiveness of a number of major Dutch products on the American market. The general conclusion was that in view of the improved international competitiveness of the Netherlands, the renewed impetus of the American economy, the recovery of the dollar, and the growing demand for foreign consumer goods, a further rise in exports could be anticipated. As it consisted of an analysis of recent general trends and, for lack of a specific export policy, participation in trade shows was principally determined by how individual manufacturers assessed the prospects offered by the American market, the committee's report had only an indirect influence on the composition of the trade show program.

The introduction in 1984 of an annual action program gave fresh impetus to the promotion of Dutch exports in the United States. The various activities in this field could thereafter be coordinated, a necessary step given the fact that only Dfl. 1 million was available for special projects in 1984. It was decided to conduct market research for certain selected manufacturing sectors in the three regions designated that year as special targets for the promotion of trade. As no more than Dfl. 100,000 was available for each region, and market research firms had to be engaged for the project, the value of the reports was limited. However, on the basis of experience with the trade show program, it was possible to refine their findings for the purposes of application, and the Chamber accordingly advised the Economic Information Division to concentrate its efforts on eleven sectors ranging from pleasure boats to medical technology and food-processing machinery.

Another area in which the Chamber was increasingly active from 1981 onwards was general publicity. Here, too, the Bicentennial was the key force, and intensive consultations were held with the Economic Information Division as the source of the necessary funds. The objective of "Holland Promotion", as it was called, was to improve the image of Dutch industry in the United States. It was not intended to create an entirely new image, but to show that Dutch manufacturers had considerably more to offer than was generally known. One of its principal components was the U.S.-Holland Trade Dinner, organized annually from 1984 by the Chamber under the auspices of the Economic Information Division to further informal contacts between Dutch and American businessmen. A magazine, Holland-USA, was launched by the Chamber in the same year, as was the Economic Yearbook, an annual account and analysis of the development of trade between the Netherlands and the United States in the previous year. With the opening of a branch office in Atlanta in 1986 and the reopening of its office in The Hague in 1987, the Chamber widened its compass and reestablished direct contact with the business community in the Netherlands.

HOLLANDUSA

Fall 1984/Volume 1/Number 1/$10

The New American Dredging Fund

Stealing the Trade Show

Avenue Magazine: Living in Style

Dutch Dreamboats

Biotechnology on a Grand Scale

Investment Paradise Regained

NEDLLOYD

G. Bresser, Pierre Dobbelmann, Ton de Boer,
James Howard, Philippe Michel, Dan Piliero,
Tom Powers, Robert Roe, Joop Swart

*First cover Holland-USA
magazine,
1984
Published by the
Netherlands Chamber of
Commerce in the United
States*

Conclusions

Economic developments after 1973 and changes in the subsidy policy of the Economic Information Division lay at the heart of the difficulties besetting the Chamber in the mid-1970s, which were only partly resolved by the restructuring which took place in 1976. While it is true that it finally produced unity in regard to policy and finances, it did not lead to the market-oriented approach envisaged by the Langman doctrine. In the late 1970s, as the world economy worsened, inflation increased and the value of the dollar declined, the Chamber could no longer defer changes in its style of management and the adoption of a more commercial approach to the services it provided for industry and commerce. New management was needed to get things moving, and the statutory transfer of executive authority from the president to the secretary in 1983 rounded off the internal changes.

Since 1981 the services of the Chamber have mainly been provided on a commercial basis. Due to the expansion of the American economy, which emerged from the recession before Europe, its income from market research, information on customs duties and import restrictions, seminars, luncheons, and participation in trade shows rose rapidly from $ 66,000 in 1980 to $ 577,000 in 1987, while the total income of the Chamber grew from $ 477,000 in 1980 to $ 1,924,000 in 1988.

It is difficult to say to what extent the new system of trade promotion contributed to the rapid growth of exports after 1980. Macro-economic factors far outweighed the influence of the Chamber. The promotion of exports is by definition an activity whose effectiveness can be measured only incidentally, if at all. If there were no means to determine how small and medium-sized businesses could best orient themselves in foreign markets, then the sole alternative was to create the widest possible opportunities for them to do so. That could only be achieved by a market-oriented approach on the part of the Chambers abroad. In pursuing the Langman doctrine, therefore, the Economic Information Division put a premium on an increase in self-earned income. Though the deteriorating economic situation made some adjustments inevitable in the late 1970s, the basic premise remained unchanged. The demonstrable interest of Dutch private enterprise continued to be the key element in the allocation of government compensations.

Notes

1. The survey covered the industrialized countries of West and East Germany, France, Britain, Switzerland, Sweden, Spain, Canada, and the Soviet Union, and the developing countries of Iran, Kuwait, Nigeria, Ivory Coast, Kenya, Malaysia, Indonesia, South Korea, Brazil, Venezuela, and Colombia.
2. The concentration on Europe probably stemmed from the fact that transportation costs were high for many of the goods exported.

ABN Amro Bank N.V., based in Amsterdam, is one of the top 20 banks in the world with more than $ 250 billion in assets worldwide. In North America, ABN Amro has more than $ 40 billion in assets and operations in 13 cities. ABN Amro's presence in North America dates back to 1941 when the Dutch bankers opened their first U.S. office. ABN Amro's North American operation is headquartered in Chicago, and includes several wholly-owned subsidiaries: LaSalle National Corp., LaSalle Talman Bank FSB, and LaSalle Cragin Bank FSB in Chicago, and European American Bank in New York, making ABN Amro the largest foreign bank in the United States.

LaSalle National Bank, Chicago, Illinois

M.Y. "Highlander", Feadship, built in 1986 by De Vries Scheepsbouw B.V., passing the Brooklyn Bridge in New York

"The Highlander", a motor yacht designed and built by Feadship and sold to Mr. Malcolm Forbes, head of the Forbes magazine group, in 1967. Feadship has continued the long tradition of Dutch shipbuilding by specializing in large and luxurious custom-built motoryachts. Feadship's trade with the United States started with the New York Boat Show of 1949. Over 100 yachts with a length between 40 and 80 feet have since been sold to distinguished American clients.

The Rabobank Group is a unique confederation of 750 cooperative banks in the Netherlands that operates as a wholesale bank for large national and international corporations. Thanks to its reputation as an international leader in banking for the agricultural sector and its AAA credit rating, Rabobank has built up a balance sheet of $ 135 billion and has offices in the United States in New York, Chicago, Dallas, and San Francisco.

The Rabobank Group is headquartered in Utrecht, the Netherlands.

Advertisement of Philips Electronics North America

Philips Electronics North America is one of America's 100 largest manufacturers and ranks among the top 50 exporters. Philips employs 35,000 people in the U.S. and manufactures consumer electronic products, lighting products, components, semiconductors, dictation systems, medical sustems and other profession-al equipment under the brand Philips, Magnavox, Philips Lighting, Philco, Airpax, Mepco, Philips Medical Systems, Signetics amd Norelco.

Akzo Nobel, headquartered in Arnhem, the Netherlands, is one of the world's leading companies in se-lected areas of chemicals, coatings, health care products, and fibers. In the United States, Akzo Nobel employs 11.000 people at more than 150 business locations.

A record-sized crew of eight (including Wubbo Ockels) is lifted toward Earth orbit as the Space Shuttle Challenger blasts from the launch pad.

Akzo Nobel, headquartered in Arnhem, the Netherlands, is one of world's leading companies in selected areas of chemicals, coatings, health care products, and fibers. In the United States, Akzo Nobel employs 11,000 people at more than 150 business locations. Akzo's Twaron fiber is five times stronger than steel and five times lighter than aluminum, while it can withstand extreme temperatures. These qualities have made Twaron an ideal fiber for use in aeronautics. Twaron is used in the U.S. Space Shuttle while other Akzo fibers are used in the uniforms of Space Shuttle astronauts.

⇒
"Untitled I", 1982.
Painting by
Willem de Kooning (born 1904)
On loan to the
Netherlands Ambassador for the United States, His Excellency Adriaan P.R. Jacobovits de Szeged, in his residence in Washington DC.
Courtesy Lisa de Kooning and John L. Eastman, Conservators of the property of Willem de Kooning.

254

"Alright, it's a deal. $24 and we'll throw in the flowers."

—Peter Minuit, *Dutch colonial leader*

Talk about a return on investment. But then, we Dutch have always had a
fondness for things that grow. So it's only fitting that we honor our historic relationship
with America here at the New York Botanical Gardens. Nice tulips.

ING CAPITAL

*Biltmore House
Asheville, North Carolina
Home of William A.
Vanderbilt Cecil,
Honorary Member of the
Netherlands Chamber of
Commerce in the United
States*

*The Biltmore House was
built by George
Washington Vanderbilt,
one of the founders of the
Netherlands Chamber in
1903.
It was designed by
Richard Morris Hunt,
who was also the architect
of New York's Grand
Central Station and the
National Observatory in
Washington D.C..
The Biltmore House was
constructed between 1899
and 1895 to contain 250
rooms and a total floor
area of 4 acres, making it
one of the largest
privately-owned homes in
the world. It comprises
about 125,000 acres and
contains extensive lands-
cape design by Frederick
Law Olmsted, who also
designed New York's
Central Park.*

*George Washington
Vanderbilt Trophy*

*The trophy is made in the
shape of a silver
"Alladin's lamp of knowl-
edge" that was used by
George Washington
Vanderbilt on the book-
mark to be found on the
volumes in the library of
the Biltmore House.*

THE GEORGE WASHINGTON VANDERBILT
TROPHY

CHAPTER VIII

1987-1993: CONSULTANCY AND REPRESENTATION

The upswing in the American economy in the early 1980s acted as a stimulus to Dutch exports to and investment in the United States. The economic stagnation setting in from 1989 had the opposite effect. In combination with the Economic Information Division's dwindling budget for export promotion, it led to a further commercialization of trade and investment promotion by the Chamber. The government subsidies of earlier days were to become a reimbursement for special programs and other delegated tasks. Under the leadership of Lane C. Grijns, Executive Vice President and General Manager of NMB Bank in New York, who was elected chairman of the Chamber in 1987, a number of large firms were asked to contribute to the Chamber's equity and working capital in order to finance new activities. In 1988 the Chamber a-warded the first George Washington Vanderbilt Trophy, named after one of the founders of the Netherland Chamber of Commerce in America in 1903, for the firm or individual making a significant contribution to the growth of trade and investments between the Netherlands and the United States. In 1991, in anticipation of the approaching dismantling of the borders between the member states of the European Community, the Chamber initiated the establishment of the European Community Chamber of Commerce in the United States, Inc., thus building further on the foundations of the Chamber.

Finances

In the early 1980s the booming U.S. economy and the accompanying high value of the dollar had encour-aged many Dutch businessmen to come to America to take advantage of the market. The Chamber's income had risen substantially. The Economic Information Division's director, Klaas A. de Jong, announced that the subsidy was to be cut to 50 percent of the Chamber's earnings, in accordance with the method fol-lowed for the Netherlands Chambers in European countries. Reduced in 1987, the subsidy arrangement was changed again in 1988, this time to cover only those time expenses incurred by the Chamber in answering U.S. inquiries about Dutch firms and products and services.

This signified a sizeable subsidy reduction, which however was more than offset by a rise in the Chamber's own revenues. Thereafter Economic Information Division payments were based on man-years spent on activities delegated to the Chamber. Amounting to approximately $ 100,000 per man-year, the amount grew smaller as the number of man-years tailed off from approximately 7.5 in 1988 to 5.0 in 1992 to 3.5 in 1993. General assistance to Dutch exporters and Holland Promotion were no longer eligible for subsidies as from 1991. The same applied in respect of trade shows, seminars, and other special projects from 1992 onward. The Executive Committee wrote to Ms. Yvonne van Rooij, the Netherlands Minister for Foreign Trade, expressing deep concern about the possible effects of these measures. Stating that while it accepted the principle of cuts in export promotion in periods showing a large Dutch trade surplus, it also hoped that in the event of a renewed deficit in the balance of trade the subsidies to Dutch exporters would be renewed. Because the U.S. economy then slowed down, the Chamber saw little opportunity to increase its own income. Dutch exports to the United States in 1989 totalled 10.5 billion guilders; they fell to 9.5 billion in 1990 and 1991 - the year of the Gulf War - and rose slightly to just under 10 billion in 1992. In December, 1992 the Chamber wrote again to the Minister, emphasizing the importance of the American market and pointing out that its dimensions and complexity demanded constant effort on the part of both the Netherlands government and Dutch private enterprise. A few months later an extra 2 million guilders were allocated for an export promotion program. With a less buoyant economy in the Netherlands, there was a sudden upsurge of interest in Dutch exports.

Through the changes in policy, government contributions to the Chamber declined markedly after 1988. Amounting in 1988 to $ 815,000 - 65 percent of every self-earned dollar - the contribution provided by the Netherlands Foreign Trade Agency, the new name of the Economic Information Division, was $ 575,000 by 1991. However, in the same period the Chamber's income from fees and services rose from $ 835,000 to $ 1.4 million, more than compensating for the contribution loss. The contribution in 1992 was no higher than 30 percent of the total budget of the Chamber, the lowest figure in all the years that the private promotion of trade in America had been government-aided. As government and private enterprise used different methods of payment, the working capital was enlarged and membership fees were raised. While the Economic Information Division paid the contribution in advance, clients paid afterwards, so a campaign was launched in October, 1991 aimed at steadily raising the Chamber's working capital. It was supported by ABN Amro Bank, ING Bank, Rabobank, AKZO America Inc., Wolter Kluwer US, Sara Lee Corporation, Vans Inc., and Van Münching & Co. The Chamber also worked in close cooperation with many regional Chambers of Commerce in the Netherlands. In 1988, 21 of the regional Dutch Chambers had joined as members, and their representatives were assisted in their study of the markets in the United States and briefed on trade policy issues, while firms in their respective regions were put in touch with American buyers and distributors.

Information

The scope of activities of the Chamber was determined to a large extent by the development of the American economy. Among other factors, this meant that around 1990 interest in the United States waned. The war against Iraq dealt a blow to confidence in world trade, the Dutch economy was flagging, and the value of the dollar declined, averaging 1.76 guilders against the dollar in 1992, just under the 1.80 guilder level that was generally regarded as the lowest level at which Dutch exports to the United States could yield a profit. The economic downturn forced many Dutch companies to retrench. Whereas with the aid of the Chamber Dutch companies had exhibited at 25 trade shows in 1988, their number dropped to 11 in 1992; of the 130 exhibitors in 1989, only 32 remained in 1992. At the same time, a growing number of

Tradingroom ING Capital

ING Capital is in the U.S. investment banking subsidiary of ING Group, one of the largest diversified financial services organizations in the world with over $ 200 billion in assets. ING Capital pioneered trading in Less Developed Countries Debt under its former name of NMB Bank and is widely recognized for its expertise in emerging markets trading and lending.

companies made use of the Chamber's consultancy services, which included market research, arranging appointments with American firms, designing and executing comprehensive market entry plans, and advising on issues such as public relations. Through its growing expertise and more market-oriented approach, the Chamber's income from these sources rose rapidly.

Other areas of increasing activity were the organization of luncheons, dinners, and seminars, the production of information videos and a *pied-à-terre* incubator service for individual companies. After the first seminars presenting the Netherlands as the gateway to Europe, commissioned in 1986 by the Holland International Distribution Center and Rotterdam Distriport, these events multiplied. In 1987 sixteen seminars on all aspects of exports to Europe were held for senior corporate executives in all parts of the United States. The Netherlands was portrayed as a country with a stable political and social structure and a well-educated population, located at international crossroads. Also in that year, in anticipation of the dismantling of the internal European Community borders, the Chamber initiated a massive campaign of 50 financial seminars on the theme of "New Financing Opportunities in Europe - a Dutch Perspective". Different organizations cooperated with the Chamber on these projects every year. In 1988 the sponsors included ABN-LaSalle, AMRO Bank, the Amsterdam Stock Exchange, NMB Bank, Rabobank Nederland, Kleynveld Peat Marwick Goerdeler, and Stibbe Blaisse & De Jong. That year, under the sponsorship of the Netherlands Foreign Investment Agency of the Ministry of Economic Affairs, the Overijssel Industrial Development Corporation, Price Waterhouse, and Stibbe, Blaisse & De Jong, the Dutch Province of Overijssel was highlighted as a promising investment area for American industry and commerce. Finally, together with the Netherlands Ministry of Agriculture, Nature Management and Fisheries, and the Export Group of the Dutch Association of Greenhouse Contractors, the Chamber organized three greenhouse technology seminars in Florida and New Jersey in 1991.

PTT, Dutch stamps celebrating Columbus discovery of America, 1492-1992

In 1988, with the permission of William A. Vanderbilt Cecil, grandson of George Washington Vanderbilt, the Chamber instituted an annual award bearing his grandfather's name for the individual or company making an outstanding contribution to the furthering of economic relations between the Netherlands and the United States. George Washington Vanderbilt, one of the founders of the Netherland Chamber of Commerce in America in 1903, was a member of one of the most prominent American families of Dutch descent. Commodore Cornelius Vanderbilt, a nineteenth-century railroad and shipping magnate who died in 1877, was the first American to leave an estate worth more than $ 100 million. The trophy is a massive silver Aladdin's lamp, the ex libris of George Washington Vanderbilt. The chairman of the George Washington Vanderbilt Trophy Committee, A.T. Knoppers, announced in September, 1988 that the first George Washington Vanderbilt Trophy would be awarded to Leo van Münching Jr. and Van Münching & Co. Inc.. Leo van Münching Sr. obtained the sole importer's rights for Heineken beer after Prohibition ended, and thereafter Van Münching & Co. Inc. so effectively promoted the product that it was distributed as widely over all fifty states as the best-known beer brand. By 1988 Heineken had a 30 percent share of the imported beer market and accounted for 5 percent of the total beer consumption in the United States. In 1988, sales of Heineken products comprised about 8 percent of the total Dutch exports to the United States. The Chamber underscored the exclusive nature of the Trophy by making no further presentation of the award until 1993, when it was awarded to Albert Heijn Jr. and Royal Ahold for their impressive investments and achievements in the U.S. retail sector.

The privatization of Dutch export promotion led almost inevitably to an expansion of the Chamber's activities. At the suggestion of the agricultural attaché in Washington, it ventured in 1988 into the promotion of agricultural products. Opening an office in Washington, it was aided by the Netherlands Ministry of Agriculture, Nature Management and Fisheries to promote high quality Dutch food products at trade shows, luncheons, dinners, and special store presentations. The Washington office already reached the break-even point in its first year.

Through the growth of Dutch exports to the United States, the Netherlands began tot take a renewed interest in the U.S. market. Early in 1988 the Netherlands Trade Promotion Center (NHC) proposed to establish an America desk and to appoint a representative in New York, but dropped the idea after consulting with the Chamber and the Netherlands Foreign Trade Agency. The Central Board for Foreign Economic relations shelved a similar plan to open an office in Washington. Agreement was reached with the

Netherlands Foreign Investment Agency to encourage U.S. companies to operate in the Netherlands. On the assumption that greater awareness of what the Netherlands could offer would result in greater interest, a promotion campaign was launched. The Agency, which already had an office in New York, opened offices and installed industrial commissioners in Los Angeles and San Francisco. Though it would have preferred to provide all investment information itself, the Netherlands Foreign Investment Agency agreed that the Chamber should continue its business-financed promotion of the Netherlands as the gateway to Europe. It was also arranged that the Chamber would receive payment for passing on the inquiries it received from American companies to the Agency. In effect the Agency was only one of the sources of information on the Netherlands available to American businessmen; both the Chamber and Dutch companies in the United States were regularly approached with queries.

Towards a Transatlantic Dialogue

Around 1990 the pending completion of the European Single Market through the "Europe 1992" program was widely anticipated as the key to wider business prospects in Europe. In the summer of 1989 the Chamber initiated a move to unite private enterprises in the member states of the European Community and in the United States in one organization to advocate free trade and investment between Europe and the United States and to inform the business communities on both sides of the Atlantic about political and economic developments.
On June 1, 1990, the Netherlands Chamber of Commerce in the United States, Inc. incorporated the European Chamber of Commerce in the United States, Inc. in Delaware, and the Netherlands Chamber urged its sister organizations representing the business community of other European Community countries in the United States to support the new platform. But it was soon apparent that the nature of the various Chambers was too dissimilar for them to work together. Moreover, most Chambers feared that they would lose members and donations to the European Chamber. In December, 1989, Ms. Margaretha Dehandschutter joined the Netherlands Chamber to assist in creating the European Chamber. While Akzo and Philips had already agreed to become founding members, at the U.S.-Holland trade Dinner held in Chicago in June of 1990, the key-note speaker, Mr. John Bryan, chairman of Sara lee, announced that he would become the first American founding member of the European Chamber. During the next six weeks several other multinationals joined the European Chamber as founding members, including Price Waterhouse, ING Bank, Siegel & Gale, and Xerox, while British Petroleum, IBM, ICI, Rabobank, Enimont, Heineken USA Inc., Merrill Lynch, Mobil Europe, Rubbermaid, Lazard Frères, and De Bandt and Van Hecke had joined as members. By the end of the summer of 1990, the European Chamber had already 42 members.

The establishment of the European Community Chamber of Commerce in the United States, Inc. was announced at a press conference in Washington D.C. on July 24, 1990. It was stated that European companies operating in the United States and American companies with interests in Europe had to speak with a single voice in expressing their needs and wishes in the development of a free and fair business climate. In 1989 European-affiliated companies in the United States represented direct investments of $ 234 billion and provided employment for 3 million Americans. In addition, United States corporations with interests in the European Community would act prudently by coordinating their activities with those of their European counterparts in order to avoid international trade disturbances. As the spokesman for the business community, the E.C. Chamber had its own part to play, different from that of the Community's diplomatic representatives, who acted on behalf of the member states. Its sphere of activities related to European investments in the United Staes, the trade and economic policies of the American government, trade disputes between the E.C. and the United States, the Uruguay Round of GATT negotiations, and the creation of North American Free Trade Agreement. The ambassador of the European Community to the United States, the former Dutch prime minister Andries van Agt was appointed honorary chairman.

At the first meeting of Members, a Board was elected. Gerrit Jeelof, Chairman of North American Philips Corporation, was elected chairman, and Dr. Gianfranco Figini, President of Enimont America, Inc., was elected Vice-Chairman. The Board of Governors whose task it is to advise and counsel the Board of Directors, is composed of Chairman John H. Bryan of Sara Lee Corporation, Shaun F. O'Malley of Price

Waterhouse, Aernout Loudon of AKZO, and Alan Siegel of Siegel & Gale. Margaretha Dehandschutter continued to be Managing Director and Kersen J. de Jong was asked to continue to lead the organization as President for the time being.

In 1991, an office was opened in Washington D.C. to handle government affairs and Sandra Taylor, Vice President at ICI, was retained to serve as executive director. In September, 1992, she was succeeded by Willard M. Berry, who also succeeded Kersen J. de Jong as president. Today, the European Chamber has grown to a membership of 100 European and American companies.

The European Chamber has since instituted the Washington Committee, composed of the government relations officers of European and American multinationals with interests in the United States. The Committee coordinates efforts to monitor legislation on investment, trade, and tax issues. It also maintains contact with the sixty major American corporations with interests in the European Community. To clarify the situation, the European Chamber sent information about the European unification process to American companies, government officials, and Congress. Just as American companies defended their interests when decisions were taken in Europe regarding economic integration within the European Community, the European Chamber likewise furthered the interests of European and American private enterprise during the debate on NAFTA in the U.S. Congress. It took part in the Congressional hearings, and set out its position in letters to the President of the United States as well as the European Commission. The members of the European Chamber are kept informed of developments in the weekly newsletter *E.C. - U.S. Abstracts*.

The Netherlands Chamber of Commerce in the United States, Inc. today bears little resemblance to the organization that functioned in the late 1970s as a source of information and on the promotion of trade and investment between the Netherlands and the United States. The offices in The Hague, New York, Chicago, Atlanta and Washington all operate on a commercial basis and operate in a wide variety of ways. Located in the major marketing areas, it is in a position to select the importer, distributor, or agent matching the profile of the most appropriate trading partner. With the founding of the European Chamber, a non-governmental lobby organization is now able to influence of the transatlantic dialogue on trade and investment. Private enterprise in Europe and the United States have joined forces to help determine the direction to be followed by economic relations between the Europe and the United States. Supported by government and private enterprise, the present-day Netherlands Chamber of Commerce in the United States, Inc. continues to focus on all aspects of commercial information, and the promotion of trade and investment between the Netherlands and the United States.

Netherlands Direct Investment Position in the United States 1950-1993 (in millions of $)

	1950	1960	1970	1980	1990	1993
Petroleum	226	639	1,311	9,265	13,627	12,424
Manufacturing Total	44	213	652			
* Food				225	7,373	3,968
* Chemicals				2,002	8,144	8,639
* Metals				170	1,448	1,137
* Machinery				1.094	3,934	5,846
* Other manufact.				1,287	3,835	3,267
Finance, Insur., Real Est	34	42	58			
* Finance				412	1,037	2,590
* Insurance				753	3,996	7,117
* Real Estate				999	4,931	4,487
Wholesale trade	-	-	-	1,307	4,674	6,253
Retail trade	-	-	-	246	1,742	1,460
Banking	-	-	-	684	2,388	3,537
Services	-	-	-	-	5,726	5,148
Other	30	53	130	696	2,176	2,604
All Industries	**334**	**947**	**2,151**	**19,140**	**64,671**	**68,477**

Top 5 Ranking of Source Countries of Foreign Direct Investment in the United States, 1992, on a Historical-Cost Basis (in millions of $)

1. Japan   96,743
2. United Kingdom   94,718
3. Netherlands   61,341
4. Canada   38,997
5. Germany   29,205

Netherlands Imports from the United States / United States Export to the Netherlands (1983-1993) (in millions of Dfl)

	1983	1984	1985	1986	1987	1988	1989	1990	1991	1992	1993
Foods and live animals	2,516	2,031	1,627	1,357	1,235	1,255	1,094	961	858	861	1,182
Beverages and tobacco	282	320	327	278	283	257	269	259	279	286	381
Crude materials, inedible, excl. fuel	2,894	3,110	2,603	1,748	1,701	1,803	1,883	1,603	1,394	1,739	1,549
Mineral fuels and lubricants	927	971	1,580	1,011	520	602	777	798	833	692	723
Oils and fats, animal and vegetable	192	238	208	106	64	91	73	82	97	125	126
Chemicals	1,669	1,846	2,363	1,840	1,880	1,975	2,358	2,307	2,378	2,414	2,609
Manufactured goods by chief material	812	873	823	810	724	845	892	979	962	961	1,010
Machinery and transport equipment	5,088	6,172	6,106	5,690	5,141	6,378	8,929	8,678	8,978	8,629	8,670
Miscellaneous manufactured articles	1,434	1,654	1,767	1,540	1,384	1,782	2,301	1,782	1,782	2,601	2,644
Total	**16,026**	**17,716**	**17,830**	**14,554**	**13,306**	**15,002**	**18,592**	**18,046**	**19,046**	**18,332**	**18,902**

United States Direct Investment Position in the Netherlands 1950-1993 (in millions of $)

	1950	1960	1970	1980	1990	1993
Petroleum	29	143	486	2,924	1,429	1,055
Manufacturing Total	6	80	843	3,142		
* Food					817	955
* Chemicals					2,825	3,406
* Metals					529	494
* Non electr. Machinery					1,101	991
* Electr. Equipment					632	468
* Trans. Equipment					61	80
* Other manufact.					582	1,382
Finance, Insur., Real Est	-	-	23	644	7,458	5,199
Wholesale trade	-	-	-	-	1,606	3,090
Services	-	-	-	-	1,679	1,845
Other	49	60	198	1329	301	923
All Industries	**84**	**283**	**1,550**	**8,039**	**19,120**	**19,887**

Top 5 Ranking of Source Countries of Foreign Direct Investment in the Netherlands, 1992, on a Historical-Cost Basis (in millions of $)

1. U.S.   18,486
2. Belgium   11,189
3. U.K.   10,270
4. Switzerland   9,567
5. Germany   6,594

Netherlands Exports to the U.S. / U.S. Imports from the Netherlands, 1983 - 1993 (in millions of Dfl)

	1983	1984	1985	1986	1987	1988	1989	1990	1991	1992	1993
Foods and live animals	518	790	733	545	506	495	556	531	500	513	598
Beverages and tobacco	566	665	696	760	655	646	614	640	649	621	697
Crude materials, inedible, excl. fuel	314	493	563	494	428	447	536	445	431	416	407
Mineral fuels and lubricants	889	656	1,027	458	489	632	618	625	327	331	196
Oils and fats, animal and vegetable	37	63	53	29	27	33	50	48	37	44	35
Chemicals	1,332	1,684	1,830	1,374	1,271	1,427	1,625	1,504	1,333	1,416	1,645
Manufactured goods by chief material	1,202	1,826	1,688	1,306	1,123	1,215	1,292	1,113	969	1,077	1,151
Machinery and transport equipment	2,424	3,641	4,227	3,456	2,818	3,062	4,067	3,681	4,346	4,513	4,472
Miscellaneous manufactured articles	571	736	865	828	782	768	1,018	955	961	1,023	1,136
Total	**7,896**	**10,610**	**11,806**	**9,325**	**8,132**	**8,768**	**10,393**	**9,562**	**9,715**	**9,982**	**10,374**

Source: Netherlands Central Bureau of Statistics (CBS)

Departure from the Dutch coast, heading for the West, which took many weeks. Etching by Ludolf Bakhuizen (1631-1708) Six Archives

264

EPILOGUE

At the foundation of the Netherlands Chamber of Commerce in the United States in 1903, the Board of Directors chose the Halve Maen (Half Moon), Henry Hudson's ship on the first Dutch voyage to America, as the logo for the new organization. Clearly, the Board was inspired by the wish to symbolize three centuries of Dutch-American trade relations. It is remarkable that the Netherlands with only 5,4 million people had the foresight and the resources to establish a Chamber in a market of 75 million Americans. In the course of the following decades, the Chamber itself came to symbolize trade and investment promotion between the Netherlands and the United States.

This book has told the tale of economic relations between the two countries and the role of the Chamber and the Netherlands government in advancing bilateral business interests. It has shown that the efforts of both entrepreneurs and the Chamber to adapt theit products and services to changing world have been highly sensitive to political and economic developments in the Netherlands and the United States.

But reading about the trials and tribulations of the promotion of the Dutch business in the United States, it is easy to forget those who have benefitted most : the thousand of companies who have sought and received assistance from the chamber over the years. Compared to their predecessors in the 17th, 18th, and 19th centuries, these companies have had a head start in having a source of valuable information at their disposal, ready to support their overseas trade and investment plans in every way possible.

The intangibles involved in assisting Dutch and American companies with their questions on overseas trade and investment make it difficult to evaluate the Chamber's effort to expand business relations between the Netherlands and the United States. To what extent is a successful entry into a market strictly the result of a price/quality ratio or when is superior insight into a market the deciding factor? Obviously, business success is a combination of both factors.

Therefore it is safe to say that in all its activities, the Chamber has made a major contribution to the strong and sound business relations between the Netherlands and the United States throughout this century. In 1988 the George Washington Vanderbilt Trophy was established to honor organizations that have made a most significant contribution to the expansion of trade and investment between the Netherlands and the United States. The Trophy has thus far been awarded to Van Münching & Co., the U.S. importers of Heineken beers, to Royal Ahold for its investments in U.S. supermarket retailling, and to KLM Royal Dutch Airlines, for its partnership with Northwest Airlines. As chairman of the George Washington Vanderbilt Trophy Commitee I feel that the Chamber wopuld be a worthy recipient in its own right.

Business relations between the Netherlands and America have come a long way since the days of New Amsterdam, and the Chamber has come a long way since its foundation in 1903. However, new time ask for new answers. For this reason, the Chamber's complete privatization of all its activities and its role in initiating the establishment of the European-American Chamber of Commerce provide a solid foundation for the future.

With confidence, then, we can look forward to ever stronger business ties between the Netherlands and the United States. All the more reason why the gardian of these ties, the Netherlands Chamber of Commerce in the United States, deseves our sincere recognition of its good work and our full support of all its initiatives.

Lane C. Grijns
Chairman,
The George Washington Vanderbilt Trophy Committee

LITERATURE

Aalst, C.J.K. van, "Levensbericht van Jacob Theodor Cremer", Leiden 1924

ABN-AMRO Bank, Met kracht naar het Buitenland. Exportmogelijkheden van het Nederlandse MKB, Amsterdam 1991

Adviescommissie inzake het industriebeleid, Een nieuw industrieel elan, Den Haag 1981

Aken, N. van, The Economic Dependence of America on the Products of Netherlands India, New York 1934

Aken, N. van, Chambers of Foreign Commerce in the USA, New York 1937

Albert, J.G., Economic Policy and Plannning in the Netherlands, 1950-1953

Albregts, A.H.M., "De omvang en de betekenis van de Nederlandse directe investeringen in het buitenland", De Economist, 1969

Ammerlaan, B.J.M., Praktische problemen uit de handelsstatistiek, Amsterdam 1930

Aldcroft, D.H., From Versailles to Wall Street, 1919-1929, Londen 1977

Arthur Young International & The Netherlands Chamber of Commerce in the US, Inc., Results of a Survey of Dutch Investors That Have Established Operations in the United States, 1983

Arthur Young International & The Netherlands Chamber of Commerce in the US, Inc., Dutch Enterprise in the USA, 1989

Ashley, P., Modern Tariff History: Germany, United States & France, Londen 1920

Baack, B.D. & E.J. Ray, "The Political Economy of Tariff Policy: A Case Study of the United States", Explorations in Economic History, 1983

Bailey, T.A., The Policy of the United States Toward The Neutrals, 1917-1918, Baltimore 1942

Bakker, A., & M.M.P. van Lent (red.), Pieter Lieftinck. 1902-1989. Een leven in vogelvlucht, Utrecht 1989

Bakker, B.A., Export en marketing, Brussel 1980

Barber, W.J., From New Era to New Deal. Herbert Hoover, the Economists, and American Economic Policy, 1921-1933, Cambridge, MA 1975

Barnouw, A., Modern Art of Holland. An Exhibition. Paintings, Etchings, Wood Engravings, Sculpture, and Batik Work, New York 1921

Baumhauer, E.H. von, "Review of the United Netherlands American Chambers of Commerce", Holland's Import & Export Trader, 1926

Baumhauer, E.H. von, Amerikaansche import-pools tegen rubber, kina en tabak, Amsterdam 1928

Baumhauer, E.H. von, "De goud-clausule in de Amerikaansche wetgeving, literatuur en rechtspraak", 1933

Baumhauer, E.H. von, "Volkenrecht en diplomatieke bescherming in zake de goudclausule", 1936

Baumhauer, E.H. von, "De dreigende Amerikaansche extra belasting op buitenlandsch effectenbezit", 1936-1937

Beaton, K., Enterprise in Oil. A History of Shell in the United States, New York 1957

Beaufort, W.H. de, "Twee rapporten over het consulaatswezen", De Economist, 1904

Bell, A.C., A History of the Blockade of Germany and of the Countries associated with her in the Great War, 1914-1918, Londen 1937

Bergeijk, P.A.G. van, Handel en diplomatie, Groningen 1990

Berghuis, W.H., Ontstaan en ontwikkeling van de Nederlandse beleggingsfondsen tot 1914, Assen 1967

Bescheiden betreffende de buitenlandse politiek van Nederland 1848-1919, Tweede periode, 1871-1899. Den Haag 1962-1972

Bescheiden betreffende de buitenlandse politiek van Nederland 1848-1919, Derde periode, 1899-1919. Den Haag 1957-1974

Beugel, E.H. van der, From Marshall Aid to Atlantic Partnership. European Integration as a Concern of American Foreign Policy, Londen 1966

Bieleman, J., Geschiedenis van de landbouw in Nederland 1500-1950. Veranderingen en verscheidenheid, Amsterdam 1992

Bierens de Haan, J. de, Van oeconomische tak tot Nederlandsche Maatschappij van Nijverheid en Handel, Haarlem 1952

Biografisch Woordenboek van Nederland, J. Charité, Den Haag 1979-1989

Blaisse, P.A., De Nederlandse handelspolitiek, Utrecht/Antwerpen 1948

Blink, H., "Economische vertegenwoordiging van Nederland in het buitenland", 1915

Blink, H., "Algemeene voorbereiding tot het economisch offensief na de oorlog", 1916

Blink, H., "Nederland in het buitenland na den oorlog", 1918

Bloemen, E.S.A., Het Benelux-effect, Amsterdam 1992

Boer, M.G. de, Geschiedenis der Amsterdamsche stoomvaart, Amsterdam 1921

Boer, M.G. de, Holland-Amerika Lijn 1873-1923, Rotterdam 1923

Boer, M.G. de, Het Bureau voor Handelsinlichtingen te Amsterdam 1903-1928, Amsterdam 1928

Boissevain, W., Mijn leven 1876-1944, Bussum 1950

Bok, E.W., Edward Bok. An Autobiography, Londen 1921

Bok, E.W., Twice Thirty. Some Short and Simple Annals of the Road, New York 1925

Boltho, A., The European Economy. Growth and Crisis, Oxford 1982

Boo, A.M. de, Nederland. Handelsnatie zonder handelspolitiek?, Groningen 1989

Boon, H.N., Afscheidsaudiëntie. Tien studies over de diplomatieke praktijk, Rotterdam 1976

Bos, R.W.J.M., Brits-Nederlandse handel en scheepvaart, 1870-1914, Tilburg 1978

Bos, R.W.J.M., "De depressie der jaren dertig: aspecten van Nederland als een kleine open volkshuishouding, in het bijzonder met betrekking tot de uitvoer van levensmiddelen naar Engeland", Amsterdam 1979

Bosch, K.D., Nederlandse beleggingen in de Verenigde Staten, Amsterdam 1948

Brakel, W., De industrialisatie in Nederland gedurende de periode der Marshall-hulp, Leiden 1954

Brands, R.F.Q., Competitive Position of Netherlands Export Products in the United States Market. An Analysis of Trends, New York 1983

Brink, J.R.M. van den, Zoeken naar een heilstaat, Amsterdam 1984

Brink, J.R.M. van den "Indicatieve planning als beleidsinstrument van de industrialisatiepolitiek in de jaren vijftig", 1986

Brouwers, G., "Tien jaar economische politiek", Den Haag 1955

Brugmans, H., (red.), Nederland in den oorlogstijd, Amsterdam 1920

Brugmans, I.J., Paardenkracht en mensenmacht, Den Haag 1961

Bruijn, J.A. de, Economische Zaken. Profiel van een ministerie, Den Haag 1989

Bruijn, J.A. de, Economische Zaken en economische subsidies. Den Haag 1990

Burk, K., Britain, America and the Sinews of War, 1914-1918, Winchester 1985

CBS, Statistisch Zakboek

CBS, 1899-1969. Zeventig jaar statistiek, Den Haag 1969

CBS, Tachtig jaar statistiek in tijdreeksen, Den Haag 1979

CBS, Macro-economische ontwikkelingen, 1921-1939 en 1969-1985, Den Haag 1987

Campo, J.N.F.M. à, Koninklijke Paketvaart Maatschappij, Hilversum 1992

Centrale Kamer van Handelsbevordering, Actie Export 1966

Centrale Kamer van Handelsbevordering, Jaarverslag 1965

Centrale Kamer van Handelsbevordering, Verslag 1971

Centrale kamer van Handelsbevordering, Made in Holland. Den Haag 1965

Chandler, C.V., America's Greatest Depression 1929-1941, New York 1970

Chernow, R., The House of Morgan. London 1990

Clerx, J.M.M.J., Nederland en de liberalisatie van het handels- en betalingsverkeer (1945-1958), Groningen 1986

Commissie voor de Handelspolitiek, "Organisatie van het consulaatswezen", 1894

Commissie voor de Handelspolitiek, "Beteekenis van de Vereenigde Staten van Amerika voor den afzet van Nederlandsche en koloniale producten", 1898

Commissie voor de Handelspolitiek, "Rapport betreffende de bevordering van de economische belangen van Nederland in den vreemde", 1904

Conybeare, J., "Trade Wars: A Comparitive Study of Anglo-Hanse, Franco-Italian, and Hawley-Smoot Conflicts", 1985

Costigliola, F., Akward Dominion. American Political, Economic, and Cultural Relations with Europe, 1919-1933, Londen 1984

CPB, Conjunctuurpolitiek in en om de jaren vijftig, Den Haag 1963

Crone, F., & H. Overbeek, Nederlands kapitaal over de grenzen, Amsterdam 1981

Dallek, R., Franklin D. Roosevelt and American Foreign Policy, 1932-1945, Oxford 1979

Delprat, D.A., De reeder schrijft zijn journaal. Herinneringen van mr. D.A. Delprat, Den Haag 1983

Denig, E., Imago van Holland. Voorlichting en presentatie in het buitenland, Muiderberg 1991

Het departement van Arbeid, Handel en Nijverheid onder Minister Aalberse 1918-1925, Alphen aan de Rijn 1925

Documenten betreffende de buitenlandse politiek van Nederland 1919-1945, Den Haag 1985-1992

Dodge, M.E.M., Hans Brinker or the Silver Skates, New York 1865

Doel, H.W. van den, P.C. Emmer & H.Ph. Vogel, Nederland en de Nieuwe Wereld, Utrecht 1992

Doorn, J., "De Nederlandse goederenexport in de jaren tachtig", Export Magazine, 1989

Dow, J.C.R., The Management of the British Economy, 1945-1960, Cambridge 1968

Drukker, J.W., Waarom de crisis hier langer duurde, Amsterdam 1990

Drummond, I.M. & N. Hillmer, Negotiating Freer Trade. The United Kingdom, the United States, Canada, and the Trade Agreements of 1938, Waterloo 1989

Duynstee, F.J.F.M., & J. Bosmans, Het kabinet Schermerhorn-Drees 1945-1946, Amsterdam 1977

Edwards, R.C., "Economic Sophistication in Nineteenth Century Congressional Tariff Debates", 1970

Eng, P. van der, De Marshall-hulp. Een perspectief voor Nederland, Houten 1987

Faith, N., The Infiltrators. The European Business Invasion of America, Londen 1971

Feld, W.J., The European Community in World Affairs. Economic Power and Political Influence, New York 1976

Fisher, F., Griff nach der Weltmacht. Die Kriegszielpolitik des kaiserlichen Deutschland 1914-1918, Düsseldorf 1961

Ford, W.J., Financiering van de export, Leiden 1970

Foreman-Peck, J., A History of the World Economy. International Economic Relations since 1850, Brighton 1983

Fortuyn, W.S.P., Kerncijfers 1945-1983 van de sociaal-economische ontwikkeling in Nederland, Deventer 1983

Galbraith, J.K., The Great Crash 1929, Harmondsworth 1961

Geschiedenis van het moderne Nederland, Houten 1988

Geschiedenis van de techniek in Nederland, Zutphen 1992

Gilpin, R., US Power and the Multinational Corporation, New York 1975

Glickman, N.J., & D.P. Woodward, The New Competitors. How Foreign Investors are Changing The US Economy, New York 1989

Graaff, A. de, De industrie, Antwerpen 1951

Graaff, B.G.J. de, "De voorlichting over Nederland en Indië aan de buitenlandse pers, 1900-1935, Jambatan 1984

Graeff, A.C.D. van, Voor u persoonlijk. Brieven van Minister van Buitenlandse Zaken jhr. A.C.D. de Graeff aan gezant J.P. graaf Van Limburg Stirum 1933-1937, Houten 1987

Gregory, R., The Origins of American Intervention in the First World War, New York 1971

Greup, G.M., Kamer van Koophandel en Fabrieken voor Amsterdam. Gedenkboek samengesteld ter gelegenheid van het 125 jarig bestaan. Het tijdvak 1922-1936, Amsterdam 1936

Griffiths, R.T., The Economy and Politics of the Netherlands since 1945, Den Haag 1980

Griffiths, R.T., "Het Nederlandse economische wonder", 1986

Griffiths, R.T., "Enkele kanttekeningen bij de eerste industrialisatie-nota's van J.R.M. van den Brink", 1986

Griffiths, R.T., The Netherlands and the Gold Standard, 1931-1936, Amsterdam 1987

Griffiths, R.T., "'Free Traders' in a protectionist World", S. Groenveld & M. Wintle

Hardach, G., The First World War 1914-1918, Berkeley 1974

Hawke, G.R., "The United States Tariff and Industrial Protection in the Late Nineteenth Century", 1975

Hayford, M., & C.A. Pasurka, "The Political Economy of the Fordney-McCumber and Smoot-Hawley Tariff Acts", 1992

Heertje, A. & N. Cohen, Export en welvaart, Leiden 1970

Hemels, J., Van perschef tot overheidsvoorlichter, Alphen aan de Rijn 1973

Hen, P.E. de, Actieve en re-actieve industriepolitiek in Nederland. Amsterdam 1980

Hine, R.C., The Political Economy of European Trade. New York 1985

Hirschfeld, H.M., Actieve economische politiek in Nederland in de jaren 1929-1934, Amsterdam 1946

Hirschfeld, H.M., Herinneringen uit de jaren 1933-1939, Amsterdam 1959

Historical Statistics of the United States, Colonial Times to 1970, Washington 1975

Hoffmann, C., The Depression of the Nineties, Westport 1970

Hogan, M.J., The Marshall Plan. America, Britain, and the Reconstruction of Western Europe, 1947-1952, New York 1987

Homan, G.D., "That 'Beautiful Tobacco': The Sumatra cigar wrapper and the American tariff, 1880-1941", 1987

Hubrecht, H.F.R., Het Nederlandsch Consulaatwezen, Amsterdam 1899

Hulsker, J., Van Gogh en zijn weg, Amsterdam 1978

Huffnagel, G.E., Economische voorlichting over het buitenland, Den Haag 1921

Jacobs, D., P. Boekholt & W. Zegveld, De economische kracht van Nederland, Den Haag 1990

Jong, L. de, Het Koninkrijk der Nederlanden in de Tweede Wereldoorlog, Den Haag 1979

Jong, T.P.M. de, De krimpende horizon van de Hollandse kooplieden, Groningen 1966

Jonge, J.A. de, De industrialisatie in Nederland tussen 1850 en 1914, Amsterdam 1968

Jordaan, L., Hollands export glorie, Schoonhoven 1991

Kamer van Koophandel en Fabrieken voor Amsterdam. Gedenkboek samengesteld ter gelegenheid van het 125 jarig bestaan, Amsterdam 1936

Katzenstein, P.J., Small States in World Markets. Industrial Policy in Europe, Ithaca 1985

Keesing, F.A.G., De conjuncturele ontwikkeling van Nederland en de evolutie van de economische overheidspolitiek 1918-1939, Antwerpen 1947

Kersten, A.E., Buitenlandse Zaken in ballingschap, Alphen aan den Rijn 1981

Klaauw, C.A. van der, Politieke betrekkingen tussen Nederland en België, Leiden 1953

Klein, P.W., "Traditionele ondernemers en economische groei in Nederland", Haarlem 1966

Klein, P.W., "Het bankwezen en de modernisering van de Nederlandse volkshuishouding tijdens de tweede helft van de negentiende eeuw", 1973

Klein, P.W., "Wegen naar economisch herstel 1945-1950", 1981

Klein, P.W. & G.J. Borger, De jaren dertig. Aspecten van crisis en werkloosheid, Amsterdam 1979

Klemann, H., Tussen Reich en Empire. De economische betrekkingen van Nederland met zijn belangrijkste handelspartners: Duitsland, Groot-Brittannië en België en de Nederlandse handelspolitiek, 1929-1936, Amsterdam 1990

Kloos, G.J., De handelspolitieke betrekkingen tusschen Nederland en de Vereenigde Staten van Amerika 1814-1914. Amsterdam 1923

Knap, G.H., Gekroonde koopvaart, Amsterdam 1956

Knoester, A., Economische politiek in Nederland, Antwerpen 1989

Koekoek, A., "The Competitive position of the EC in Hi-tech", Weltwirtschaftliches Archif 123, 1987

Kohnstamm, G.A., Toekomst van Nederlands industriële ontwikkeling, Den Haag 1948

Kok, A., Exportmanagement, Deventer 1987

Kooy, T.P. van der, Hollands stapelmarkt en haar verval, Rotterdam 1931

Kottman, R.N., "Herbert Hoover and the Smoot-Hawley Tariff: Canada, a Case Study", Journal of American History, 1975

Lake, D.A., "International Economic Structures and American Foreign Economic Policy, 1887-1934", World Politics, 1983

Lake, D.A., Power, Protection, and Free Trade. International Sources of US Commercial Strategy, 1887-1939, Ithaca 1988

Lammers, A., "Post uit Washington", De Gids, 1985

Lammers, A., God Bless America, Amsterdam 1987

Lammers, A., Uncle Sam en Jan Salie, Amsterdam 1989

Leffler, M.P., The Elusive Quest: America's Pursuit of European Stability and French Security, 1919-1933, Chapill Hill 1979

Leuchtenburg, W.E., The Perils of Prosperity 1914-1932, Chicago 1958

Leuchtenburg, W.E., Franklin D. Roosevelt and the New Deal 1932-1940, New York 1963

Lenstra, R., "Jacob Theodoor Cremer, het koloniaal beheer en het Nederlands belang in Atjeh", 1986

Liagre Böhl, H. de, J. Nekkers & L. Slot (red.), Nederland industrialiseert!, Nijmegen 1981

Lieftinck, P., Overzicht van de ontwikkeling der handelspolitiek van het Koninkrijk der Nederlanden van 1923 tot en met 1938, Haarlem 1939

Lindblad, J.Th., "De Handel tussen Nederland en Nederlands-Indië", 1988

Lindblad, J.Th., & J.L. van Zanden, "De buitenlandse handel van Nederland, 1872-1913", 1989

Lipsey, R.E., Price and Quantity Trends in the Foreign Trade of the US, Princeton 1963

Luykx, P., & A. Manning, Nederland in de Wereld, 1870-1950, Nijmegen 1988

Lynden, C.D.A. van, Directe investeringen in het buitenland, Den Haag 1945

McDougall, W.A., France's Rhineland Diplomacy 1914-1924, Princeton 1978

McElvaine, R.S., The Great Depression. America 1929-1941, New York 1984

Maliepaard, C.H.J., De Nederlandse landbouw, Antwerpen 1952

Manen, C.A. van, De Nederlandse Overzee Trustmaatschappij, Den Haag 1935

Mansvelt, W.M.F., Geschiedenis van de Nederlandsche Handel-Maatschappij, Haarlem 1925

Marcks, F.W., Wind over Sand. The Diplomacy of Franklin Roosevelt, Athens 1988

Maritieme geschiedenis der Nederlanden, Bussum 1978

Messing, F., De Nederlandse economie 1945-1980, Haarlem 1981

Metz, Th.M., Fünfzig Jahre Niederländische Handelskammer für Deutschland 1905-1955, Den Haag 1955

Milward, A.S., The Reconstruction of Western Europe, 1945-1951, Londen 1984

Milward, A.S., The European Rescue of The Nation State, Londen 1992

Morgan, D., Merchants of Grain, Londen 1980

Moquette, F.G., Van BEP tot BEB, Leiden, 1993

Motley, J.L., The Rise of the Dutch Republic, New York 1875

Muiswinkel, F.L. van, Handel, markt en beurs, Amsterdam 1969

Muiswinkel, F.L. van, De handelsonderneming, Amsterdam 1966

Mulder, J., Sidney van den Bergh. Een liberaal, Utrecht 1975

Murray, R.K., The Harding Era. Warren G. Harding and his Administration, Minneapolis 1969

Nederbragt, J.A., "Economische voorlichting", Nederlandsch Fabrikaat, 1920

Nederbragt, J.A., Herinneringen, Den Haag 1950

Nederlandsche Maatschappij voor Nijverheid en Handel, "Handel met het buitenland. Bron van Welvaart", Haarlem 1966

Nederlandsche Studiegroep New York, De economische, financiële en sociale ontwikkelingsgang van de Vereenigde Staten van 1940 tot 1945, Amsterdam 1946

Nekkers, J., & W.H. Salzmann, "Een 'heilzaam orgaan in ons staatsleven'",1990

The Netherland Chamber of Commerce in America, The Dutch in New Netherland and the United States 1609-1909, 1909

The Netherlands Chamber of Commerce in the US, Inc., Yearbook 1950

Nieuwkerk, N. van, & R.P. Sparling, The Netherlands international direct investment position, Dordrecht 1985

NIPO, Export naar de Verenigde Staten, 1986

Nusteling, De Rijnvaart in het tijdperk van stoom en steenkool, Amsterdam 1974

Offer, A., The First World War: An Agrarian Interpretation, Oxford 1989

Oud, P.J., Honderd jaren, een eeuw van staatkundige vormgeving in Nederland 1840-1940, Assen 1979

Parrini, C.P., Heir to Empire: United States Economic Diplomacy. 1916-1923, Pittsburgh 1969

Pollard, S., The Development of the British Economy, 1914-1967, New York 1969

Ratner, S., J.H. Soltow & R. Sylla, The Evolution of the American Economy, New York 1979

Riemsdijk, A.K. van, The Netherlands Chamber of Commerce in Londen 1898-1951, 1950

Roeterink, A., Economische voorlichting in Nederland, Amsterdam 1936

Rink, O.A., Holland on the Hudson, An economic and social history of Dutch New York, Ithaca 1986

Rogge, J., Het handelshuis Van Eeghen, Amsterdam 1949

Roon, G. van, Kleine landen in Crisistijd, Amsterdam 1985

Rydell, R.W., All the World's a Fair, Chicago 1984

Russell, F., President Harding. His Life and Times 1865-1923, Londen 1969

Sand, G.W., "Clifford and Truman: A Study in Foreign Policy and National Security, 1945-1949", St. Louis 1972

Sangers, W.J., Structuur- en Conjunctuurverschijnselen in de Nederlandse tuinbouw, in het bijzonder ten aanzien van de groenteteelt, Wageningen 1963

Schaik, A. van, Crisis en protectie onder Colijn, Alblasserdam 1986

Schendelen, M.C.P.M. van, De markt van politiek en bedrijfsleven. Den Haag verklaard voor ondernemers, Deventer 1988

Schram, J., "Nederland en het Marshallplan." P. Luykx & A. Manning, Nederland in de Wereld, 1870-1950.

Opstellen over buitenlandse en koloniale politiek, aangeboden aan Dr. N. Bootsma, Nijmegen 1988

Schreurs, W., Geschiedenis van de reclame in Nederland, Utrecht 1989

Seegers, J.J., "Produktie en concurrentievermogen van de Nederlandse industrie in het Interbellum", 1987

Seringhuasen, F.H.R., & P.J. Rosson, Export Development Promotion: The Role of Public Organization, Boston 1991

Schlesinger, A.M., The Coming of the New Deal, New York 1958

Schlesinger, A.M., The Politics of Upheaval, New York 1960

Smit, C., De handelspolitieke betrekkingen tusschen Nederland en Frankrijk 1814-1914, Den Haag 1923

Smit, C., Nederland in de Eerste Wereldoorlog (1899-1919), Groningen 1971-1973

Smit, C., Tien studiën betreffende Nederland in de Eerste Wereldoorlog, Groningen 1975

Sneller, Z.W., De geschiedenis van den Nederlandsche landbouw 1795-1940, Groningen 1943

Sobel, R., The Age of Giant Corporations. A Microeconomic History of American Business 1914-1970, Westport 1972

Sociaal-Economische Raad, Advies inzake de organisatie van de handelsvoorlichting en exportbevordering, Den Haag 1970

Staatsalmanak voor het Koninkrijk der Nederlanden, Utrecht

Stokvis, P.R.D., "Some American views of The Netherlands during the Nineteenth Century", 1982

Stubenitsky, F., American Direct Investment in the Netherlands Industry, Rotterdam 1970

Taams, A.S., De exportmanager, Assen 1991

Taussig, F.W., The Tariff History of the United States, New York 1931

Tamse, C.A., "The Netherlands Consular Service and The Dutch Consular reports of the Nineteenth and Twentieth Century", 1981

Tijn, Th. van, "Geschiedenis van de Amsterdamse diamanthandel en nijverheid, 1845-1897", 1974

Treub, M.W.F., Oorlogstijd, Haarlem 1917

Treub, W.M.F., Herinneringen en overpeinzingen, Haarlem 1931

Vajda, M., "Het Fordney-McCumber Tarief", De Economist (1922)

Vajda, M., "Douane- en handelspolitiek der Vereenigde Staten", De Economist, 1924

Valk, J.P. de, & M. van Faassen, Dagboeken en aantekeningen van Willem Hendrik de Beaufort 1874-1918, Den Haag 1993

Vatter, H.G. The Drive to Industrial Maturity: The US Economy, 1860-1914, Londen 1975

Veenendaal, A.J. "The Kansas City Southern Railway and the Dutch Connection", Business History Review, 1987

Veenendaal, A.J., "Nederlandse kapitaal plaveit de weg van Kansas City naar de Golf van Mexico", 1989

Veenendaal, A.J., "An Example of 'Other People's Money': Dutch Capital in American Railroads", 1992

Verseput, J., Kamer van Koophandel en Fabrieken voor Rotterdam. 1928-1952, Rotterdam 1955

Vries, Joh. de, De economische achteruitgang van de republiek in de achttiende eeuw, Tilburg, 1959

Vries, Joh. de, Herinneringen en dagboek van Ernst Heldring 1871-1954, Utrecht 1970

Vries, Joh. de, 1811-1961 met Amsterdam als brandpunt, Amsterdam

Vries, Joh. de, De Nederlandse economie tijdens de 20ste eeuw, Antwerpen 1973

Vries, Joh. de, "Een welbespraakt reiziger in oppositie", Den Haag 1977

Vries, Joh. de, Een eeuw vol effecten, Amsterdam 1976

Vries, Joh. de, Geschiedenis van De Nederlandsche Bank, Amsterdam 1989

Vries, W. de, "Export-experiment rond 1900." Maandschrift Economie, 1967

Ward, G., A First-Class Temperament. The Emergence of Franklin Roosevelt, New York 1989

Wels, C.B., Aloofness and Neutrality. Studies on Dutch Foreign Relations and Policy-Making Institutions, Utrecht 1982

Wentholt, A.D., Brug over den oceaan. Een eeuw geschiedenis van de Holland-Amerika Lijn, Rotterdam 1973

Werking, Richard. H., "Selling the Foreign Service: Bureaucratic Rivalry and Foreign-Trade Promotion, 1903-1912", Pacific Historical Review, 1976

Westermann, J.C., The Netherlands and the United States, Den Haag 1935

Westermann, J.C., Kamer van Koophandel en Fabrieken voor Amsterdam, Amsterdam 1936

Weststrate, C., Economic Policy in Practice: The Netherlands 1950-1957, Leiden 1959

Wetenschappelijke Raad voor het Regeringsbeleid, Plaats en toekomst van de Nederlandse industrie, Den Haag 1980

Wever, J.A., Les institutions d'expansion commerciale des Pays-Bas, Parijs 1927

Wielenga, F., West-Duitsland: partner uit noodzaak, Utrecht 1989

Wilkins, M., The History of Foreign Investment in the United States to 1914, Londen 1989

Wilkins, M., The Maturing of Multinational Enterprise: American Business Abroad from 1914 to 1970, Londen 1974

Wilson, J.H., American Business and Foreign Policy 1920-1933, Lexington 1971

Winter, D., Haig's Command. A Reassessment, Londen 1991

Winter, P.J. van, Het aandeel van den Amsterdamschen handel aan den opbouw van het Amerikaansche Gemeenebest, Den Haag 1927

Woestijne, W.J. van de, "De goede jaren die aan de depressie vooraf gingen", Tijdschrift voor Geschiedenis, 1969

Zanden, J.L. van, De economische ontwikkeling van de Nederlandse landbouw in de negentiende eeuw, 1800-1914, Utrecht 1985

Zanden, J.L. van, De industrialisatie in Amsterdam, Bergen 1987

Zanden, J.L. van, "The Dutch economic history of the period 1500-1940", 1989

Zanden, J.L. van, & R.T. Griffiths, Economische geschiedenis van Nederland in de 20e eeuw, Utrecht 1989

Zanden, J.L. van, "De economische ontwikkeling van Nederland en België en het 'succes' van de Benelux, 1945-1958", Amsterdam 1992

Zwaag, J.S. van der, Verloren tropische zaken, 1991